Some Blaine Ethridge Books on Latin America

HISTORY, SOCIAL HISTORY, DAILY LIFE, ARTS, SOCIO-ECONOMIC STUDIES

THE DEATH THORN: Magic, Superstitions, and Beliefs of Urban Indians in Panama and Peru. By Alma M. Karlin. (1933) 1971.

HISTORY OF ANCIENT MEXICO: Anthropological, Mythological and Social. By Bernardino de Sahagun. Trans. by Fanny R. Bandelier. (1932) 1971.

LIFE IN BRAZIL; or, A Journal of a Visit to the Land of the Cocoa and the Palm. By Thomas Ewbank. Heavily illustrated with engravings of artifacts, costumes, furniture, persons, events, etc. (1856) In preparation.

MEXICAN POPULAR ARTS. By Frances Toor. New illustrations. (1939) In preparation.

PERU IN FOUR DIMENSIONS. By David A. Robinson. Geography, economy, demography, government. In CHOICE's 1969-70 list of "Outstanding Academic Books." (1964) 1967.

PERU'S OWN CONQUEST. By Fernando Belaunde Terry, former President of Peru. Unfulfilled plans for solving age-old problems in a developing country. 1965.

RIO IN THE TIME OF THE VICEROYS: Daily Life, Customs, and Institutions. By Luiz Edmundo da Costa. Translated by Dorothea H. Momsen. (1936) In preparation.

A SHORT HISTORY OF BOLIVIA. By Robert Barton. The only complete study in English. Heavily illustrated. 1969.

THREE DOLLARS A YEAR; Being the Story of a Typical Zapotecan Indian Village. By G. Russell Steininger and Paul Van de Velde. Informal and knowledgeable social anthropology, with resource and need accounts. Good plates. (1935) 1971.

THE WAR IN NICARAGUA. By General William Walker. (1860) 1971.

Write for list of Latin American books in
reference and bibliography

BLAINE ETHRIDGE—BOOKS
13977 Penrod Street, Detroit, Michigan 48223

LIFE IN BRAZIL;

OR,

𝔄 𝔍𝔬𝔲𝔯𝔫𝔞𝔩 𝔬𝔣 𝔞 𝔙𝔦𝔰𝔦𝔱

TO THE

LAND OF THE COCOA AND THE PALM.

WITH AN APPENDIX,

CONTAINING

ILLUSTRATIONS OF ANCIENT SOUTH AMERICAN ARTS

IN RECENTLY DISCOVERED IMPLEMENTS AND PRODUCTS OF DOMESTIC
INDUSTRY, AND WORKS IN STONE, POTTERY, GOLD,
SILVER, BRONZE, &c.

BY THOMAS EWBANK.

WITH OVER ONE HUNDRED ILLUSTRATIONS.

NEW YORK:
HARPER & BROTHERS, PUBLISHERS,
PEARL STREET, FRANKLIN SQUARE.
1856.

Republished by Blaine Ethridge—Books, Detroit, 1971

GEORGES P. VANIER LIBRARY, LOYOLA COLLEGE, MONTREAL

204475

AUG 28 1974

Entered, according to Act of Congress, in the year one thousand eight
hundred and fifty-five, by

HARPER & BROTHERS,

in the Clerk's Office of the District Court of the Southern District of
New York.

Library of Congress Catalog Card Number 75-165653
International Standard Book Number 0-87917-007-7

PREFACE.

THE present times are the beginning of a fresh chapter in man's history, and look not unlike the opening of a new epoch in the development of his being. Habits and impulses, hitherto rudimental seem ready to burst into maturity, as if the larva state of his existence was closing, and he was about to use wings as well as feet—an age of locomotion, and the prelude to one of flight.

Nature always presages marked changes in the condition of her diversified offspring, and by indications not easily mistaken. The appearance of new, or an advanced elaboration of existing organs, is invariably preceded or accompanied by corresponding instincts. A lepidopter is no sooner fitted for action in an element different from that in which its previous constitution delighted, than it finds itself impelled to the exercise of newly-born powers, and anon is off in quest of untasted pleasures. The phenomenon of metamorphosis is common to every form of life. Man is but an aspiring insect, and the addition of instruments of volitation would scarcely surpass in novelty transformations which the species, according to some authors, has already undergone.

As on the approach of migratory seasons with lower tribes, a general restlessness pervades society. Classes and masses heretofore inert are beginning to move and to flutter, agitated by latent influences. Pede-locomotion is growing obsolete, and a disposition to soar every where manifest. Harbingers, too, of something like a general flight may be noticed in those gentlemen musicians and ladies of song now tripping over the earth and making professional tours round it. Histrionic artists rivaling old circumnavigators!

Such facts the world never witnessed before. What they forebode Heaven best knows. If precursive of a breaking up of the old recluse' habits of the species, and introductory of a system by which distant branches of the human family will become better known to, and be led to the interchange of sentiments and civilities with, each other, who would be among the last to feel the generous impulse? Indeed, who, with health and leisure, can now stay at home inactive—be content to grow, remain, and die upon one little spot of this glorious sphere, when even females dance and sing, and music-masters fiddle round it?

These questions the writer put to himself; and the result was a determination to cast off for a season the instincts of home, and hie away to a region of butterflies and flowers. Inclination led him across the equator to the verge of the southern tropic, where he found a succession of novelties in the moving panorama of a Brazilian city that supplied subjects in abundance for both crayon and pen.

As I give my impressions regardless, in this politic age, of the policy or impolicy of so doing, there are doubtless among them opinions with which every reader will not sympathize. But what then? The Creator never designed us all to think and feel, see and speak, reflect and write alike. It is absurd to expect it, and worse than Manchegan folly to get angry about it. This would be a tame world if all things on it were modeled after one or two patterns, and men were fac-similes of each other.

I am told that I should have kept silence on ecclesiastical matters; that it is improper for laymen to meddle with them. I can only say I did not go out of my way to find them. In Brazil, religion, or that which is so called, meets you every where; you can do nothing, observe nothing, without being confronted by it in one shape or another. It is a leading feature in public and private life. Festivals and processions constitute the chief amusements of the masses—are their principal sports and pastimes, during which the saints themselves come out of their sanctuaries, and, with padres and people, take part in the general frolic. To pass by them would be omitting the most popular acts, and neglecting the favorite actors in the national drama.

I have occasionally commented freely on facts, but I have distorted none—not one; nor have I forgotten that South American superstitions were once common, and that their rejection by our ancestors is of no remote date. The world is still " a ragged school." Of the races and nations that make up its classes, few have got through the horn-book of knowledge; and it is certain they never can be seated on the same form in religion any more than in arts, sciences, and civil polity. The dogma of uniformity is opposed to the organic law of diversity.

In whatever light the physique of Romanism may appear to others, it is full of interest to me. Almost as purely heathen as before the advent of Christ, it is a living and luminous exponent of pagan mysteries and ceremonies. Restore the old terms "temples" and "gods" for "churches" and "saints" (they are strictly synonymous), and there is scarcely aught in it but what was in common use ages before the times of the Cæsars. Churches, their internal arrangements and accessories, their store-rooms for machinery, chests and closets for dresses, ornaments, insignia, and jewels belonging to the images; artists to take charge of and repair these; several shrines located in one temple, forms of worship at them, candles on the altars, mass-bells, vows, penance, flagellation, pilgrimages, pocket and household images; the various orders of priests, of monks and nuns, habits of the priests, rosaries, the Inquisition and its tortures, the tonsure, ex votos, holy water and its applications, professsional attributes of saints, bodily cures wrought by and character of miracles ascribed to them, &c., all belong to classic and anterior epochs. Bulls of excommunication and commination, involving confiscation of property and death, are versions of those issued against Alcibiades and other alleged heretics; so, also, exceptions taken by enlightened Romanists to such wholesale cursing are finely illustrated by Theano, who excused herself, saying she was " a priestess for prayer and not for execration."

It is impossible to witness for the first time ecclesiastical pageants without calling to mind the same things established by the Gentiles, and which constituted a cherished source of their entertainments. Now, as then, the business of a city is ever and anon arrested, its streets are swept and strewed with leaves, the fronts of the houses decked with evergreens and drapery, women and children throng the windows, country people flock in to the sight, and groups of both sexes are every where waiting for it. At length appear full-sized statues painted to the life, mounted on platforms, and borne in triumph on men's shoulders, amid crowds of officials in their varied costumes. Mitred pontiffs, with their trains held up by pages, walk under canopies, accompanied by civil magistrates and escorted by battalions of soldiers, the whole preceded and followed by cohorts of priests, monks, lay-brothers, and acolytes, with music, banners, flambeaux, staves, censers, symbols on poles, &c., while from the mixed masses of spectators proceed *sotto voce* remarks, reverend and profane, as each wooden deity and its perspiring supporters pass by. What is all this but a continuation of the pomps of Isis and Cybele—of festivals celebrated in honor of the gods and goddesses of Egypt, Assyria, Asia Minor, Carthage, Greece, and old Rome ? Similar scenes and performers at Nineveh, Babylon, Corinth, Delphos, and Athens pass literally before one ; at least so it seemed when the sight first opened upon me in Rio.

I believe Romanism, as it exists in Brazil and South America generally, to be a barrier to progress, compared to which other obstacles are small, and there are native statesmen alive to the fact; but, incorporated as it is with the habits and thoughts of the people; transfused, as it were, through their very bones and marrow, unless some Kempis or Fénélon, Luther or Ronge, arise to purify it, generations must pass before the scales drop from their eyes, and they become mentally free.

Of those who think differently, I trust none will suffer their ire to glow at this expression of an opinion, or at recitals of facts upon which it may be based. I am for every one telling his own stories and commenting on them in his own way; and while he who, in doing this, expects to please every body, is a miller or the son of a miller, those who insist on his seeing things only through their glasses are verily allied to the companion of Æsop's two grinders of grain.

Besides Church affairs, I noted whatever interested me, and that, in sooth, was nearly every thing: arts, manners, customs, buildings, trades, tools, pottery, food, slaves, animals, agricultural products, climate, diseases, population, antiquities, &c., &c.; hence this volume will be found a miscellanea of tropical life. It was in preparation when the late President Tyler honored the writer with an official appointment in Washington; the sheets were then laid aside, but, as they relate to matters that are all but unchangeable, there is nothing to regret in the delayed publication.

WASHINGTON, D. C., 1855.

CONTENTS.

CHAPTER I.

New York to Hampton Roads: Passports.—Wrinkled Faces.—Bataleurs.—Richmond.—Market.—Mules.—Lotteries.—James River.—Floating Boarding-house. —A Virginian Job.—Crippled Slave.—The Roads .... Page 17

CHAPTER II.

Ten Days' Sail: Beat out.—New Sensations.—Captain in Costume.—A Gale.—Sea-sickness.—Water Rams.—Gulf Stream.—Christmas Carols.—Human Daring.—Ship hunted by marine Demons.—Hard Life of Seamen.—Cook and Captain.—Enchanting Skies.—Minute Crabs........................... 26

CHAPTER III.

Twenty-four Days' Sail: Sea Sorrows.—A Genoese.—Rough Weather.—A Flying-fish.—Flowers of Death.—Oceanic Skies.—The Atmosphere charged with red Dust.—Firmamental Paintings.—Flying-fish Latitudes.—Cream-colored or Quaker Skies.—Flying-fish again.—A Meniscus.—A Squall.—A ship in Distress.—A young Fly.—In the Variables.—The Ocean unchangeable.—Temperature of Air and Water.—Brazilian Coasts 35

CHAPTER IV.

Diagram of the Ship's Motions.—The Ravels at Sea.—Sailing in Elysium.—Worlds are Ships of the Almighty Merchant.—The Nebulæ his Ship-yards.—The Ocean a Type of the Sea of Life.—Abrolhos and Squalls.—Cape Frio.—Land-breeze.—Sea-breeze.—Sugar-loaf.—Enter the Bay.—Former Treatment of Foreigners.—Table of Latitudes and Longitudes during the Voyage..... 47

CHAPTER V.

The Bay, City, and Suburbs from the Ship.—The Forts.—I land alone.—The Cattete.—A Brazilian Parlor.—Meeting of two Brothers 57

CHAPTER VI.

Almanacs.—Livery Stables.—Carriages.—Honorable H. A. Wise.—The Host.—Booming of the Surf.—The Matadoura.—Beeves.—Assist at Mass.—Esmola Box.—Apollonia.—A Funeral.—Funeral Customs.—Mourning.—Cost of Masses for the Dead 62

CHAPTER VII.

The Military Arsenal: its Manufactures.—Fine old bronze Ordnance.—School. —Ceremony of the Hat.—Larangeiras.—Cattete Brook and Washerwomen.—A Brazilian Chacara.—Old Portuguese Customs.—Butterflies.—Fountains.

—Indian Medicine-tree.—A Dessert after the manner of Eden.—Uniformity of tropical Heats.—Iron Collars on Slaves.—Shoes and Neckcloths symbols of Freedom.—The Vicar and Sneezing.—The public Garden an earthly Elysium .... Page 71

CHAPTER VIII.

Sudden Floods and their singular Inconveniences.—Discovery of Brazil.—Indians and early Navigators. — Rio founded by French Protestants.—Their religious Disputes.—An Indian Chief knighted. — His Descendants. — Location of the City.—Saints of the Hills.—Streets and Pavements.—Houses.—Jalousies.—Roofs.—Chimneys.—Spouts.—Street Lamps.—Substitute for Bells and Doorknockers.—Signs.—Markets.—Fountains.—No Sewers or Sinks.—Rio a City of Quarries.—Neighboring Mountains.—Names of Streets, etc. 81

CHAPTER IX.

Sedans.—Removing Furniture to new Dwellings.—Street " Cries."—Peddlers.—Large Lizard.—Penny Portraits of Saints.—The Intrudo and its Sports.—Of Hindoo Origin. — Death and Burial of the Secretary of the Institute. — The Church, Coffin, Corpse, Cemetery, and Orations 90

CHAPTER X.

The Marimba.—Procession announced.—Unloading Lime-boats.—Lapa Convent and Lady at Confession.—The Campo and Lavandeiras.—Dog-killers.—Customhouse.—Trucks.—A Slave chained to one.—Young and old Women in Chains.—Coffee Carriers.—Crippled Slaves. The Spectacle given up.—An Angel.—The Musuem.—-Antiquities, etc.—Fathers of Snuff and the Snuff-trade.—Original Snuff-mills and Sniffing Apparatus. — Slave-traders.—Monastery of San Bento : its Monks, Chapel, Cells, Library, and Bookworms.—Sopping.—Great Wealth of this Monastery 111

CHAPTER XI.

Diversity of Complexion in one Family.—Sabbath Diversions.—Street of Silversmiths.—Its staple Manufactures.—Amulets.—Figas.—Lock and Key.—Passage in Shakspeare explained.—Eating-houses. — Charges.—Sneezers " blessed."—Priests.—Free colored Men.—Great Consumption of Pork.—National Dish.—Pastry and Confectionery.—Heavenly Bacon.—Francis of Penitence.—Brotherhoods akin to modern Odd Fellows.—Terms of Admission.—Advantages.—Who this Francis was.—Garden, and Electric Eel.—Current Philosophy respecting the Sex.—Divination.—Provincial Nicknames.—Dowries in Cocoa and Coffee-trees.—Vegetable and other Sobriquets. — Horsewomen.—Officers' Wives on Drill in Military Costume.—Morals of the Priesthood 130

CHAPTER XII.

Visit to Christoval : native Sheep.—Palace of a Peddler.—Imperial Quinta.—Rapacity of the old Queen.—Miguel.—A Viscount and his strange Employment.—Emperor's Apartments.—Objects of Natural History.—Collection of Coins.—Peruvian, Egyptian, and Roman Antiquities. — Laboratory. — Theatre, and Garden 144

CONTENTS.

CHAPTER XIII.
Poor Anthony robbed.—Ex Votos.—Their Manufacture.—Humming-bird and Bouquet.—Affronted Image and wicked Painter.—His Punishment, and Process of " disaffronting" the Image.—Imperial Chapel and its Shrines.—Turk's Head.—Barefooted Friars.—Estaçio de Sá.—Slab over him.—Chief of the Capuchins.—Virgin's Shoe-sole.—Architectural Remains.—Ajuda Convent.—Dumb Waiter.—Glimpse into the Interior.—Vestals.—Nuns in the Ajuda, and their Treatment .... Page 151

CHAPTER XIV.
Candelaria Church.—Jacks of the Clock.—Peccary.—God's Stepfather.—Botanic Garden.—Snake.—Fences.—Dinner and its Cost.—Catalogue of Plants in the Garden... 169

CHAPTER XV.
Goddess of the Blind.—Her Church, Shrines, and Symbols.—A Slave consulting her.—Interview with her Sacristan.—Ex Votos.—Our Lady of the Cape of Good Hope.—Insuring Friars.—Other Professional and Competing Saints.—Street Images 176

CHAPTER XVI.
Rain.—Mechanical Professions.—Labor versus Respectability.—Effect on young Men.—Building.—Hammer-gamut.—Working Hours and Wages.—Rejoicings over Rafters. — Masons and Masonry. — Scaffolds.—Walls.—Antiquity of the Tools.—Plummet.—Hatchet or Adze.—Carpenter's Bench.—Saw and Planes.—Mode of laying Floors.—Doors, Shutters, Hardware.—Pavers.—Lithography.—Coppersmiths.—Lamp.—Slave Artisans.—Merchants. — Barbers.—Beggars.—Lawyers.—Lotteries 183

CHAPTER XVII.
Maté and Cups.—Sunday Scenes.—Gloria Church.—Images, Vestry, Ex Votos, and Paintings.—Miracles in behalf of Pedro I. and one of his Daughters.—Lady of Gloria and a Larangeiras Absalom.—Chapel of the Ajuda grated like a Jail.—Its Shrines and Images.—A Penitent licking the Dust.—Public Notice of a Procession.—Images, Angels, and Pomp described..................... 198

CHAPTER XVIII.
All Fools' Day.—Streets flooded.—Breaking down Mountains.—Notices of Festivals.—Flying Visit to Francis Paula, St. Anne, Joaquim, St. Rita, Bom Jesus, and the Candelaria.—No Animal Oils burned in Churches.—Carmelite Procession with full-grown Images.—The Nimbus and its curious Origin 208

CHAPTER XIX.
Palm Sunday : Ceremonies and Customs.—Eunuch Singers.—Specimens of Ecclesiastical Advertisements.—Benedictine Chapel.—Dark Wednesday.—A Merçēeiro.—Juno Lucina of Rio.—Lady of Civilities.—Holy Thursday.—Matracas.—Silver Plate in the Carmo Church.—Kissing a dead Christ in the Candelaria.—Appearance of the Interior.—Kissing the Floor and Steps in the Bom Jesus.—Plate in the Paula.—Mine-finders.... 217

CONTENTS.

CHAPTER XX.

Good Friday.—Capuchins preaching.—Burial of God.—Dresses and Jewels of the Angels.—Allelulia Saturday.—Blessing Fire and Water.—Paschal Candle.—Killing Judas.—Church Machinery.—Cinerary Urns and Commemoration of the Dead.—Symbols carried by Angels.—Boy Monk.—Little Prospect of Protestant Missions succeeding in Brazil.—Mary of Nazareth........... Page 227

CHAPTER XXI.

Amulets: the Church a Mart for them.—Measures of Saints.—Royal Touches and metallic Tractors.—Bentinhos.—Pictures of Saints.—Indulgences.—Hindoo Pictures. — Portable Images. — Medals of Saints. — Bedini.—Symbols of the Cross. — Crossing Manual. — Pieces of holy Rock.—Hippocanthus.—Figa.—Ashes of Palm.—Rue.—Love Powder. — Sieve and Shears.—Curing the Bewitched.—Negro Witches. — Cures for Whitlows and Toothache.—The Evil Eye.—Rio Poulterers troubled with it.—Horns quench it............... 241

CHAPTER XXII.

Begging for the Holy Ghost.—The Symbols.—Mr. Barboza.—An afflicted Mother.—The City agitated through Mistake.—San Jorge.—Market.—Church of Peddlers.—Burying-ground of Heretics. — Small Water-craft. — Beeves of the Sun.—Lady of Navigators.—Mozambique tribal Marks.—Church of Boa Viagem.—Ex Votos and Miracles.—Curious Lavatory.—View of the Harbor and Mountains.—Alms-box.—Ships' Sails vowed to Our Lady, and sold on her Account.—Indian Boy.—Wax offered to Marine Deities by old Pagans.—Other Heathen Types of Romish Customs................................. 250

CHAPTER XXIII.

People of Color. — Twilight and Climate.—Barbonos Monks.—The Ex-Nuncio.—Henry A. Wise recalled.—Arrival of the Emperor and Anxieties of Courtiers. —A new Saint.—Mask.—Market Incident.—St. Peter's Church.—N. S. Conceição.—Plaster Images proposed.—Collecting-days and Collectors.—Church of the Mother of Men.—Fat Ladies and Gentlemen.—Unctuous Worship of N. S's. Shoe-sole.—Bedini, the new Nuncio................................. 267

CHAPTER XXIV.

Pluvial Deity. — Aqueduct Records. — Pope John. — Ecclesiastical "Cries." —Slaves.—Army Recruits.—The Emperor opens the Legislature.—Fires and Fire-engines. — Slaves. — Suicide. — Begging for the Holy Ghost. — Auction of Slaves... 275

CHAPTER XXV.

Winter.—New Saint.—Lady do Parto.—An English Monk.—Black and white Infants in Purgatory.—Auction at a private Dwelling: its Furniture, Garden, Lares, Oratorio, and Slaves.—Barber's Basin and Shaving-cloth.—Mass and Capuchins.—Church of the Rosary, its Images and Ex Votos.—A sick Man.—Old Slave. — Uncertain Origin of the Negro Saint. — Ramble through Nictherohy.. 284

CONTENTS.

CHAPTER XXVI.

Inauguration of a new Saint: how the alleged Bones were procured.—Buried in a waxen Figure.—The Bishop's Letter.—The Affair generally condemned.—Bedini and Miranda. — The Emperor declines joining the Procession. — The Pomp.—The "Arca" and Saint within.—Official Account.—Newspaper Puff.—A Visit to Priscilliana.—Miranda's Circular.—A French Tribunal on Religious Impositions.. Page 294

CHAPTER XXVII.

A Day for getting Souls out of Purgatory.—Trip to the Falls of Tejuca.—Character of the Country.—Anacharsis and Charcoal.—Fat Pigs and Morphea.—Mills.—Cotton-tree.—Coffee Plantation.—Tailless Dogs and Fowls.—Process of preparing Coffee for the Market.—Early Notice of Cauphe.—The Falls.—Dinner and Dessert at them.—Inscriptions on the Gavia...................... 305

CHAPTER XXVIII.

Church Advertisements.—Auction and Fire-works at St. Rita's Church.—Articles sold.—Official Puff.—Horse-racing in honor of the Holy Ghost.—St. Gonçalo the Friend of the unmarried.—Capuchin preaching.—Two Slaves given to the Friars, and their Baptism by Bedini.—Chief Capuchin.—Priscilliana.—Famine in Ceara.—Indians bought and sold................................. 312

CHAPTER XXIX.

Winter and Western Islanders.—Brazilian Names: their Derivation and Import.—Primitive Patronymics.—Combinations.—Names in connection with Professions.—Names of Ships.—Pigs and Pig-stealing.—Invitation to Tea..... 324

CHAPTER XXX.

St. Anthony of Padua: his Monastery and Miracles.—His Rank and Salary as a Soldier.—Shameful Treatment of his Images.—Feast of the Holy Ghost.—Auctions and Fire-works, etc.. 329

CHAPTER XXXI.

Vicar and Vintems.—Theatricals.—Barbonos Monks and the troublesome Blacksmith.—Priscilliana.—Host and drunken Bellman.—Proceedings of the National Senate arrested.—Slave-trader's Office.—Anthony of the Poor: his Festival and Tablets.—Mosquitoes and Lizards.—Corpus Christi and St. George.—Showmen and the Burial... 349

CHAPTER XXXII.

Crockery-wares: Talhas.—Monkey.—Moringues.—Furnaces, Flower-pots, etc.—Water-baril.—Scrubbing-brush.—Mortars.—Fuel 357

CHAPTER XXXIII.

A Trip to Macacu.—Steam up the Bay.—Prospects.—Slaves.—Sambayratiba.—Dense Mist.—Bed-chamber.—Attacked by Rats.—Extent of the Pest.—Sugar-house.—Stingless Bees.—Sheep.—Dogs without Tails.—Visit other Estates.—Wasps' and Ants' Nests.—The Rats again.—Scenes in the Forest.—Sipos.—Spoon Wheels.—Female Slaves making Brick.—Chigres.—Muleteers camping.—Estate of the Carmelites.—Mules 361

CONTENTS.

CHAPTER XXXIV.

Macacu.—A large Tree.—Its Form, Dimensions, and extraordinary Roots.—Why so few old Trees.—Vegetable Origin of Forms and Ornaments.—Singular Forms of Boles.—Natural Moulding.—The Sloth-tree and Sloth.—Fabrication of Farinha.—Cultivation of the Plant.—Grating and pressing the Pulp.—The Tipiti. —Musical Wagons.—Rats keeping Carnival.—Return to the City ... Page 371

CHAPTER XXXV.

Apollonia and Carasco.—Divinations.—Beatified Galens.—The Mizericordia.— Meeting of Isabel and Mary.—The Chapel.—Emperor.—Foundlings.—Isabel the Representative of a Pagan Goddess.—Manual and tibial Worship.—Fourth of July.—Lame leading the Blind.—British Chapel, Preacher, and Prayer-Book. —Nictherohy.—Fine Estate and its small Cost.—A Paca.—The Nuncio denounced.—Lost Image.—Shrine in a Brothel.—Legislation invoked.—Theatrical and sacerdotal Exhibitions... 384

CHAPTER XXXVI.

Capuchin Attractions : Fireworks, Music, Auction, etc. — The Mint. — Lantern-bellows.—Lady of Lampadoza.—Balthazar.—Peter Coelho.—A winged Monk.— A dead Christ by a Negro Artist.—Ceara.—How the Emperor was anointed.— More Galas.—Conveying Presents.—Interior of a Drawing-room.—Proverbs.— The Neckcloth.—Bedini.—British Embassador.—Chamber of Deputies.—Jaunt to the Gavia.—Inscriptions.—Tailor.—Dead Slave.—Pride and Piggishness.— God's Grandmother.—Bedini again.—Lady of Snows.—Birth of a Princess.—A Wizard's Stock in Trade 395

CHAPTER XXXVII.

The Corcovado Mountain and Carioco Aqueduct : View from chamber Window.— Aqueduct Arches.—Ascent of the Tereza Hill.—Conduit and receiving Basins. —Romantic Character of the Work —Section of Conduit.—Mother of Waters. —Paineiras and Pic-nic.—Forest Features.—Ascent of the Corcovado.—Vegetable Instincts.—Summit of the Mountain.—Prospects from it.—Descent.—The Paineiras tributary to the Mother of Waters.—Reach Home by Lamp-light.— Subsequent Visits to the Aqueduct.—Its Length and Fall.—Section of Channel over the Arches.—Entire Length of the Aqueduct and Feeders.—Water furnished by it.—Might be conveyed through Tubes into every dwelling.—No Reservoirs 407

CHAPTER XXXVIII.

Population of Brazil.—Diseases.—National Income.—Police.—Literature.—Library.—Newspapers.—Character of Brazilians.—Slaves.—Voyage Home   430

APPENDIX 445

SKETCHES

OF

LIFE IN BRAZIL.

CHAPTER I.

New York to Hampton Roads: Passports.—Wrinkled Faces.—Bataleurs.—Richmond.—Market.—Mules.—Lotteries.—James River.—Floating Boarding-house.—A Virginian Job.—Crippled Slave.—The Roads.

FREE travel and free trade are not yet. The barbarism that in the Old World prevents man from traversing the earth and communing with his species at his pleasure prevails over South America. Tourists are not allowed to step on nor to leave the shores of Brazil without passports. I had, therefore, to call on the Brazilian consul, and pay him for an invoice, or pen-and-ink sketch of myself. With it I left New York on the 2d of December, 1845, by rail for Richmond, Va., to join the bark Mazeppa, in which I had engaged a passage to Rio. In passing through Jersey, crowds were assembled in every village in expectation of the President's Message. It met us at Bristol, when every one responded to the sentiments concerning Oregon. The feeling was universal that not another foot of North America should be polluted with monarchy; that here, come what may, people should be free from the evils of hereditary rulers, primogeniture, tithes, and a state priesthood.

From the corrugated countenances of two loquacious old gentlemen, I was led, for want of something else to think on, to infer that the diversified wrinkles in the human face are produced pretty much in the same way as are similar marks in the leathers of bellows. The movable board, like the movable jaw, ever stretching and collapsing the flexile material, at length determines and defines the lines. No two faces are crimped alike, neither are two bellows. Both cheeks and leathers are smooth when new, and it is only by long-continued action that the creases become stereotyped in either. To be sure, the living skin requires more working to take and retain the impressions than that prepared by the tanner, but then how vastly more is it worked! The muscles of the mouth and the play of the lower jaw scarcely have a moment's rest from the beginning of life to the end of it. The lines in the hands are formed in the same way.

Night traveling is favorable to revery. There were some three hundred passengers in the train—politicians, editors, ladies, and ladies' maids, place-hunters, merchants, planters, military and naval officers, artisans, and engineers—every one more or less absorbed in cogitation. In fact, we are all itinerant *Bataleurs*, proprietors of little cosmoramic exhibitions, which we carry about for our individual entertainment, and whose value varies with the pictures put into them. How large a part of life is spent in working these, and what pleasure they impart when Hope fingers the strings!

After a short stay in Philadelphia, we rushed on, through Baltimore, to Washington, where I spent a day over the lions, and left for Richmond. We descended the Potomac in a small steamer, some forty miles, to Aquia Creek, whence the cars ran us, in a few hours, to the capital of Virginia. The landscape for a hundred miles presented a uniform icy arborescence. Gusts of wind rustled through clumps of trees and shrubbery, shaking down showers of crystals, which came whirring in waves over the glassy fields toward us.

Arriving according to appointment, I learn that the vessel—loading with flour nineteen miles below on the Appomattox—will not complete her cargo for several days. Not expecting to stop here twelve hours, and to be detained perhaps a week, is enough, in such weather as has now set in, to give one mental chills and bodily ague-fits. The air is tangible from excessive moisture, and at night darkness is literally felt. The fog is so dense as completely to hide from view buildings on opposite sides of the street. If "in thick mists the devil is smoking tobacco," this must be a favorite place for taking his pipe in. But travelers should not be discouraged nor readers frightened off by preliminary disagreeables.

Richmond is picturesque in its location, occupying both high and low grounds. The river at its feet is crowded with rocks, which nothing but a canoe can thread; the longest bridge in the state, a very high one, crosses immediately below them. The canal sweeps along the banks at an elevation of some forty feet, presenting enviable sites for hydraulic motors, and in these sources of wealth rivaling the water-power of Paterson and Lowell. The houses, of diverse fashions, run up and cross precipitous streets, while the State House, on an eminence, overlooks the city and surrounding scenery. "Main Street" is two miles long, its lower end terminating at "Rockets," the nearest place to which steamers and small craft can come up. The middle portion of this avenue—the old business part of the city—is steep, and occupied on both sides with substantial stores and dwellings. In other parts the edifices are poor. I was surprised to find decent white people living in very mean apologies for dwellings. Several old streets are not paved, neither middle nor sidewalks. I am told no marked changes have been made in the city during the last thirty years.

The State House is a handsome structure. In the hall stands Houden's statue of Washington, in citizen's dress, and a walking-cane in his hand—a perfect picture in marble of a Virginian gentleman of the eighteenth century. True to life, it will convey to posterity a far more correct idea of the Father of his Country than the half nude Roman figure at Washington.

The market is well supplied, and prices are moderate. Beef and mutton from $4\frac{1}{2}$ to 6 cents per pound; pork, 6 cents; turkeys, 75 cents each, and ducks the same per pair. Fish averages 3 cents per pound.

A numerous class of animals killed here and elsewhere, but seldom eaten, are mules—the cheapest, easiest fed, and most enduring beasts of draught and burden. It is surprising how they climb icy acclivities with loads so disproportioned to their slender frames. Some streets have a rise of eight or ten feet in a hundred. The Exchange Hotel opens on one, and it is painful to witness them tacking from side to side as they pass it, for ascend direct they can not. See those two small ones struggling with a ton of building-stone from the river side, straining as if their limbs must become disjointed and their sinews torn asunder! Scalding vapor pours from their nostrils and rolls over their panting sides. Their clinched teeth are wide exposed, for their quivering lips are drawn apart and corrugated by their efforts. Conscious that if they ceased their exertions the load would drag them backward and whirl them down the steep, how spasmodically they strike their toes into the ground to secure a footing! It is wonderful how their delicate pastern joints endure without snapping such violent grapplings with the pavement. The driver now turns their heads across the street, and blocks the wheels to allow their palpitation to subside. In many streets they can not ascend over twenty feet without thus resting. Richmond is the mules' Tartarus. There was some reason, if not piety, in the reply of the old Spanish hybrid to his young associate in harness as to the preference to be given to level or to undulating roads. His answer was, "A curse on both, and on the fiends that made them."

Lotteries, expelled from Northern States, still flourish here. Every day, Sundays excepted, a new one is announced. The 290th of "The Alexandria Lottery for Internal Improvements in the District of Columbia" was drawn on the 5th instant. Three more have since been issued, and the 294th is to be drawn to-day. "The Virginia Leesburg Lottery, for endowing the Leesburg Academy and other purposes," was drawn on the 8th. Men, it is said here, will gamble, and why not direct the business into beneficial public channels? They assuredly will, wherever the laws stimulate the passion, and authorize hosts of agents to carry it into every corner of the land. At best, lotteries are crusades against public morals—legislative schemes to convert men into blacklegs—making worthy citizens worthless in every sense. For every lottery-gambler enriched, a score have been made insane and a thousand beggared. But inconsistencies and their vindication are natural to man, else these devices for improving public lands by impairing public morals, and debauching a people's virtue to endow schools for their children, had not been so long tolerated.

Considerable business is done in Richmond, but not what is due to the capital of the largest and earliest-colonized state of the Union. Its population, though nearly double that of any other Virginian town, is under 21,000—less than that of Lowell or Rochester, not half that of Cincinnati, and falling, in this respect, behind northern and western cities of yesterday. The people of the "Old Dominion" are said to be awakening to the fact of other states, less favored by nature, shooting so fast ahead of her, and some of the youngest leaving her in the rear.

December 15. The bark having started yesterday in charge of the pilot for Hampton Roads, along with a Bremen brig bound for Bahia, I left Richmond, with Captain Smith, in a Norfolk steamer, glad in view of getting to sea after so long a detention. After steaming twenty-five miles down James River, we overtook the Mazeppa at anchor only half way to the Roads, while the Bremen vessel was ahead and under sail, having passed a long bend where the wind that arrested our progress was favorable to hers. She left the Capes four days before us, and was probably seven hundred miles on her way to the equator ere our pilot left us. So much for a few hundred yards start on a crooked river. Here we were detained two days. A strong gale, with snow, set in, and increased till additional anchors had to be thrown out to prevent our being blown ashore.

To pass the time, suppose we glance over the floating boarding-house. There is something pleasing in the idea of occupying rooms in one of those hotels that take their inmates out to see the world, and more especially the wonders of the deep. The dining and drawing rooms are one. Built on deck, it extends from the stern to near the mainmast, where the entrance is. The ceiling-beams are elevated sufficiently for men of ordinary stature, except when carrying their heads too high, in which case they act the part of moral monitors, and reprove the haughty. The side walls are made up of painted doors with Venitian panels, each opening into a sleeping chamber. Look into one, and you see all. Five and a half feet long, the same in height, but less in width; each is a double-bedded room. Those two shelves are the bedsteads; one, three feet above the floor; the other, fifteen inches over it, and the same distance below the ceiling. The narrow ledges in front are to keep the occupants from rolling out. Were they deeper, no person could get in nor out, and, as things are, it is not easy for strangers to introduce themselves between the mattress and the coverlet.

There may be those who with dignity get into and out of bed ashore, but it is not to be done at sea.

A wash-stand is wedged fast at one end of the chamber, and as you raise your face out of the lavatory, a miniature mirror meets your eye. A space, four feet by two, is left for you to move in. A prismatic strip of glass lets in light at the ceiling, while air from the drawing-room circulates through the panel-slats.

The dining-table is fastened to the floor, and has raised edges to keep dishes from sliding off with their contents. The sideboard is overhead—a long and wide swinging shelf, in which are perforations for every variety of table glass-ware. A fire, in weather like this, is indispensable, and there glows the stove, chained to the floor, with its pipe ascending through the roof. Two skylights illumine the room by day, a lantern and lamp by night. A ship's largest saloon is named the "cabin," a word of low orgin, from *cavea*, a den, characteristic, no doubt, of primitive conveniences at sea. But now marine philology more than keeps pace with improvements in shipping; passengers' berths are "state-rooms," though the poorest of all places for stately people to show off in.

Two more distinct dwellings are on the main deck; one near the bows, in which the sailors sleep, and sup, and hold soirées —in naval nomenclature, the "forecastle," to distinguish it from the captain's mansion, anciently known as the "rear," or "hindcastle." The other is located amidships, and accommodates a number of friendless passengers, of whom few will live to see Rio. It is an independent floating dwelling, namely, the long-boat, having its sides raised with neat carpentry, in which are two windows, a cubit square, with shutters, and the whole covered in with a tight roof, a copy, on a small scale, of Noah's ark, and somewhat resembling it in its tenants too.

On either side of this abode is lashed a row of huge water-casks, leaving but a narrow path for the sailors between them and the ship's bulwarks. Forward of them rises a square structure, black inside and out as the iron chimney projecting from it—a marine kitchen. Here the cook presides, close to his living larder. As if sensible of his vicinity, and of the daily onslaughts to be made on them, how his victims scream! and well they may. A huge black fellow, wearing a high-pointed red cap, a shirt of the same ominous color, with sleeves rolled above his elbows, bare-legged, and knife in hand, he is enough to scare others besides the chicken-hearted.

The cellars of the establishment are so well stocked with flour, apples, hams, cheese, and other edibles, that we might "put a girdle round the earth" before running out of victuals. The family is not large—the captain, two mates, steward, cook, and six men: eleven in all—myself, the only boarder, making out the dozen.

17*th*. After drifting down twelve miles with the tide, we are again at anchor opposite a small building of one story, at the foot of an excavation in the left bank—a country store owned by an acquaintance of the pilot. The steward suggested some additions to his stock, and the captain, pilot, and I went ashore. We found the proprietor a good, easy soul, and wondered how so mild a man had lost an eye. Short, thick, and fifty, he wore a fox-skin for a cap, a docked gray coat, and had both legs and thighs incased in leather leggins. To one heel a rusty spur was strapped. He had nothing in his store save a little chewing tobacco. His wife was tall, thin, and obviously an energetic helpmate. She was miserably dressed, considering the weather. Her hair was streaming through rents in her cap, the sleeves of a light calico gown stopped before they reached her elbow, and, with the skirts, were scolloped without the aid of scissors. The dwelling part seemed desolate as the store. The only thing approaching to ornament was a huge heart-shaped red pincushion, pendent from the mantle-shelf. Upon the latter lay a stalk of dried tobacco. Our host pulled off a leaf, bruised it in his hand, charged a pipe, and invited us to follow his example. A black girl brought in an armful of wood, threw it on the fire, and took a stand behind her mistress, of whose gown she grasped a handful, and with two fingers in her mouth glared at us as if we had come to buy her.

Major J—— gave us a sketch of his life. He began the world with nothing; the day he married, seventy-five cents was all he and his wife possessed; they had not a scrap of furniture; a friend lent them a bed. In twenty-five years they had made $12,000 by hard labor, and now it was nearly all gone.

He had become surety for neighbors; his house, on the site of the present one, was burned; a steam-boat captain cheated him out of a cargo of fire-wood; a sloop shared the fate of his house; he lost two negroes, and had no children. Troubles came so thick that he thought Providence was trying to see how much he could bear; he could not tell why, for he defied the world to show he had cheated any one of a cent.

General challenges may sometimes be just; they are seldom prudent. There is no telling when nor where the author of mischief may pick up an opponent. Sometimes he succeeds among the appellant's friends, which is bad enough, but it is much worse when his own wife springs into the lists in answer to the summons. At the innocent boasting-point of this Virginian Job's recital of his woes, his lady said his assertion was not true! He *has* cheated somebody, and he knows it! Moreover, she had told him he would be punished before he died. Hitherto we had sat silent as Bildad, Eliphaz, and Zophar over their friend, but one of us now asked how he lost the slaves. Both, he said, were young and promising; one, a girl, worth $150; the other, a smart fellow, was cheap at $300. He never knew what ailed them; they took sick, and died on his hands.

The only effects of the felonious charge were a slackening of the puffs, a half withdrawal of the stem from his lips, and a placid stare at the accuser. He immediately returned to sucks and puffs again. For my part, I was greatly relieved, but not so his mate. "Yes, he has cheated somebody;" here I felt like going out; but her next shot hit the mark and cleared away the mist. "He had cheated *himself*—he had trusted every body."

At a short distance back of the house stood a miserable hut. While looking toward it, I observed a movement in the bushes above, and every now and then caught a glimpse of something working its way through them. As it drew near, it proved to be a negro moving on his knees, and with the aid of a stick, dragging two withered and bandaged legs through the ice and snow behind him—a harrowing spectacle. By skipping some and wading more, I reached the open entrance of the hut, but could see nothing of him. All was black and chill within. There was no opening for light save the low, door-way. A flickering flame at length broke out, and showed he had crept into a corner, where he was fanning a few half-extinct embers. Poor fellow! he was but twenty-five, and quite intelligent. He lost the use of his limbs twelve years ago through rheumatism, was soon after sold, and had been traded away many times since. What a fate is his!

On coming out, his mistress was feeding a crowd of turkeys, pea-hens, common fowls, and pigeons. The hawks, she told me, got more of her chickens and pigeons than her own family. They have now, she observed, only five slaves, and the cripple I had seen was worth all the rest; he cuts down more cords of wood a day than any man in the county; they bought him six years ago for $50, and he had earned them a thousand; he was a good hand at fishing, and at almost any thing.

Although the captain obtained no eggs for money, he got a fine black cat for nothing. I thought him joking when asking for it, and am half sure the lady had no idea of being deprived of it on giving an indirect affirmative; but he forthwith snatched up the astonished animal and took it aboard.

Two tedious days more elapsed ere we reached the Roads, and anchored amid a fleet of vessels waiting for a change of wind. The village of Hampton lies on our left, Norfolk at the right, and Old Point Comfort three miles ahead of us. Yon massive battery, rising out of the water opposite "Old Point," and three quarters of a mile from it, is the famous "Rip Raps"—an expressive sobriquet. The water between it and the Norfolk side of the shore is too shallow for large craft to float through. All must pass in and out between the two forts whose names are so diverse; one offering you consolation, if a friend; the other ready to knock and tear you to pieces, if an enemy.

CHAPTER II.

Ten Days' Sail: Beat out.—New Sensations.—Captain in Costume.—A Gale.—Sea-sickness.—Water Ram. — Gulf Stream.—Christmas Carols.—Human Daring.—Ship hunted by marine Demons.—Hard Life of Seamen.—Cook and Captain.—Enchanting Skies.—Minute Crabs.

December 20. We are still lying opposite the mouth of Chesapeake Bay, after spending a week in descending the lowest of the five parallel streams of which it forms the basin. The barometer has suddenly fallen from 30°.25 to below 28°, a certain indication of a change in the weather. Our detention makes heavy draughts on the captain's patience. He swears he will pass Cape Henry before night, let what will happen: a pretty piece of blasphemy this would have been in an ancient mariner; but, alas for Neptune! instead of bulls reeking on his altars, he receives little from sailors now but exhausted quids thrown in his face.

After two unsuccessful attempts, we at last beat out, and by 5 P.M. the forts were miles behind us. Now fairly off, with the wind abaft, the ship, hitherto so sober and demure, moves as if mad with joy at getting into her element, rolling and pitching from pure exuberance of spirits. A stranded whale just floated over a sand-bar could not make off more merrily. Her very timbers creak in concert with the flapping sails and whistling in the rigging. Eheu! But this is a change! If she minced and minueted down the river, she is leaving it in a gallopade. How the ocean roars, and how the water hisses where she cuts it, as if her bows were red-hot plowshares! She's going to "make a night of it"—to treat us to a ball. All things are preparing for one, and not a few have begun rehearsing.

The captain, as master of ceremonies, dressed early. Retiring after dinner in citizen's dress, he sprung forth a singular-looking sea beau. I did not recognize him, and was on the point of asking who the stranger was, when he announced himself *viva voce*. A glazed hat with a hemispherical crown covered his caput; the wide and flexile brim was drawn at two opposite points close to his florid cheeks by spun-yarn ribbons, tied in a slip-knot under the inferior maxilla. An oil-skin coat, or cloak, or shirt, or chemise—it had properties belonging to all four—reached from chin to ankles: of the color of bees'-wax, it was not more supple than stiff paper; the upright collar embraced his neck, and was made to hug it closer by a fillet cut from the same web as the hat-bands. But the strangest portion of his costume were his French boots. Inflexible as marble, and the legs thick almost as the soles, he raised his skirts, and showed his knees sunk in them, with scollops cut out behind. I had supposed nothing rigid should be about a sailor's dress, nor could I perceive how in such things he could act the skipper. He did, though, and in style too.

The wind rose to a gale, and, blowing directly astern, caused the vessel to roll most fearfully. From no other quarter could the effect be so distressing. I no longer could withstand the general tendency to change of place and posture. Much against my will, my feet began a series of ungraceful steps toward the cabin, where matters were no better than outside. Several trunks had got loose, and, with a dozen stools, were rushing with violence from side to side. The pantry-door flew open, and a soup-tureen, with dishes, and a score of sound and maimed plates, came sweeping over the floor. The steward, securing his erratic charge, threw the fragments overboard, and blessed the ship, the wind, or something else, in subdued but bitter terms.

Night is fast letting down her curtain, and the lamps above are kindling, but I am sick already of the evening's entertainments. They agree not with my head nor legs, and against them I feel my stomach rising. The taste more than a feast suffices; but the worst thing about sea-revels is that, however desirous one is to be excused, no excuse is taken, no begging off allowed, no "not at homes" admitted.

It is impossible to convey to those who never left the land an adequate idea of the distresses of a sea-sick voyager; but let them imagine a person like myself approaching the ocean, and, when launched upon it, half smiling at his previous fears, yet sensible while he smiles of a *je ne sais quoi* sensation flitting about his epigastrium, so very slight, however, that he tells himself it is mere imagination. A struggle between this new feeling and his fears goes on, it may be, for an hour or two, when there is no mistaking either. He now no longer rules his inner or his outer being; his faculties are flying and his feet forsaking him. Creation reels: he looks out, and lo! the earth has left her orbit, and the heavens are rushing with her into chaos. His nature seems dissolving; electric halos play round his bursting eye-balls; he feels the sutures of his cranium open, and his viscera about to leave him—his soul seems taking her departure. Suppose the victim seeks his bed, beyond question the best place for him in such weather as this, yet even there he is rolled and tossed, jerked and shaken, till he becomes indifferent to life, and even wishes for its extinction.

Though some persons get over sea-sickness in a few days, many are never rid of it till they step on shore. Old sailors have slight attacks after remaining a few months on land. The pilot told me he was fourteen years at sea before it wholly left him, and he named some who had died from its violence. I designed fairly to test during the voyage a few alleged specifics. I did so, and the result was, *none* were of any or of marked avail. Lying horizontally mitigates the evil, and if the vessel does not roll, nausea and retching then subside. One proposed remedy is a fillet or belt drawn tightly round the abdomen. With some, this may possibly prove beneficial; with me, it might as well have been strapped around the mainmast. Another is —what has, in fact, been tried ever since the disease was known, every patient by a natural impulse practicing it—to *mesmerize* the enemy: divert his attention to distant matters, and *will* him to be gone. "Be firmly persuaded he can not approach you, and he wont." I have known preachers of this doctrine have opportunities of testing it, when they found that fools and philosophers were alike prostrated, and equally reduced to helplessness.

At midnight the storm, for the stiff gale had risen into one, was raging. At intervals the captain's voice was heard amid the bellowing elements, and feeble and indistinct replies, as from a great distance, came down from aloft. Hail pattered on the skylight and kept whizzing among the rigging. I wondered how the men withstood its fury. The fowls and pigs sent forth cries of distress, and the bewildered cat kept scratching and miauling at my room door for admittance. There was no keeping her out afterward.

My pillow was within a few inches of the water, and, of course, I heard as well as felt it booming against the planks, and boiling and gurgling as it rushed by. While ideas of foundering, running on rocks, or against some other vessel, were invading me, there came suddenly such a blow, somewhere beneath me, as made the vessel stop and fairly spin again. Shaken by the jar, I involuntarily shouted "What is that?" but a stentor's voice could not, at the time, have been heard on deck. It was so short, sharp, and tremendous, that I knew not to what to attribute it except that the hull had been struck by the fluke of a whale. These creatures have crushed in ships' timbers—what if some sound or rotten plank has been knocked off, and I about to drop, unseen of any one this dark night, into the abyss! Then I thought of sword-fishes plunging their nasal weapons clear through the sides of vessels—what if one should transfix me here! Well, such a death is preferable to sinking slowly down among marine monsters that would tear one asunder, and fight over one's disjointed limbs before sensation left them. Of the two kinds of death, give me the quickest.

As if taken at my word, there came another shock, close to where I lay, that made the ship and all within her shiver. She could not have been more stunned if the blow had come from a battering-ram propelled by giants. It was succeeded by others during the night, and not till morning did I learn they were indeed blows from water-rams—huge waves snapping directly under and against her.

21*st*. Wind still high and snow falling. We are dashing across the Gulf Stream, which, like a boiling caldron, is covered with thick-ascending vapor. Ere entering it, the steam rose like a high wall before us. The central portion of the current is, of course, the warmest, the heat diminishing as the volume spreads out on either hand. At 8 A.M. its temperature was 66°, at noon 72°, the air meanwhile below the freezing point. Unfortunately, the temperature of the sea before reaching it was not taken.

I was anxious to ascertain some particulars of a body of water that circulates incessantly round the globe, and silently works great changes on it, but could not keep the deck. A counterpart of the aerial current of rotation, the main stream and its branches modify the configurations of continents, and thereby diversify its own action and effects. Besides its dynamic powers and whatever influence it may have on piscine life—the natural abode of some tribes, and perhaps an occasional and necessary retreat for others—its thermal influence is obvious. But for it the Arctic seas had not been open. The volumes of heated waters from the torrid zone which it pours without ceasing into high latitudes not only serve to moderate the heat of one and cold of the other, but they prevent the polar ice from enlarging its dominion.

A fine lesson in mechanical science might long ago have been learned from it. If the reader has kept up with modern progress of the arts, he is aware of a system recently introduced for heating public and private buildings by hot water. It is indeed a fact, and ever will be one, that in *every* operation of nature, magnificent or minute, simple or complicated, an important invention is anticipated or suggested. There is no valuable device but what may be found in God's museum of machines. Thus, in the warm channel we are rushing through, we behold one of His "hot-water circulators," by which the coldest latitudes are tempered with heat drawn from the hottest. The furnace and boiler are on the equatorial belt, equidistant from the regions to be warmed. "Mains" proceed toward the poles, sending out branches as they proceed, and, after yielding up their warmth, return circuitously for a fresh supply, precisely as do their artificial imitations. The principle of action—the diminished gravity of a fluid or portions of a fluid by heat, in both is one. But how different is Nature's mode of carrying it out. She uses no metallic or other stiff tubing as we do, but conveys the hot liquid through channels formed in the cold, the most flexile, and lasting, and yielding of conduits. The one we are floating in varies in width from twenty to two hundred leagues.

22*d*. The cold moderating. Thermometer at 8 A.M., 55°. Wind still abaft, and no mitigation of the tormenting rolling. Pale, faint, and feeling low enough, loathing all food, and sickening at the sight of a glass of hot toddy kindly pressed on me by the captain, I had to retire after trying repeated cures for sea-sickness. It appears to me that no human power can cure it, but that, like the storm without, it must be left to exhaust itself. During the night I staggered from a sofa to the cabin door; one glimpse showed the sky falling and the sea rushing up to meet it. That was enough. I reeled back, and, the first time for three days, fell asleep in the mammoth and roughly-rocked cradle. Petrels and other oceanic birds pass their nights on the waves. Tossed to and fro, now down in a watery glen, and now on a mountain crest, they sleep on. Can man do this? He must, if he sleep at all at sea. The only difference is, he has a plank between him and the billows.

24th. We are passing into warmer and calmer latitudes. The wind is light, with a splendid day overhead. During the night we passed within one hundred and twenty miles of Bermuda.

25th. Awoke to Christmas by a dismal carol. How evanescent are human hopes! How quickly are they blighted! We hailed yesterday as a harbinger of fine weather through the holidays, and it has ushered in as rough a time as we have had yet. Long before day the wind rose to a hard gale, which drove the vessel headlong. Every plunge she made a sea went hissing over her, while dark waves and boiling foam danced round her. In the cabin, the barometer kept swinging with a violence that threatened to throw it out of the gimbals—one moment perpendicular, the next parallel to the ceiling. [Of course this was an illusion; it was the ship that was vibrating, the instrument being comparatively at rest.]

Of the restless, daring, danger-defying nature of man, there can be no better proof than a few individuals thus riding over the trackless and turbulent deep, pursuing their solitary way with unerring certainty, through storms and darkness, even to antipodal seas and harbors, and turning, as they go, the warring elements to their purpose! Without witnessing something of the kind—taking a few trips in an ocean phaeton, and marking the skill of the charioteers—it is not easy duly to appreciate the value of nautical science and of nautical men.

Noon, on deck. So great is the commotion, that the distant horizon all round us is seen jagged and broken with the heaving waters. The poor ship, like a wounded sea-bird hunted by shoals of marine demons, struggles hard to escape. I can compare the scene to nothing else. One moment panting she flies, and the next is overtaken and pulled shuddering over, her joints and masts creaking as if crushed by their fangs. Encouraged by the helmsman, she rights herself and proceeds, but soon they fasten on the other side, and down she groaning leans. Again she recovers herself and throws them off. Next, leaping at her throat, she raises her bows till half her keel is out of the water, and then plunges in desperation on them. Staggered and trembling, it would seem as if she must be torn to pieces. But a short lull ensues, as if her foes were wearied. She breathes a while, her wings are freshly braced, and as the howling of the pursuers reaches her, she takes to flight as with renewed determination to escape them. In this way the pursuit has been kept up, and, with little variation, will be till she find safety in Rio Bay. Then she will refit, and thence lead them another steeple-chase of five or six thousand miles home again.

How the cook managed to prepare dinner passed my comprehension. The steward brought in soup, approaching one moment as if climbing a ladder, and the next as if descending one behind him, so precipitous and declivitous became the base he trod on. Before reaching the table, a sea was shipped that burst in the cabin door, floored him and the *bouillon*, deluged the pantry and several state-rooms. Midnight passed before the water was bailed and swabbed out. The rest of the dinner had been washed away. Thus the sea-sprites, if they could not sink the ship, knew how to spoil our victuals. A hundred times I have wished myself out of their hands, were it only to waste time in coquetting with Virginian Naiades down James River.

Verily, the life of common seamen is a hard one. Night brings them no discharge from duty, and in rough weather all must be on the alert. When relieved from watch, they retire to dark and loathsome forecastles, whose atmosphere would produce asphyxia in persons of weak nerves, thaw and change their garments, if a change they have, and catch what sleep they can. Unused to the amenities of social intercourse, without leisure or taste for mental improvement, no stimulus to ambition, but kept to their labor as oxen or horses are, they can not but become more or less animalized (that is, the great majority, for there are noble exceptions). The sea is designed as a theatre for human enterprise, and the profession of a sailor is as honorable, and now almost as indispensable, as that of a tiller of the soil. Constituting, as both classes do, essential and important links in civilization's chain, the day can not be distant when they will be permanently elevated in their own and in the world's estimation.

A watch, with a loose pendent ribbon and seal, hangs from a nail in the cabin. Going to wind it up, my mind, meanwhile, engaged on other thoughts, I put forth my hand, and was somewhat startled to see the key come deliberately six or seven inches from the wall to meet me—a feat as unexpected at the moment as would be that of a walking-cane anticipating its owner's wishes. The incident may be thought a common one, and so it was, but at the time I was not prepared for it.

27*th.* Yesterday the wind was light and fair, but the troubled ocean had not lost the effects of the previous day's tantrums, and now another gale has come, and more ground and lofty tumbling. The temperature steadily increases. At 6 A.M., thermometer 68°, which a shower of rain reduced in an hour to 64°. The cabin feels close, and the state-rooms more so. New substances, as cheese and other stores, are volatilized, whose odors, mingling with those exhaled from staple bases of every ship's perfumery, are exceedingly distressing; every draught of the horrid fluid received into lungs already sore is inexpressibly sickening.

The cook has given out, having been unwell for some days. The captain now acts the physician, and the steward apothecary. One prescribes, the other prepares the medicine. The patient was called aft to state his case, to place his hands where his pains were, open his mouth, and show his tongue. Prompt as Galen, the captain dictated a prescription, which after seeing prepared, I besought Heaven to spare my health till I could get ashore.

30*th.* The gale of the 27th lasted two days, during which the vessel rocked and plunged so violently, there was no sitting at the table or keeping any thing on it. More libations and offerings were made to the divinities of rough weather. Yesterday the ship was easy, and ran before the wind southeasterly, as if for the coast of Guinea. This morning bright and fair. "Turned out" early. This phrase is quite appropriate. There is here no rising from or sitting up in bed. To enter and emerge is literally to turn in and out. The sky at sunrise inexpressibly beautiful, and introductory to an enchanting series of dissolving views.

At first the entire canopy was gray and dotted, almost uniformly, with fleecy masses, each slightly shaded with umber. Soon these, and the most distant of them, were set off with golden borders, in which livery they hailed the rising monarch of the day, and kept varying their forms and positions as he rose, as if for joy at his arrival. His own robes of burnished gold were next exchanged for those of radiant silver, and anon each cloud was fringed with the like. These now gathered round the horizon, leaving the vault a pure ethereal azure, in which the god, in undimmed glory, mounted. In this manner the ball opened for the day, and the dance of cirri and cumuli began. With a scene as glorious, the evening entertainments ended.

The horizon in fine relief all day. What rather surprised me was its apparent nearness. The circle looked as if not more than four or five miles across, suggesting the idea of neighborhood, and of new objects coming into view on our approaching the outline, as when journeying on land. The surface of the sea helped to strengthen the illusion: in the morning it presented a series of moderately-sized hills, with here and there a narrow valley stretching along between green sloping ridges, while toward evening the whole became a lively representation of undulating meadows.

31*st.* Wind light, water smooth, and sky overcast. "Sungalls," resembling small patches of rainbow, and indicative of squally weather, appeared. Picked up specimens of sea-weed, the little berries and leaves incrusted with microscopic shell, or, rather, cell-work, done by coral artists. Living *crabs*, some not larger than a pin's head, were sticking to and starting life's voyage on them. We have accounts of enterprising human travelers, but what an array of strange facts and incidents would the lives and adventures of a few of these marine foundlings furnish!

CHAPTER III.

Twenty-four Days' Sail: Sea Sorrows.—A Genoese.—Rough Weather.—A Flying-fish.—Flowers of Death.—Oceanic Skies.—The Atmosphere charged with red Dust.—Firmamental Paintings.—Flying-fish Latitudes.—Cream-colored or Quaker Skies.—Flying-fish again.—A Meniscus.—A Squall.—A ship in Distress.—A young Fly.—In the Variables.—The Ocean unchangeable.—Temperature of Air and Water.—Brazilian Coasts.

January 1. The old year expired in convulsions, and the new one has come forth in a storm. The wind is bellowing with rage, rain falling in torrents, and we bounding on a dark and raging ocean. A bad night, during which sleep was impossible, is succeeded by a worse morning. Unable to stand, too sick to sit up, no resting in bed, and no resting-place out of it, loathing all food, and bereft of all strength—what more can sea-sickness do? Could the feeling be got up artificially in prisons, it would be mightier than the *douche* in taming rebellious spirits. For three days more we had both rough and moderate weather, with wind for us and against us; now running for the Cape of Good Hope, and next driven toward Gibraltar.

6*th.* Nothing could be more grateful than our progress yesterday. With the air at summer-heat, we sailed over placid waters beneath a glorious sky. It repaid us for a week's bad weather, and gave us a taste of the sailor's paradise. This morning I was on deck at early dawn, and watched the dark gray canopy slowly turn into a light dull green, out of which swarms of brown masses came; a little while, and vivid red spots grew out between them, and then each cloud appeared with a crimson fringe; both spots and fringe increase in brightness, short streaks of vermilion next appear at the eastern horizon, and now, shooting far above it, enliven the whole firmament. They are rays of the rising monarch's crown, and yonder comes his glowing face! We shall have the pleasures of yesterday repeated. So I thought; but lo! in seven minutes he retired, and a sombre leaden screen enveloped all. So quick a change in Nature's kaleidoscope I have seldom seen. A brig hove in sight, and by noon we exchanged signals. Her flag is little known in these seas, and yet it ought to be no stranger, since under it Columbus sailed for several years. She was a Genoese. By 5 P.M. we had run her out of sight, her sailing qualities being little better than those of the rickety *Nina*, or the dull flag-ship of the world's great admiral.

8th. Yesterday the barometer presaged bad weather, and it came. The sea ran higher than ever. As the opportunity was favorable for observing the height of the waves, I spent some time in watching them. Instead of mountains, they were moderate-sized hills. None appeared over twenty feet high. In reality, their altitude was only about twelve feet, because their bases were sunk about as much below the general surface as their peaks rose above it. The ship, with most of her sails furled, is tossed about almost like a feather in a whirlwind. Racked and shaken as she is, with 300 tons or more of cargo liable to displacement, it is surprising to me how she holds together; one moment careening till the water spouts through the scuppers, the next her bows rising as if to rest on her stern, and the next plunging as if to stand on her head. These movements are so irregular, and often so suddenly arrested, that, as when a sea breaks under her, she quivers to her centre.

Two stormy-petrels kept flitting at the stern. Restless, these tiny lovers of the troubled ocean know no rest. Superstition makes them unhappy souls of departed sailors, while the huge gull and huger albatross are those of wicked mates and masters.

The sun tried hard to-day to push aside the watery screen; but a few short, ochre-colored beams, which had a singular effect on the hazy atmosphere, was all he could do in the morning, and then but for a few moments. The general aspect of the ocean is remarkable. It might be compared to a calico pattern of black and white spots. The waves are black, their crests pure white, and, at a distance, both appear in equal numbers and dimensions.

A flying-fish came on board; but for its wings I should have taken it for a mackerel. Common to seamen and familiar to naturalists, it was new to me, and may be to some readers, hence its portrait, a pretty accurate one, is introduced.

FLYING-FISH.

From the nose to the extremity of the tail, twelve inches; deepest part of the body, two inches; the longest side of each wing, seven. The lower lobe of the tail prolonged beyond the other, designed, no doubt, to facilitate the act of springing from the water. The wings—enlargements of pectoral fins—have their translucent membrane strengthened by rods or rays, which diverge with the expanding surface, and still farther to distribute their support, each one becomes split about half way up the wing, and the two branches, after spreading apart, become in like manner divided as they approach the margin. Having nothing else to do, I began to moralize on the unhappy fate of the pretty stranger. If it flew on board to escape a dolphin's jaws; how fatal its mistake! and if allured by the ship's lights, it is an emblem of many a country youth, whom the glare of city life has drawn from home to his destruction. While thus musing, the captain told the cook to fry it for breakfast. There was nothing outre in this, but it grated strangely on my meditations and dispersed them.

9*th*. Wind moderated, but the swell little abated. It takes time for an uproarious ocean to settle down after the disturbing cause has ceased to act. I noticed three or four delicate yellow flowers, less than a pea, growing out of a partition joint in the cabin. They were "the flowers of death," the "*Immortelle*" of French florists and undertakers. Cultivated in grave-yards, of them wreaths for the dead are formed. Welcome at sea as every trifling incident is, there are those, in whom ancient superstitions live, that would have construed the appearance of these pretty things into an intimation that the fate of Cloudesly Shovel, and the myriads who have found coffins in cabins and cemeteries in sunken ships, was about to be ours. The vessel had taken a cargo of cotton to Europe, the cabin having been filled as well as the hold, and in that way the seeds probably found their way into her.

10*th*. A swelling sea, but a glorious day. Hitherto we have received the wind on the starboard, but having this morning crossed the edge of the great trading current, the larboard side is turned to it.

I pity those who could sail in such a day as this, and under the canopies that covered us, without perceiving God's love of the beautiful, and the means every where provided to foster the taste in man. Were I a painter, I would fill portfolios with oceanic skies, from the gorgeous to the plain, dark, and awful. Copies will in time be required by philosophy. Of several rich scenes, I jotted particulars of one: a narrow, slate-colored ribbon circumscribed the horizon, and upon it reposed a broad belt of vermilion, interspersed with soft dashes of India-ink, shaded with umber. This glowing field merged insensibly above into a bright *cream* or yellow—a new firmamental tint—and this into a delicate pale green, which deepened upward as it approached the summit of the dome, while over all amber-stained masses floated, diminishing in size, but deepening in tone as they descended, and varying in figure every where.

12*th*. Another gale, and the ship practicing the polka. Sun veiled since yesterday morning, when we entered the tropic. As the captain and I were conversing just within the cabin-door, something came flashing between us and dropped on the floor—a flying-fish, allured by the lamp. Nearly killed by the blow, it died before a bucket of water to put it in could be drawn. Others came on board during the night. We are approaching latitudes 13° and 14°, called "Flying-fish Latitudes," from the fish abounding in those parallels. Such is the velocity of their motions, that a portion of the nose or scalp is left wherever they strike; marks are numerous on the ship's sides.

13*th*. The sun just showed his face and left us. Thermometer, at sunrise, 72°; noon, 73°; sunset, 72°. For the last ten days the rise of the mercury has seldom exceeded three degrees between daylight and evening, often not two. The wind is strong from the east, and brings with it a red impalpable powder, whose presence is visible on the windward side of the sails and rigging, and is thought to have been collecting for the past two days. It is only by bringing the burr or loose fibres on the outside of a rope between the eye and the sun that its presence and color are made manifest. The captain calls it "African sand"—says he has observed the like before. The moon this evening, as well as the sun during the day, obscured by mist; supposed to be, in some measure, caused by the atmosphere being surcharged with the dust.

14*th*. Air, at sunrise, 72°; at 2 P.M., 76°; at sunset, 74°. A blandness not felt before prevails. Sun obscured all day. Spent most of it watching the movements of flying-fish. Schools of fifty to a hundred every now and then sprang up and darted off on either hand as we approached, reminding one of coveys of quails and other game disturbed on moors or prairies. I could hardly persuade myself they were not birds.

At and after sunset appeared panoramic paintings, which no human pencil could approximate, nor human pen portray half their beauties. Imagine the zenith of azure diminishing in tone down one third of the vault, and there blending into living emerald, which, as it descended, vanished through a straw tint into brilliant white at 25° above, and continued with increasing brightness near to the horizon. The heaving waves at our feet, constituting the dark and bold foreground of the picture, had dwindled into rest, and a pale band of misty brown, 5° or 6° in depth, ran, as usual, round the horizon, its upper and broken edge, of course, in strong relief.

Upon it rested, in one line, two adjoining streaks or short strata, of unequal length, densely black, and shaded mellow with umber. Two smaller lay just above, between one of which and the longest below the glowing orb peeped out. They did not open sufficiently to show the perfect ball; portions of its upper and lower boundaries were hid. Three more small strata, of a deep chocolate hue, were gracefully arrayed above, in manner of an eyebrow. Behind, and stretching far above, was something like a fawn-colored fan, half opened, whose leaves were marked with silver rays, proceeding from and centring in the orb. A similar fan reversed was unfolded immediately beneath, but assumed a darker shade from the misty belt over which it spread. And now the finest trait—some eight or nine cumuli, picturesquely shaped, and of the purest *cream* color, formed a broken arch over the whole. The crown of this wide curve reached high into the emerald field; its wings of smaller masses descended through the glistening cream and white nearly to the dark band at the base of all. The highest portions of it were of a lighter tinge than those below, so much so that in the varying backgrounds the whole appeared in equal relief. I never saw nor imagined a scene so purely chaste and captivating, and never expect to see the like again.

As the sun sunk, the scene changed into another about as rich and novel. The clouds gradually turned to chocolate, and the groundwork to cream, which lightened in tone upward.

Again, the zenith next was purple, which merged below into crimson, this into pink, and this into a light and dead yellow, which touched the narrow band at the horizon, now between cinereous and slate. Clouds, varying in figure and magnitude, floated over this gorgeous groundwork, all of deep umber, their lower sides showing edges of red more or less vivid.

15*th*, 6 A.M. Air, 74°; rose during the day to 76°, and was at that two hours after the sun went down. By 7 A.M., the ash-tinged curtain vanished. At 8, the king of day was still concealed by a moderate-sized cloud, which rose with him. By 9 he threw it off, and shone in undiminished glory. The phenomenon of his being thus accompanied with a rising screen, as if to conceal him till his toilet is completed, is common. In evenings, similar attendants wait on him till he sinks out of sight.

Flying-fish numerous. Flocks, of from twenty to a hundred, in one case twice that number, spring up as the ship plows in among them. They seem to take the air for pleasure as well as to escape danger, groups and individuals being observed leaping and making short trips as if in mere wantonness. They fly low, seldom mounting higher than six or eight feet, but they have the power to rise and fall with the heaving surface, and to change their direction laterally. While the greater part of a group goes off in a right line, individuals turn aside and pursue different courses, just like birds disturbed in a rice or wheat field. Sometimes you are ready to swear they are swallows skimming along for flies, so strongly do they, in certain lights, resemble them. When going in a direct line from you, their black backs are foreshortened, and the wings in relief. In some positions the fluttering of these organs is distinctly visible, resembling trembling plates of mica.

The distance they pass over varies with the impulse that rouses them. While some descend not far from you, others, more timid, dart far away. The ordinary flight of a group may be averaged at two hundred feet, but some proceed four or five times that distance. I have seen single fish pass over three hundred yards.

At 11 A.M., the sun again obscured by a dark brown cloud of moderate size, beneath which a drab curtain stretches out, bordered with a wide cinereous hem below. From the concealed orb, white and cream-tinted streams descend, producing a soft and singular contrast with the bright blue and green grounds above, with their light floating masses. In the afternoon another rich groundwork of cream appeared, and upon it a numerous flock of chocolate fleeces, all edged with white and silver—a glorious picture! The day's drop-scene was almost as ravishing as that of yesterday, exhibiting much the same colors, but differently disposed. A few particulars may give artists an idea of its character. The zenith blue, vanishing into greenish white, and thence into vivid white at about half way down the vault; then a light cream tint commenced, and continued increasing in depth of tone to the ribbon of slate at the horizon. Words are wanting to describe the richness of this cream below, its delicacy above, and purity throughout. The sun was about $8°$ above the horizon, glowing as yesterday like an eye of molten gold between eyelids of densest jet.

Six or seven degrees above him lay a dark brown fleece not

less than 20° in length and 4° in depth, and, but for some patches resembling dark tortoise-shell, might be called a raven black. In front of this shot up from the orb a fan of rays, and a similar one opened below him. Each did not exceed a sextant, or sixth part of a circle. Their effect, relieved and modified as they were by the different-colored media, was of course indescribable. Then, on either hand, and all above, were seen single clouds of varying forms and sizes, all of a rich chocolate hue, their under sides being darkest, and edged with silver. Those lowest were deeper toned than those above. Their longer axes were inclined to the departing luminary, and moved after him, as if hastening to bid him good-night.

These cream-colored scenes might be named "Quaker skies," for here the heavens, in their loveliest costume, not only sanction, but adopt the very hues that pretty sisters of the sect prefer. Can George Fox, William Penn, or other voyaging patriarchs of the Friends, while on missions over seas, have received their canonical colors immediately from above? caught the idea and inspiration literally from the clouds?

Happily was the solar orb made patron of the fine arts. Unrivaled scene-painter as he is to this and some scores more of worlds, it is to me inconceivable that he can turn from planetary easels pictures excelling those of yesterday and to-day.

16*th*. Air, at sunrise, 76°; at sunset, 78°; water, 79°. The red dust obviously accumulating; one of the fore-sails, an old one, looks as if it had received a coat of light brick-colored paint, so much and evenly has the dust collected on it. We are opposite Senegambia and Soudan, which border on the Great Desert, whence the captain thinks the shower comes. He sent a man aloft to collect specimens for me, but, after several ineffectual trials, I sent up a sheet of foolscap paper, which he rubbed over the sail, and sent it down coated over with a light reddish or pale brick-colored tint. The particles are so minute, and adhere so firmly to the villous nap, that no other way occurred to me to obtain them.*

* Most of this colored sheet was distributed to friends. Professor Girard, of the Smithsonian Institution, identified the dust with the atmospheric infusoria, of Ehrenberg. To it the predominance of the cream color in the celestial paintings was most probably due. See "*Red Fogs and Sea Dust*" in Maury's *Winds and Currents*.

Flying-fish are exceedingly numerous. Every where they are darting out of and playing over the liquid furrows, obviously enjoying themselves as they spring from wave to wave, and turning their pearly sides and snowy abdomens to view. There is no watching them frisking over the green uneven surface without reverting to wrens and linnets in their native meads. Voice only is wanting to perfect the illusion; but, though terrestrial glades resound with vocal melody, the ocean has no songsters.

Kirby, Roget, and other naturalists, who teach that the wings of flying-fish are only buoyant, not progressive organs, are mistaken—decidedly so.

The ground of the evening's drop-scene was a light and dead yellow.

17*th*, 6 A.M. Air, 78°; water, 79.5°; barometer, 30.1°. The wind wavers as if about to leave us. Sea smooth; air balmy, but very damp. Toward evening the solar disk shone feebly through the dense mist unaccompanied by a single ray.

18*th*, 6 A.M. Air 79.5°; water, 80°; barometer, 30.1°. A universal haze. We are moving through a sea of vapor; our clothes are damp as if wetted with a sponge. More symptoms of having reached the southern border of the northeast trades. The water moves in light swells, resembling waving grain, while here and there a solitary fish springs up like a lapwing in a coppice. Toward evening some dull fawn, cream, and chocolate tints came out.

The sea and sky present the figure of a meniscus: I am probably mistaken, but I fancy I can detect the liquid convex beneath the ethereal concave. Perhaps the illusion, if it be one, is partly due to watching vessels coming up the watery curve before us, and passing down it in our rear, as one did yesterday.

Noon. Barometer, 29.5°. The men, reclining at ease in their Sunday attire, are roused in a twinkling to take in sail. Ere they succeeded, a portentous whizzing reached us, and the ship at once changed her easy, lounging pace into a dancing one; the sky meanwhile, shrouded in blackness, poured down rain as from a broken waterspout. In four minutes the thermometer fell from 82° to 77°. The change was not less in the *personnel* of men and officers. They were drenched, and the captain, in his oilskin chemise, appeared as if he had been plunged in copal varnish, hands, face, and all—a marine Achilles dipped in water-proof.

By 1 P.M. the squall was over. As the atmosphere cleared, a vessel was seen coming up in the horizon before us. As she rose, her topmast was missing, and soon a signal to speak us was hoisted. She was a British bark, laden with copper ore from Peru; had lost a mast, two jib-booms, and *two men* in rounding the Horn. In a ragged condition, and short of bread, Captain Smith supplied her with flour, for which he refused pay. She crossed the line yesterday. After learning that she was in need of nothing more, we hoisted sail, and went on our way with gladness and lightness of heart, conscious of having done good on this Sabbath-day.

19*th*, 6 A.M. Air, 78°; water, 80°; barometer, 30°. The sun rose in resplendent beauty. The scene drew forth exclamations of wonder and delight. The entire expanse was profusely studded with every variety of celestial ornament. Snow-white figures floated in azure; others, of dark tortoise-shell and ruby, over grounds of green and cream, while rich chocolate masses moved over a lighter cream and white. Beneath all were dashes of jet amid beams of molten gold.

In half an hour the whole was rolled up and a leaden screen let down. Now in the region of "the Variables," we have every kind of weather in twenty-four hours. Early this morning we were making three knots; at ten, six; at eleven, a calm. At seven, a sky to enchant an angel; before eight, one of unbroken gloom. The clouds cleared away for a few minutes at noon, affording an opportunity to ascertain our position, viz., forty miles north of the line, having passed the rocks of St. Paul, for which we had been looking out.

Gulls hovered about us to-day. While they and a nautilus or two enlivened the scene without, a young house-fly amused us at dinner. Flitting from dish to dish, it enjoyed itself. Whence it came we knew not, unless it left New York in the vessel in a torpid state, and is now resuscitated by the genial heat, while chill winter reigns over its native place.

Cream-tinted clouds appeared for the last time to-day. The red dust is also going; the rains have washed nearly all of it away.

20th. Showers, squalls, and calms. Air, at sunrise, 78°; water, 78°. Surprised at the equality, Mr. Little, the mate, a young officer of superior talents and attainments, and I repeated the experiment with fresh buckets hastily drawn up, but the result was confirmed. Can the rain have wrought a diminution of 2° in the ocean's temperature since yesterday? This region is properly named; it is one of smiles and tears, gloom and brightness, of feeble gusts and prolonged stillness. Vessels are sometimes becalmed for weeks, and, with their occupants, become parboiled or half roasted. More fortunate, a light broken breeze kept us on the move until a genuine southeast trade caught us at 1° south, when the ship's head was turned southwest. South America resembles, as all know, a lean ham, whose Patagonian shank and knuckle terminate at Cape Horn, and the eastern side of its shoulder at Cape Roque, round which we now are edging.

Although the sea is here a boiler of hot water, and the fire that heats it glowing overhead, the air is not so much heated as might be supposed. The dense mist acts as a screen that mitigates the fierceness of the solar shafts—blunts them where they are keenest. And—what never fails to excite admiration in me—when this screen becomes attenuated and about to be dispersed, portions collect into clouds in front of the sun, *rise with him,* and thus mellow his ardent rays by veiling his resplendence. We have not yet got directly under him, as he is running the southern line of the ecliptic, but we soon shall meet him, and then every one of us will be in the predicament of "the man who lost his shadow."

We took leave of the north star a few nights ago, and now a new heaven opens on us. The "Magellan clouds" were visible last night. There are those who pride themselves on having stood on Cheops and in classic capitals. "God," say the people of Cairo, "has such a love for their city that he casts his eyes in complacency on it seven times a day." "See Naples and die, since nothing else is worth looking at," observe others. I would say, "Cross an ocean," and then you may conclude that nothing more ancient, unique, and sublime is to be seen—nothing more suggestive of new ideas, pleasures, feelings, hopes, fears, &c. " Unstable as water" is a saying as old as the Pharaohs; but, for all that, nothing has been more permanent: it is the only element that remains so. A grand agent in changing the condition of other things, it remains itself unchanged. The ocean is now what it was when its waves laved the shores of a lifeless world.

21st, 6 A.M. Air, 78°; water, 79°; barometer, 30°. At noon, air 83°, the highest range yet attained. At 6 P.M., air, 79.75°. Water precisely the same as before the sun rose. Clouds collected rapidly at the east to receive him; not one in the west. The day, on the whole, a pleasant one, notwithstanding the sun was veiled, like the flame of a parlor lamp within a frosted globe of glass.

22d. Air and ocean alike in temperature. I can not detect the slightest change in the thermometer when plunged into the sea. Noon, air 82°, and the sky mottled with white and blue —very like the haunches of fat gray horses. This has been a heavenly day—one fitted for the blessed. Sea-birds fluttered round, and occasionally flying-fish diverted us. In making off, some took to leeward, and others went directly against the wind. Some kept along parallel with us, and were occasionally canted half over by the wind blowing against their sides. Examples of progress by successive bounds, and of varying their course when in the air, occurred. Each flock follows a leader, and when he changes the direction of flight, the rest conform to it. Passed to-day the island of Fernando Norohna. At 6 P.M., air and water 79°.

24th. Yesterday, at 6 A.M., air and water 79°. This morning they are 79.4° and 80.1°; barometer, 30.1°. The day opened with the first of a new series of paintings; the blue expanse was thickly sprinkled with fancy masses of purest white, which became tinged and edged with red, brown, chocolate, and gold. The ocean was gently rippled, and over it played a moderate breeze. Another day's sailing in Elysium. At noon, air 82°. A two-feet rule suspended by a thread cast a four-inch shadow. 6 P.M., air, 80°; water, 80°.

25th, 6 A.M. Air, 79°; water, 80°; barometer, 30.1°. 6 P.M., air, 80°; water, 80.5°. Air, at noon, 82°. Sailed to-day as steadily as if traveling on a rail-road, and under a sky minutely mottled in blue and white, in imitation of the prettily-rippled water. For two weeks we have had twenty-one sails exposed to the motive currents, and seldom have they been disturbed except when tightening the ropes.

Brazilians have here a splendid theatre for steam navigation, extending over thirty degrees of latitude, and bordering one of the choicest departments of the earth—one comparatively free from storms, and where the severities of northern seas and climes are wholly unknown.

CHAPTER IV.

Diagram of the Ship's Motions.—The Ravels at Sea.—Sailing in Elysium.—Worlds are Ships of the Almighty Merchant.—The Nebulæ his Ship-yards.—The Ocean a Type of the Sea of Life.—Abrolhos and Squalls.—Cape Frio.—Land-breeze.—Sea-breeze.—Sugar-loaf.—Enter the Bay.—Former Treatment of Foreigners.—Table of Latitudes and Longitudes during the Voyage.

COULD the complexity and infinity of curves one's person is compelled to go through be transferred to paper, they would convey to landsmen a better idea than could otherwise be imparted of the pitchings, swings, and shakes seafarers undergo; of the intricate and erratic lines their heads, without ceasing, trace in air. The best apology for sea-sick travelers, it would excite surprise that the brains of many are not addled.

Standing close to the mainmast and looking up, its topmost extremity is seen to sweep from star to star, or cloud to cloud, tracing in the firmament diagrams that truly mark the vessel's movements. To imitate this would serve the purpose, and the barometer, freely suspended on gimbals, with a heavy mass of mercury at its bottom, suggested the ready means. Its top reached nearly to a level with the beams of the cabin-roof under the skylight. This was removed in fine weather, and a pencil (point upward) fixed to the instrument, six or seven inches from the point of suspension. An edge of a letter sheet pressed firmly upon one of the two beams between which the pencil was, and the opposite edge borne gently down to bring and keep the under surface and central parts of the paper in easy contact with the moving style, was all that was necessary to obtain a faithful chart of the vessel's motions, except her progressive one, and, consequently, of our own.

48 SKETCHES OF

The paper supplied the place of the firmament, and the pencil acted the part of the mast (though, in point of fact, the operation was reversed). The action of the point was of course distinctly seen on the upper surface of the paper, as the diagram progressed on the under side. The slightest lurch or pitch, and every variation from the horizontal which the vessel's deck underwent were thus accurately delineated and recorded; their direction and comparative extent also.

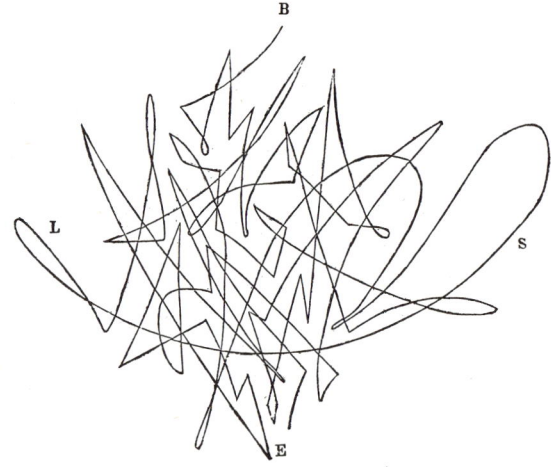

DIAGRAM ILLUSTRATIVE OF THE SHIP'S MOTIONS.

The annexed figure is a specimen from scores taken during the voyage. The letters denote the position of the vessel: B, her bows: E, the stern; L, the larboard, and S, the starboard side. If a line were drawn from L to S, and another from B to E, they would intersect in the middle of the deck, where the pencil was. Hence all deviations from that point, on either hand, indicate rolling or lurching, while the rising and falling of her bows are shown by the lines above and below L S. Most of the movements, it will be seen, are combinations of pitching and rolling. There is but one decided roll—the long sweep that passes beyond L and S. The paper first touched the pencil at B and left it at E. The time it was in contact, from twenty to thirty seconds. When the time was prolonged, the lines became too much involved to be traced without difficulty.

Such are the motions of a ship in even moderate weather,

while the changes in them are endless and infinite. Through eternity no two diagrams could be found alike, and yet to the motions represented by them every individual on board must conform to preserve his centre of gravity over that of motion—to keep his head above his feet. If it ever become worth while to underwriters, vessels could be made to register every strain they may be subjected to. A roll of paper unfolding, as in the electric telegraph, has only to be adapted to a pencil properly suspended.

Some phrenologists insist on organs of flexibility and perpendicularity. Such must be largely cultivated in seamen, for two of our men rival feline tribes in suppleness of spine, climbing like cougars, and accommodating themselves to the rolling base they tread on with enviable felicity. Insensibly turning, twisting, leaning, they preserve their balance like what they really are—systems of walking gimbals. Whatever the art or faculty be, it differs from that of tumblers on shore. These, when at sea, often dance and tumble against their will, having no fixed base to start from or return to, and no regularity in a ship's pitching to time their movements by. Captain S—— took out the Ravel family to Pernambuco, and found the most elastic and agile on the stage mere louts on board. They who trod the tight rope confident as on a pavement, who, with bodies pendent, skated along ceilings, and even he who, with preternatural springs and climbings, rivaled monkeys, scrambled over the deck on all fours.

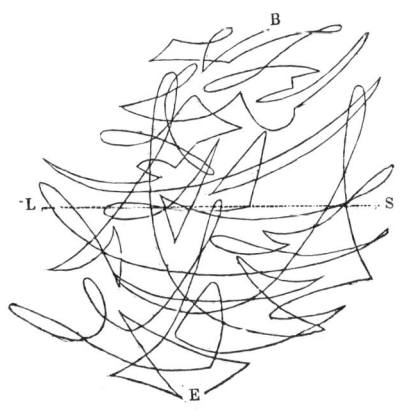

During a part of the voyage I slept in a cot suspended from the cabin ceiling, and, from curiosity, attached a pencil to it, whose point acted on a yielding sheet of pasteboard. Of the diagrams the annexed one is an example.

26*th*, 6 A.M. Air, 70°; water, 80.4°; barometer, 30.1°. At 11 A.M., air,

82.5°. Noon, air, 82°. 6 P.M., air, 80°; water, 80.2°. The shadow of a flour-barrel, at noon, was 4 inches; that of a three-legged stool fell within its feet. Did the Oriental greeting, "May your shadow never be less," mean, "May you never leave home," or does it allude to man in sickness as a prostrated gnomon, and in the grave to a buried one? The moist air makes sad work with our stores and clothing. It tests the quality of silver-ware; some new pieces showed a large dose of copper, parts being green as verditer. A few dolphins and bonitos played at the bows, and a sword-fish, twelve feet long, with a weapon one third of that, came near, and, after a reconnoisance, departed.

27*th*, 6 A.M. Air, 79°; water, 80°; barometer, 30°. 6 P.M., air, 79°; water, 80.1°. Passed Bahia yesterday. There are those whose minds illumine others, and whose virtues warm into life the best affections of their kind, but who shrink from notoriety and vulgar gaze, content to bless unseen, happy without acknowledgments. Of such was the sun an emblem to-day; he vivified, adorned, and placed in relief all things but himself.

A night serenely beautiful as ever elicited admiration from or kindled devotion in a patriarch's breast—mild as an evening in heaven. Myriads of orbs in undimmed radiance shine above us, while cooling zephyrs delightfully waft us onward. The horizon, shifting imperceptibly as we near it, courts us forward, and happily conceals the liquid immensity we float on. In the larger planets, how much more extensive must be views at sea —how much more capacious the celestial canopies! Treading the deck on such a night as this, it is impossible not to forget the petty grovelings and selfishnesses of life in the awful grandeur of the scene, or not to feel a relationship between us and the inhabitants of the worlds in sight. For my part, I can not but believe that at this very moment navigators are crossing oceans in yonder spheres, bearing, like us, the products of one clime to another, and serving as a bond of brotherhood to peoples in districts the most remote. Sailors and trade in other worlds! Yes; why not? Physical beings must have physical employments, and wherever variety is the law of mind and matter, diversity of pursuit must follow. For every type of genius and class of intellects congenial theatres of exertion are undoubtedly provided.

The idea of navigation is singularly apposite to the heavens, and is suggested by them. What are all those floating orbs but ships of the Almighty Merchant; ranged in fleets, loaded with passengers and provisions; varying in their tonnage, courses, distances, and speed; in their freights, accommodations, and destinations? Why has God launched us in the same ocean, given us powers of vision to perceive, and intellects to comprehend their magnitudes, densities, and movements, if not to accustom us to look out of our own small bark and identify it as one of them? Why else has he implanted within us desires to know something about others who are sailing in them? As they and we are children of the same Parent, how natural the desire to become acquainted with them! Seamen are glad to recognize vessels belonging to the same port or country with themselves, and when too distant for verbal communication, with what alacrity they run up their flags! Now it is but an extension of the same social principle that leads us to inquire after those who, embarked on other planets, belong to the same owner and fleet with ourselves. Is it not an innocent wish to have a peep into their vessels, and know how they do? or to exchange signals with them, and, if possible, with those sailing in more distant parts of the same ocean?

Then we might extend our thoughts to yonder nebulæ, the ship-yards of God according to some astronomers, where vessels are in the early stages of construction—some barely framed, others just coming into form, others more advanced, but not prepared for passengers, because not yet provisioned. Oh! for the removal of another film from the mind's cornea, that we might draw nearer to the Divine Builder, and clearer contemplate his doings! But hold! were the screen withdrawn, we should possibly become dissatisfied with and unfitted for our duties here. Enough is shown to make us scorn ourselves for neglecting kindred themes within our reach for the paltry and sordid pursuits that too generally absorb us. But better times are opening. Long-imprisoned Hope has gained the quarter-deck, and our earth's ship-fever—mental squalor—will be driven from her holds.

Leaning over the ship's rails, I could not but think how like the ocean is the sea of life—a very picture of it. The surface of life's waters is never free from agitation. Its waves of hopes and fears are ever raising and depressing man; smiling and frowning skies alternately hang over him, while breezes, favorable and adverse, checker his course, and render it erratic as that of a tacking ship. An illusive horizon encompasseth, and rocks and lee-shores await him. Here all mortals are embarked, and how diverse are their actions! Some float listlessly along and drift among breakers, others sport in fine weather, and, neither looking for nor prepared for squalls, are suddenly ingulfed, while others, again, brace their sails and steer direct through fleets and wrecks of loiterers, in spite of calms, opposing winds, and currents. Upon this sea, human spirits, numerous and restless as the waves, are always rising; and, like these watery forms, they fume and fret a while, and vanish—jostle and dash against each other, and sink unheeded. Each wave is a type of a living man and of his brief career. Soon all that now live will disappear and be forgotten; for, notwithstanding Notoriety is busy as ever in elevating here and there her favorites, wherein do most of them differ from yon solitary swellings, whose crests puffs of wind have raised, and but for a moment, above the general level? What a dark void is the past! We know little more of the successive shoals of human beings that have moved over the earth's surface than of the heavings of ancient oceans.

28*th*. In the vicinity of the Abrolhos—the region of fogs, squalls, and showers. No seeing over a hundred yards ahead. At 5 A.M., air, 79°; water, 80°; barometer, 29.9°. At 6, rain fell, and by 7, the air reduced to 75°; and before noon, to 73°. Washing in sea-water is now like taking a warm bath.

29*th*, 6 A.M. Air, 77°; water, 80°; barometer, 29.9°. Little or no variation during the day. We have passed the sun, for shadows begin to show themselves in opposite directions than heretofore—at our right instead of the left—in front instead of behind us. We are running parallel with the shore, about one hundred and fifty miles from it. A stiff breeze from northeast enables us to plow onward magnificently, throwing up furrows high on either hand. For an instant, near noon, the sun came out again, and while waiting for another glimpse to determine his position and our own, the horizon behind us thickened, a dark patch separated and began rapidly to ascend. In a twinkling all hands were furling sails ; before they were through, darkness overshadowed us, rain in large drops came down, and the ship moaned as if sensible of what was coming; another moment, and she writhed, leaped, lay down, recovered, and shook herself, and then sprang forward at a bounding rate. Bereft of most of her wings, she flew over the roaring waters, while spray kept sweeping the deck. In ten minutes all was quiet except the billows. At 4 P.M. we had a similar flare-up that lasted longer.

30*th, sunrise.* Air, 77°; water, 78°. A fall of 2° in the temperature of the water since last night: a sure sign of our approaching soundings. Luminous streams, as from ten thousand ajutages, are gushing upward from the solar fountain, still below the horizon; like jets d'eau, they spread as they ascend, and break at the zenith into golden spray. What mysteries science has to unfold in yon celestial spring (now just emerging into view), whence flow rivers of light and life upon an assemblage of planets!

In one short hour the sky was in sackcloth and the sea in a fury; rain poured, and the vessel danced more violently than ever. It was impossible to stand without clinging to spars and rigging, and even then you tremble lest the hull, already half capsized, become wholly so. I expected to see the masts snap close to the deck, so fearfully did they swing. The rain increased, and had a marked effect on the waves. It smoothed down their crests and outlines, and prevented collisions. Instead of dashing one another into spray, they now fumed inwardly, like the contents of a caldron near the boiling-point. There was something in this, combined with the unnatural darkness, that made one both feel and fear.

By noon the weather cleared, and we began to look out for land. Sounded with a fifty fathom line without finding bottom.

Throughout the voyage the ducks and geese invariably cackled and screamed in answer to the ship's bell. They mistook its sounds for those of their native villages, and imagined the ponds and fields they were brought up in close by: so the sailors say. Four sickly ducks, all that survive, were let out. As rain fell, it was pleasing to see how they enjoyed it—washing and nestling in it, and running after what fell as the lurching vessel threw it from side to side. The oily matter secreted by water-fowl for the dressing of their feathers must be expended in them, or its sources dried up, for they were soaked with water like wet rags; yet, for all that, it was evidently a treat.

31*st*. By 7 A.M. the weather cleared a little, and Cape Frio, hardly to be distinguished from a cloud, hove in sight—the first land seen since starting. At 8 A.M., water 76°; at 11 it was 75°; at noon, 73°; by 4 P.M., the Corcovado and Sugar-loaf in sight. At 6, the wind left us some twelve or fifteen miles from the harbor's mouth. Air 68°, and the water down to 64°; a difference of 16° from its temperature a hundred and fifty miles out!

From where we lie, the marine gateway presents a wide opening between two mountain walls that rapidly converge to a narrow opening at the distant apex, where the water meets the sky, and where the left wall terminates in a slightly-leaning conical mass—"the Loaf," which rears its head far above the wall, and, with the Corcovado, a higher mass at the other extremity, reminds one of look-outs at the angles of fortifications. The boundary on the right appears continuous, the effect of distance, for several detached islands stand out from it. Raza Island, on which is the harbor light-house, nearly faces the middle of the passage, but now is far to the left. This opening into the port of Rio is so clearly defined that there is no mistaking it, and so easy of access at all seasons that pilots are unknown. Every skipper, foreign and native, runs his own craft in and out.

8 P.M. No chance of getting in to-night. Thunder and lightning—the first we have seen and heard since leaving home. More rain, too, is falling, but the sight of port makes such things trifles, and tempts one to snap the fingers at past sufferings, and send them to the winds that caused them.

February 1. Made sail at 3 A.M., but had to anchor before reaching the Loaf. A morning more beautiful than this never ushered in a summer's day in Eden. The water is smooth as glass, and yet most singularly etched, in squares as small and uniform as those of a plaided garment: the effect of imperceptible waves crossing each other at right angles.

6 A.M. Yonder comes the *land-breeze* down the bay: an up-

right wall of wind, hundreds of miles in thickness, sliding deliberately toward us, and marking its progress over the silver surface by a line of minute ripples. It now has reached the bows, and passes over us at the same moderate pace. It was twelve seconds in going the length of the ship.

Something like a triangular piece of sheet iron was observed protruding above the water and silently cutting through it— the fin of a shark, which hovered about us for several hours. A more agreeable sight was hundreds of small gulls whirling in the morning sun; and still more gratifying, some half dozen palm-trees—specimens of tropical vegetation I was most desirous to see—in fine relief on three mountain islands, Pāi, Māi, Menina—Father, Mother, Child.

Noon. The thermal balance now preponderates in favor of the land, and the aerial current of the morning is reversed. The *sea-breeze*, for which we have been waiting, has set in, and bears us gently on. When near the Sugar-loaf—a bare, black mass of granite nearly thirteen hundred feet high—we tacked and crossed over to within hailing distance of the Fort of St. Cruz, whence three interrogatories were blown at us through a speaking sarbacan. What vessel? Where from? How many days? The captain sent such replies through his trumpet as brought forth the prolonged blast of "Vara wale-e," the signal for us to pass on.

Now within the bay, I supposed we should not stop till abreast of the city, whose spires and windows were glittering on the left shore, a few miles ahead; but harbor regulations required us to anchor near the small island and fort of Villegagnon, whence a covered barge brought alongside the port physician. Without stepping on board, he inquired if any were sick, required all letters and newspapers, even those for the consignees; asked for my passport, and directed me to call in three days at the police-office, where I would find it with an endorsement authorizing me to take board and lodgings in the city; ordered the captain to wait till visited by the Custom-house boat, which might be expected about 4 o'clock, and took his leave. The sun is scorching hot, and the idea of lying here inert for three hours or more is any thing but agreeable.

The treatment of masters and passengers was formerly insulting in the extreme, and even officers of national vessels did not escape. Krusenstein speaks of strangers being treated with the same insulting jealousy as in Japan, while the accounts of Captain Cook and Sir Joseph Banks excite disgust. It is not so now, though boarding-officers are occasionally complained of. That, however, is the case, more or less, in every port, and will be till the Dayspring arise, when not a Custom-house exists to interfere with man of one clime visiting and exchanging commodities with his brother of every other.

The voyage having ended, a table of the daily progress of the ship is annexed, as it may be serviceable with reference to the meteorological facts noticed.

VOYAGE OF THE BARQUE MAZEPPA FROM HAMPTON ROADS TO RIO JANEIRO.

Date.	Latitude.	Longitude.	Remarks.	Date.	Latitude.	Longitude.	Remarks.
1845.	° ′	° ′		1846.	° ′	° ′	
Dec. 21	36 38	72 44		Jan. 11	21 12	33 57	
" 22	35 43	69 01		" 12	18 52	32 56	Red dust.
" 23	35 03	66 01		" 13	16 07	31 13	" "
" 24	34 58	65 23		" 14	13 14	29 39	" "
" 25	34 50	63 20		" 15	10 27	29 00	" "
" 26	34 50	61 25		" 16	7 44	28 31	" "
" 27	34 40	58 26		" 17	4 57	27 43	" "
" 28	35 08	55 33		" 18	2 31	27 23	" "
" 29	34 50	53 20		" 19	00 40	27 55	" "
" 30	34 12	51 40		" 20	— 40 S.	28 19	Turned the ship to
" 31	33 37	49 53		" 21	2 43	29 19	[S.W.
1846.				" 22	4 50	30 37	
Jan. 1	31 51	47 47		" 23	7 23	31 48	
" 2	31 32	45 50		" 24	9 40	32 40	
" 3	30 58	44 00		" 25	11 50	33 36	
" 4	32 01	43 02		" 26	14 15	34 36	
" 5	32 28	42 02		" 27	16 20	35 30	
" 6	31 31	40 09		" 28	18 22	36 30	By dead reckoning.
" 7	28 59	37 58		" 29	20 22	38 00	
" 8	27 10	35 54		" 30	22 30	39 55	
" 9	24 54	34 37		" 31	23 05	42 48	7 P.M., at anchor
" 10	23 33	34 37					off the Sugar-loaf.

CHAPTER V.

The Bay, City, and Suburbs from the Ship.—The Forts.—I land alone.—The Cattete.—A Brazilian Parlor.—Meeting of two Brothers.

ALL is not evil that seems so. While detained, the prospect is favorable to obtain a correct idea of the *locale* of the Brazilian capital; and I have a personal object to accomplish, which makes a reconnoisance before landing desirable. We have time to take a general sketch.

The bay is triangular in its outline, and admitted to be one of the safest and most beautiful harbors which the present disposition of the earth's waters has formed. It is a basin over a hundred miles in circumference, scooped in granite and walled in by mountains whose sides and crests are clothed in perpetual verdure. But for the small opening through which we have just come, it would be a lake hermetically sealed. Its godfathers mistook it for the mouth of a large river, hence the current misnomer.

It is a bay of islands, being studded with seventy, large and little, of which some might well have been taken for "Islands of the Blessed"—those happy abodes of departed virtuous spirits formerly located on the borders of the Western World. Its shores are deeply scalloped—a feature very conspicuous where we lie. The water runs in behind the Fort of Santa Cruz, and, spreading there, nearly insulates it. A mountain island, shaped like a hay-stack, with a small church on its summit, separates this fine cove from another that stretches with some irregularity up the bay to a projecting point, on which the village of San Domingo stands. Immediately above it the shore again trends inward, forming a handsome semicircular beach, the site of the town of Praya Grande, or city of Nictherohy, immediately opposite Rio. Two little steamers have crossed and recrossed several times to-day.

Without peering farther in that direction, since remote objects become indistinct, let us turn to the other side, which has more attractions. On coming up with the Sugar-loaf, a long, narrow strip of rock is seen stretching from its base. Upon the extremity of this strip is the battery of San João, directly facing that of Santa Cruz; hence crews and vessels attempting to come in without leave are maimed and slain, shattered and sunk, under the patronage of the beloved apostle at the larboard, while, under the emblem of salvation, they are blown to pieces at the starboard. The boys of Zebedee were named "sons of thunder:" was it on that account one of them was chosen to preside over this establishment for hurling material thunderbolts at enemies' heads?

Soon as San João is cleared, the water is seen to sweep in and beyond the Sugar-loaf. With map in hand, this is at once recognized as Boto-Fogo Bay, and the white houses skirting the beach the village of Boto-Fogo. The upper horn of the crescent is marked by a bluff, precipitous hill, whence the shore slightly curves onward to another eminence, on which a handsome white church conspicuous stands. It and the hill are dedicated to "Our Lady of Glory," and a glorious site for a dwelling they have given her. Between the hills is the Cattete, a suburb connecting Boto-Fogo with the city.

From the church the beach shoots forward a mile in a more irregular curve, ending in a point that juts far into the bay. In this stretch part of the city is seen—a swarm of houses, crowding and turning through a narrow passage between two hills like troops rushing through a defile and treading on each other's heels. With the aid of a glass a double tier of arches—the aqueduct—is seen. On the point the arsenal is located, facing San Domingo. Immediately above the point, and behind the two hills, one of which is Castle Hill, with flag-staffs and marine telegraph on it, the old part of the city of Rio and the shipping lie. Beyond the city the bay widens into several leagues in breadth. The immediate background of Rio, and up the bay as far as the eye can reach, consists of mountains. Nothing but sky and peaks are seen. An opening occurs in looking over the small bay of Boto-Fogo, but there peaks behind peaks rise in the distance.

Such are the outlines of the Bay of Rio between the city and the sea. Every prominent landmark is so easily recognized, that, with this rapid glance, I am prepared to thread my first steps on Brazilian ground without a guide, and only wait the opportunity.

Four o'clock has come and brought no relief; on the contrary, it has induced something not very creditable to the captain and me. Instead of enduring the detention with smooth faces, we are making excessively wry ones—in place of reasoning with Seneca, or gathering consolation from Kempis, we are invoking blessings on the visiting officers' heads not altogether canonical. But the sun is oppressive; he is already broiling pitch out of the deck-seams, and to him should be attributed a portion of the heat distilling in our bosoms. Another hour elapsed, and the officer, a very polite gentleman, came. Requiring every loose parcel and package, even to a hat-case, to be entered on the manifest, he took the ship's papers, and gave us leave to go ashore. In three minutes the captain and I were in the jolly-boat, and, as I did not wish to go up to the city, he landed me, at my request, at the foot of the Gloria Hill. Pushing the boat in, I succeeded in springing on the beach without a ducking from the surf, and, stepping up briskly into the street, passed along in the direction of Boto-Fogo as if no stranger.

The houses are low, faced with colored stucco, and roofed with the old red tile; not a paneled front-door, stoop, knocker, or bell-pull, and many windows without glass. Coming to a small garden-plot attached to a showy corner house, I stopped a moment to look at white, red, blue, yellow, green, and gilded screens and trellis-work, vying in colors with the flowers; while the walks, bordered with shells, were crowded with something like a hundred painted statues and statuettes.

Being Sunday evening, and very hot, I met few people, but observed, through the open windows and in some gateways, families playing at cards and chess. After winding along for half a mile, with mountains often in the immediate rear of the houses, I inquired of a young man for Rua do Cattete. I was in it. Soon I came to a green, open spot on the right, in which stood a fountain vase, and at it negroes filling vessels. Assured that the residence I wanted was not far off, I passed on. A young gentleman and some ladies were at an open window, and, at a venture, I asked if that was the residence of Mr. E——.

"Si, senhor," was the reply. A table-bell tinkled, a smart negro opened the heavy door, I entered, and was invited to a seat with the company I had just saluted—a very handsome lady, three sprightly young ones, and their brother—a Brazilian mother and her offspring.

The head of the family, whom I had asked for, it was said, would be in presently. He was taking a siesta. Before he came, I had time to observe that the features and furniture of the room were indicative of a tropical clime; high ceiling, matted floor, chairs and sofas with cane-seats, walls papered, but nothing like carpets, rugs, curtains, fire-places, and other essentials of our parlors.

Presently, through an inner door, a tall gentleman made his appearance. Dressed in white linen, and, withal, gray-headed, he formed a perfect contrast with the deep black in which I was draped. A miller and a sweep could not have set off each other more distinctly. Rising, I introduced myself as just come in from New York, and the bearer of letters and other matters from his brother, who had insisted that the first threshold I crossed in Rio should be this one.

"Pray be seated. And so T—— and you are old acquaintances?"

"Yes, sir—bosom friends."

"Orestes and Pylades, eh?"

"Why, not exactly; still, I never was in distress but he sympathized with me, and I may safely say the same for myself and family whenever he or his tasted of trouble."

"Is he stout?"

"Not so much so as you, sir, nor so tall. He is nearer my size. I presume you would not know him, since I understand you were separated in early youth."

"It is forty years since we parted; but, though we have not seen each other in that time, I think I should know him at sight. He talks of paying me a visit. Can I be of service to you?"

"I am desirous of engaging apartments for a brief season. It is getting dark, too, and, without your aid, I shall be in trouble to-night: though I have succeeded in finding your dwelling, I have misgivings, in going from it, of losing myself."

Here there was a movement among the ladies at the farther end of the room, and one addressed two or three words to him in Portuguese. Our eyes again met. I could act a part no longer, and we sprang into each other's arms.

This was followed with such laughing and crying, clapping and shaking of hands, such impassioned greetings, that—But neither the scene nor the feelings are for the public eye.

CHAPTER VI.

Almanacs. — Livery Stables. — Carriages. — Honorable H. A. Wise. — The Host. — Booming of the Surf. — The Matadoura. — Beeves. — Assist at Mass. — Esmola Box. — Apollonia. — A Funeral. — Funeral Customs. — Mourning. — Cost of Masses for the Dead.

February 6. The Rio almanac is a necessary handbook for strangers, while to natives it is indispensable, to enable them to keep the run of the saints' days. Not till to-day have I felt well enough to go out, though some things have occurred which I should have liked to witness. On the 2d inst. was a high festival, in which the emperor usually performs a part, but he is absent in Rio Grande, endeavoring to soothe political troubles there. The 3d inst. was the anniversary of St. Braz. Public honors are paid him in a monastery where his statue is. Celebrated for removing tracheal complaints, he is consulted literally as doctors are.

Livery-stables are here what their name imports. The proprietors furnish plain and showy traveling equipages, with servants in various styles of livery. Having some letters to deliver, a "carro" was ordered, and in a few minutes I was off in a large, well-built and easy chaise. A mule in the shafts drew it by a broad belt across his chest. The saddle mule was simply attached by a hook to the carriage axle. The dress of the postillion, a dark mulatto, eclipsed the plated mountings of the carriage and harness: a polished jet hat, with golden band and edging, yellow vest, light-blue jacket faced with red, and a red collar; white breeches, half lost in boots extending up his thighs, and at his heels brass spurs with rowels two inches over. He wielded a monster cow-hide, and laid it across the shaft animal's back with a ferocity that, had it been an edge-tool, would have cut the beast in two.

We entered Engenho Velha, the name of a district exceedingly rural and picturesque. The driver cracked his thong, whirled through a gateway, dashed up a short avenue bordered with shrubbery and flowers, and brought up at the front of a handsome mansion. Here, after an hour's ride, we were not half the distance we had passed over from the place of starting, the circuitous route being unavoidable to get round intervening mountains. Ascending the piazza, I was the next moment in conversation with the Honorable Henry A. Wise, United States Minister in Brazil, to whose kindness and hospitality, on this and subsequent occasions, my warmest acknowledgments are due.

Walking out in the evening with a friend, we met a bareheaded priest in a carro, accompanied by three half-naked negroes. One, with a large candle, went by each wheel, and the third trotted in advance, ringing a bell. This, I was told, was "the Host," which the priest was going to administer to some sick or dying person. "But where is the wafer?" I asked. "In that little crimson bag suspended from the padre's neck."

7th. I started out alone this morning on a miscellaneous ramble, and shortly became puzzled to account for a slow succession of deep booming sounds that shook both the ground and air. As no one in the streets stopped to notice what I took for subterranean thunder, I followed the sounds down to the Flamingo Beach, and there the riddle was solved by the surf. Wind and tide combining had caused the noise of its breaking on the shore to be unusually loud and powerful.

Winding along the beach to Gloria Hill, I tripped down its farther side (where I landed from the ship's boat), and, continuing toward the city, stumbled upon a revolting scene: a large inclosure full of cattle, adjoining a barn-like structure, whose long and broad roof was supported by stone columns, the spaces filled up with picket gates and railings. Four half-naked men, wielding long spiked poles, were forcing certain of the beasts through a gate between two of the central columns. These fellows wore red pointed caps, their legs and arms were bare and bloody, their hallooings and their cruelty were enough to make one shudder. They thrust the goads at random into the poor distracted victims; blood was oozing from wounds in the sides and necks of several. One dropped exhausted, nor could blows, nor digging the iron points into the most sensitive parts, make it rise. Some twenty to thirty had now been forced through, when the gate was closed—to them the gate of death; for, as I suspected, this was the public slaughter-house. It is located on the edge of the bay.

As I had no wish to revisit the place, I concluded to take a first and last look at the *Matadoura*. Passing round to the end of the building facing the street, I found the administrador at his desk, with the whole interior open before him, and separated only by a low partition no higher than a counter. And what a sight! The immense floor strewed with expiring oxen in all imaginable positions. Those that had just been driven in were leaping hither and thither over the bodies of the slain. Two tall, athletic negroes, with nothing on but short pantaloons of coarse canvas, stained with gore, held axes vertically, at arm's length, over their heads, and kept moving slowly about. Six other men, with poles armed with spikes, were heading the bewildered animals. Whenever one remained a moment steady, or passed slowly by, an axe was buried in its neck behind the horns, and in an instant it dropped. Thus they proceeded till all had fallen, when a negro, with a piece of rag round his middle, bled them by plunging a knife in their throats.

Not less than sixty were now lying prostrate. The gates were again opened, and as I left, the moans of the dying and the bellowings of the living were mingling with the click of the axe as it sunk into their vertebræ—the identical mode of Homer:

> "As when some vig'rous youth, with sharp'ned axe,
> A pastured bullock strikes behind the horns,
> And hews the muscle through."—*Il.*, xvii.

The naked figures of the butchers; their shouts as they faced and frightened the trembling creatures into positions to receive the blow and submit to death; these roaring from pains inflicted by the prongs, and their distress at beholding their comrades sink and quiver, were truly horrible. One evaded the blow, and sprang nearly over the platform, but, ere it recovered from the effort, its head was half severed from the trunk. The axemen moved unconcernedly about, one with a cigar in his mouth, the spikemen affording them sufficient protection. The instant an ox turns on them, he is met by an array of points, which, without mercy, are thrust into his breast and face. By twelve o'clock the work is over for the day, and the flesh borne off to the licensed meat-shops in every part of the city.

The cattle were long-horned, of medium size, various colors, but mostly red, and looked somewhat lean. I subsequently ascertained from the administrador that the number slaughtered last year was 45,000, including the supply for the foreign shipping. There is a municipal impost of 320 reis, or 16 cents, per head. Pigs are slaughtered up the Bay. A few sheep are killed and dressed in town.

8th. I was pressed to attend mass at a chapel close by, where the old vicar, an intimate friend and daily visitor of the family, officiated. He went through the Latin services in a low, monotonous tone. In some parts one could only infer that he was reading by the movement of his lips. His manner was impressive, save the crossings, bowings, courtesyings, and kissings, which were puerile enough in my eyes, and any thing but gracefully done, nor can they be, by a man in a gown, with his back to spectators. The ceremonies were over before fatigue or listlessness wished them at an end. Over the altar stands Nossa Senhora da Gloria, to whom the place is dedicated. Twen-

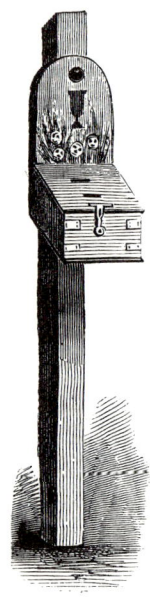

ty inches high, dressed in silks and frills, with necklace and ear-rings, the mopsey lady presides with tranquil dignity at her shrine. The congregation consisted of less than twenty persons, half of whom were blacks. On returning, I was complimented for having "honored God and our Lady."

Four or five feet in front of the chapel door, a post is fixed in the pavement, and against it an alms-box, bound with iron and secured by a padlock. On the raised back a cup is painted, and under it heads rolling in flames. On the box is written, "Esmolas para as almas" — alms for drawing souls out of Purgatory.

9*th*. This is the anniversary of Apollonia, one of those saints who, after leaving the earth, continues through all time to bless it. No pains are more excruciating than those she removes. "Advogada contra a tossé" — she cures toothache. Jaw-bones of wax are offered to her here.

An invitation came for J—— to attend the obsequies of the Condessa d'J—— at 6 P.M. The letter was bordered with symbols of death, and in the centre a shrouded urn, under which appeared the Lusitanian version of Horace's universal adage:

"Entra com passo igual pelas ufanas
Casas dos reis, e miseras choupanas."

On returning from a ramble I met the funeral procession: a long string of chaises, followed by twenty horsemen carrying lighted candles; an elegant coach-and-four came next, guided by a charioteer in light livery, and in it the coffin, whose ends projected through the doors. Carriages of every style followed, some with outriders and lackeys behind; last of all, a coach-and-four, with attendants in white and scarlet costumes, the driver and footmen sweating under enormous triangular hats with red feathers. Except the coffin and candles, there was nothing to indicate a funeral.

In conversations during this and subsequent evenings, particulars relating to funeral customs were mentioned, and may as well be given here.

Soon as a person dies, the doors and windows are closed—the only occasion, it is said, when the front entrance of a Brazilian dwelling is shut. The undertaker is sent for, and as the cost of funerals is graduated to every degree of display, he is told to prepare one of so many milreis. Every thing is then left to him. The corpse is always laid out in the best room, is rarely kept over thirty-six hours, and not often over twenty-four—the number required by law. If the deceased was married, a festoon of black cloth and gold is hung over the street-door; for unmarried, lilac and black; for children, white, or blue and gold.

Coffins for the married are invariably black, but never for young persons; theirs are red, scarlet, or blue. Priests are inhumed or borne to the tomb in coffins on which a large cross is portrayed. Lay people can not have the use of these. In fact, few persons, rich or poor, are actually buried in coffins; their principal use being to convey the corpse to the cemetery; and then, like the hearse, they are returned to the undertaker.

Fond of dress while living, Brazilians are buried in their best, except when from religious motives other vestments are preferred. Punctilious to the last degree, they enforce etiquette on the dead. These must go into the next world in becoming attitudes and attire: married females draped in black, with black veils, their arms folded, and their hands resting on their opposite elbows; the unmarried, in white robes, veils, and chaplets of white flowers; their hands closed as in adoration, with palm branches between them. The hands of men and boys are crossed upon their breast, and, if not occupied with other symbols, a small cup is placed in them, and removed at the tomb. Official characters are shrouded in official vestments, priests in their robes, soldiers in their uniforms, members of the brotherhoods in their albs, sisters of the same societies in those appropriate to them; *e. g.*, those of the Carmo in black gowns, blue cloaks, and a blue slip for the head. The lady entombed to-day was a maid of honor to the empress. Her sepulchral dress was the "livery of the maids of honor." "And, pray, what may that be?" I inquired. "A white silk gown embroidered with gold, a train of green silk similarly decorated, a plume of ostrich feathers, necklace, bracelets, ear-rings, etc.:" raiment adapted to make impressions on worldly monarchs, but not to secure special greetings from the King of Hades. (The countess was young, in health, and playing an hour before she died.)

Children under ten or eleven are set out as friars, nuns, saints, and angels. When the corpse of a boy is dressed as St. John, a pen is placed in one hand and a book in the other. When consigned to the tomb as St. José, a staff crowned with flowers takes the place of the pen, for Joseph had a rod that budded like Aaron's. If a child is named after St. Francis or Anthony, he generally has a monk's gown and cowl for his winding-sheet. Of higher types, Michael the Archangel is a fashionable one. The little body wears a tunic, short skirts gathered at the waist by a belt, a golden helmet (made of gilt pasteboard), and tight red boots. His right hand rests on the hilt of a sword. Girls are made to represent madonnas and other popular characters. When supplementary locks are required, the undertaker supplies them, as well as rouge for the cheeks, and pearl-powders for the neck and arms.

Formerly it was customary to carry young corpses upright in procession through the streets, when, but for the closed eyes, a stranger could hardly believe the figure before him, with ruddy cheeks, hair blowing in the wind, in silk stockings and shoes, and his raiment sparkling with jewels, grasping a palm-branch in one hand, and resting the other quite naturally on some artificial support, could be a dead child. But how was the body sustained in a perpendicular position? "Generally in this way," said Senhora P——, who had often assisted on such occasions: "a wooden cross was fixed on the platform, and against it the body was secured by ribbons at the ankles, knees, and under the arms, and at the neck." Twenty-five years ago this practice was common. It is now confined chiefly to the interior.

No near relative accompanies a corpse to the cemetery. It is given at the door into the hands of friends, to whom its final and respectful disposal is confided. No refreshments of any kind are furnished.

On the death of a father, mother, husband, wife, son, or daughter, the house is closed seven days, during which the survivors indulge in private grief. They wear mourning twelve months. For brothers and sisters, the house is closed four days; the period of mourning four months. On the last of the four or seven days, mourners attend mass, and then resume the business of life. For first cousins, uncles, and aunts, the established rule is to wear mourning two months; for second cousins, one; for other relatives, from fifteen to eight days. By an old law, survivors can be compelled thus to respect the dead according to degrees of consanguinity. The poor contrive, by aid of friends, and sometimes by selling what articles of furniture or clothing they can spare, to comply with the general custom.

Large sums are occasionally consumed in dresses and jewels for the dead. Generally, the embroidery, tassels, cords, spangles, tiaras, etc., are of French gold or gilt tinsel, but in some cases pure metal and real gems are entombed. The cost of funerals ranges from $50 to $1000. Some go to the expense of putting the parish church in mourning. If the deceased owned a carriage, it is generally used to convey him to the tomb—to give him his last ride. To save the expense of a hearse, people in moderate circumstances frequently borrow a friend's carriage. Not long ago, a hearse, all velvet, feathers, and gold, was imported from France, and a few days after a rich man lost his wife. He spent $1500 on the funeral, exclusive of mourning dresses, and, to give *eclat* to the pageant, hired the new funeral-car for $200.

Widows never lay aside their weeds unless they marry. Till recently, they were never known to dance, such an act being deemed scandalous, no matter how long their husbands had been dead. And now, old people shake their heads and repeat an ancient apophthegm: "Widows should ever mourn their first love, and never take a second." They complain of modern degeneracy and the disappearance of old Portuguese virtue. But the young folks contend that they are as good as their grandams, and insist that if widows seldom remain such now, it was much the same formerly, as the proverb more than intimates: "*Viuve rica cazada fica.*" Clusters of a small purple flower are here known as "Widows' Tears." They bloom but once a year, and soon dry up.

A lady living near us recently became a widow, and, at the instigation of a fresh applicant for her hand, induced her only child, a lad of eighteen, to enter a convent, under the pretense that she had in his infancy dedicated him in that way to God, and that he would be the means of delivering his father's soul out of Purgatory. He consented, and she and her legal paramour now riot on his father's wealth and his own. But widowers are not much better. Mention was made of a neighbor who lost his wife, and cried himself almost to death in four days. His friends, alarmed, got him to a ball, where he met a lady, and married her in two months.

When the corpse of a husband is laid out, custom requires his surviving partner to appear before consoling friends in a black woolen gown, train, and cap, crape veil, a fan in one hand, and a handkerchief in the other. Old Senhora P——, who ought to know, says the *mouchoir* often hides smiles as well as tears; and, further that some widows have no cause to cry, their losses being no losses at all. Those who cry loudest, she remarked, are often the soonest comforted, and mentioned a senhora who, on the fifth day, being told that her beauty as well as her health was suffering, looked up and naïvely said, "If that was the case, she would stop," and she did: a parallel to the rich heir who, bending over his parent's coffin, exclaimed, "Father, I'll mourn for you hereafter; I can not now."

Visits of condolence are attended with fashionable formalities. Unless you call in deep mourning you are thought disrespectful. A full dress of black is a *sine qua non* for both lady and gentlemen visitors, and, unless very near neighbors, etiquette requires a carriage and a footman. Enlightened Brazilians are awake to the evils of these expensive follies, and, as in other lands, are making efforts to reform them.

With the exception of holy water, priests are paid for every thing—for christening and burying as well as marrying. When a person is not interred in the district he lived in, the fee is exacted all the same. The Gloria parish has a very insufficient cemetery, at the Lapa Church, and many are entombed elsewhere. In these cases the vicar attends in a carriage, immediately behind the corpse, till it reaches its destination. He then bows to his reverend brother, into whose charge he thus delivers the body, according to ecclesiastical or civil rule, and retires, receiving the legal fee of twenty milreis—the rich frequently giving more. Previous to the transfer, the doctor's certificate of the cause of death must be obtained and countersigned by the vicar, for which the latter receives two milreis—he often gets twenty.

Whatever they may be in life, lay people are profitable to priests when they cease to live. Masses, many or few, are then to be offered for them, and masses are always paid for. The usual charge for one at which a family attends soon after a burial is two dollars, the wealthy, of course, not being limited to that. For subsequent ones a special agreement is made. J—— observed that he and another gentleman were executors of an acquaintance who left five hundred milreis to be expended in masses for the repose of his spirit. They agreed with a priest, and, as usual, at so much for each. Now every mass, to be effective, must be performed fasting and before noon; and in the case referred to one only was to be celebrated in one day, and for the exclusive benefit of the soul of the payer. In a very short time the priest brought in his bill, ready receipted, and asked for his money. Objections were raised on the ground that half the period had not elapsed which was necessary honestly to perform his part of the agreement. He insisted that all he had bargained for had been properly done. They winced, but paid him.

CHAPTER VII.

The Military Arsenal: its Manufactures.—Fine old bronze Ordnance.—School.—Ceremony of the Hat.—Larangeiras.—Cattete Brook and Washerwomen.—A Brazilian Chacara.—Old Portuguese Customs.—Butterflies.—Fountains.—Indian Medicine-tree.—A Dessert after the manner of Eden.—Uniformity of tropical Heats.—Iron Collars on Slaves.—Shoes and Neckcloths symbols of Freedom.—The Vicar and Sneezing.—The public Garden an earthly Elysium.

10*th*. Visited the Military Arsenal, and breakfasted with the polite commandant, Colonel V. Lisboa. His family was from home, and he performed the part of hostess. This is common. In merchants' city establishments, not a female, black or white, is employed. They and their clerks do all the honors of morning, noon, and evening meals, while in private dwellings it is customary with gentlemen visitors to relieve ladies of the teapot. Here were large standing water-jars from Bahia, and the popular " monkey"—a peculiar formed earthen vessel of aboriginal origin. [See figures of water-pots.]

The repast wound up, as all repasts do here, with passing round the paliteiro—a fancy piece of silver holding tooth-picks of orange-wood. Not a little ingenuity is displayed in the designs: e. g., a peccary or porcupine, from which the picks stand out as quills; a disk of the sun, in which they represent his rays; a pine-apple, held by an Apollo; a column of muskets, on which they stand for bayonets, &c.

In the yard were the usual piles of balls and iron guns, all of English make; also quite a number of old Portuguese bronze pieces, one fluted and richly ornamented, another twisted spirally with loops of alligators: it had been two hundred and fifteen years in Brazil, and is a splendid specimen of ancient founding. These had been baptized, as usual in old times, with scriptural appellations. How much more appropriate had one been christened, " The bringer of bad news," after a Dutch thirty-two pounder, or " The Devil," after a French one.

We entered the cooper's shop, where buckets, kegs, and canteens were in process of development. The foreman could not comprehend or believe in our pail and barrel making machinery. " Não, senhor," he exclaimed, shaking his head; " não, senhor, uma impossibilitado."

Leaving the infidel, we came among the tinmen, a dozen blacks and whites, making canisters for grape-shot, horn lanterns, and huge tin crowns and globes—imperial arms to put over the entrances of public establishments. Bugles and trumpets, with and without keys, and equal in finish to any, are made here. One room is dedicated to philosophical instruments. A theodolite of superior workmanship was in progress; also a large electrical machine, the plate from a window of the old king's state-coach. The foreman was employed at a very handsome bench-vice, with a sliding jaw, of his own invention. A model was presented to me. It is now in the collection of the Franklin Institute, Philadelphia. There was not in the carpenters' shops a common hand-saw. Not one is said to be used in the country; nothing but the old classic buck-saw. In Spain and Portugal, the tools and processes current in Greece and Rome in the days of Numa are preserved unchanged. It is much the same here. At a forge were bellows such as Vulcan used: they will be found figured on a subsequent page.

In the turning-shop were some excellent French lathes. Three or four fine bronze presses were at work stamping cap and epaulette plates; one is one hundred and twenty years old, and ornamented with the arms of Portugal—a beautiful thing. In the leather department is made every article for cavalry and infantry—saddles better and cheaper than can be imported. The barrels and locks of muskets are of foreign manufacture, but all are stocked and mounted here. Founders and finishers were fusing and filing belt-buckles and sabre-handles. The model-room is crowded with devices for civil and military engineering.

In the school-room were two hundred lads, from six to thirteen years old, whites, blacks, mulattoes, and Indians, as thoroughly mingled on their seats as the ingredients of mottled granite. They are taught reading, writing, arithmetic, and drawing. When fourteen, each names a trade he prefers to follow—one of those carried on in the arsenal; *that* is taught him, and at a certain age he enters the artillery. In this manner a supply of carpenters, smiths, saddlers, founders, machinists, &c., is secured for the public service.

This military establishment is admirably organized, and under an effective administration.

At noon the workmen went to dinner, each taking off his cap as he passed the outer gate—a piece of ceremony enforced on every one, high or low, stranger or native, at every government building. Hence, at the shabby entrance to the Custom-house, merchants, captains, and every one else who wears a hat must remove it in passing in and out, and fifty times a day, if they go in as often. This Oriental mode of securing reverence for rulers appears to be a Gesler kind of homage. He put his chapeau on a pole, and required those who passed to bend the knee; so here, wherever a tin copy of the Emperor's head-gear is stuck up, every one must uncover in obeisance to it, the same as if entering a church.

12th. Walked out with E—— to the Larangeiras, *Anglice* orange-groves, a suburban district adjoining the Cattete, and bordering on a brook that comes rippling along, scarcely any where over five feet wide, and the depth in most places only a few inches. When told this was the Cattete *River*, I thought a humbler appellation a fitter one, but I have since seen how two or three hours' rain converts the quiet streamlet into a wide, dashing, tumbling, and overwhelming torrent.

All the way up for nearly a mile one is reminded of a characteristic Spanish and Portuguese custom, of classical and scriptural antiquity too; for

"Where, gathering into depth from trickling rills,
The lucid fluid a spacious basin fills,"

there, in the pools, stand bevies of African nymphs, employed precisely as were the daughter of Alcinous and her maids ere their romps and laughter awoke the shipwrecked Ulysses. This stream is resorted to daily by lavandeiras from adjacent districts. Glance at the one we are approaching—it will not do to stop and look. Her sole dress is a garment which ought to be an inner and never an only one. In the middle of the brook, and midleg deep in it, she is handling a linen coat by the collar; now plunging it at her feet, and now raising it, she furiously rubs it till the arms fly out and strike her as if the owner were within. Another plunge, and she continues as if she had his ears in her hands, and was resolved to have them off. Another dip, and she twists him into a coarse rope, thrashes a smooth boulder with him, reversing her hold, brings his head and spreading arms down on the stone with loud flops, and anon lays him on the grass to dry.

Here we reach a couple who have joined their labors. One does the washing: she is using handfuls of saponaceous leaves in place of soap. The other is wringing, flopping, and spreading out frocks, shirts, and pants to bleach and dry. Yonder comes one who has finished her task, and is returning home with the blanched vestments piled up in that huge wooden bowl on her head—a load little less than Mrs. Ford's buck-basket when on its way to Datchet Mead. A few rods farther, and behold a lavandeiro. Probably the family that own him have no female slave, or his master may be a bachelor. See! there are half a dozen negroes in that pool in petticoats alone, and those distressingly curtailed. Except one, who has thrown a towel over her shoulders, the whole group is nude above the waist. When Homer's girls got through a family batch of linen, they washed their own; so these, having finished their owners' things, are giving their own a rinsing. As we passed on, variations in the scene occurred that spoiled the poetry of the picture. Of natural or acquired delicacy these Rio washerwomen exhibit none. Their manners, more than their garments, want purifying.*

Crossing the brook by a bridge, we entered the grounds of Senhor J. L——a, with whom we had been invited to spend the day. The house is a low stone structure, with the usual tegulated roof and stuccoed walls. The upper story, agreeable to a singular style of building yet prevalent, recedes from the lower. The estate is extensive, and, from its location, picturesque. A mountain quarry is on it, and a stream runs through it. We climbed the hills to the old farm-house, whence we had a view of the bay and the mouth of the harbor. The property has been in the family many generations, and here we learned some of the patriarchal customs of the old Portuguese planters. The mother of the present proprietor, a venerable lady of ninety, recently deceased, kept them up to her death. Carefully instructing the slaves, the first thing she taught them was to address the Virgin. Every night the bell on the portico, which awoke them to work and called them from it, summoned them to prayers, which, as surviving head of the family, she read. As soon as they were concluded, her children, grandchildren, and any other relatives present saluted her, and each slave, in passing out, asked and received her blessing for the night. She sometimes roused all, blacks and whites, to matins at two in the morning. One old negro troubled her exceedingly: "Work, work, work all day," he would say, "and pray, pray, pray all night—no negro stand that!"

As a party of us wandered over the grounds, besides many

* "Now the history tells us that the page was very discreet and sharp, and, being very desirous to please his lord and lady, he departed with a very good will for Sancho's village; and being arrived near it, he saw women washing in a brook, of whom he demanded whether one Teresa Panza, wife of one Sancho Panza, squire to a knight called Don Quixote de la Mancha, lived in that town. A young wench who was washing started up and said, '*That* Teresa Panza is my mother, *that* Sancho my father, and *that* knight our master.' 'Come, then, damsel,' quoth the page, 'and bring me to your mother, for I have a letter and a present for her from that same father of yours.' 'That I will,' answered the girl; and, without putting any thing on her head and feet, for she was disheveled and bare-legged, she ran skipping before him."

smaller, a few large blue butterflies tempted us to chase them. I captured one six inches across the wings, and after keeping it an hour concluded that, as I was no naturalist, the sins of naturalists should not be mine. Having no sufficient reason to deprive it of the pleasures of life, I let it go.

We strolled up the road to where it changes its name to Cosme Velho. Here a dozen houses had come sociably together, as if tired of keeping, like their old neighbors, so far aloof. A spring of cool water gushes from a neat design of masonry, built against a spur of Mount Martha, one of the chief eminences at the base of the Corcovado. It is named "Bica da Rainha," or Queen's Spout. Its refreshing fluid is not more exhilarating than the scenery. Half a mile farther we came to a medicinal spring inclosed in a very neat structure. On a bronze plate let into the pediment, is inscribed "Agoa Ferrea, 1835." This font is the foreground of a landscape no painter could pass. Palms, bananas, orange, and other trees, with shrubbery and flowers, are every where; snow-white walls and red-tiled roofs glisten on distant hills, a romantic brook comes dancing down the glen, and a glorious mountain boundary incloses all; to say nothing of living figures—birds, insects, and, not least worthy of notice, lizards darting from rock to rock quicker than the eye can follow them.

On returning to the grounds of Senhor L——a, we stopped at the decaying roots of a celebrated tree, recently cut down, against his protestations, to make way for a road. At the discovery of the country this noble forest production was visited by Indians for its medicinal bark, and ever afterward known as the "Páo Grande," or Great Tree. It was three metres in diameter, and of a proportionate height. The Indian name is Jequitiba.

After dinner we adjourned outside, and partook of a dessert after the manner of Eden. Reclining under venerable tamarind and cinnamon trees, we knocked fruit off them and off widespreading mangoes. We ranged among cloves and pimentos, bananas and plantains, oranges and lemons. Here red coffee-berries were pendent from the stems of tall and slender bushes; there stands the caja, a species of Indian palm, and near it the caju, yielding a yellow plum, the jaça, with its gourd-like nuts, the patinga, on which grows a scarlet or purple cherry of a sweetish acid taste; the favorite mamao, with its egg-shaped treasures hanging like cocoas from the boll. Here are garlic-trees, so named from the odor their crushed leaves give out; soap-trees, bearing saponaceous berries, and wax or candle plants that secrete cereous substances: the leaves of the last are fan-shaped, three to four feet over, and from their curved edges radiate bayonet points a foot in length.

As the evening closed in, we took leave of our kind friends and returned home, after a day of unalloyed enjoyment.

13*th*. The weather is oppressive, and yet the thermometer has ranged since I landed between 80° and 86°; but then, neither night nor day has it been below the former or above the latter, except to-day. At 6 A.M., 84°; noon, 87°; 10 P.M., 86°. How slight and sluggish these movements are, compared with the range through which the mercurial column sweeps in our latitudes! Summer heats in New York rise often over 90°, but at night we pass, as it were, into cool and refreshing baths. Here, night brings little relief to one's parboiled lungs and viscera. It is not, therefore, so much the high temperature that distresses one as its unbroken continuance.

This uniformity of tropical heats may be conducive to bodily health and old age, but I suppose it is also to intellectual quietude. There is an obvious connection between meteorology and mind; energetic spirits thrive best where heat and cold, calms and storms alternate. I feel an increasing tendency to mental

as well as to physical supineness, and can readily understand why those who visit the tropics grow tired of unvarying verdure, longing for snow and ice, and the renovating influence of a northern spring.

A Portuguese in the neighborhood has the reputation of being unusually cruel to his slaves. One goes past the window for water three or four times a day, in an iron collar, with an upright prong at one ear, and a shorter one under the other. There he is again! and behind him a lad, not over twelve, belonging to the same owner, wearing a similar instrument, with the prong behind.

15th, Sunday. Rain last night has brought down the temperature to 80°. As the omnibus from Boto-Fogo stopped at the door, I observed three blacks seated among white gentlemen. This is common. A free negro in decent attire—implied by the expression "wearing shoes and a neckcloth"—can take his seat in places of public resort and conveyance as freely as persons of the lightest complexion. The Constitution recognizes no distinction based on color.

At ten the vicar, having got through mass, which must be performed fasting, came in to breakfast. Presenting his caxa, I tried a pinch, and instantly repented, but he grasped my hand, and, with glistening eyes, congratulated me on the happy *omen:* he was as exhilarated as Penelope when Telemachus, without snuff, had a fit of sneezing. Rising from the table with a palito stuck behind an ear, he asked for cards. To oblige him, two ladies sat down to *bisca*, nor would he release them till the dinner-hour. I took up his square cap, made of pasteboard and covered with serge; three segment-shaped ridges radiated from the centre of the crown to three of the four corners. Suspecting a mystic signification, he was told of my surmise. Using the palito as he turned in his chair, he said the ridges represented the persons in the Trinity, and, with the tuft in the centre, the Trinity in unity.

16th. Devoted the day to the City Park—o Passeio Publico —an irregular piece of ground, extending some three hundred feet along the Bay. It is inclosed by high walls, on which are vases for flowers at regular distances. Gravel-walks cut up the ground into fancy plots, on which tropical shrubbery and trees luxuriate. Here is the entrance, in Rua do Passeio, opening on a wide path that runs straight through the middle to the Bay. Let us step in. As we proceed, the view at either hand becomes more and more confined by the foliage. Arriving near the end of the walk, a triangular pyramid of granite, thirty or more feet high, rises on each side from a basin of water. An oval cartouch on one has the inscription, "A Saudade do Rio;" on the other is, "Ao Amor do Publico." The Passeio was completed and presented to the city by a wealthy merchant on retiring from it to end his days in Portugal. In the first inscription he gave expression to his patriotic feelings in a sentiment not easily translated. We have no word, nor half dozen words, equivalent to "Saudade." It not only implies remembrance and good-will, but a doting upon and a yearning after an object. It includes every thing that affection can desire for the absent, and hence is in common use in the correspondence of relatives and lovers.

The prospect is still limited within the walls, and will be until we ascend one of those two flights of marble steps facing us, which converge to a platform above. The triangular space between them has been tastefully improved. An artificial mound, covered with cactus plants and verdure, is built against the wall; a basin of water is confined in front by an antique-fashioned rim of highly-wrought granite. At the foot of the mound, two bronze crocodiles, partly concealed by shrubbery, turn their heads to each other, and, resting them on the beach, throw jets of water from their nostrils. Above the mound rises a fanciful terminus, on which are carved the crown and arms of Portugal, and beneath them a bust of Diana in relief.

We ascend the stairs; the handsome balusters are iron, the hand-rails bronze. Reaching the platform, a pretty fountain-device arrests attention on the back of the wall, on whose front we have below been contemplating Diana and her crescent. A Cupid grasps in his right hand an inverted tortoise by its tail, and from the struggling creature's mouth the jet falls into a small granite barrel. In his left hand the little laughing god holds a scroll, the motto on which can not be surpassed. As if anticipating rebuke for torturing the testudo, he exclaims, "*Sou util inda brincanda!*"—though playing, I am useful. "And so you are," I told him, as I plunged a tin tumbler, standing near, into the sparkling fluid.

And now, by simply turning round, we are on a terrace close to the Bay, which, for its beauty and enchanting prospects, if any where equaled, can not be excelled. Three hundred feet long, forty-five wide, paved with white and colored marble; inclosed by low walls, in which are continuous seats, except where interrupted by short columns bearing flower-vases, and both columns, backs and fronts of seats—the whole interior surfaces of the walls—lined with painted and enameled tiles. Near each extremity of the promenade, a light octagonal structure offers shelter from the sun's rays, and seats for all who choose to enter. Stairs here also communicate with the garden. A spirited Mercury, with his caduceus elevated, stands at the head of one flight, and the god of music, with his lyre, at the other. Both are in bronze, of the natural size, and, with the rest of the works in metal, were brought from Portugal.

Here the eye takes in the islands of Cobras and Villegagnon, the lower bay, entrance of the harbor, and the open sea beyond, ships coming in, others going out; at the right, Boto-Fogo, Cattete, and the Corcovado; on the left, the hills of Nictherohy, down to the rocks and Fort of Santa Cruz. Small gulls whirl round and light on the water near you, pigeons are running along the beach as if they here acquire aquatic tastes, boys are playing in the surf, and canoes, skiffs, and crafts of all descriptions are moving over the water. Yonder rises the black, gigantic Sugar-loaf before us. Ten minutes since it was wholly relieved by the light blue sky behind it, and so it is yet, except that small cloud, white as driven snow, and the only one in the wide firmament, which is descending upon its peak. In five minutes the dark apex emerges, the aerial visitor turns gray, losing its density as it spreads itself over the widening mass. Now, half way down, it is but a thin gauze, and now it has vanished, yielded up its moisture. In this way mountains here are almost daily seen to draw down clouds and *milk* them, as Mr. Wise beautifully remarked.

In the Passeio is a large vegetable edifice. Vines and tendrils form its walls; dense foliage, dressed as thatch, its roof. Within is a table, at which citizens can dine or lunch on refreshments brought with them, or indulge in fruits and *doces* bought of negroes at the gate — a slab of granite, ten inches thick, four feet wide, and thirty long, resting on carved pedestals, each weighing a ton. A seat of the same massive material and character completes a piece of furniture calculated to endure as long as the city shall exist. Upon it I am penciling these remarks.

I did not leave this earthly elysium till sundown, and was not a little surprised that so few visitors made their appearance in it. Two or three young men straggled in and out occasionally, but not a family or a female; open to every body, and comparatively enjoyed by nobody. True, it is located at one side, and not the most populous one, of the city; but the fact is, not till within a few years have ladies begun to appear in the streets. The old Moorish seclusion of the sex has but lately been invaded, and latticed jalousies pulled down.

CHAPTER VIII.

Sudden Floods and their singular Inconveniences.—Discovery of Brazil.—Indians and early Navigators. — Rio founded by French Protestants.—Their religious Disputes.—An Indian Chief knighted. — His Descendants. — Location of the City.—Saints of the Hills.—Streets and Pavements.—Houses.—Jalousies.—Roofs.—Chimneys.—Spouts.—Street Lamps.—Substitute for Bells and Door-knockers.—Signs.—Markets.—Fountains.—No Sewers or Sinks.—Rio a City of Quarries.—Neighboring Mountains.—Names of Streets, etc.

18*th*. Rain fell all night, and still continues, *sans* intermission. The Larangeiras Washerwomen's Brook is now bearing all before it. It has risen over a stone bridge in the Cattete, and is sweeping roots and stems of trees down the avenue. The low streets running off to Flamingo Beach resemble millraces. The occupants of the vicar's recent dwelling probably spent the night as he spent one a few months ago. Torrents from mountains in the rear suddenly flooded it, and at midnight, unable to escape, his only resource was to spring from his couch and mount a chest of drawers, where, like another patriarch, he waited the abating of the waters; and where, seated and undressed, his negro and the neighbors found him in the morning. Preferring safer quarters, he has hired an upper room on higher ground, and is no longer in danger of being roused to meditate in dishabille and darkness on the motions and forces of fluids.

As there is no going out, the opportunity is favorable for posting up a few notes on the origin, outline, and some particulars of the city.

Brazil was discovered by chance. On the return of the pioneer to India by way of the "Cape of Tempests," the Portuguese government sent out Cabral with a fleet to take advantage of the discovery. Instead of creeping down the African

F

coast, where calms were known to prevail, he pushed out into the open Atlantic, and continued in a southwest direction till startled by land looming in the distant horizon. On the 1st of May he went ashore on the coast of Espiritu Santo—the province north of and adjoining that of Rio. On the 3d he erected a wooden cross, named the country *Santa Cruz*, and took possession of it in the name of his sovereign. This occurred in 1499 or 1500.

The coast was farther explored by Gonzalo Coelho in 1501. Nine years afterward a Portuguese vessel was wrecked near Bahia, and Diego Alvez Correa the only individual saved. On falling in with the natives, his presence of mind saved his life. He showed them the effect of a musket by discharging it at a distant object. They named him *Caramuru*, the man of fire.

In 1515, John Diaz de Solis, a Spaniard, discovered Cape St. Augustine, a little south of Pernambuco, though Vespucius, from his own account, was on that coast fourteen years before. De Solis, in 1512, entered the great river De la Plata, and, according to some authorities, he was, in the course of that or the following voyage, in the Bay of Rio. Brazilian writers assert that the first Europeans who entered it were two Portuguese navigators in the service of Charles V.

It is certain that he who was second only to one in the galaxy of daring spirits that opened the true epoch of geography and navigation—he who first passed through the eastern gate of the Pacific, gave a new ocean to his compatriots, and taught them to girdle the planet—Magalhanes—called in here on his immortal voyage. He and his associate, Ruy Faleiro, entered the harbor on the 13th of December, 1519. They named it St. Luzia, that being her anniversary : this was the first designation conferred on the place by Europeans. Pigafetta describes native Indians flocking round the ships in canoes, bartering refreshments ; for a king out of a pack of playing-cards they freely give six fowls.

In 1530, John III. sent out Martin Affonza de Souza to take possession of the country. He first touched at the north, ran down the coast, and passed in between the Sugar-loaf and opposite wall of rocks on New-Year's day, 1531, and christened the gulf or bay "*Rio* de Janeiro." Had it been explored, it had not been taken for the mouth of a fresh-water river. The Indian name was "Nictherohy." Bahia and Pernambuco were founded in 1535. Governor de Souza resided at the former; the first Brazilian land-proprietor, he possessed eighty leagues along the coast. He introduced the sugar-cane, and from his plantation it became dispersed.

The *city* of Rio is of French origin. The Portuguese had attempted no settlement in its neighborhood when Villegagnon, in 1555, began, under the auspices of Coligny, to found a Protestant colony there. On the return of his vessels, large numbers, including ministers and students, embarked, like the Pilgrim Fathers of the North, to escape from religious intolerance. But, alas for poor human nature! while unmolested without, quarrels began within—and such quarrels will ever begin and never end while any one class of fallible mortals are permitted to dictate to others what they shall believe or disbelieve. Doubts and disputes arose about the real presence, diluting the wine, using salt and oil in baptism, etc. These things, apparently sanctioned by Villegagnon, were denounced as rank popery, and the dissentients celebrated the sacrament as rigid Calvinists did in France. These squabbles, and the bitterness of spirit accompanying them, ruined all. Like people flying from the cholera, with its seeds lurking in their systems, they bore the spirit of persecution with them, and at length fell victims to it. In 1567 the Portuguese took possession, and expelled them on the anniversary of St. Sebastian, and under his protection it has ever since been placed. The name then given to it is still retained in official documents—"The most loyal and most heroic city of St. Sebastian."

Two neighboring tribes, the Tumoyos and Tupinambas, gave the settlers much trouble, but the musket at length frightened away those it had hitherto spared. A friendly chief named "Ararigboia" essentially aided the colonists. He was converted, and made a "Knight of the order of Christ." Lands at Praya Grande were ceded to him, and some of his descendants now occupy the village of St. Laurence, located on them. The government was recently about taking a part, but was prevented by the Indians producing the original grant. Dwelling within sight of the Brazilian capital, the modern descendants of Ararigboia are said to be strongly tainted with the original sin of warm climates—aversion to labor. They plant barely enough for necessaries, and spend the bulk of their time in sleeping, lounging, and smoking.

Location of the City.—Its site is the first piece of level ground met with on the left shore on coming in from sea—the first open spot between the mountains. Instead of being built "upon a hill," as a modern work informs us, Rio may more properly be said to be located in ravines. The face of the country is a succession of hills and mountains, and an irregular patch, hardly exceeding half a mile wide, opening upon the bay, is the principal site. Streets wind in among the hills on either hand. The pavement generally is but little above the bay. Water is every where met with in digging a few feet; hence there is not such a thing as a cellar.

All the chief eminences were early dedicated to the Church, and still are occupied and chiefly owned by her functionaries. If angels lived with men, they could not have finer sites for dwellings than have the monks and nuns at Rio. On the north side the Benedictine convent crowns San Bento's hill, and is one of the most valuable properties of the city. Behind it, the Bishop's palace rises on " Mount Conception." Opposite San Bento, to the south, ascends " St. Sebastian," now Castle Hill. On one spur of this mountain the ancient Jesuits dwelt ; on the other, the first church was built, and is at present in possession of Capuchins. Close by tower the hill of St. Anthony and his monastery. A little to the south, upon a higher one, the nuns of St. Teresa are cloistered ; and southwest, where the land shoots into the bay, soar the hill and the church of our Lady of Glory. Then, on Mounts Livramento, Diego, N. S. da Saude, and Madre de Deos, are chapels named after each. Mediators between the inhabitants of heaven and earth, the reverend occupants are thus, like ancient seers, located between both. The prosperity of the city is still believed to depend no little on the prayers and mortifications of these saints of the hills.

Streets and Pavements.—The streets are generally straight, yet Rua Dereita is crooked. As an apostle boarded in a thoroughfare thus designated, most Catholic towns have, in common with Damascus, "a street which is called straight," no matter how devious its direction. Laid out for the most part at right angles, some are found running from every point of the compass—a circumstance due to mountains insulated by them, and to the angular and indented shores of the bay. They are narrow: Custom-house Street is just eighteen feet wide from wall to wall—the general width in all the old parts of the city. If a few are found to exceed it, others are mere alleys. The ancient mode of grading is general; that is, the pavement inclines from the houses at each side to the middle of the road. But workmen are engaged modernizing this feature. No curb-stones are used; they could not be, as carriages, in passing one another, sweep close to the fronts of the houses: for the same reason, no steps or other projections are permitted.

Rozaria is a genuine old Moorish street, twelve feet between the fronts of opposite houses. The carriage-way is just six feet. The gutter, as usual, is in the middle, and full two feet below the side-flagging, so that on either side the surface has a fall of two feet in three. How distressing for mules to drag carriages through such avenues! But if so, what shall be said of the sacrifices of human sweat and sinews incessantly offered on them as on so many altars—of slaves yoked to massive trucks, whose wheels, creaking under more weighty loads, cause adjacent walls and floors to quiver—of slaves gasping in their slow and tortuous progress, and straining their life-strings to rending? The whole business part of Rio is singularly well adapted for railways, and if the people determine to continue blacks as beasts of draught, it would be to their interest to have them. A rail might be laid along every street at a very moderate expense; even wooden rails alone would quickly pay for themselves in the prolonged vigor of slaves now daily broken down and ruptured. The subject is worthy of the reputed humanity of the emperor.

Houses.—These are mostly two stories, some three, and many one, all grotesquely mixed as in most old cities; not a block is uniformly built. There is not what our builders would call a handsome front, nor any thing approaching to one; nor can there be, since all entrances are on the pavement level, and no steps nor porticoes allowed. There is not a brick nor a wooden house in Rio. The walls, universally, are of rough stone (like our foundation walls), coated with a stucco of lime and loam, which makes them appear as if whitewashed. Posts and lintels of coarse mottled granite border every door and window. Some owners show their taste by coloring the stucco in panels or otherwise; light blue and pink are favorite tints. *Gilt* scrolls and rosettes, running below the cornice, are to be met with. Though the houses are not showy, they are far more substantial than ours. Fonseca, the great slave-trader, one of whose vessels got in a few days ago with a full cargo, by which he is said to have cleared nearly two hundred thousand dollars, has a splendid dwelling nearly finished in Rua Quitanda. The front is paneled, and colored light blue, pink, and white. The spouts which shoot the water from the roof are gilt and burnished. The house is next door to his dry-good store, in which he commenced life.

Balconies at the upper windows are common. Formerly they extended across the front of each house, and were inclosed with lattice-work. Within these "gelosias" the females of a family were confined, as if in Turkey, or in ancient Greece, where females were not permitted to go out except under particular circumstances, nor to show themselves at windows. A few balconies remain, with their fronts removed. Every lower door and window was latticed, and a majority are so still. No stores have glass windows, the light being admitted between granite posts, which form open doorways. Probably not more than a dozen fancy stores can be found with glass windows. There are a few in Ouvidor (the Broadway of Rio), but in some of them the glass frames are removed at night, like the goods behind them. Of course, such a thing as a store bow-window is unknown; the wheels of carriages would whirl through it.

The *tiled roofs* are more or less concave, the result of large cornices projecting out of the line of the general pitch. This feature gives an Oriental cast to the buildings, and the more so when birds or other figures terminate the overhanging angles. The ribbed appearance of the tiles, their waving edges at the eaves, and the contrast of their color with that of the walls, have a pleasing effect on strangers to this style of architecture.

Chimneys.—Take a view of New York from the top of a church, and chimneys appear as thick as forest trees. Do the same in Rio, and you see none, or very few. Perhaps, by close inspection, a small one may be detected low down in some open area, and here and there a stove-pipe with a cowl.

Another trait likens the buildings still more to those of Greece and Rome. Rain collected on the roofs, instead of being brought down, as with us, to the pavement, shoots out of spouts at the eaves. This is the universal practice. The spouts are copper tubes, three or four feet long, in fanciful forms—a fish is very frequent—the fluid escaping from its open mouth. The gaping head of a tiger or of a bird also occurs. These pour the water on the middle of the street. Smaller pipes project from the bottom of balconies (which are almost as numerous as windows), and discharge it on the side-walks. How actively a foot-passenger in wet weather is kept dodging to and fro to avoid these torrents, at either hand of a narrow street, can readily be conceived.

Street lamps are suspended over the pavement from iron brackets secured to the sides of the houses. They are trimmed by lowering them; hence lamp-lighters here are armed with a rope instead of a ladder.

Street doors have no bells nor knockers. A gentleman raps at a door with his cane, or draws the end smartly across the slats that commonly fill the upper panel. When a family resides on the upper floors, a visitor, on entering the passage below, communicates notice of his presence by *clapping his hands*, which soon brings some one to the stair-landing above.

Street signs are not numerous, nor is any thing like taste displayed on the best of them. Often they announce combinations unusual with us: Dry Goods and Lottery-tickets; Printing and Cigars; Crockery and Tea. Over one door was printed,

> Entrada franca,
> Gosto pago,
> Saida livre.

The sense in English requires more words. It amounts to, Enter and welcome, select what you please, pay and depart free.

The *Fish-market* is a very convenient structure. At each of its four sides is a wide gateway, and in the centre a fountain plays. One side only is taken up with fish-stalls, the rest being occupied by dealers in other edibles and kitchen conveniences. Here are piles of fruit; fowls, turkeys, and roasting-pigs in cages; monkeys and wild birds; little shops of native earthen and wooden wares. Of the fish I have recognized none except mammoth shrimps and young sharks, both always found on the stalls. The side next the Bay, not over a hundred feet from it, presents an exciting scene. While crowds of boatmen and handsomely-formed canoes are waiting to be hired, there is coming in, every now and then, a falua with fish, when stout negroes, all but naked, with baskets on their heads, plunge through the surf (here black and thick with mud) to meet her, rivaling and rushing past each other to get a portion of her cargo first on shore; their shouts, screams, and quarreling equaling any thing on the Niger.

There are no *Wells* in Rio, though shallow pits, reaching to the surface-water, which is used for scrubbing, etc., are common. Except in very severe droughts, the city is well supplied with water. Here, close by the market, is the Chafariz* of Palace Square. It is a rather small, but an elaborately-wrought structure of cut stone, four square, surmounted by a pyramid, and capped with the Brazilian crown. The water is discharged at the pinnacle of a little stone mount, down which it streams into a shell-formed basin, whence it issues through five spouts at each of three of its sides; hence fifteen vessels can be filling at the same time. This spreading out the fluid and exposing it to the rays of a vertical sun necessarily heats it to a disagreeable degree, but old people say it is not good to drink water that is not agitated. "Beaten water" is better when warm than cold water not "beaten." On the side facing the bay is a tablet, stating that the fountain was erected for the benefit of the "People of Sebastianopolis" in 1789. But the subject of fountains is too copious a one to be treated of in this volume.

Here are no *sewers* nor *sinks*—no privies—no, not even where spacious yards and gardens are annexed to dwellings. The use of close-stools is universal even in the rural suburbs! Borne on the heads of slaves, they are emptied into certain parts of the Bay every night, so that walking in the streets after 10 P.M. is often neither safe nor pleasant. In this matter, Rio is what Lisbon is, and what Edinburgh used to be.

* A Moorish word signifying fountain—in universal use in Brazil.

Rio is a city of quarries. It is built of, paved, and inclosed with granite. Its hills, shores, and mountains are all granitic; no other rock is to be seen. It could supply the world with this material, and yet thousands upon thousands of cargoes of stone have been imported. All the old side-walk slabs, the channel for the Carioco Aqueduct, materials for churches, and scores of houses, were brought from Europe. Formerly, a very coarse and dull mottled granite seems only to have been worked. The city is built of it. It is incapable of a smooth surface. I have picked laminæ of mica three fourths of an inch over, and half-inch crystals of feldspar from it. A much better kind is now in vogue. It has a fine and uniform grain, and is nearly white.

It is curious to observe the extremes of condition in which adjacent granitic masses are. If all belong to one epoch and rose together, by what means are some preserved indurate and compact, while adjoining ones are crumbling, and others softened to the centre, and changed into a *red* tenacious loam—the color of the soil not only about Rio, but to the Andes and the Equator? The tint is bright and deep as that of our salmon brick. Castle Hill is, among others, thus decomposed.

A map of the country round Rio would, if the mountain bases were all laid down, be marked like a leopard's skin—the spots equally numerous, and diverse in dimension and outline. Such, it is said, is the surface of a large part of Brazil, as if the whole continent had once been fluid, and in an instant stiffened during ebullition.

Of the high mountain crests, that of the Corcovado is nearest the city. In a straight line, it is four miles from the Customhouse. The Tejuco and Gavia are each two hundred feet higher; the former is nine miles from the city, and the latter somewhat more, but to reach any one of them considerable more ground must be passed over.

From the religious education of the discoverers and early occupiers of the great southern peninsula, its provinces, mountains, rivers, lakes, cities, towns, parishes, avenues, squares, alleys, and, in fact, almost every thing and every person, were christened out of the calendar. Most of the streets of Rio are thus consecrated, as well as its eight parishes and forty-eight (large and small) churches. The meaning of other names attached to a few districts is not very well settled. Flamingo Beach is supposed to have been frequented at the discovery by birds of that name. Cattete is understood to be the Indian word for the peccary or paca. Engenho Velho from the location of the first sugar-mill. Boto-Fogo from vampyre bats. The common bat is seen here every fair night, but neither cattle nor men are tormented with the monsters so numerous in the northern provinces.

Of *Public grounds*, the Passeio has been described. The "Campo," the most spacious area, will be noticed in another chapter.

CHAPTER IX.

Sedans.—Removing Furniture to new Dwellings.—Street "Cries."—Peddlers.—Large Lizard.—Penny Portraits of Saints.—The Intrudo and its Sports.—Of Hindoo Origin. — Death and Burial of the Secretary of the Institute. — The Church, Coffin, Corpse, Cemetery, and Orations.

HAD custom not prevented ladies from promenading the streets, they could not indulge the exercise with any degree of comfort. The thoroughfares of few cities are less adapted for it than those of Rio. Their contracted width, the danger from wheels of trucks and carriages, imperfect side-walks, and sometimes none, to say nothing of the indecencies of blacks, and the offensive condition of places bordering on thoroughfares—the Gloria Beach, for example, and, worse still, that facing the palace and palace square—are enough to keep the sex in-doors. In suburban avenues ladies can air themselves, but not in the city. They have less inducements than with us to appear abroad. To the attractions of shopping they are strangers. If an article is wanted which the street-peddlers have not, a note is sent by a slave to a store, and samples are returned by him to choose from.

When a lady has occasion to visit the business part of the city, a carriage or a *cadeirinha* is called. The latter is a sedan. All are built on the same plan, and differ only in ornament. *Cadeira* is the Portuguese word for chair, and *cadeirinha* is

BRAZILIAN SEDAN.

literally "little chair." They are derived from the *sella gestatoria* of Rome, probably fac-similes, and are infinitely more elegant and commodious than the old English box or Opera hand-barrow chair.

I entered one to examine its construction. The annexed cut  shows the skeleton. On an elliptical board thirty inches by twenty, a high-backed chair is fixed, the rails of which extend up to a hoop of the form and dimensions of the base. The curved pole is connected to the base by small iron rods as represented.

The two bearers of a *cadeirinha* never go in a line; the one at the rear is always more or less to the right or left of his leader. This is easier for themselves and the person they carry. They do not stop to rest, but shift the load occasionally from one shoulder to the other as they proceed — not by actually changing their position with regard to it, but transferring the pressure, by a stout walking-stick thrown over the unoccupied shoulder, and passed under the pole. I met one with a dome of polished leather and a gilt dove on it, the curtains highly embroidered; the ends of the poles were gilt lions' heads. It was a private one. The slaves that bore it were in a flaming livery. The lady's colored maids walked behind, as in the preceding sketch.

Sometimes a *cadeirinha* is sent out without its owner. I saw one of a blue color, all but covered with gold embroidery; a broad engrailed band of Cordovan went round the top; two elegant horns or finials arose in front and rear, and on the convex roof a silver or silver-gilt eagle stood. The curtains were drawn aside, exposing the chair within, and upon it an enormous bouquet, a present from the owner of the sedan, its value augmented by this complimentary mode of transmitting it.

Another time I met one with a light green dome crowned with a silver dove. The curtains were crimson, the mourning color for children: the corpse of a child was being taken in it to the cemetery.

20*th*. Almost pushed into the Bay, the street along the Gloria Beach is the only passage from the city to Boto-Fogo. On entering it, I turned aside to an alms-box fastened to the corner of a mean venda, close to where I first sprang on shore. It was apparently for the relief of infant souls. Fat Dutch cherubs had been painted on it, but time had well-nigh extinguished the flames and bleached them into snow-drifts. While looking on, a yell and *hurlement* burst forth that made me start as if the shrieks were actually from Tartarus. From dark spirits they really came. A troop of over twenty negroes, each bearing on his head one or more articles of household furniture—chairs, tables, bedsteads, bedding, pots, pans, candlesticks, water-jars, and crockery—every thing, in fact, belonging to a family moving to a new domicile. Chanting only at intervals, they passed the lower part of the Cattete in silence, and then struck up the Angola warble that surprised me. There they go, jog-trotting on! The foremost, with pants ending at the knees, a red woolen strip round his waist, upon his head a mop, whose colored thrums play half way down his naked back, and in his hand a gourd-rattle, fringed with carpet-rags, beats time and leads the way.

The "cries" of London are bagatelles to those of the Brazilian capital. Slaves of both sexes cry wares through every street. Vegetables, flowers, fruits, edible roots, fowls, eggs, and every rural product; cakes, pies, rusks, *doces*, confectionery, "heavenly bacon," etc., pass your windows continually. Your cook wants a skillet, and, hark! the signal of a pedestrian copper-smith is heard; his bell is a stew-pan, and the clapper a hammer. A water-pot is shattered; in half an hour a moringue-merchant approaches. You wish to replenish your table-furniture with fresh sets of knives, new-fashioned tumblers, decanters, and plates, and, peradventure, a cruet, with a few articles of silver. Well, you need not want them long. If cases of cutlery, of glass ware, china, and silver have not already passed the door, they will appear anon. So of every article of female apparel, from a silk dress or shawl to a handkerchief and a paper of pins. Shoes, bonnets ready trimmed, fancy jewelry, toy-books for children, novels for young folks, and works of devotion for the devout; "Art of Dancing" for the awkward; "School of Good Dress" for the young; "Manual of Politeness" for boors; "Young Ladies' Oracle;" "Language of Flowers;" "Holy Reliquaries;" "Miracles of Saints," and "A Sermon in Honor of Bacchus"—these things, and a thousand others, are hawked about daily.

Vegetables are borne in open, fowls in covered baskets; pies, confectionery, and kindred matters are carried on the head in large tin chests, on which the owner's name and address are

painted; dry-goods, jewelry, and fancy wares are exposed upon portable counters or tables, with glass cases fixed on them. These are very numerous.

Proprietors accompany silver-ware, silks, and also bread, for blacks are not allowed to touch the latter. When a customer calls, the slave brings his load, puts it down, and stands by till the owner delivers the articles wanted. The signal of dry-goods venders is made by the yard-stick, which is jointed like

a two-foot rule. Holding it near the joint, they keep up a continual snapping by bringing one leg against the other. The Brazilian yard is the *vara*, equal to 43⅓ inches English. The *covado*, an old Portuguese measure, is also in use, equal to 28¼ of our inches; hence the *vara* of the streets is divided unequally, the long leg being a *covado*. These are the only measures used by shopkeepers in Brazil. Fine goods, such as silks, lawns, crapes, and the like, are sold by the *covado*, and others by the *vara*.

Young Minas and Mozambiques are the most numerous, and are reputed to be the smartest of *marchandes*. Many a one has an infant added to her load: she secures it at her back by a

wide piece of check wound round her waist. Between the cloth and her body it nestles and sleeps; and when awake, inquisitively peeps abroad, like an unfledged swallow peering over the edge of its nest. To protect her babe from the sun, she suspends a yard of calico at the rear end of the case on her head: this serves as a screen, and, from its motions, acts somewhat as a fan. Dealers often solace themselves with lighter companions—paper cigars—which, when called on to display their wares, are disposed of in a curious place. One of these gentlemen, with a strangely miscellaneous stock, was called into the passage to-day. He had combs, soaps, needles, perfumes, inks, quills, thread, blacking, books, paper, pencils, matches, English china tea-sets, cards of fine cutlery, and I know not what else, so crammed was his glass counter. Before coming in, he stuck his cigar behind one ear, and on his stooping down, I perceived a tooth-pick projecting from the other.

The way customers call street-venders is worth noticing and imitating. You step to the door, or open a window, and give utterance to a short sound resembling *shir*—something between a hiss and the exclamation used to chase away fowls; and it is singular to what a distance it is heard. If the person is in sight, his attention is at once arrested: he turns and comes direct to you, now guided by a signal addressed to his eyes—closing the fingers of the right hand two or three times, with the palm downward, as if grasping something—a sign in universal use, and signifying "Come." There is here no bawling after people in the streets; for in this quiet and ingenious way all classes communicate with passing friends or others with whom they wish to speak. The custom dates, I believe, from classical times.

Here comes the tallest and blackest man-milliner I have yet seen; his dress, the usual brown shirt and trowsers, ending at the knees and elbows. His case contains Leghorn and fancy silk bonnets—nothing else. These he cries, and at every few steps turns to this side and that in quest of fair customers.

Yesterday a young negro came along with a couple of *Seguise*, or miniature monkeys. He stopped and held up the wicker cage, not over six inches square. "Tres milreis?" I said. "Não, senhor, seis milreis," putting forth his spread dexter hand, from which, sure enough, *six* fingers grew. This was the only itinerant Macáco merchant I met in the streets; there are several in the market.

On nearing home, I met a negro coming in from the country with a walking-stick much taller than himself, and to it lashed a lagarto—a species of lizard considered a table delicacy, and much preferable to any flying game. I bought it, intending to bring it to the States, but it was lost in the voyage home. It was two feet and a half long, and six inches across the thickest part. A slap of its tail across the breast of the slave who helped to secure it in a box took away his breath.

A crier of confectionery was called in a few mornings ago. Among *doces* and fancy wares was a lot of saints—coarse woodcuts in penny frames, three inches by five. Taking up Dominic, I asked the price. The sable merchant shook his head. "It had been blessed; it could not be sold; only exchanged; it cost two patacas." It is in this way the value is put on holy things. You are told they cost so much, and will be exchanged for an equal sum. I could not purchase the founder of the Dominicans for 32 cents, but at that rate I could have him and a dozen more saints, if I would view the transaction as a reciprocal convenience between the vender and myself, and without the taint of worldly merchandising in it. Then, as no profit must be made by the pious traffic, venders necessarily accompany the offer of every article with a flam—telling you, with a seriousness and devotion which for the moment the article calls up, they paid the amount you are expected to give for it.

THE INTRUDO.

21*st*. For a week past I have noticed colored balls exposed here and there on plates for sale. The green ones might be taken for small apples, the yellow for oranges and lemons. Some are formed like pears, others like melons. An acquaintance made with some this morning has banished the indifference with which I have passed by them. Another article has also been pressed upon my attention. It is native *starch*, not granulated like ours, but an exceedingly white and fine powder, put up in paper cylinders six inches long, and half an inch in diameter. When used, one end is opened, and the contents shaken out.

While sitting at breakfast, S—— passed behind J——'s chair, and, to my amazement, emptied a couple on his head and shoulders. The operation was performed so quietly, and the dust fell so lightly, that he knew not what was going on till a handful was applied to his face and ears. He sputtered, sprang up, and, half-blinded, was saluted with liquid shots from a long-necked cologne-bottle. Half in anger, and amid much laughter, he made a quick retreat, dressed, and went to the city.

While wondering what this could mean, a particle or two dropped from my forehead. Raising a hand, I found my own hair had also been powdered—a discovery that elicited a general screech. I rose to decamp, but this had been foreseen, and the only door through which escape was possible was locked. Now beset by a host of female foes, I dodged and ran till well-nigh exhausted, in trying to evade incessant volleys of starch and water. At length I protested if the unrighteous war was continued I must and would come to close quarters, and, *vi et armis*, capture and play their own ordnance upon them. This was received with fresh peals of merriment and fresh broadsides; but, at last, an armistice, to endure through the day, was agreed on. I now was told that *the Intrudo* begins to-morrow, when all classes, in-doors and out, dust and sprinkle one another; and that it is usual to do a little, by way of preface, the day before.

I retired to change my dress, but had not taken five paces ere I was overtaken by a storm of colored balls, charged with some liquid, similar to those I had noticed in the city. Surprised at this open breach of faith, and at the red and blue fragments with which I was bespattered, I lost no time in reaching my room and securing the door. I took from the shelf an old Portuguese dictionary for information. It derives *Entrudo*, or *Intrudo*, from the Latin *Introitus*—" Entrance, or Beginning;" and describes the festival as one in which people, like Bacchants, romp, feast, dance, and frolic in-doors, and play all manner of tricks out, wetting and powdering one another. Of the origin of the feast—of which I had been treated to a foretaste—I could learn nothing. Neither the vicar nor any one else appealed to could impart the smallest glimmer of its history. That it dates back to remote times is admitted.

It may be a question whether the Intrudo and the Carnival of Italy are the same. Though associated with the great Quadragesimal fast, there are striking points of seeming difference. The former, in its etymology, has no reference to abstinence from butcher's meat, of which the latter is the literal expression. *Carni*, " flesh;" *vale*, " farewell." Carnival time extends from the first of January to the beginning of Lent; whereas the Intrudo occurs in the latter part of February, and lasts but three days, invariably beginning on the Sunday previous to Ash-Wednesday. Moreover, throwing dust and water is its special characteristic, the most conspicuous of its rites.

Intrudo-balls—for so the colored shot are named—instead of fruit, which they resemble, are mere shells of wax filled with water. They are sufficiently tenacious to retain the liquid, to bear gentle handling, and to be thrown to a considerable distance. Like more fatal bombs, they explode when they strike; the wax is shivered, and most of it sticks where it hits. I received a present of specimens of a superior kind, formed like bottles or decanters, and decorated with paint and gilding. The necks were closed in imitation of corks sealed over. When used, they are charged with cologne or other scented waters.

22*d*. This is Intrudo-day. On rising, my friend R—— found the lower extremities of his pants sewed up. It is not unusual to lodge half a dozen balls in each leg; but as he is rather unwell, these singular marks of affection and foot-baths were spared him. In the act of shaking hands, I had one or two balls crushed in mine. At breakfast one had his coffee without sugar, another found it sweetened with salt, a third began to pick threads out of his mouth, which caused fresh explosions of laughter; of two plates of toast, fine thread had been drawn through and through every piece, so that the teeth became unavoidably entangled in the meshes. Some foreign merchants came up, on their way to the Botanic Garden. T—— invited them in. The simpletons! Their riding-costumes were soon like bathing-dresses. One got out without his hat, and actually rode off bareheaded! He returned in the afternoon with a slave bearing a large basket of the cereal missiles, and, quietly entering the rear, repaid his foes with interest.

The vicar came, and was saluted with cologne; they spared his *sutain* the infliction of the starch. He mentioned instances where he had been half drowned after receiving the most solemn pledges that he would not be molested. That I can fully believe; and, turning to some ladies, asked how *they* could, and on a Sunday too, tell such ——. "Oh!" they replied, "Intrudo lies are no sin." There is no believing any one while it lasts. The padre wisely took his departure; he did not dare to stay for dinner, lest his rooms should be robbed by friends sending, in his name, for every valuable in them. Doña F——, by a ruse of this kind, obtained a dozen bottles of porter from J——'s carpenter, who had charge of them. He himself tricked the vicar last year; and, by the aid of a slave, deprived a friend of a turkey and fowls, upon which the owner and his family dined as guests, without dreaming of having contributed to the feast. It used to be a custom to set before guests joints of wood, pies of sand, custards and puddings of kindred inedibles, dishes out of which leaped frogs, etc.; but the Intrudo, like other festivals, is not kept up as formerly.

Senhor F—— rose to depart, but was induced to drop again into his seat, on which a neighbor had slipped a quantity of flour, and water balls. He sprang up as these nest-eggs crushed beneath him, while the mischief-loving projectors were in convulsions. Nor was the tumult one whit lessened by his manner of relieving the parts affected. Finding it impossible now to remain, he good-humoredly waved an adieu with one hand, and with the other placed his hat upon his head—and snatched it off again. It had been lined with the current ingredients of the day. Two extremities of his person were now in the condition of Quixote's head when he suddenly called for his helmet at an inconvenient moment for Sancho to deliver it.

Retiring to my room, I found a strange lady writing at the table. I paused and addressed her. No answer or motion. I advanced. The intruder was a bolster, furnished with sleeves, skirts, bonnet, shawl, etc., very artistically got up. Opening the drawers, I found the sleeves and neck of every shirt sewed up, and other garments hermetically sealed, so as to require both time and patience to get into them.

Both sexes are expert in calming a person after an attack, and throwing him off his guard. Ladies will show their open palms, rub them down their sides, to prove that they have no concealed missiles; sit down by you, express fatigue, and say that a little frolic is well enough, but this excess is foolish, and very vulgar; look innocent as Madonnas, and conclude with "No more Intrudo." Your suspicions are lulled; but, ten to one, that same moment a couple of waxen wash-balls are applied to your face in the manner of soap and water, and a paper of cassava starch emptied on you. Your fair enemy springs from you with a shriek, and your surprise now takes another turn. She draws from her person ball after ball, and paper after paper, till you are ready to conclude she is made of them, or has some machine about her for producing them.

Employing parties on fool's errands is practiced. An unsuspicious person is sent on what he imagines a confidential matter of great moment to his friend — to borrow money, on an emergency, perhaps. The substance of the letter he carries is, "Send the fool to Senhor B——, and ask him to forward him with a like request to others!"

An example has been given of a family being feasted on their own victuals. A reverend sweet-tooth revenged himself for a similar trick played on him by indulging largely at a neighbor's table. His hilarity became more enhanced when a splendid cake was brought in and placed before him. With sparkling eyes he cut deep into it, and when three fourths had disappeared, some hint was dropped which caused him to rise, stand aghast, and pray for patience! The cake — a highly-valued present from a female friend—had been filched from his own larder!

I walked out toward the Passeio, and saw few individuals molested. One gentleman in a new suit received two or three balls, and was quite indignant: he addressed some remarks to me, and pointed to the window whence the shots came. It is useless to get vexed; those who do are sure to have their anger cooled by a fresh shower.

Youths, here and there, were playing with syringes. For some time past I had noticed huge tin implements hanging by the door-posts of "Funileiros," and occasionally met an individual carrying one home. Wondering for what they were made, I stopped one day to examine them. All I could make out from the laughing tinman was, "Two milreis"—the price of one. They were quart and half-gallon Intrudo-squirts. Young black rascals, who charge them in gutters, seldom molest any except their own color; but white boys use no ceremony in washing the Ethiops. B—— told me of acquaintances who have concealed garden-engines to salute their friends with. He has one himself, but it is out of order.

The subjoined illustration, by a Rio artist, is a fair represent-

ation of playing the Intrudo in the street. I saw one negro laden with water from the Carioco Font attacked in precisely the same way. He stumbled, and fell headlong, fortunately without being injured.

On retiring for the night, I could not find the way into bed. The sheets and coverlet had been formed into a sack whose contracted mouth was under the bolster. Relighting the candle, I unraveled the sewing, and finally laid down to rest, heartily tired of the Intrudo, and little thinking what cause I had to be thankful that half a bushel of balls had not been deposited at the foot of the sack.

Puerilities of the Intrudo would hardly be worth noticing did they not illustrate ancient manners. Like other sports, they have outlived institutions they were designed to celebrate; and very naturally too, for all people love gayety and mirth, and none ever willingly gave up stated periods for enjoying them.

The remarkable coincidences in language, customs, and other matters that go to establish an intimacy, if not identity, between the ancestors of the people of Western Europe and those of Central Asia, have been often observed. I am not aware that the Intrudo has been thus elucidated. There seems, however, little room to doubt of its being the *Hohlee* of Hindostan—a festival dating from mythic epochs, and, consequently, involved in dense obscurity.

Some writers have supposed the Hohlee refers to the victorious return of a famous hero from battle. Others think it was founded on the orgies of Krishnu, a god more licentious than the Grecian Jupiter. Others, again, imagine it had reference to the close of the old year and the approach of spring, when nature scatters over the earth her blossoms. The epithet of *purple* was given to the spring by ancient poets, and the same season is supposed to be typified by the red powder which the Hindoos, in celebrating the Hohlee, sportively throw at each other.

A graphic account of the part he took in celebrating this festival at the court of a Hindostanee prince is thus given by Mr. Broughton:

"Playing the Hohlee consists in throwing about a quantity of flour made from a water-nut called *singara*, and dyed with red sanders: it is called *abeer*, and the principal sport is to cast it into the eyes, mouth, and nose of the players, and to splash them all over with water tinged of an orange color. The abeer is often mixed with powdered talc to make it glitter, and then, if it gets into the eyes, it causes a good deal of pain. It is sometimes inclosed in little globes made of some gelatinous fluid, about the size of an egg, with which a good aim can be taken at those you wish to attack; but they require to be dexterously handled, as they yield to the slightest touch........

"A few minutes after we had taken our seats, large brazen trays filled with abeer, and the *little balls* already described, were brought in and placed before the company, together with yellow-colored water, and *a large silver squirt* for each individual. The Muha Raj himself began the amusements by sprinkling a little red or yellow water upon us from goolabdans—small silver vessels for sprinkling rose-water at visits of ceremony. Every one then began to throw about the abeer and squirt at his neighbors. It is contrary to etiquette for any body to throw at the Raj; he had, however, been told that we had declared our resolution to pelt every one who pelted us, and good-humoredly replied, 'With all his heart, he was ready for us, and would try which could pelt best.' We soon found, however, that we had not the slightest chance with him; for, besides a cloth which his attendants held before his face, he had in a few minutes a large pipe of a fire-engine put in his hands, filled with yellow water, and worked by half a dozen men. With this he played about him with such effect that in a short time there was not a man in the tent who had a dry thread on his back.

"Sometimes he directed it against those who sat near him with such force that it was not an easy matter for a person to keep his seat. All opposition to this formidable engine was futile. Whole shovelfuls of abeer were cast about, and instantly followed by a shower of yellow water, and thus we were alternately powdered and drenched, till the floor on which we sat was covered some inches in depth with a kind of pink and orange-colored mud. Such a scene I never witnessed in my life.*

"Figure to yourself successive groups of dancing-girls, bedecked with gold and silver lace, their tawdry trappings stained with

---

* See also WARD's "*View of the Hindoos*" for this use of the syringe and throwing of red powder.

patches of abeer, and dripping, like so many Naiads, with orange-colored water—now chanting the Hohlee songs with all the airs of practiced libertinism, and now shrinking, with affected screams, beneath a fresh shower from the Raj's engine—the discord of drums, trumpets, fiddles, and cymbals, sounding as if only to drown the other noises that rose around them—the triumph of those who successfully threw the abeer, and the clamors of others who suffered from their attacks—the loud shouts of laughter and applause which burst on all sides from the joyous crowd—figure to yourself, if you can, such an assemblage of extraordinary objects, then paint them all in two glowing tints of pink and yellow, and you will have some conception of a scene which absolutely beggars description."

In other respects the Intrudo and Hohlee agree. The latter, we are told, "takes place nearly at the same season as our Ash-Wednesday, and it also precedes the Lent or Hindoo season of expiation"—a coincidence of time and purpose as remarkable as that of both festivals being celebrated by dust and water—by missive balls and syringes. The Hohlee is kept up by all classes throughout India—an occasion of universal merriment. Among the staple divertisements is also that which characterizes the 1st of April with us.

In several respects the Asiatic festival resembles the ancient Saturnalia and the modern Carnival, the utmost license being accorded to all ranks. It has been compared to the *Hilaria*, celebrated in Rome at the vernal equinox in honor of the Mother of the Gods, her statue being carried in procession, accompanied with crowds in masquerade, every person assuming by his dress and manners whatever character he pleased.

In fact, nearly all our old Church festivals are allied to similar institutions of India, Egypt, Greece, and Rome.

To conclude this curious subject: within late years India-rubber has been applied to a multitude of useful purposes. It has contributed many valuable additions to medical and philosophical apparatus. Bottles of it form a new and unique species of exhausting and compressing instruments. Neat aids to breast and cupping-glasses, and substitutes for syringes. The last device is due to the aborigines of Northern Brazil. In Para, the country of caoutchouc, gum-elastic squirts have for ages been common, and, during the Intrudo, may be seen in the hands of Indians, whites, and negroes.

Curious enough too, a *yellow* earth or ochre is thrown about, as well as cassava starch.

BURIALS.—CEMETERIES.

In Rio, as every where else, life is a medley. Tragedy and comedy, death and diversions, farces and funerals, are mixed up together. No matter how popular the amusements, innocent the sports, or universal the joys, the Great Intruder can neither be softened nor cajoled, and to him monasteries are as attractive as masquerades.

In the midst of the Intrudo-revels, the Friar Barboza, Secretary of the Historical and Geographical Institute, expired. His demise is deemed a loss to the country, he having been considered the most devoted man in it to literature and science. I attended his obsequies at the Paula Church, and there witnessed the transition from childish gambols to the solemnities of a funeral; from the heyday of life to contemplate its extinction. Variable in his nature, man alternates between grief and joy; the poles of his existence—toward one or the other he is ever veering.

A friend of the deceased and I went early, and had time to look about before the ceremonies began. The church stands at the head of Ouvidor Street, flush with the pavement, and is relieved by poor-looking dwellings on either hand. It is of the prevailing style. Two square towers support the central part, whose peaked pediment is surmounted with a huge bronze cross. The towers run up a story higher, each finished with a dome, resembling a boy's inverted top, the peg set off with a brazen chanticleer—the symbol of Peter and of vigilance.

The interior is a long, high, and airy saloon; the floor clear of encumbrances; no aisles, columns, pews, nor aught else to intercept the view or interrupt one's movements. Light is admitted at the sides, near the arched and richly-carved roof, through semicircular windows, through the street doors, which as usual constitute the entrances, and also at three windows over them. The farther end is wholly taken up with the high altar, a rich affair, with numerous candles burning. Above them stands the saint, carved, draped, and painted to monkish life. Against the side walls are six more shrines, three on each side, with their images of natural dimensions, so that in this place are seven altars, where seven distinct saints can be invoked, and where all, or nearly all of them, are consulted daily.

This temple honors ignorance as well as superstition in the person of its patron, Francis Martotile, a Calabrian monk, who, burying himself in a cell, acquired, as Fakirs acquire, notoriety by disgusting mortifications. He renounced fish, wine, meat, stockings, shoes, beds, soap, and razors, besides rigorously cultivating mental destitution. The usual result followed; he, like other dirty gentlemen who lived and died in the odor of sanctity and filth, wrought miracles. His fame induced that old tiger Louis XI. to drop on his knees before him, and implore his intercession with the saints for a prolongation of life—a miracle too great for the monk and too good for the culprit. What he can do for people here of whose country he never heard, it is not hard to tell.

The only sign of a funeral was a kind of sarcophagus-looking stand in the middle of the floor, similar to the article furnished by undertakers. Four feet from it, on either side, stood a row of nine gilt candlesticks of classic patterns, five feet high, with candles to correspond. A negro mason was at work, cutting a door-way into the left wall, some fifteen feet above the floor, and near the altar, for an entrance to a new pendent or swallow-nest pulpit, to correspond with one opposite. About a dozen persons were in, and all moving and looking round as if on change, except an elderly female, who came in and seated herself upon the matted floor within the balustrade. Three colored women, also in black veils, appeared and seated themselves beside her. These were the only females present. As I leaned on the rails close by them, a well-dressed man of fifty came up, and, kneeling near me, touched with his right thumb his head, eyes, nose, cheeks, chin, mouth, shoulders, and breast. Then, without rising, he gazed round, looked at the negro working in the wall, nodded to me, and kept twisting himself about to see what was going on behind him.

Negroes brought in huge trays of mammoth candles, and piled

them near the door. A number of gentlemen soon after entered, and, with those already in, ranged themselves three deep on either hand, forming a living passage from the door toward the altar; and presently we all held lighted tapers, resting one end on the floor, and inclining the upper one forward to prevent the swealing material from descending on one's hands. Two hundred of us thus stood, like soldiers at drill with muskets, in the same position. As currents caused the melted wax to accumulate beneath the flame, it was unceremoniously thrown on the floor by bringing the tapers to a horizontal position. The officiating priest next entered, followed by others bearing the coffin, which they quickly placed upon the stand.

Coffins here are not like ours, being of the same width and depth throughout, and so shallow that the face, folded hands,

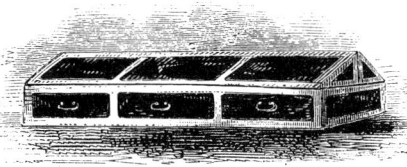

and feet of the corpse appear above the edge. The covers are peaked, like the roofs of houses, consisting of two boards meeting in the middle at an angle. Hinged at both sides, they open along the ridge, so that either one half or both may be thrown back. When finally closed, the only fastening is a small padlock.

When placed on the stand, the folding lids were laid back,

and the deceased secretary, from where I stood, appeared as in the accompanying sketch. While the priests walked round the coffin, chanting, swinging censers, and sprinkling the corpse, the black mason above, resting on his crow-bar, was a conspicuous spectator.

We now were about to witness the mode of burial; one of classical antiquity, and which to my mind commends itself as far superior to ours. The cemeteries of Rio adjoin the rear or sides of their respective churches. They are not seen from any street, not opening directly into any. At first I wondered where they were, and when I found them, I wondered more at their limited dimensions. The dead are not interred in graves, nor concealed below the surface; instead of extensive burial-grounds or subterraneous excavations, room for four thick walls, of which the side of a church commonly answers for one, is found sufficient. As these places are on one plan, a description of this of St. Francisco de Paula will give a general idea of all.

Passing out through a side door, we entered a quadrangular area bounded by four high walls, with a continuous shed or roof projecting inward, leaving a central space open to the sky, occupied by a few marble tomb-stones. The niches for the dead, wrought in the walls, were a little over six feet by two and a half, eighteen inches high at the ends, and two feet at the middle, the roof forming a low arch. All are plastered and whitewashed. In hot weather they would be no bad resting-places for the living. I was no longer surprised that people

CEMETERY OF THE PAULA CHURCH.

here are mostly buried without coffins, and especially as all are entombed in their clothes.

Here were three tiers of niches, each continued round the place. Those that are occupied have the fronts bricked up and plastered over. All are numbered; no other mark or lettering. Their tenants occupy them too short a time for inscriptions or eulogies to remain.

The coffin was placed on a temporary platform close to a niche in the middle tier, into which it was slid with the covers open. A handkerchief was spread over the face of the deceased by one of his friends; then, in succession, priests and friends stepped up, one at a time, and, with a silver sprinkler handed by the sacristan, threw holy water on the body, and emptied a small scoop of powdered quick-lime, which an attendant held ready, upon it. A bushel or more of lime was thus disposed of, until it entirely concealed the body, and was heaped over the trunk. A priest used the silver sprinkler once more, poured something out of a small perforated box, and the church ceremonies were over. We now put out our candles, and leaned them against the walls, whence black attendants removed them.

A gentleman now drew a paper from his bosom, and for half an hour read a eulogy on the dead. A second, third, and even a fourth oration was thus delivered; at the close of which the President of the Institute closed the coffin lids, locked them, and handed the minute key to a relative of the defunct. Thus closed the interesting rites. Several officers of state, of the military, and members of the Senate were present.

In half an hour the front of the niche was bricked up, and covered with a coat of white plaster.

In this mode of inhumation nothing like corruption takes place. The lime consumes the flesh, and in two years the bones are taken out and placed in a rosewood or marble vase, or burned, and the ashes preserved. The niche will then be whitewashed, and ready for another tenant.

The cemeteries of Rio are literal copies, on a smaller scale, of the sepulchral structures of the Greeks and Romans.* The

* See Moses' collection of vases, tripods, altars, etc. Plate 114 represents one discovered in Rome in 1746. It has six rows of niches. Plate 113 exhibits another belonging to the Livia family—all above the surface of the ground.

form of coffins here is also of remote antiquity. Originally of stone, and placed in the open air, their roofs were formed after those of houses, and with the same view—to allow rain to run off. Stone sarcophagi of this description are counted among the oldest of ecclesiastic monuments in Europe.

Two of the orations were published. The style is too figurative for colder latitudes, but is characteristic of the genius of Brazil. The deceased had been ambitious of political, as well as of scientific and monastic fame. He was a member of the Chamber of Deputies, took an active part in the Revolution, and urged Pedro to assume the title of " Emperor," as one more imposing than that of " King." An extract from the best of the panegyrics is added:

"Almost a quarter of a century after the consummation of the famed fact—the creation of a new empire on the earth—Death has come and snatched away a chief actor in the great drama, of which the principal actor was the son of kings, the beloved Prince of Liberty in the Old World and the New.*

"He is dead who, in that epoch of enthusiasm, proposed to the new sovereign the title of Emperor, and who, undaunted, raised his voice in the midst of bayonets, to anathematize an oppressive policy, designed to reconquer in America the irreparable past, to suspend chains in the throne where kings had been seated, and from which flowed facts that rendered a regress to slavery impossible.

"The New World was not shaped to be measured by the hands of a pigmy. The mouths of the Amazon, Madeira, Xingu, and Guayba, were designed by Providence for a people of giants; and for a prince who, from the summit of his throne, must one day have conference with the universe, and mark the track of his high destiny! The conception of this grand idea was not sufficient for the genius of the man who now rests in the bed of death, but day and night, with his ardent and creative soul, he worked to complete it.

"Twenty-six honorary titles adorn his memory, and in eighteen illustrious societies was his name proclaimed that of a sage.

"Brazil must shed tears for the loss of the Canon Januario da Cunha Barboza."

* This was Pedro I., whom the Brazilians expelled for his tyranny.

CHAPTER X.

The Marimba.—Procession announced.—Unloading Lime-boats.—Lapa Convent and Lady at Confession.—The Campo and Lavandeiras.—Dog-killers.—Customhouse.—Trucks.—A Slave chained to one.—Young and old Women in Chains —Coffee Carriers.—Crippled Slaves. The Spectacle given up.—An Angel.— The Musuem.—Antiquities, etc.—Fathers of Snuff and the Snuff-trade.—Original Snuff-mills and Sniffing Apparatus.— Slave-traders.—Monastery of San Bento : its Monks, Chapel, Cells, Library, and Bookworms.—Sopping.—Great Wealth of this Monastery.

25*th*. This morning a slave came along with a load on his head and both hands in a large gourd, out of which he drew a fashionable waltzing tune. I took the opportunity of examining the popular *Marimba*. Every African nation has its own, so that a Congo, Angola, Minas, Ashantee, or Mozambique instrument is recognizable, but the differences are not great. A series of thin steel rods, from ten to fifteen, are fixed on a thin

board, five or six inches square, in the manner of flute-keys, which they resemble. A long and a short one alternate; sometimes they diminish like Pan-pipes. The board is secured in the larger half of a dry calabash. Grasping it with his fingers beneath, and his thumbs on the keys, he produces, by pushing them down at one end and letting them fly back, a soft humming sound allied to that of the Jews'-harp. The city is an Ethiopian theatre, and this the favorite instrument of the orchestra. Slaves are daily met playing African airs on it, and groups returning to the country have commonly one or two among them. In the preceding illustration, a couple are, like Jewish captives by the river of Chebar, reviving recollections of home in the songs of their native land.

As this is Ash-Wednesday, there is to be a procession, toward evening, from the Church of "St. Francis of the Penitence." Fourteen images, and among them "Black Benedict," are to come down the hill and parade the streets. *Angels*, too —real, living, winged spirits—will, it is said, join the pageant.

The lime of Rio is made of shells scooped out of the Bay, and, of course, is in powder. See that falua—a light boat of one mast—riding at anchor some fifty feet from the Gloria Beach. She is charged with lime, and, dancing on the swell, is unloading her cargo. The slave on her bows, keeping her head to the shore with a long bamboo, is captain; the other, on the gunwale, raising the dust on the blade of a hoe, is her deckhand. Observe those four blacks, with empty tea-chests on their heads, wading toward her, and as many coming from her with their boxes filled. How steadily they move, where the waves would take a stranger off his feet! The water is at the arm-pits of him who is lifting his load from the edge of the vessel; and see, as he turns and breasts that retiring swell, it swashes over his eyes. Now he comes dripping out, ascends the bank, and, crossing the street, empties his chest on the floor of an establishment for the sale of building materials. As he does, so do eight or ten more, keeping the hoe (used in place of a shovel) in constant motion.

Their dresses are too primitive for laborers on our wharves. Some are, like the skippers on the craft, in shirts minus both sleeves and skirts; others wear a petticoat that neither reaches the knees nor meets behind; and two have aprons not one whit wider than aprons usually are. White as their contents, the boxes contrast strongly with their moving pedestals, while these increase in height as they near the beach, and all but disappear at the falua. One, while his box was being filled, plunged over head and washed himself; then tore off a part of his pinafore, and fastened it over his shoulders, to protect them from the caustic dust. The scene altogether is a novel one, though common enough here. One old man's head is so whitened with the dust as to remind one of a cauliflower on a coal-sack.

Wending along, I came to the Lapa Church, and convent behind it. A genteel young man, certainly not out of his teens, was at the door, in a prim white alb just from the laundress. The little shaven spot on his head glistened within its comate boundary like a disk of pearl inlaid in ebony. As I had inferred from repeatedly passing that the interior was in ruins, I stepped in. The old rough walls were bare, the floor unflagged and piled up with rubbish. The only part finished was the ceiling, upon which the "Lady of Lapa," with legendary attendants in vivid colors, contrasted strangely with the desolation below them. Turning to the right, a little chapel appeared, in which a solitary monk was reading on a bench, and near him three females seated on the floor. Another door opens here into the cemetery. I passed through it into a passage, and followed on into the sacristy. Here were three shrines, and, as no one appeared, I examined them rather closely; but, on passing round the second to the third, lo! the skirts of a lady at confession behind a chair, and the handsome young friar reclining in it with his ear at the strainer.

I retired, and continued on to the Campo—a spacious square, on the sides of which several national buildings stand, including the Senate-house. Covered with stunted grass, and the site of one of the principal fountains, it is the city's great washing and bleaching establishment, and is ever alive with lavandeiras. More than two hundred are now scattered over the field, exclusive of crowds at the fount. From the surrounding mountain peaks they must appear like clamorous daws or restless magpies. How busy all are, each in the centre of a ring of drying garments! The huge wooden bowl, which, in coming and re-

H

turning, serves as a basket, is now a washing-tub, and "the

baril" a bucking-stool. Most are, like their Larangeiras sisters, slightly draped. A single vestment with most suffices, and with its purification the wearer winds up her labors. Some are Minas and Mozambique girls, as evinced by their superior forms, and attentions to attire. If others are naked to the waist, these are so seldom. Figures graceful as any seen at the wells of the East occur among them.

With this business of the Campo the heavens sympathize; for, while the grass is half concealed by garments bleaching in the sun, the blue welkin is dappled over with snow-white patches, as if it was drying-day above. For the oldest and thickest settled parts of Rio this is the only washing-place; as such it is never clear, except in rainy weather, when we may suppose Celestials are wringing out wet linen.

The fountain supplies a wide district with water, and hence no small part of the colored population is constantly passing to and from it. Let us draw near. What a hubbub! A Hottentot fair can not surpass it. These two military policemen may prevent a lusty negro squeezing in before his turn and pushing aside the half-filled baril of a weak one, but they can not silence the oral clamor. The fluid not borne off runs into two stone cisterns, thirty feet by fifteen, and keeps them knee-deep filled. They are bordered with granite coping, which, sloping outward, forms continuous washboards for the negroes within. A dozen or more are busy in each. Splash, swash, go shirts and sheetings! Plunged, pounded, twisted like a rope, swung overhead, and flap, slap, down they come upon the coping. A score of these thongs are whirling in the air at once, wielded by infuriates, whose laughings and screaming interjections break the monotony of the ceaseless gabble at the fount. Soap Street appropriately runs into the Campo.

Lavandeiras have no saint assigned them, yet they deserve

one, were it only to relieve them once a year from the washing-tub. No class have stronger claims upon the Church, nor on the saints themselves. A mass can not be performed nor a festa kept without them. Festas are hailed as blessings by all others, but what do they for these? Drawing near they demand additional toil, and in departing leave them naught but piles of dirty linen.

Invited to dine in the city that I might witness the procession, I now turned down Ruo San Pedro, a long and narrow street, in which iron and copper smiths, hatters, and guitar-makers were at work. And here I again observed how dogs are sacrificed to Sirius. The priest devoted to this service used to dispatch his victims, like a Roman cultrarius, with a mall or bludgeon, insidiously pursuing them from street to street; but now, to avoid the evil omens of evasive blows, he drops little balls made of flour, fat, and nux vomica, which are eagerly devoured by the unsuspecting animals. Convulsions and death quickly follow. I have passed to-day no less than four expiring and expired, and here was the fifth.

I emerged from the long avenue in Dereita Street, not far from the Custom-house, where street-passengers have to run a muck through piles of bales, barrels, packages, crates, trucks, and bustling and sweating negroes. Here are no carts drawn by quadrupeds for the transportation of merchandise. Slaves are the beasts of draught as well as of burden. The loads they drag, and the roads they drag them over, are enough to kill both mules and horses. Formerly, few contrivances on wheels were used at the Custom-house. Every thing was moved over the ground by simply dragging it. A good deal of this kind of work is still done. See! there are two slaves moving off with a cask of hardware on a plank of wood, with a rope passed through a hole at one end, and the bottom greased or wetted! Such things were a few years ago very common.

Trucks in every variety are now numerous. Some recent ones are as heavily built and ironed as brewers' drays, which they resemble, furnished with winches in front to raise heavy goods. Each is of itself sufficient for any animal below an elephant to draw; and yet loads varying from half a ton to a ton are dragged on them by negroes. Two strain at the shafts and

one or two push behind, or, what is quite as common, walk by the wheels and pull down the spokes. It is surprising how their naked feet and legs escape being crushed, the more so as those in front can not prevent the wheels every now and then sinking into the gutters, and whirling the shafts violently one way or the other. One acts as foreman, and the way he gives his orders is a caution to the timid. From a settled calm he in a moment rages like a maniac, and seems ready to tear his associates to pieces.

A slave was chained to one heavy truck. He had been absent when it was wanted, and his enraged owner took this method of preventing him from losing another job. The links of the chain were three quarter inch round iron.

Neither age nor sex is free from iron shackles. I met this morning a very handsome Mozambique girl with a double-pronged collar on; she could not have been over sixteen. And a few evenings ago, while standing on the balcony of a house in Custom-house Street, a little old negress, four fifths naked, toddled past, in the middle of the street, with an enormous tub of swill on her head, and secured by a lock and chain to her neck. "Explain that, Mr. C——," I said. "Oh, she is going to empty slops on the beach, and being probably in the habit of visiting vendas, she is thus prevented, as the offensive vessel would not be admitted. Some slaves have been known to sell their 'barils' for rum, and such are sent to the fountains and to the Praya accoutred as that old woman is."

With a friend I went to the Consulado, a department of the Customs having charge over exports. Gangs of slaves came in continually with coffee for shipment. Every bag is pierced and a sample withdrawn while on the carrier's head, to determine the quality and duty. The tariff, based on the market price, is regulated every Saturday. At present the duty amounts to eleven per cent. on coffee and seven on sugars. The instrument used to withdraw samples of coffee is a brass tube, cut precisely like a pen. The point is pushed in at the under side of the bag, and the berries pass through the tube. A handful is abstracted. On withdrawing the instrument, its point is drawn over, and closes the opening. The operation occupies but a few seconds. The samples amount to some tons in a year. They, with those of exported sugars, are given to the Lazaretto.

Every gang of coffee-carriers has a leader, who commonly shakes a rattle, to the music of which his associates behind him

chant. The load, weighing 160 lbs., rests on the head and shoulders, the body is inclined forward, and the pace is a trot or half run. Most are stout and athletic, but a few are so small and slightly-made that one wonders how they manage to keep up with the rest. The average life of a coffee-carrier does not exceed ten years. In that time the work ruptures and kills them. They have so much a bag, and what they earn over the sum daily required by their owners they keep. Except four or five, whose sole dress was short canvas shirts, without sleeves, all were naked from the waist upward and from the knees below; a few had on nothing but a towel round the loins. Their rich chocolate skins shone in the sun. On returning, some kept up their previous chant, and ran as if enjoying the toil; others went more leisurely, and among them some noble-looking fellows stepped with much natural grace.

A gang of fourteen slaves came past with enormously wide but shallow baskets on their heads. They were unloading a barge of *sea-coal*, and conveying it to a foundry or forge. The weight each bore appeared equal to that of a bag of coffee (160 lbs.). This mode of transporting coal has one advantage over ours, since the material is taken directly from the vessel to the place where it is to be consumed. As with coal, so with every thing; when an article is once mounted on the head of a negro, it is only removed at the place where it is to remain.

A couple of slaves followed the coal-carriers, each perspiring under a pair of the largest sized blacksmith bellows—a load for a horse and cart with us. A week ago I stood to observe eight oxen drag an ordinary wagon-load of building stone for the Capuchins up the steep Castle hill; it was straining work for them to ascend a few rods at a time; to-day I noticed similar loads of stone discharged at the foot of the ascent, and borne up on negroes' heads.

No wonder that slaves shockingly crippled in their lower limbs are so numerous. There waddled before me, in a manner distressing to behold, a man whose thighs and legs curved so far outward that his trunk was not over fifteen inches from the ground. It appeared sufficiently heavy, without the loaded basket on his head, to snap the osseous stem and drop between his feet. I observed another whose knees crossed each other, and his feet preternaturally apart, as if superincumbent loads had pushed his knees in instead of out. The lamplighter of the Cattete district exhibits another variety. His body is settled low down, his feet are drawn both to one side, so that his legs are parallel at an angle of thirty degrees. The heads of Africans are hard, their necks strong, and both, being perpendicular to the loads they are called to support, are seldom injured. It is the lower parts of the moving columns, where the weights are alternately thrown on and off the jointed thighs and legs, that are the weakest. These necessarily are the first to give way under excessive burdens; and here are examples of their having yielded and broken down in every direction.

Dereita Street is the chief scene of religious pomps. By four P.M. the balconies began to fill with ladies in full dress, the heads of several adorned with flowers, and the necks and ears of all with chains and pendents. In the whole street there was not a cap or a bonnet to be seen. By five, the crowds on the side-walks became anxious and restless, for the sky was overcast and increased in gloom. At six the clouds dissolved in rain, and the spectacle was given up.

On the way home I overtook some of the actors in their acting dresses, and in one couple beheld a vivid symbol of ethereal essence chained to mortality — a short, fat lay-brother, bare-headed, his face glistening with perspiration, and the skirts of his black alb or gown draggling on the wet pavement, over which he was hastening with a speed and gait any thing but attractive. In one hand he held an open umbrella, and with the other pulled after him an "angel of the festival"—a little, pretty girl of six or seven. Her face was painted; a diadem surmounted her flowing ringlets; she wore a short scarlet frock, the stomacher glittering with gems, and the skirts expanded by elastic hoops; tight yellow boots inclosed her tiny feet, and a pair of Cupid's wings fluttered at her shoulders. There was no looking at the little Houri without admiring her as she tripped along buoyant as air. The springs in her wings and skirts inflated them, and at every step she seemed ready to rise and soar away the instant her captor let go her hand.

27*th.* H—— and I devoted this day to the Museum, which faces the Senate-house in the Campo. The curator, a Carmelite friar and professor of chemistry, received us cheerfully. In the yard was a caged king-vulture, the handsomest of accipitrines; his body was cream-color and slate, with roseate tints; his head and neck, protruded from an ample frill, were variegated with crimson, green, yellow, and some darker patches. In a long box near him lay snugly coiled a twelve-foot boa, from Minas Province. Close by was a curiosity of another kind, a mounted cannon, four and a half feet long, three inches

bore, composed of two longitudinal slabs of hard and heavy *wood*, strongly bound by numerous wrought-iron rings. It had evidently been used. It was taken from the rebels at Para during an attempt at revolution there, some eight or nine years ago.

Zoology and ornithology are the chief features of the Museum. The native feline tribes, from the jaguar to the smallest of tiger-cats, are fully represented; so are the quadrumana. One sloth is nearly four feet in length; the rest are less than three. In the brilliant assemblage of birds are representatives from every province, including, of necessity, a numerous deputation from those fairies of the forest, humming-birds.

For students of numismatics, here are ancient and modern coins and medals. The collection of minerals is extensive, and a laboratory for the analysis of ores is provided. Some interesting Egyptian antiquities have also been procured.

Native antiquities are few and not of much interest; but this feature of the institution will improve. There are a few embalmed heads from the Amazon. The Tapajos thus preserved the skulls of their enemies, and on special occasions carried them suspended on the breast as amulets.

They look horrible enough, worse than New Zealand specimens placed near them. The sockets of the eyes are filled with a dark resinous matter, in which are imbedded small pieces of bone or shell. Into the open mouths are inserted the ends of strong corded loops, and the whole filled flush with cement.

A ridge of black hair remains on the crown, and at the occiput considerable quantities adhere. Large and handsome feather rosettes conceal the ears, like similar ornaments of ribbon worn by modern ladies.

In one case were specimens of musical instruments. Double flutes were extensively used by the classical ancients, and here they are as constructed by American aborigines. The bones of which they are made are yellow, jagged, and far from inviting to delicate lips. Their tones, however, are singularly soft and mellow.

A represents the largest. Each bone is twelve inches long, and three eighths of an inch bore. They are united by twine, neatly wound and worked. On the back of the lower parts are finger-holes—shown at B: these were stopped up; perhaps they were experimental additions of some Brazilian Pronomus.

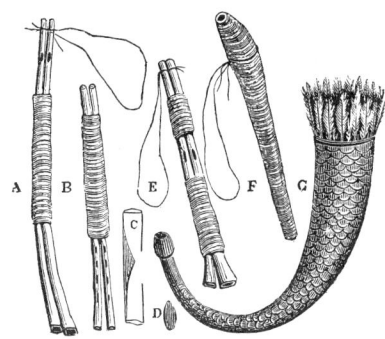

The construction of the sounding, or whistle part, is seen at C, a cone of resinous cement being secured immediately under the orifice. The ridge of cement rises to the centre of the tube. The instrument is played by blowing through the upper end, as in a clarionet. E is a smaller flute, to be blown at either end. F has a swelled wooden mouthpiece, and no side-opening. Dual bone flutes, with finger-holes, are yet in use in the northern provinces, besides bamboo flutes, and instruments with which the voices of wild beasts are imitable with singular accuracy. Single and double flutes of Greece and Rome were of bone. The "Ossea Tibia" was made of the leg-bone of a crane.

A cazique's trumpet is figured at G. The substance, hard as iron and black as jet, appeared to have been handsomely carved. The diverging orifice is furnished with a double row of scarlet and yellow feathers, which add to its length, and by their vibration probably affected the notes. Through age they are mostly stripped. While attempting to revive its long-silent tones, the deputy curator asked if we knew what it was made of. It was the end of an alligator's tail! Rams' horns were the primeval clarions of the East, but no quadruped of South America supplied any thing of the kind; hence these amphibious substitutes.

The next thing was an article of female ingenuity, a comb, in which the teeth, set edgeways, are thin slips of hard wood, uniform in size and shape, and, by means of four transverse pieces, firmly strung together by thread. 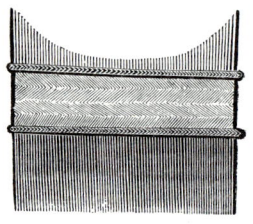 The needle-work forms a broad band, with raised borders, reflecting waved figures; the whole is smooth and regular, as if woven, and the instrument is strong as modern ones. The thread is round, well twisted, and uniform as silk cord. Its material is from the *macaya*, a species of cocoa, whose fruit produces a shining white fibre, stiffer than silk and stronger than cotton. Specimens of the undressed fibre, of thread made of it, and of stockings, are in the Museum.

Combs of rosewood, sometimes attached to coronals of feathers and other head ornaments, are still common among the Indians, and display both taste and skill in the hands that put them together.

The only sample of ancient native earthenware in the Museum was disinterred between twenty and thirty years ago on the Praya Flamingo, while digging foundations for a house. The internal diameter at the rim is eighteen inches, the depth six.

ANCIENT BRAZILIAN BASIN.

The thickness of the bottom and of the sides exceeds an inch. It was probably used as a caldron, the under side being blackened as with fire. No signs are observable of the wheel in its formation, though the circle is tolerably correct. The material is a grayish-yellow clay, and imperfectly burned. The inside has been profusely decorated. A band of dark red goes round just below the rim, and the rest is covered with complicated lines, that are more like a mass of serpents entangled together than any thing else. Small dots are mingled with them. A light and poor kind of glazing has been put on, of which remains are left. The surface, inside and out, is covered with an infinity of minute cracks, like old teacups thus disfigured. The outside has been colored red, the inside a palish yellow, the ornamental lines brown.

In another case were mills for triturating leaves of a popular plant, of which large quantities were manufactured by the ancient natives; also a couple of philosophical apparatus by which the prepared material was conveyed into dark, tortuous, and precipitous caverns.

Previous to unlocking the case, our courteous attendant opened and gracefully offered his snuff-box—a common Brazilian practice. It reminds one of relators of long or dry stories beginning with lighting a pipe, or treating themselves with a pinch. Suppose we imitate them on this occasion:

Modern lovers of the pipe seldom think of the worthies to whom they are indebted for its free enjoyment; and of those who delight in nasal aliment, how few ever call to mind the Diocletian persecutions their predecessors passed through for adhering to their faith in, and transferring to their descendants the virtues of tobacco. Europe frowned, and Asia threatened. Pagan, Mohammedan, and Christian monarchs combined to crush them. James I., foaming with rage, sent forth his "Counterblast;" the half-savage ruler of the Muscovites followed suit; the King of Persia, Amurath IV. of Turkey, the Emperor Jehan-Geer, and others, joined the crusade. They denounced death to all found inhaling the fumes of the plant through a tube, or caught with a pellet of it under their tongues. Those who used it as a sternutative only were to be deprived of nostrils and nose. To perfect the miseries of the delinquents, Urban VIII. went in state to the Vatican, where, tremulous with holy anger, he shook his garments, to intimate that the blood of the offenders would be on their own heads, and then thundered excommunication on every soul who took the accursed thing in any shape into a church.

Loss of life for lighting a pipe! Mutilation for taking a pinch! Tortures here, and endless torments hereafter, for a whiff or quid of tobacco! One wonders how the sufferers managed to pass through the fire unscathed, or even to escape annihilation; yet most of them did escape, and they did more—they converted the Nebuchadnezzars who sought to consume them.

What a spectacle! The world in arms against an herb, and anon prostrate before it! Proud rulers worshiping the idol whose admirers they had so fearfully menaced, and lawgivers avowed violators of their own laws! The modes adopted to exterminate the plant increased the demand for it, till it was sought for with an avidity that no penal enactments could suppress. Royal and sacerdotal clamor had raised its consumption ten thousand fold. The tide turned, and all began to praise the magic leaf. Ladies joined their lords in smoking after meals; boys carried pipes in their satchels to school, and at a certain hour pedagogues and pupils whiffed together. Not a bad subject for a painter. Mothers in the sixteenth century filled their sons' pipes early in the morning, to serve them instead of breakfast. People went to bed with cigars or pipes in their mouths, and rose in the night to light them. All classes became consumers; even priests were not excepted, provided they refrained till after mass. To accommodate travelers, poor and transient persons, *Tabagies*, or smoking-houses, were licensed on the Continent in every marine and inland town, where sailors and itinerants could, on moderate terms, be made happy, either by inhaling the vapor of the popular stimulant or tickling their nasal membranes with it. The ambitious sought fame by associating themselves with the introduction of the plant and its cultivation: hence we find it named after cardinals, legates, and embassadors, while, in compliment to Catharine de Medicis, it was called "the Queen's herb." Kings now rushed into the tobacco-trade. Those of Spain took the lead, and became the largest manufacturers of snuff and cigars in Christendom. The royal workshops in Seville are still the most extensive in Europe. Other monarchs monopolized the business in their dominions, and all began to reap enormous profits from it, as most do at this day.

Much has been written on a revolution so unique in its origin, unsurpassed in incidents and results, and constituting one of the most singular episodes in human history; but next to nothing is recorded of whence the various processes of manufacture and uses were derived. Some imagine the popular pabulum for the nose of transatlantic origin: no such thing. Columbus first beheld smokers in the Antilles, Pizarro found chewers in Peru, but it was in the country discovered by Cabral that the great sternutatory was originally found. Brazilian Indians were the fathers of snuff, and its best fabricators. Though counted among the least refined of aborigines, their taste in this matter was as pure as that of the fashionable world of the East. Their snuff has never been surpassed, nor their apparatus for making it.

The following is their milling and sniffing machinery—machinery, we believe, never figured and published before.

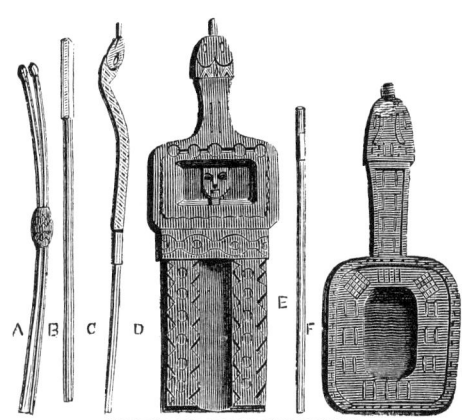

ANCIENT BRAZILIAN SNUFF-MILLS.

F is a slab of *jacaranda* (rosewood), ten inches long, of which five are taken up with the handle. The blade is nearly half an inch thick, with a cavity in the middle. The extremity of the handle represents the head of a serpent, with the tongue protruded. E is a cylindrical stick of rosewood, nine inches long and three fourths of an inch in diameter. These two constitute a mill. The owner takes out of a "*chuspa*"—a pouch, commonly slung over his right shoulder—a few pieces of dried tobacco leaf, places them in the cavity, and, grasping the stick, grinds them by rubbing its end to and fro upon them, and in a few moments reduces them to a rich and fragrant snuff; nor is the fragrance wholly due to the substance ground, but to the material of the mill. The heat developed by the friction of two pieces of odorous wood evolves a pleasant aroma that impregnates the powder.

The article being thus prepared, the next thing is to transmit it to its destination ere it grows cold, or the odor becomes weakened by evaporation. The apparatus for this part of the business is shown at A; it consists of a double tube, consisting of two light cylindrical bones united by thread, having the upper ends tipped with small wooden bulbs. The reader has anticipated the rest: no sooner is the triturating process ended than the pestle or stick is thrown down, the plain ends of the tube are plunged into the smoking powder, the others inserted into the nostrils, and by a smart inhalation the warm-scented dust is diffused in a trice over the olfactory palate! D represents another mill, in which the grinding receptacle is in the shape of a gutter running out at the end of the blade; C is an edge view, and B the rubber.

Suspended by a string round the neck, an Indian had this apparatus always at hand. At the back of one or both is an angular recess for the purpose of producing fire by friction, thus uniting in each a snuff-box, mill, and tinder-box.

Modern Indians are as fond of snuff as their ancestors; their apparatus for making and taking it are also similar to those described. I have seen neat circular mills from two to five inches across, with short conical and pyramidal pestles or mullers; sniffing-pipes also, more portable than those figured. Sometimes three bones are united—one to put into the snuff, connected with two for the nose—like one pipe serving two suction-pumps.

An ardent enemy to all stimulants, wet or dry, might, after reading the foregoing, be disposed to ask, And has not tobacco avenged, to some extent, the New World for the blood of her children slain by those of the Old—in its Circean effects, physical and moral; in the wealth it has drawn and continues to draw from consumers? All the conquerors have become tainted with the poison; the most ruthless are the most deeply polluted. Formerly the first powers of the earth—now contemptible for their weakness, dissensions, and crimes — slaves to blighting superstitions, to ignorance, poverty, pride, and a poisonous weed.

28*th*. A slaver arrived on the coast the other evening, and yesterday her cargo was landed a little north of the city, with slight attempts at concealment. J—— says the largest fortunes here, with few exceptions, are realized by the traffic. Passing lately a new castle-like structure in Mata Cavallos, he remarked, "The blood of negroes built that." A Brazilian lady observed more than once to me that the great slave-merchants do not flourish long, and never prosper to the last. "They die early, or their wealth leaves them; they live unhappy, and seldom leave children. With them the smell of gain is good, but like ice it melts away."

Met H—— according to appointment, and started with him to visit the Monastery of San Bento, the oldest one in Brazil. Male visitors are admitted from nine to twelve. To females the entrée is tabooed. Climbing the wide zigzag steep, we reached the plateau. The building appears rather small and mean. The front of the church looks like the gable end of an old Dutch house, except that two square towers run up a little higher, and are set off with low pyramidal termini. We entered on a corridor paved with plain and lettered tomb-stones of monks and abbots: one bears the date of 1560. A colored man was standing by the chapel door; he told us the fathers were at prayers, and would soon be out. Presently they came rushing forth, not the aged and emaciated beings I had anticipated, but smart young fellows, fat and fair. There were fifteen, of whom not one could be over twenty-three, and some had certainly not seen eighteen. In long-sleeved gowns, nothing but their heads and hands were visible. All bore the Church's mark, but scarcely two of their tonsures were alike.*

H—— recognized an acquaintance in one, and by a low *shr* arrested his attention; then, closing once or twice the fingers of his right hand without raising it from his side, the young father came directly to us. An affable and good-looking youth of about seventeen, he led us into the chapel, the richest in ancient carvings and gilding in the city. It seemed all gold, but much worn and tarnished. In the naves are statues of four kings, and eight bishops of the Benedictine order, in the midst of arabesques, flowers, and figures in high relief. San Bento himself stands at one side of the altar, and Our Lady on the other. One lamp

* Anciently a mark of infamy inflicted on felons and slaves, shaving the head was adopted from a mistaken humility, to show that those who bore the stigma were slaves to the Church; but then the razor swept the whole scalp. In time, portions were excepted, and eventually a circular spot on the crown was alone made bare, and now it varies in dimensions, as in these young friars, from a shilling to a saucer.

is remarkable for its design and ornaments. Two other antiques of the kind weigh between three and four thousand ounces of silver.

The monks' cells are arranged along both sides of wide passages on the second floor. Neat little rooms, each is furnished with a bed, bureau, table, chair, and looking-glass. They are kept in order by male slaves. The organ-gallery has some fine old Gothic furniture : a reading-table on a spiral stem is worthy of special notice. At the back of the organ, and facing the choristers, is a large statue of Christ on the cross, horrible to look at, on account of the wounds, blood, and the agony depicted in the features. In one of the gallery passages, among lumber, stood another statue, nearly full size.

Our young friend obtained permission to show us the library —a large, commodious room on the highest floor, with prospects opening from its windows enough to enchant an anchorite. Before the agitation of independence, here were fourteen thousand volumes ; at the close of commotions incident to it, not half remained. Great numbers of the missing volumes are said to be in the public library—a place more favorable to their preservation and to public access. With few exceptions, the shelves were laden with massive Latin tomes of the fathers, canon law, legends of the Church, lives of the saints, &c. Baronius, in 34 immense folios, besides 3 of indices ; Albertus in 21 ; Orders, Acts, and Annals of St. Benedict, in 12 or 14 more ; a valuable work, in 40 or 50 folios, on the Antiquities of Italy and Greece. Montfaucon, Aristotle, and a few treatises on Philosophy.

To what extent reading is enjoined by the abbot we did not learn, but no private or public collection bears stronger marks of bibliothecal taste or literary voracity. We read of recluses wearing out missals, but here one fifth, one fourth, and, in some cases, one third of every leaf has disappeared, and the remainder left as free from backs and covers as if they had never been glued together. Ponderous folios have been reduced to shapeless sheets, varying between quartos and octavos. As may be surmised, these persevering seekers after knowledge are of Formican descent ; children of a race proverbially wise ; industrious too, for to them Solomon sent sluggards for instruction.

Now, near twelve, we descended and looked for a moment into the kitchen, where a negro was hopping about on one leg, aided by a crutch. Some years ago he applied for charity, and is now cook. A laughing lad of sixteen, a friar, was attending, in his turn, on such poor visitors as might come a sopping. "And have any come?" "Si, senhor," he replied, and beckoned us to the open door of the refectory: four rather respectably-dressed white men were busy, each with a heaped plate of rice and fish. Common beggars bring their own spoon and calabash, and receive sops and porridge outside. Recollecting how Cervantes and poor Spanish scholars often depended on victuals thus doled out of monasteries, I suggested, in order more fully to realize the thing, that we should go in and be indebted to Saint Benedict for a dinner. The young father was delighted with the proposition, and was on the point of calling on the wooden-legged provider, but my companion was inflexible.

This monastery is reputed here the richest in the world. Besides the greater parts of some streets, and the whole of others, where stores bring the best rents, the fathers have estates in each of the eighteen divisions of the empire. Their principal lands are in the three provinces of Rio, Bahia, and Pernambuco. On some plantations they employ a thousand slaves. On Ilha do Governador, the largest island in Rio Bay, they have a large farming establishment, over which a number of friars regularly preside. A numerous brood of colored boys and girls are there raised till old enough to be sent to labor on the estates in the interior.

I

CHAPTER XI.

Diversity of Complexion in one Family.—Sabbath Diversions.—Street of Silversmiths.—Its staple Manufactures.—Amulets.—Figas.—Lock and Key.—Passage in Shakspeare explained.—Eating-houses. — Charges.—Sneezers "blessed."—Priests.—Free colored Men.—Great Consumption of Pork.—National Dish.—Pastry and Confectionery.—Heavenly Bacon.—Francis of Penitence.—Brotherhoods akin to modern Odd Fellows.—Terms of Admission.—Advantages.—Who this Francis was.—Garden, and Electric Eel.—Current Philosophy respecting the Sex.—Divination.—Provincial Nicknames.—Dowries in Cocoa and Coffee-trees.—Vegetable and other Sobriquets. — Horsewomen.—Officers' Wives on Drill in Military Costume.—Morals of the Priesthood.

March 1, *Sunday.* A Mozambique Mercury arrived from Senhor N—— with a dispatch, stating that he, his wife, two sons, and five daughters were on the way from Nictherohy to spend the day with us. In half an hour they came, and presented a diversity of complexion and features that surprised me. The youngest, a lad of fourteen, was very fair; the color of the rest veered between cinnamon and olive. H——, to whom I spoke on the subject, said tints so variegated and strongly marked in one family were not common, nor yet rare; adding, "If you want to see fair and handsome women, go down to Rio Grande."

The hair of all, no matter how light in infancy, becomes black. B—— showed me specimens taken in early life from the heads of his own children. Some were nearly white; all now have raven locks.

The old vicar came, and, as usual, joined a party at cards till dinner, after which, dancing and music till nine, when tea was served, and then more dancing till eleven P.M. I am thus particular to show how very differently Romanists here and Protestants in colder climates view the Sabbath. The former accuse the latter of making it, by stringent rules and tedious services, the most miserable of the seven, whereas, say they, it ought to be the pleasantest. Hence, after morning mass, social amusements and hilarity are deemed not only innocent, but meritorious. On this subject a lady observed to me, "God, in making the world, worked every day till Sunday, and then he

LIFE IN BRAZIL.

took his pleasure; so must we; he would be angry if we did not."

2*d*. Visited with H—— several shops in Silversmith Street. The staple stock in all consists of amulets, jewelry, paliteiros. spurs, and Church ornaments. Neither forks, pitchers, trays, or tea-sets are made in Rio. One pair of spurs, with chain and straps, weighed four pounds. The shops are small, without glass windows, and, with a small additional room, bring an average rent of $40 a month.

More or less of classical jewelry is to be found in all the Latin nations: much of it is current in Brazil. Ancient charms and amulets, including the *figa*, are as common as ever they were in Thebes, Ephesus, or Rome. Although I had repeatedly observed the small perpendicular case hung out against the door-post of each shop, it was not till my attention was turned to amulets that I stopped to examine the contents. They are very much the same from one end of the long street to the other. Besides crosses, crucifixes, crowns, palms, glories, and other little sacerdotal bijouterie, every case contains staple amulets in gold, silver, stone, ivory, etc. In some, these constitute the principal—in all, a prominent item. Specimens are subjoined.

The amulets marked *a, b, c* are known as the "Signs of Solomon," and are very popular; *f* is another, much worn by children; *d, d* are *figas*—one in gold, the other cornelian. I have seen them of horn, bone, wood, and lead. They are decidedly the chief of amulets, being worn by all classes and all ages, from teething infants to second childhood. They, as well as others, are blessed by priests before being worn;* *e* I suppose to be the tooth of some animal; one precisely like it was taken by the police, with other paraphernalia, from an African conjuror; *g* is of coral; the artist explained its virtues, but I did not understand him; *i* represents a pair of eyes; groups of these stare at you from every case, varying in size from those in the illustration to two or three times as large; they are composed of thin strips of gold and silver, struck in dies; and resemble those given out at the Festival of the Protectress of Eyes—St. Luzia. They keep off the evil eye; *k* is a "Dove Amulet;" *l, l* are keys of ancient form, and are quite common; *m* is a *bulla* within a ring; *n* is another form, much worn by children; Minas and Mozambique women sport large ones, and so do most fashionable white ladies; *o* is a cock's spur—also made of brass, tin, silver, etc. In the same case was another amulet, resembling it in form, but much larger; *p* and *q* are rings, with locks, keys, hearts, crescents, hour-glasses, etc., suspended upon them, each having a significance of its own.

Anxious parents protect their children by a number of these preservatives. The device is neither due to modern nor mediæval ingenuity. We find it exemplified in Pharaonic necklaces, and other relics of past epochs. Images of gods, shell-beads, birds, beasts, and scores of symbols were strung round the neck and attached to various parts of the body. The same thing was formerly in vogue in Europe. Finger-rings decorated in this manner are in high esteem in Brazil. They are met with in most of the jewelers' shops. Fig. *h* is one; a miniature figa, bulla, padlock, key, crescent, cockspur, &c., were attached to the one from which the illustration was taken.

Here are necklaces and bracelets which look like charms

---

* The old practice of "making the fig" to express insult or contempt is referred to by DANTE in his *Vision of Hell*, Canto xxv. See also DOUCE's *Illustrations of Shakspeare*.

against hunger rather than against witchcraft. One of the former before me—a gold one—is made up of knives, forks, a padlock and key, a stew-pan, water-jar, plates, dishes, ewer and basin, and twenty other culinary and domestic things. The best work of this kind comes from Bahia. Doña E—— has a bracelet made there, three inches wide, and divided into four compartments, in which kitchen utensils to the number at least of fifty are arranged. All are of gold, attached to the band by loose rings. These bracelets are in great repute in the country, and are not entirely out of date in the cities. There are morals in ear-pendents: an hour-glass worn at each lobe was an old European fashion. It is not out of date in Brazil. But, though common in the interior, many city belles have a distaste for such monitors of their fleeting charms and the flight of time. When watches came into vogue, efforts we know were made to secure for them the same favorable regard which the sex had accorded to those primitive chronometers; and, strange as it may seem, ladies then sported real ticking horologes at their ears. For the benefit of those who have never dreamed of trinkets teaching ethics, and are incredulous of the union of piety and fashion in our great-grand-dams, also to do justice to the moral and mechanical ingenuity of the old jewelers, I add the following from an old writer:

"The wit of man hath been luxuriant and wanton in the inventions of late years. Some have made watches so small and slight that ladies hang them at their ears like pendents and jewels. The smallness and variety of the tools that are used about these small engines seem to me no less admirable than the engines themselves; and there is more art and dexterity in placing so many wheels and axles in so small a compass, than in making clocks and greater machines; for some French watches do not exceed the compass of a farthing."

Locks and keys were once common auricular pendents, and are still sometimes seen. Doña L——, a lady of my acquaintance, wears the lock at the right ear, and the key at the left. Others have both at each ear. The sentiment embodied in the device is apparent—lock up what you hear. Thus Othello to Emilia:

"There's money for your pains;
I pray you turn the key, and keep our counsel."

Warburton, not aware that ear-jewels in these forms were once common, makes a mistake worthy of Dogberry himself, in attempting to elucidate the following observation of that learned dignitary: "And also the watch heard them talk of one Deformed; they say, *he wears a key in his ear, and a lock hanging by it.*" On this the bishop remarks: "They heard the conspirators satirize the Fashion: whom they took to be a man surnamed Deformed. This the constable applies with exquisite humor to the courtiers, in a description of one of the most fantastical fashions of that time—the men wearing rings in their ears, and indulging a favorite lock of hair, which was brought before and tied with ribbons, and called a *love-lock.*" Malone has a note to the same effect. I am not aware that any commentator has properly explained the passage.

Keys were symbols of confidence and secresy among the ancients. They were presented by husbands to wives, and worn on finger-rings. See Montfaucon, tom. iii., part i., book iii., cap. iii.

There are three or four eating-houses in Rio. I beg the reader's pardon for having fatigued him so long without asking him into one. Here is a Casa de Pasto, patronized by merchants, silversmiths, and shopmen. We pass through a little apartment in front, into a rather dark and moderate-sized one behind. Drawing chairs to an unoccupied table, a printed bill of fare, with prices, is laid before us.

The charges are low: for 98 cents two of us had soup, beefsteaks, boiled tongue, a ragout, pudding, and a bottle of wine. I refused to have any thing to do with the ragout, recollecting Santillane supping on one. I believe there was no cause to fear fishing up such ingredients as he did, but there was no getting rid of certain impressions where so many things recalled the adventures of the godson of Gil Perez. Besides, it was the conscience of a Lusitanian that served up cat instead of rabbit, and who, without owning a goat, managed to sell kids. Then every thing that has life and substance is caught and cooked in the interior, if not in the cities of Brazil, Levitical distinctions between clean and unclean being wholly disregarded.

After the table was cleared we fell into conversation with two gentlemen who had joined us. A snuff-box was passed round,

LIFE IN BRAZIL. 135

and one of the party sneezed, on which another exclaimed "*Dominus tecum*"—a common salutation in such cases, and always acknowledged with a polite inclination of the head. A priest came in and took a seat near us; in citizens' dress, I did not recognize him as one till he removed his hat and exposed his tonsure. Although Lent, he did not confine his meal to Lenten fare. Priests are here reputed free livers. Nearly all have families, and when seen leaving the dwellings of their wives— or females who ought to be—they invariably speak of them as their nieces or sisters, verifying an old Peninsular device, *Ida y venida por casa de mi tia*—It is my aunt's house at which I call.

Young colored men came in, sat down without hesitation at the same table with whites, and, on a perfect equality, took part in the conversation.

The prominent feature in dietetics here is the enormous consumption of pork. It is used by the highest and lowest, and used every day. And then what pork! It is all fat; at least what lean appears is but a film—a slip of pink blotting-paper lost in a ledger. One is surprised to find the strongest reasons for prohibiting swine's flesh in warm climes in the East so successfully set at naught here, and under the equator itself. European physicians of long standing here admit that it is as wholesome in Brazil as in any part of the earth. Brazilians are a fat and sleek people, and though the enervating influences of the climate, and the lassitude it induces, prevent them from working off superfluous flesh by labor, as our pig-eating farmers and others do, their general health, and the great age to which many arrive, corroborate the doctors' views.

The active native hog—the peccary—secretes little fat.

Pork, always held in high esteem in Europe, was particularly so by Spaniards and Portuguese. With them and other people it was usual to begin the Easter feast, in celebration of the expiration of Lent, not with a sirloin or rump of beef, but with a gammon of bacon—a dish often ushered in by a laughable representation, in dough, of Lenten fare and its departure—a dried herring on a galloping steed. The great Spanish dish is the olla, composed of fowls, mutton, beef, and other matters, but never without bacon; hence, "An olla without bacon is no olla." And so with the Portuguese and Brazilians—A dinner without toucinho is next to no dinner at all. *Feijaõ com toucinho* is the national dish of Brazil.

For the information of ladies, and of some future Mrs. Glass, the names of a few popular articles of native pastry and confectionery are added. Those on the bill of fare awakened curiosity, as well they might: *Celestial Slices*—fine bread soaked in milk, and steeped in a hot compound fluid of sugar, cinnamon, and yolks of eggs. *Mother Benta's Cakes*—an angelic dainty, invented by an ancient nun of the Adjuda convent; the ingredients, rice-flour, butter, sugar, grated meat of the cocoa-nut, and orange-water. *Widows*—sweet paste, thin as tissue-paper, piled an inch thick on each other and baked. Then here are *Sighs, Lies, Angels' Hair, Egg Threads, Weaning-pills, Young Negroes' Feet*, and another, *Baba de Moça*, which I shall not translate. *Rosaries* are eight and ten-inch rings or strings of praying-beads, by which the Credo may be acquired with incrusted almonds, and Ave Marias counted with pellets of jujube paste.

A word on "heavenly bacon," *toucinho do ceo*—a species of light pudding, composed of almond-paste, eggs, sugar, butter, and a spoonful or two of flour—because its name reminds one of olden times. The glorification of bacon is of very ancient date, and arose partly from prevailing enmity to Jews, but oftener from the estimation in which it was held. The most popular and esteemed of carneous aliments, it was given as rewards for rural, and particularly for connubial virtues. *El tocino del Paraiso el casado no anepiso*—Bacon of Paradise for the married who repent not—is a medieval proverb.

3d. Visited the Hospital of the "Third Order of St. Francis of Penitence," in company with H—— and a brother of the order.

Every church here, as in Lisbon, has affiliated with it a *Lay Brotherhood*, whose members are pledged to promote the interests and uphold the honor of its patron saint. They collect alms, in their turn, through the parish (though, of late years, this duty has been, in a great measure, transferred to the sacristans), provide candles, see to the dressings of the altar and images, and to the decoration and illumination of the church during festivals, receive contributions on these occasions, and issue to the donors pictures and medals. They provide angels for processions, walk in official costumes, and endeavor to rival other "Irmandades" in these spectacles. Through a board of managers they direct all fiscal and secular affairs.

Every brotherhood is a mutual benefit society, resembling somewhat a modern Odd Fellow's association. From the "Rules of the Order of St. Francis" (a pamphlet now before me), it appears that any respectable white Catholic can be admitted. If under thirty, the initiation fee is $25; if over forty, $80. No annual dues nor any subsequent demand is made; but "he who enters into the service of God and of our father, holy Francis, must concur with all his power to the augmentation and splendor of the order." Initiation takes place in the chapel, the altar is lit up, the candidate kneels before the officiating padre, while the image of the founder and the brethren look reverently on.

Independent of its religious character, this institution is a noble one. It annually distributes from fifteen to twenty thousand milreis to decayed and distressed families of its members. To give so much implies that its funds are large. It owns considerable real estate in the city, and also in the country. Numerous legacies have been left it. Rich merchants and others become members with the view of adding to its funds. Some of the wealthy men of Rio joined it in early life when poor clerks. When a member is sick, he can enter the hospital of the order, or be attended at home, and when he dies his brethren bury him.

The hospital is a spacious and pleasantly-located structure, near the monastery of St. Anthony, to which it is in some way allied, for the abbot is *ex officio* patron, and draws a stipend from its funds. Three stories high, the lowest is, with the exception of four small and strong rooms for maniacs, devoted to lumber and storage, being deemed, as all ground floors are, too damp to be healthy. The second is occupied by the sick and their attendants. The ward contains over twenty curtained beds, with a table, chair, and writing materials to each. A neat private bed-room, and an airy sitting one, await the convalescent. The physician came in, and, besides the "Rules," gave some interesting facts. None but brothers of the order are admitted.

There are fifty-three individuals at present in the institution, including officers. Of the patients, nineteen have ordinary complaints, and two are insane. Of the latter class, *twelve are admitted on an average each year*, and the terms of confinement vary *from four to sixteen days*.

The 17th of September is the anniversary of the order, " being the day on which the wounds of Christ were impressed on the body of our holy patriarch." The election of the board is to open with the vesper of the " Solemnidade das chagas de N. S. Padre," and invocations are to be addressed " to the Holy Spirit, our Lady, and our Father Saint Francis."

This Francis, founder of one of the four companies of Begging Friars, was an Italian devotee of the twelfth century. The son of a respectable merchant, he, to the distress of his parents, gave himself up to the severest austerities, excited by ambition or religious phrensy. His townsmen considered him hopelessly insane. His father, anxious to cure him, induced the bishop to order him to give up all claims to the paternal estate. Nothing loth, he went farther, and instantly stripped himself completely naked, and offered his garments, including his shirt. In one of his rhapsodies he had an interview with a seraph, and thence his followers assumed the title of " the Seraphic Order."

On the upper floor are the store-rooms, pantry, kitchen, and apartments for the menials. 'In the garden, a pleasant arbor, perpetual shrubbery and flowers, solicit the convalescent to walk and rest. Water spouts from a brazen face into a stone cistern; and in a wooden one an electric eel, from Para, was slowly moving. Two feet long, its head is two and a half inches over, and its body proportionally thick. Two small eyes, like dots, appear on its head. On first touching it I felt nothing, but attempting to grasp it I received a smart shock, and another on touching it with a pencil-case. Most of the water was drawn out, when it was difficult to awaken its anger; the discharges were feeble; and when the whole was let out, it gave no proof of electrical power.

Females, or " Sisters of the Order," are admitted on payment of the same initiation fees as men. They are not received into the hospital, but, when poor or sick, are provided for and attended at their homes.

4*th.* Confined within doors, I was amused with some current philosophy respecting the sex, and the influence of natal months. New to me, it may be so to the reader. Females born in March are commonly inquisitive; those who come crying into the world in April, in after life shed many tears; while such as postpone their appearance till May are oftener happy than sad. Those whom June brings forth have an awkward gait, and the children of July take long strides. The daughters of August turn out chatterers, and to those who first open their eyes on earth in September, the proverbial rebuke is commonly applicable—" More respect, if you please, and less familiarity." Although science may not yet be sufficiently advanced to solve these problems, there is little difficulty in the way of explaining another: In February, women talk less than in any other month.

Divination is as much in vogue here as it was in Europe centuries ago, especially on St. John's eve; but as it is after old formulas, examples are not worth quoting.

A love of humor is a part of our nature, and is amusingly exemplified in the universality of national and provincial nicknames. Unlike personal burlesque, there is nothing in them to wound individual sensibilities. The people of equatorial Brazil are named *Cocoas*, from their fondness for the fruit, and eating it with every dish. The provincials of Bahia and Pernambuco are, however, more generally known as *Manoel Cocoas*, the etymology of which is thus given : It was formerly, and still is the custom, in making devices, settling dowries, &c., to fix the amounts in cocoa-trees, whose current value was as well understood as coin itself. A southern native married the daughter of a wealthy Bahian, who promised him twenty thousand dollars for a marriage portion. The young husband reminded him of this. " True," said he; " go into the plantation, and take the amount in cocoa-trees."

" Cocoa-trees! Why, sir, I don't want cocoas, but what you promised—dollars."

" Very well; every tree is worth half a dollar; go and select forty thousand; they are the dollars I deal in, and they are worth more than all the dirty silver ones you ever saw, or will see."

From the prenomen and prudence of this dealer in nature's

specie, his countrymen are named Manoel Cocoas. It was hearing the term applied repeatedly that led me to ask for the explanation.

As with cocoas at the north, so it is with coffee-trees here. A planter promises to a son or daughter a certain number of cruzados, and they take them out in plants; the current value of each being a cruzado, or twenty cents. When an estate is sold, its trees are reckoned as so many cruzados certain.

The Portuguese, who are said to have little affinity for soap and water, call the citizens of the capital "*Cariocas*" and "*Ducks*," because of their fondness for ablutions. This the Fluminenses admit, and in reply concede that their Lusitanian brethren do wash themselves once a year—on St. John's eve, the celebration of which is preceded by washing or bathing.

The people of the Province of Rio de Janeiro are generally known as "*Bananas*," because, say the Paulistas and others, they are soft and lazy. The stem of the banana never hardens into wood. The hale and active Rio Grandees call them "*Women*." Weak and sickly young people are Bananas. Fops, who must have slaves to do every thing for them, even to the drawing on of their stockings, are thus designated. A young lady, complaining of being unwell to an intimate, is often saluted with, "Oh! you're a Banana." But the appellation, applied seriously, is a gross insult.

Many persons in Rio are natives of Gibraltar, descendants of Portuguese settled there. They are named "*Rock Scorpions*," from the numbers of those reptiles in the neighborhood of the fortress. (The English at the Rock baptize the Portuguese "*Salads*," and these, in return, christen their godfathers "*Herrings:*" both terms from favorite relishes of the respective parties.)

Orange-trees are of rapid growth; hence, when a person becomes suddenly rich or prosperous, "he's an orange-tree."

Meeting one day a lady, handsome and (as nearly all are) *embonpoint*, with a small, meagre man, my companion, who knew both, remarked, "What a shame for such a woman to be married to that *pilchard !*"

The inhabitants of Rio Grande—the most southern province, bordering on Paraguay — are known as "*Guascas*," from the thongs or narrow strips of hide they carry in their hands. The ends of the lasso, by which they take wild cattle, consist of guasca strips. A spirited race, they resent affronts by lashing the shoulders of offenders. Brave, hardy, and imbued with Republican principles, they have been in rebellion eleven years, and were but recently induced to lay down their arms. Should they continue an integral branch of the empire, they will probably exercise a controlling influence in its administration.

Rio Grande belles are expert horsewomen. Except in cities, they use no side-saddles, but ride as the sex still rides in Asia, and as once all rode in Europe. Twenty years ago it was common for officers' wives to accompany the troops on horseback. They sported boots, spurs, and masculine hats, and when in towns or at parades, mounted military caps and epaulettes, to denote the rank of their husbands, and consequently their own. Old Senhora P—— made a two years' campaign thus equipped with a regiment her husband commanded. She says the ladies of St. Paulo and Minas provinces followed the same custom, as well as her countrywomen of Rio Grande. My aged friend retains other camp accomplishments; oftener than once she has sent, or rather told Pompey to go to what the Portuguese call the Englishman's heaven—a place antipodal to the abode of the righteous.

5th. The disappearance, sudden and inexplicable, of a young lady espoused, with her parent's consent, to a merchant of her own age, has for the past fortnight caused some excitement. The police were employed, but neither they nor the friends of the afflicted family could discover a clew to her fate. Three days ago her distracted father attempted suicide. Last evening information reached the city verifying the worst of fears. The late priest of the Gloria church, having received an appointment in another province, has been met on his way thither, and with him the ruined girl.

I did not intend to say a word on the morals of the priests, but hearing so much as I do daily, it is impossible to refrain. The depth of their pollution I should not have suspected, nor would any stranger, unless in a similar position with myself to have his eyes opened. The following language of an enlightened native is not introduced to denounce individuals, but the system that makes them what they are. "The priesthood of this country is superlatively corrupt. It is impossible for men to be worse, or to imagine men worse. In the churches they appear respectable and devout, but their secret crimes have made this city a Sodom; there are, of course, honorable exceptions. but they are very few." An old inhabitant of Rio, who has neither inducement nor disposition to misrepresent the country or its morals, added, "Every word is true, and much more than you can well conceive." He continued, "With country priests concubinage is universal, and, if possible, they are worse than the 'sacred crowns' of the city!*

Another, whose authority would not be questioned if it were prudent to give his name, observes, "They are assuredly the most licentious and profligate part of the community. The exceptions are rare indeed. Celibacy being one of their dogmas. you will find nearly the whole with families; and it is a substantial fact, which admits of no argument, that in their amours they are ever partial to women of color—blacks or mulattoes."

Within a few days, a gentleman holding office under government was requested to give away a young couple about to be married. On returning from the church, he said, in reply to inquiries, "All I know about the bride and bridegroom is, they are both the offspring of priests;" the latter being, in fact, a son of the Vicar of San José, who is known to have a large family, and who, to his credit, does not disown it. He takes no offense when asked how his niece and her children are.

Within the last month another priest sent out invitations to friends to attend the funeral of a young man who he openly avowed was his son. A little noise arose, but it soon blew over.

St. Anthony's Convent was the scene of a direful tragedy. A young woman of doubtful reputation was visited by several of the monks, and subsequently introduced into the monastery in one of their dresses. After some days the affair became public; the police interfered, and found her in one of the cells in a dying condition. It is not a year since this transpired.

A current story respecting a sick lady and one of the Capu-

* This term, derived from the tonsure, is applied in derision to all priests and friars.

chins, recently brought over by the empress, I shall not relate. The villain barely escaped the fatal vengeance of her son.

Women constitute the chief part of the Church's charge, and they are taught to believe, and do believe, that the crimes of a priest do not affect his efficiency as one, nor the duty of confessing to him. I have heard several native ladies maintain this.

Pedro I. cared little for monks. He made inroads into their privileges, and under him a law was passed forbidding any more novices to enter the monasteries. His son, brought up by monks, has sanctioned its violation, as we have seen in the youths at San Bento's.

In all sects and countries immoral clergymen are found, but in Brazil evils consequent on the celibacy of the priesthood are admitted to be general, and of the most revolting character. It is believed that the government will be compelled eventually to carry out the intentions of the late regent Feijaō—suppress every convent, and adopt the system of the Greek Church in requiring priests, other than bishops, to marry.

CHAPTER XII.

Visit to Christoval: native Sheep.—Palace of a Peddler.—Imperial Quinta.—Rapacity of the old Queen.—Miguel.—A Viscount and his strange Employment.—Emperor's Apartments.—Objects of Natural History.—Collection of Coins.—Peruvian, Egyptian, and Roman Antiquities.—Laboratory.—Theatre, and Garden.

March 7. This morning a carro drew up at the door, and in a few moments Senors R——, B——, and myself were whirling down the Cattete on a visit to the country palace. Soon we were skirting the Bay along the Praya da Gloria; then, inclining to the left, passed through Rua das Mangueiras (street of leather pipes), leaving the roaring surf on the opposite hand; dashed under the aqueduct arches into Mata-cavallos, or horse-killing avenue; turned again into another, named after sick people (Rua dos Invalidos), which terminated at a corner of the Campo, whose area was alive with lavandeiras. Rattling through Mata-porcos (pig-killing street), we came to a point where the road merged into two others, one leading to the imperial Quinta.

Groups of mules, with their skin-covered panniers filled with charcoal, vegetables, and other matters for city consumption, every now and then passed by; also a flock of sheep, long-necked, with little wool, and that hairy; but most observable was the variety of their colors, black, white, brown, bay, etc., and spotted just as oxen often are with us. Handsome cottages and country-seats occurred: one, a perfect palace, belonging to a widow whose husband began life by peddling a few pieces of nankeen, and at whose death she received, as her share of the estate, six hundred thousand dollars in cash. Some half a mile off arose the Lazaretto, with its cupola and white glistening walls, on an eminence close to and overlooking the Bay.

We now were trotting along a road bordered with thorn and other living fences, paved, and planted with lamp-posts, so exactly like suburban streets we had come through that I was not aware of being on the emperor's grounds till the palace itself rose in sight. An hour's ride brought us to it. Its location is delightfully romantic, on an elevated plateau. A square building of three stories constitutes its left wing and prominent feature; the other wing is a story lower. Its composite character is due to its origin. The old king, in his country drives, took a liking to the place, and was once or twice entertained by its owner, who at length, in a fit of enthusiasm or from some other impulse, begged his acceptance of it. Whether this sacrifice to the first anointed head seen in the country—admitted on all hands an unusually thick one—was ever suitably acknowledged, my informants could not say; but instances are current of members of the family sending messages to Brazilian Naboths, and following them up with acts much in the manner of Ahab and his lady. Among enlightened natives, the old queen, sister to that incarnation of royalty, Ferdinand VII., is spoken of as a Jezebel in no wise behind her Jewish prototype.*

---

* Of Portuguese scions of royalty, Miguel, the brother of Pedro I. and uncle to the present emperor, equals any of the anointed carnivora of ancient or modern times. Many are the anecdotes current of him. He used to go to the market with profligate associates, and, among other tricks, snatch a sucking pig, swing it aloft in the air, and receive it on his sword's point. To vary the diversion, his companions would throw up the squeaking victims that his highness might with less exertion flesh his weapon in them. Such was the way he gratified his taste for blood here before he caused so much to flow in Portugal. If the *jure divino* rulers of our earth do not lap blood, most of them sport with it.

Ascending a flight of stairs, we found ourselves on a corridor running along the four sides of an open area, and communicating with the principal rooms of the edifice. The housekeeper, an old lady busy with her needle, took our cards to a gentleman who was walking to and fro on the corridor with a child in his arms. He came directly to us. This was a viscount. Left in charge of the infant prince during the absence of its parents in Rio Grande, he has been isolated here for several months. He spoke English well, had traveled in Europe, and was alive to "the wonderful progress" (his own words) of the people of the United States in national greatness. He inquired respecting the connection of the great lakes by canals, of the states by rail-roads, and telegraphs, and rather surprised me by asking the price of labor. When told that ordinary mechanics had from $1 50 to $2 50 a day, and that in some branches from $3 to $4 were earned, he opened his eyes—wages of Brazilian artisans and salaries of government officers being very low. I explained that what he deemed extraordinary wages was an element of American prosperity, inasmuch as it awakened and stimulated thousands of keen intellects to the invention of labor-saving machinery, whereas, in countries where labor costs almost nothing, there can be but little inducement to make it cost less. On giving us in charge of an attendant, he observed that Nature had done every thing for Brazil, but as yet man had done next to nothing.

In the prime and vigor of life, able and accomplished, I could not but pity him as he left us with his charge in his arms. And is it for employments like *that*, I thought, for which such a man was made? Instead of being the head of a province, or, as chief magistrate of the whole, unfolding the resources of the country, and identifying himself with the progressive influences of the age, to be acting as dry-nurse to another one's baby! But such is the philosophy of monarchy, and men here, as in Europe, in thus unsexing themselves, do not dream that they surpass Alcides when spinning flax among Omphale's maids.

Our cicerone led us into a passage lined with pictures of Madonnas, friars, and ghastly saints, mixed in with modern heroes and Napoleon's battle-scenes. A small group of Indians by a native artist was, in my view, worth all the rest. The floors of a suit of three principal rooms are laid in native woods, worked into coarse mosaics—satin and rose woods preponderate. In one apartment is a large painting of the Portuguese first landing on the coast. A lady presenting her two sons to Alphonse, an incident well known in Lusitanian history, is the subject of another. The conductor called my attention to a French "Pendule Mechanique," and, winding up the spring, a number of minikin figures danced, to his great admiration. The side-table on which the toy stood possessed greater interest. It was on it that Pedro I., on the 17th of April, 1831, signed his abdication. In consequence of his ideas of divine rights, power was taken from him, and he was forced to leave the country—a remarkable example, considering where it happened, of the progress of the doctrine of popular rights.

The third apartment was the imperial bed-room, fitted up, like the others, with French furniture. A native feature consists of two jaguar skins spread on the floor, the tails, legs, feet, and claws expanded, and the heads perfect and stuffed to resemble life. These face the bedstead—guardians of its occupants. This delightful dormitory is thirty feet above the ground, while its folding windows open upon forests, groves, and gardens in perpetual bloom.

The "Throne-room" is a large and dark one, and only used by candlelight. Brazilians are tenacious of the solemn fooleries of the Portuguese and other European court ceremonies, which it is hardly possible to witness without feelings of contempt for the actors; and a deeper emotion on beholding American ministers paying a humiliating homage to monarchy, which the republics of Greece would not allow their embassadors, even at the court of Persia, to offer. Commodore Wilkes, when here, on his passage out, saw but a little, yet sufficient to excite his disgust.

In the "Guard-room," a fluted column, surmounted by a wivern, occupies the centre, and round it swords and halberts are tastefully arranged. Several statues stand about: Diana, Pomona, a Medicean Venus, and another leaving the bath. Here are also two spirited statues, of polished marble, of Egyptian divinities, of the human size. The next door opened into the chapel, a shabby affair, but soon to be superseded by a new one.

"Our Lady of Pains" stands on the altar, and St. Anthony, with the baby, near her. Two large paintings hang on the walls: one, St. Peter of Alcantara, the patron of Portugal; the other, a monk in an excruciating state of mortification—more pallid and ghastly than death itself.

At length we came to a place devoted to science, antiquities, mineralogy, etc. Part of the room is occupied with objects of Natural History, among which humming-birds are conspicuous, the cases containing a male and female specimen of every known variety.

Another department is exceedingly interesting in medals and coins: money current in the days of Socrates, Plato, Themistocles, Aristides, Alexander, Hannibal; coins of Rhodes, Heraclea, Achaia, Ithaca, Rome, Thrace, Laconia, Macedon, Syracuse, Tarentum, etc., serving to call vividly before the mind the great acts and actors of antiquity, through whose hands some of these very pieces may have passed.

Native minerals and metals are largely represented and well classified. In one case was huddled a large number of ancient moringues, chiefly Peruvian. Most of them were ornamented in colors or relief. See specimens in the annexed group.

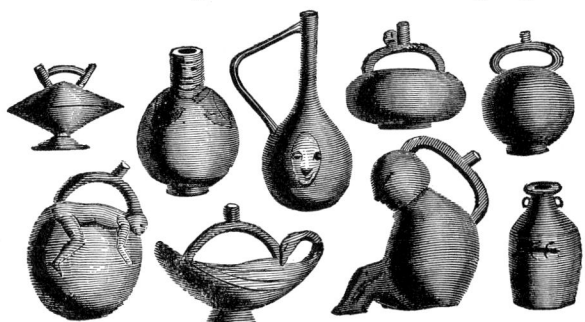

ANCIENT PERUVIAN POTTERY.

The first figure at the left, on the upper row, is a fac-simile of one recently disinterred and presented to the Hon. H. A. Wise. In the two spouts, one through which to fill it and the other to drink from, it resembles the "Pitcher of Brazil," which has been dug up, in one shape or another, in most parts of South America. Similarly-formed vases have also been found in the catacombs of Rome. The next vase, if placed in a collection of Egyptian relics, would be received as a genuine canopus, so striking is its resemblance to some Pharaonic vessels. The third is a long-necked bottle, moulded at opposite sides into protruding fish-heads. The fourth is in the form of a spheroid, with the neck united to it by two curved tubes; a feature common in old water-flasks of Meridional America. The fifth is another, elaborately decorated with colors. Of the second row, the first is very like two antique Bolivian bottles engraved in *L'Homme Americain*, Paris, 1839. Of the two next, one is figured after a bird; the other, after a man in a sitting or bent position. The last is a neat bottle with loops for a cord to suspend it. A lizard has been painted on it between two bands —(omitted by the engraver).

On a window-sill were antiques from Herculaneum and Pompeii, sent over with the empress as a present from her brother, Bomba of Naples. All are covered with a hard green crust, of which a little is scaled off on one vase, showing the metal underneath as smooth and polished as a modern tea-urn just finished.

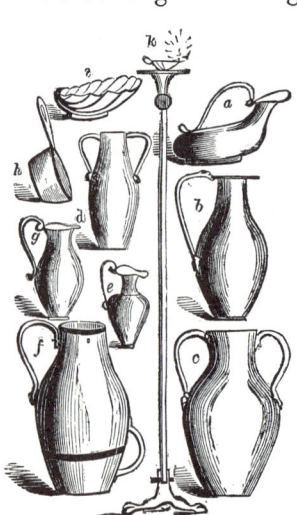

At the first glance of Fig. *k* I took it for the one engraved in the work on Pompeii in the Library of Entertaining Knowledge; but in design and ornament it is far inferior to that. Of very plain pretensions, it probably belonged to the commonest of metallic lampstands. About five feet high, the shaft might be taken for an old inch copper bolt. Its lower end is secured into a socket in the tripod by an iron wedge-key. Part of the socket next to the wide end of the key is gone, having evidently been burst off by driving in the latter too hard. The whole weighs not less than thirty pounds, being solid throughout, but not of solid *bronze;* for, on turning up the feet, I found solder (lead and tin) had been run into the centre of each. Whether this had relation only to the better security of the shaft to the tripod, and whether the former, like the latter, was cast hollow, I had no means to determine.

The small lamp has nothing to distinguish it either in shape, size, or ornament. Of very thin metal, I judged it to have been struck up by dies, and the top soldered on.

The largest of the vases, c, is of the capacity of about four gallons, as near as we could judge; b, two gallons; d, one; e, three pints; and g, a quart. These are all fine specimens of ancient coppersmiths' work. The handles generally are ornamented. The one belonging to Fig. g is broken off, showing an imperfection in the soldering. There are two vases similar to d. On taking up Fig. a I was confident of having before seen its portrait, but I was mistaken. The one resembling it in its general outline, in the second volume on Pompeii, is elaborately enriched with ornament, whereas this is wholly destitute in that respect. It will hold about a gallon. There is another, identical in shape with it, in the Collection of Antiquities by Count Caylus, of a capacity less than a pint. The shape seems to have been common. The skillet, h, has been cast complete in one piece. It resembles, in that respect, our light hollow-ware, but excels it in the distribution of its metal. While the handle is just stout enough, the sides, which are little subject to wear by fire or friction, are quite thin, and the bottom, which has every thing to endure, is remarkably thick. But, not to consume material unnecessarily, a series of grooves, close to each other, have been cut out by a lathe on the underside. They are nearly one eighth of an inch deep, of the same width, about an equal distance apart, and extend from the centre to near the circumference. Were our copper kettles and stewpans made thus, they would last almost forever.

The same feature is observable in the bottoms of the other vessels; hence it was not confined to those for heating liquids. The grooves are cut square down, leaving the edges and angles sharp, as if the tool had just been withdrawn. The rings left between the grooves are in some instances worked into ovolos and astragals.

Besides the skillet figured, there is a smaller one, made as our copper saucepans are, and, like one of them worn out—its bottom is half separated from the sides.

The shell-formed scoop or mould, Fig. *i*, is of very thin metal, and of uniform thickness. It has been struck up—just as such things are with us, out of sheet brass and tin plate.

Our attendant, who is a Portuguese, observed that Figs. *b*, *c*, and *d* were understood to be Roman *measures*, adding that they were very like those used in Portugal. On returning to the city, I had an opportunity of verifying this in the examination of an official "*almude*," the standard measure for liquids, imported from Lisbon for the government. It is represented at *f*. Its capacity is four and a quarter gallons. "Twenty-six almudes make a pipe." By the almude the Portuguese sell all their wines. Identical in shape, it has a feature not found in those ancient vessels—a small hole in the side, near the brim, to mark the full measure—a device which has this advantage: as wine *froths* much in decanting, the surface of the liquid beneath is at once ascertained when risen to its proper elevation. The disposition of the handles in so large a vessel is a farther improvement.

The Laboratory is a room set apart for experiments in natural philosophy and chemistry. An air-pump, electro-magnet, electrical and other apparatus, were standing about. Here, much to his honor, the young emperor is said to spend considerable time. He is fond of books, and all admit his private character to be irreproachable. An adjoining room is fitted up as a theatre: the subject of the drop-scene, "The landing of the Portuguese." To the astonished natives on the foreground, a priest holds out a cross, while frowning warriors, with spears and battle-axes, stand by him—a vivid representation of the system of the conquerors, and of that twofold power which has all but depopulated this half of the earth, and under the influence of which man is a blighted being in the other half.

My associates were fatigued and anxious to leave. Past dinner-time, they quoted the popular hungry apophthegm, "An empty sack can not stand." After making a proper acknowledgment to our obliging cicerone, we descended a flight of some sixty stone steps to a level with the garden, through which we passed. Citron, cinnamon, and tamarind trees presented nothing remarkable in their appearance, but some short, thick boles, with crowns of pendent feathers, were interesting; they were sago-trees. Up the face of a low wall, over and down its other side, lizards, from three to eight inches long, darted quick almost as the lightning's flash.

We passed an oblong pond or lake—a small but handsome sheet of water. Vases and statues alternate along its sides. Near one end is a square cistern in the ground—the prison of an electric eel. On reaching the opposite end of the lake, two negro women were knee deep in it washing, and within five feet of them two black men, perfectly nude, engaged in the same operation.

CHAPTER XIII.

Poor Anthony robbed.—Ex Votos.—Their Manufacture.—Humming-bird and Bouquet.—Affronted Image and wicked Painter.—His Punishment, and Process of "disaffronting" the Image.—Imperial Chapel and its Shrines.—Turk's Head.—Barefooted Friars.—Estaçio de Sá.—Slab over him.—Chief of the Capuchins.—Virgin's Shoe-sole.—Architectural Remains.—Ajuda Convent.—Dumb Waiter.—Glimpse into the Interior.—Vestals.—Nuns in the Ajuda, and their Treatment.

March 10. Walked to town early with a special object. In passing through Rua dos Invalidos, I hoped to get a view of the interior of the little old church of Antonio dos Pobres, as it is opened in mornings during Lent, but I was too late. Except his effigies on his alms-box, I have not yet seen this patron of mendicants. The founder of the church sold all he had to build it, including his own children by his slaves. He was nicknamed *Panela*, from having been a dealer in crockery. Two years ago the church was robbed of its plate and some gems on the image. The witty thief added sarcasm to sacrilege. He took from the head of Anthony a "splendore," and put in its place an old straw hat, with a label attached, signifying that those who beg should not wear jewels. Next morning the sacristan was electrified on beholding the metamorphosis of the saint, and wondered still more on finding him perusing a slip of paper in his hands, on which was written

Quem hé Pobre não tem vicios:

a proverbial sentence, implying that the indigent have not the means to commit current follies, and that their exemplar should not sport silver and gold. The moral burglar was not discovered.

Passed on to and entered the Paula Church, now undergoing extensive renovations. Surely nothing can disturb Rio worshipers: here are individuals, male and female, on their knees, praying alongside of busy masons, carpenters, painters, glaziers, and upholsterers, amid planks, ladders, mortar, paints, webs of gimp, and I know not what, while spectators like myself lounge about, and master tradesmen, with unsuppressed voices, give their orders.

But none of these things brought me here. I have been repeatedly told that in every church more or less votive offerings for miraculous cures are to be seen, and as often I have replied that I could find none. Last evening I learned that, though formerly suspended about the altars, they are now almost invariably confined to vestries and side passages. Here is an inner door through which lay brothers occasionally pass; let us cross its threshold, and get, if possible, a glimpse of one of the most singular sights in ancient temples. A few steps, and we are in a wide and high passage. The walls are white-washed, and broken into compartments by pilasters, and suspended between these are the very things we are in search of. They are not exactly what I expected, but who that has read of classical Ex Votos would not be pleased to look on modern copies?

Some ten feet from the floor long strips of wood extend, and from them the offerings are suspended by twine and ribbons. Here are forty-nine *votive tablets*, each recording the name of the devotee who dedicated it, the complaint which had prostrated him, and the saint who had restored him to health. They are little painted boards, averaging eight inches in length and five in width, cut into every fanciful form. Many have gilt borders, and on most the inscriptions are in gold letters; some are half of one color and half of another. Taken altogether, the diversity of tints reminds one of calico manufacturers' pattern cards. A few appear of recent date, but the greater part are old. On some a face is drawn, to indicate the location of the disease. Sixteen have bed-chambers portrayed, and the sick languishing on couches. In several of them St. Francis appears in a cloud in a corner of the room, telling his suffering friends what to do. In others, beatified monks and nuns peep through holes in the ceilings and dictate prescriptions, the writing beneath declaring that their heavenly physicians appeared thus visibly, and *viva voce* delivered their advice. To transcribe the inscriptions would be to copy the language on similar tablets in the temples of Egypt, Syria, Greece, and old Rome. Each one begins with *"Milagre"* or *"Milagroso."* Some record deliverances from shipwreck.

Pious pagans did not confine themselves to written acknowledgments of the interposition of medical divinities, but hung up in their temples figures in bronze, wood, etc., of the diseased members. So it is here. *Heads, hands, arms, feet, legs,* etc., of natural dimensions, but moulded in *wax*, mingle with the tablets. Here are five hands, three feet, two legs, four arms, as many heads, a female's breasts, a pair of eyes, jaws, and parts which I can't make out. On two of the hands are wens, an excrescence on the breast, and some of the feet are distorted. None of these are colored. A couple have recently been put up, the wax being clean, and the light blue ribbon by which they are suspended quite fresh. The rest are brown with age and dust.

EX VOTOS IN THE PAULA CHURCH.

After I had contemplated them a little, a gentleman came out of the vestry, and walked to and fro, watching my movements. I thought he was displeased, but perhaps he was not. The objects were too interesting to be abandoned.

Offering to gods metallic and other representations of evils from which the parties were freed is of extreme antiquity. The earliest example on record is a remarkable one. 1 Sam., vi., 4. Tavernier observes of India, "When a pilgrim goes to a pagod for the cure of disease, he takes with him a figure of the member affected, made of gold, silver, or copper, and offers it to his god." See also Montfaucon, tome ii., for ex votos in temples—some to Neptune for safe voyages, to Serapis for health, Juno Lucina for children and happy deliveries, pictures of sick patients in bed, and eyes, heads, legs, limbs, and tablets without number to Esculapius and other popular medical saints among the heathen.

On leaving, a friend went with me to a wax-chandler's store, where I found, in addition to members just named, abdomens, breasts single and in pairs, thighs, hearts, cheeks, toes, knee-joints, and faces, all of full size, but hollow and extremely light. Here were babies, also, from ten to fourteen inches high. The proprietor told us there were twenty-one chandlers in Rio, but only seven that fabricated these things, and that the demand for them in the interior is considerable. They are formed in plaster moulds, and constitute a regular branch of business. Pointing to specimens on the counter, I inquired the price. "That," said he, "depends on circumstances: we have no fixed charge." He was assorting large candles, such as are used at funerals and in churches. They are sold at 54 cents per pound. Smaller, for family use, 60 cents.

11*th*. T——'s birth-day, and celebrated in Brazilian fashion. In the morning complimentary notes and presents poured in. One bouquet contained a thousand floral beauties. Another came from Miss L——, of the Larangeiras, and to it was attached by a thread what the Indians call a sunbeam!—a guanunbi—in other words, a golden-breasted humming-bird. The little flutterer soon after escaped and darted back to its native groves.

12*th*. A red curtain in the doorway of the church of the Military Order in Dereita Street intimated that the place was open. The front of this structure is low, and of rather elaborate design. There is some good carving on the heavy door, and two statues occupy niches above it. The narrow sidewalk in front was crowded with colored women and their baskets of fruit; and near them were the most horribly decrepit beggars I ever saw; some pushing out arms, and others legs, from which the fingers and toes had dropped away by disease.

As persons kept going in and out, I pushed aside the screen

and entered. Besides the main one, here are only two side shrines. The image over one of these is the Virgin, in what character I could not make out, nor who the presiding genius of the other was. No priest was visible. From fifteen to twenty men, women, and boys were within, and most of them in front of the left-hand altar, the panel of which was removed, and exposed an image of a dead Christ, the head, hands, and feet marked with gore. Worshipers were kissing it. While one crept up, another knelt behind him to be ready, and in this way ladies and gentlemen, negroes and negras, succeeded each other. Every one contributed something to swell a pile of coppers and milreis bills on an immense salver. It is said that ladies will not kiss an image after a negro; I saw three do it here.

This image has acquired great notoriety. Almost every one goes to see it. At one time it was called the "Insulted" or "Affronted;" it is now known as the "Disaffronted Image."

Some time ago the interior of the church was undergoing repairs and a refitting. The images were removed to the vestry to be painted. Several workmen were employed on them, and one, a Portuguese from the Azores, subject to epilepsy. Among topics of conversation, the daily one of lotteries came up. Every person gambles in them, and this man was asked by his companions if he had bought a ticket in one then about to be drawn. He said he had not; it was of no use; he had purchased many, and got nothing but blanks. "If it had not been for this (using an opprobrious term, and pointing to an image he was painting), who had a spite against him, he would have drawn a prize in the last." In the course of the day, though some say it was not till a subsequent one, he had a fit; the priests heard of his blasphemy; it became noised abroad with additions; the city was in uproar, and crowds of devotees rushed from all directions to punish the blasphemer. Fortunately for him, some prudent persons got him on board of a small vessel in the Bay, or he would have been torn in pieces. It was said he had not only reviled one sacred image, but had stuck his cigar in the mouth of another.

The bishop and clergy took up the affair, and formally excommunicated the offender. He was arrested, and, to escape punishment, readily consented to make every concession. Preparations were made, and a day appointed for his penance. This took place, and the public mind, awakened to the subject, was not allowed to forget it. Sermons were preached; pamphlets, with portraits of the image and its reviler, circulated; and the wonderful manifestation of the wrath of Heaven against the despisers of holy images set forth. The feelings of the superstitiously devout were excited. They flocked to do homage to the abused image; contributions poured in; and a colonel in the army, named Castro, took the insult so much to heart, that he presented to the brotherhood two government bonds of a thousand milreis each toward founding a perpetual mass, to be celebrated every Friday before and in honor of the injured image.

The contributions on the dish this morning evince that the excitement is not over, nor are efforts wanting to keep it up. Like other associations, the brotherhood and board of managers know the value of newspaper notices. A few days ago the following appeared in the *Jornal do Commercio:*

"Depois do dia 29 de julho do anno passado, em que o infeliz Augusto Frederico Corrêa, apoderado do espirito vertiginoso de impiedade, blasfemou e ridicularisou a sagrada imagem de Nosso Senhor Jesus Christo, da igreja da Cruz, foi pela imperial irmandade dos militares e louvaveis membros da mesa, com mais fervor animada a adoração da mesma Imagem, estabelecendo a missa do desaggravo em todas as sextas feiras. A mesa actual, não menos zelosa e religiosa, nada tem esquecido para com todo o asseio, respeito e solemnidade continuar com esse Santo Sacrificio da Missa, que attrahe cada vez maior numero de devotos.

" Este proceder da mesa e da imperial irmandade não póde ser indifferente a um catholico que reconhece os importantes serviços daquella irmandade, fazendo respeitar a Religião, e transmittir aos nossos vindouros pela missa semanal a historia do desacato feito á Sagrada Imagem.

" Estas poucas linhas sejão aceitas pela irmandade, como tributo de gratidão e respeito que lhe consagra.   UM DEVOTO."

" On the 29th of July of last year, the unhappy Augustus Frederick Correa, instigated by a demon of impiety, ridiculed and blasphemed the sacred image of our Lord Jesus Christ of the

Church of the Cross, upon which the Imperial Brotherhood of the Military and the worthy members of the board established a mass, to be celebrated every Friday, for the purpose of disaffronting the image, and to animate the pious to adore it with increased fervor. The present board, not less zealous than their predecessors, have neglected nothing calculated to add to the respect and solemnity of the holy sacrifice of the mass, and to attract a large number of devotees.

"These proceedings of the Board of the Imperial Brotherhood can not be indifferent to Catholics familiar with the important service of the brotherhood in inducing respect for religion, and transmitting to our descendants by this weekly mass the history of the insult offered to the sacred image.

"These few lines will be accepted by the brotherhood as a tribute of gratitude and respect which have consecrated to them
"A Devotee."

A rich contributor has, with a view still farther to "redress the wrong" inflicted by the painter, had a handsome lithograph executed of the altar and "the Disaffronted Lord" prostrate within it. I am indebted to the politeness of the artists for a copy.

Desirous of seeing an official account of the affair, the *Jornal* of August 13, 1845, was put into my hands, and from it the following extract is taken:

"On the evening of the 29th ultimo, a painter, named Augustus Frederick de Almeida, aged 23, and born in the Azores, was employed in the Church of the Holy Cross of the Military. While at work with other artists in the consistory, he, possessed by the devil, blasphemed an image of the Lord Jesus Christ, nor desisted when reprimanded by his companions. As soon as he left the consistory to work at the altar of our Lady of Pains in the Church, a horrible shriek was heard, and he was seen falling to the ground. He struggled violently, and lost the use of his speech, which he did not recover for three days.

"Yesterday, at 10 A.M., his excellency the bishop, Count of Iraja, etc., accompanied by the clergy of the parish, went to disabuse the holy image of the insult offered it at the very place where the crime was committed. The clergy of the Candelaria, with the Imperial Brotherhood of the Military, were also in attendance, and in their presence the image was uncovered and exposed to public veneration.

"The Canon Moreria, master of ceremonies to the throne, read a pastoral letter of the count bishop, in which were narrated all the particulars relating to the insult, and wherein his excellency speaks largely of the worship (*culto*) of images, and elucidates the practice from ancient custom. The unhappy delinquent, with a most contrite countenance, then made a public confession of his guilt, and was absolved by his excellency from the penalties he had incurred. He made his profession of faith, and recited the Apostles' Creed, and after it an article upon the worship of images, according to the Piana faith. The Liturgy of the Saints was chanted by the clergy, and the whole concluded with the oration Pro Excelsia.

"Then followed the adoration of the sacred image, every person present prostrating himself before it and kissing it. The concourse of people was very great. The church and consistory could not contain the faithful who crowded to the ceremony. During the day great numbers rushed to 'adore the image of the Lord.'"

As the door of the Imperial Chapel on the opposite side of the street was open, I crossed over and entered. I had been in before. Externally, the old structure is inferior to its next-door neighbor, the Carmo Church, being built of rough stone like common stores, and plastered; but within, it is rich in carvings, and showy as paint and gold-leaf can make it. The official fane of the court, a wooden statue of St. Sebastian, protector of the empire, stands conspicuously over the high altar. His naked body is covered with bleeding wounds left by the arrows. Below, and alternating with the altar candlesticks, are small figures (30 inches) of the apostles, most of whom have halos—silver wires springing from and returning in circles to their heads. A *coat of arms* is wrought on the pedestal of each.

On the floor stand the usual chancel candlesticks. They have plain cylindrical shafts, and square bases, being the plainest-looking things of the kind in Rio, and the only *silver* ones. I had been told they were of solid metal, but I had ocular proof that they are of the same material as the equally large and more tastefully-designed golden ones of other churches—solid wood.

Belonging to the state chapel, and the only specimens coated with silver leaf, they have acquired the reputation of being all *prata.*

Six subsidiary altars, furnished with appropriate appendages, are in the body of the building. Each has its presiding genius: The Baptist, San José, St. John Nepomuceno, St. Anne, and our Lady of the Head, every one of whom holds a festival here once a year, and receives petitions every day. As it would be a slight to the Portuguese hero, the " Padroeiro de todo O Imperio do Brazil," to refuse him a shrine in the national temple, accommodations have been made for San Pedro d'Alcantara in a large recess within the chancel, where, on the 19th of October, he holds his annual levee.

Across the entrance end of the church is a small music gallery, where is also an old organ, and connected to it is a Turk's head projecting from the front of the gallery. By some mechanism, when the music plays the eyes of the whiskered and mustached infidel roll in ecstasy.

13*th.* Called on H——, who asked if I had seen the barefooted friars. I had not. " Come along, then ;" and off we started for Castle Hill. There are two ridges on this eminence, both occupied at an early period by the Church. On one is the old Jesuits' Chapel and some splendid remains of the cathedral begun by them. On the other is the homely little fane of St. Sebastian. Long neglected, it has, through the influence of the empress, been recently granted to a troupe of Capuchins, her countrymen, whom we are on the way to visit.

Gasping and panting, we climb the zigzag path, and, when two thirds up, to cut off a long sweep, dash up a precipitous bank and land upon the green summit. Close by the little whitewashed temple a large and massive structure is going up, part of the erections contemplated for this central establishment of Capuchin missions in Brazil, for such it is avowed to be. " Who finds the money ?" I inquired. " The government has granted the friars a lottery by which to raise it."*

An ancient marble post stands three feet out of the ground near one corner of the church. Its date, if it had any, has be-

---

* For this fact, see Report of the Minister of Justice to the Legislature, May, 1846, p. 31, 32.

come obliterated. On one of its four sides a cross of Malta, and on another the arms of Portugal are about to disappear. We stepped within, and found three friars reading to themselves within the altar rails. Outside, eight elderly men and women were seated on benches—the first seats I have seen on the floor of a church here. In this little space were no less than five shrines, each with its presiding divinity—Sebastian, Veronica, another female whose name I did not learn, but at her feet and side was quite an assortment of heads, necks, hands, feet, eyes, jaws, breasts, and kindred specimens of wax chandlery. At one shrine are thirty-inch figures of the Virgin and child: King David is taking off his crown to the latter; and the three Magi, one of whom is a negro, are making their offerings and salaams. Here hang a cereous arm, and a hand without fingers. The other shrines are little more than old-fashioned tables placed beneath ancient dolls.

A couple of "confessionals" stand by the box pulpit. They resemble large invalid chairs, with broad sides carried up as high as the high backs. Into each side is let a sheet of tin, painted yellow and perforated with small holes, through which a penitent breathes her shortcomings and the friar whispers penance. In this class of chairs a priest occasionally shrives two at once by inclining the right ear to one strainer and the left to the other.

Lithographic saints hang on the walls along with old portraits in oil of St. Bernard and other Capuchin worthies. Alms-boxes solicit contributions. On the back of one is a miniature of "Nossa Senhora da Paz."

We fortunately met here Senhor Barboza, a gentleman connected with the State Department, and, as far as I could learn, the only antiquary in Rio. On the church floor are ancient monumental slabs. One with shield, helmet, and crossed arms lies within the chancel, and is of historical value. With some difficulty we made out the inscription: "Aqui jaz Estaçio de Sá 1º Cass^m. i Conquistador d'isla, terra i Cidade. Ea campa mandou fazer Salvador Corr^a de Sá seu primo i 2º Cass. Govor^r. . . . . Capella achabou un . . . . . 1583." A few words in my MS. are illegible, but they are unimportant. The sense is complete. "Here lies Estaçio de Sá, first captain-general and conqueror of the isle of Villegagnon, land and city. This tomb was erected by Salvador Correa de Sá, his cousin, and second captain-governor. This chapel was finished in 1583."

As the occupant of the tomb died sixteen years before the church was built, a note may here be added, taken substantially from a popular abridgment of the history of the country, recently published in Rio:

"Estaçio de Sá, nephew of Mendo de Sá, governor-general of Brazil, was sent out by the Queen-regent of Portugal in 1564, with orders to his uncle to assist him with forces to expel the French at Rio. In the following year Estaçio came down from Bahia with the required assistance, landed near the Sugar-loaf, and was defeated. He sent for farther aid to his uncle, who placed a squadron under the command of Christopher de Barros, joined it himself, and arrived at Estaçio's camp on the 18th of January, 1567. They put off the attack till the 20th, St. Sebastian's day, and then attacked the French, slew the whole of their Indian allies, the Tamoyoes, took the fort Uracumini, and afterward Fort Coligny and island of Villegagnon. In the attack Estaçio received an arrow in his face, which caused his death a month after. His cousin, Salvador Correa de Sá, second in command, and named by the queen his successor in case of his demise, then drew up a plan and laid out a city on the edge of the Bay, naming it after the saint on whose anniversary they had recovered the place. The French thus expelled went to Pernambuco, but not succeeding in making a landing, returned to Europe.

"Estaçio was buried on the beach, and his remains were subsequently removed by his cousin to their present resting-place."

While stooping and turning about to decipher and copy the inscription, I forgot Sebastian and Veronica. Senhor B—— requested H—— to remind me of the impropriety of turning my back on them, and to beg that I would keep at least one cheek toward them while tracing the letters.

Every body seemed to go into the vestry, and we followed. The great attraction was the chief of the Capuchins. He was engaged at a chest of drawers, selecting fresh linen for the shrines and images, opening first one drawer and then another,

L

till he got a piece to suit. He then shook it out before him, took it to a shrine, and came back for another, making a leg to the altar as he passed in and out. A score or more of both sexes came in, and almost every one went up and snatched his hand and kissed it, or, rather, his wrist-joint, for that is the part saluted, the owner facilitating the operation by bending the hand inward.

Between thirty-five and forty, there were few of the elements of comeliness in him to make ladies dote upon his person: a wedge and freckled face, small, keen, and restless gray eyes, a thick and reddish beard that spread like furze up to his ears. He wears no body-linen, but is clothed in a russet gown tied round his middle. At his left side swings two feet of knotted cord, and at the right a string of rough beads. His gown has no collar, leaving his tanned neck exposed, while the opening in front shows his hairy breast. The cowl hangs down his back, its peak reaching to the cord round his waist. No stockings, of course, but his feet are pushed into tamancos—wooden-soled slippers—in which he shuffles about, showing his bare heels wherever he moves. As he is dressed, so are his associates.

Among the treasures on the vestry walls brought over by the Capuchins was one that, from its insignificant appearance, arrested my attention, as well as from the fact that almost every person who came in went up and kissed it. A little black picture-frame, with a piece of glass in front, was the rough casket of the precious relic, namely, "An exact outline of the Virgin's shoe-sole," which fell from heaven near Padua in 1543. The particulars, in fine writing, are given within the contour. Clement VII. or VIII., and another pope, are quoted as verifying the particulars.

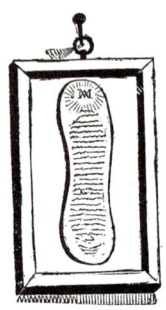

The shape is not over handsome—see the cut—if it had reference to that of the wearer's foot. The length is 7½ inches, and breadth from 2½ to 3. Many Brazilian ladies have smaller shoes. One of the men who kissed it told us the fathers have recently received from Rome some very holy and miraculous images, which will soon be exposed to the pious.

On the other spur of Castle Hill is the old

Jesuits' chapel. The date of its erection is over the door—
"1567." Though quite small, it has four altars. Loyola, in
full stature, occupies the chief one; Francis Borgia and Xavier
stand by him. Every thing looks worn and faded. Capitals,
friezes, cornices, pilasters, etc., of cut stone, lie about the place
—unused portions of materials for structures begun before the
expulsion of the order in 1753. The entire grounds and property are now in the possession of the government, appropriated
to an observatory, telegraph, and other public institutions.

AJUDA NUNNERY.

On reaching the foot of the hill, we observed, on the opposite
side of the street, one of the heavy doors of the Ajuda Convent
open, and stepped into a paved area around which the dark
walls arise. Of the two tiers of windows, the lowest is fifteen
feet from the ground, and all inclosed with massive gratings that
remind one of the condemned cells of Newgate. At the side
farthest from the street is the apparatus by which persons without communicate with the interior. I had read of the ancient
device. A rectangular opening, about four feet high and two
and a half wide, is cut through the thick wall, the upright edges
being worked concave. A strong wooden cylinder or drum is
made to revolve vertically in the opening, and to occupy it wholly. Suppose the staves of the cylinder be removed for one
third of its circumference, you have then a revolving cupboard,
into which any article put in at one side of the wall is instantly received at the other on simply pushing round the opening,
and without either sender or receiver having a chance to get a
glimpse of each other. The sides of the drum enter the concave sides of the wall, and its bottom and top extend within
the stone-work. The width of the opening into the drum is
only half the thickness of the wall, so that in no position of
the drum can a spectator see any one within.

While we stood by, a negro brought a parcel, put it in the
closet, clapped his hands as a signal, and turned the dumb waiter half way round. Thus money, letters, food, and all articles
required are passed within. If sweetmeats have been ordered
by friends or visitors, the price is put on the shelf, and the next
moment the bon-bons come out.

We strolled to the farther extremity of the same side of the square, where there was a similar machine, and near it a strong door with a small brass plate, full of minute holes, through which the invisible abbess, or her deputies, can see who stands without. Casually touching this door, it yielded to slight pressure. Here was a temptation to step into a nunnery, for none but our two selves were within the spacious area. To have some color for pushing the hinged valve back, one of us gently knocked. No one answered, but some object behind moderately opposed its being opened. By little and little the opening was enlarged, and our courage with it. We squeezed in, when my companion, in a whisper, said, "This is the office of the portress. She has left for a moment, and, not dreaming of intruders, placed her old high-backed chair against the door. She'll return anon, and give the alarm if she find us here."

But the way into the interior was not so clear as we imagined; still, we got a view of the machinery adopted in such places to prevent intrusion and desertion. The small apartment opened into a large, long, and, verily, a strong one. A paved floor, high whitewashed walls, with nothing to break their monotony or let in light, that we could see, save a single opening, eight feet square, and level with the ground. This communicated with a wide and dim passage into which we could not get; for there was no entering the large opening in front of which we stood. The stone wall through which it is cut is four feet thick, and on *each side* hangs a gauze curtain whose threads are inch bars of iron: those forming the woof pass through loops in the warp, and the ends of all are buried in the granite blocks. The interstitial spaces are between three and four inches. A rather larger aperture is at the bottom, and through it small things are passed across on the blade of a wooden shovel, as appeared from one lying ready for the purpose.

If, as is said, nuns are happy in their cells, for what purpose then, in lands were law prevails, are these massive walls, gratings, bolts, locks, and other devices? Even shackles, it is admitted, are not wanting in this place. No felon-prison can have a better system of securities. What alliance can there be between the gentle, willing spirit of the Gospel and so much iron? Penal statutes suffice to prevent people from breaking in; what need of such devices, if not designed to keep those confined from breaking out? These thoughts I addressed to my companion, who said I might stay till the door-keeper returned, and ask her! In two minutes more we were in the street. Through what passage she had disappeared, after blocking her door, we could not imagine.

This was the first and last time I got into a nunnery. Into the chapel fronting the street I often stepped.

There is no entering ecclesiastical institutions here without being reminded of their heathen originals, and of the little change they have undergone. Every popular phase of ancient worship was early adopted. Rituals of the temples, and the temples themselves; the different orders of priests, and their imposing costumes; the entire system of symbolism; of praying through the medium of images and other physical representations; praying for the dead, and to the dead. The various religious orders, too, including mendicant and monastic, are of pagan parentage, with all their peculiarities of dress and discipline—their shaven crowns, knotted cords, relics, rosaries, and squalor.

The institution of Vestals was reverenced at Rome. Numa, the consuls, and the emperors patronized them; the rich made presents, the pious bequeathed legacies, and the superstitious sought admission for their daughters. Commanding general respect, they were introduced, under Christian appellations, into the Church. Substituting the Virgin for Vesta, the old rules, penalties, peculiarities, etc., seem to have been received without material revision, and also the plans, arrangements, securities, general economy, and management of the nunneries.

The cloistered virgins of the Ajuda pass their lives in much the same way as their sisters of antiquity: separated from the world, from parental and family influence, dedicated to a goddess "Nossa Senhora da Ajuda," donning a particular habit, their initiation accompanied by cutting off their hair, vowing chastity, and subject to death for its violation, strictly secluded, extraordinary means employed to prevent their communicating without the walls that inclose them, under the surveillance of a matron and a system of espionage that sifts out their very thoughts, subject to the control and punishment of the bishop, no male persons allowed to visit them except those interested in retaining them, and permitted to hold free converse with none else.

The Pontifex Maximus chastised pagan nuns for offenses, and his modern representative does the same thing. If Christian nuns are not now put to death for violating their vows, they once were, and, but for the increasing intelligence of the age, would undoubtedly be again.

The inmates of nunneries, it is asserted, "are happy"—"even those who enter reluctantly become reconciled and content." Here are a few Rio facts in illustration:

1. H—— told me he was acquainted with four sisters, all of whom were forced by one or both parents into the Tereza Convent. Years elapsed, and the father died, when three, all that were alive, by appealing to the Pope, eventually got out.

2. A merchant, whom he also knew well, took an only daughter out one day a visiting. The carriage stopped at the Ajuda Convent. The young lady tripped up the three or four outer steps without observing the place, the doors closed on her, and her parent drove off. She had refused a husband selected for her, and was immured two years before she yielded her consent and was let out.

3. A poor woman, with a slight peculiarity of manner, is occasionally seen in the Cattete. She passed the window twice yesterday. "Sister Paula" and her melancholy history are known to many families in the Gloria parish.

Of respectable lineage, she was born and brought up in the country. Amiable and intelligent, she unfortunately became rich in her own right on the death of her mother. Her father and brothers coveted her wealth, and found means to gain over the abbess of the Ajuda. A chest, perforated to admit air, was provided by the unnatural villains, and in it the poor victim was hurried from her residence (some leagues distant from Rio) to the convent. She resisted all attempts made to force her to take the veil, and in a long course of years managed to escape three times, but implored in vain, with a heart bursting with anguish, for mercy from her kindred. The last time it was her brothers who drove her back, the father being dead. Nature at length gave way. The punishments to which on these occasions she was subjected—chastisement, want of food, shackles, and other tortures, known only to the fiends that inflicted them, broke her down. Reason fled, and she became irrevocably insane. Her persecutors took undisturbed possession of her property; and some, it is said, still enjoy it—if, indeed, they *can* enjoy it or any thing else. Of her they know nothing. A nun has neither worldly relations nor wealth. Every thing, even her name, is taken from her, and all natural ties are forever sundered.

The abbess permitted her—imprudently, as many think—to go at large. She is over fifty. Her disease is of a mild type. For several years she has made out, by charity and her needle, to hire a room and buy the little food she wants. She constructs wax and feather flowers, makes "baby saints," and assists in dressing images for the festivals. Dwelling near the Lapa Church, she is employed every Christmas to fit up in it "the Cradle and the Baby God." All churches have, at that season, an exhibition of this kind. Most have new bedclothes and dresses, but some have the old ones furbished up and used again. Sister Paula sometimes quarrels with the brotherhood, and loses an order " to dress Our Lady and her Son." At lucid intervals she will speak with a few confidential friends of the inhuman treatment of her brothers and the abbess. At other times she says an evil spirit possesses her—" one too strong for the friars of St. Anthony to drive out." Poor lady! she is right. Hers is a wounded spirit, which requires a higher power than that of any dead or living saint to heal.

4. Senhor L———a, of the Larangeiras, ex-councilor of state, has an aged relative in the Ajuda Convent, a first cousin to his mother. She has at present charge of the garden, which is as much concealed from the public as the interior of the building. Having been abbess, she is known as *Mother* Anne Tereza. This venerable lady was in her youth one of the handsomest girls of Rio. She formed an attachment which her father did not approve of, although her lover was every way worthy of her. By the influence of her parents he was shipped off to India, and she carried directly to an endless imprisonment in the awful Ajuda. Distracted beyond endurance, for months horror and despair preyed on her: she was tempted to end her miseries by suicide. A year passed over—another, and others, till her soul,

crushed by griefs, yielded to her fate. Urged to take the veil, she consented; but, ere the ceremonies were quite over, she awoke as from a lethargy artificially produced, and burst into such a torrent of abuse of her parents and family, who were witnessing the rite, the abbess, convent, and the whole system of ecclesiastical fraud and tyranny, that for a moment all stood aghast. And but for a moment! It was evident she was possessed! Under this belief she was gagged, borne off to her cell, confined by cords, and punished no one living knows how but herself.

Time, that subdues all things, at last tamed her. Forever excluded from the world, and without a friend, relative, or acquaintance in it—to her all was lost—she consented to live and adapt herself to her hard lot. She became a favorite, and was twice elected abbess, which office she has filled for eight years (an election takes place every four years). Let us hope that the victims sent in under her administration were differently treated than she had been.

It must not be supposed that the law could interfere. No civil officer could (nor can) enter a convent to serve process there; and under the old régime, a father had unlimited power over his daughters. The only redress was: 1. Through the bishop; but while the abbess was in collusion with parents, the victim might wear her fingers to the bone in writing petitions before one could reach him. Not a scrap can enter or pass out without her consent. 2. The bishop had to appeal to Lisbon; and, 3. Through the ecclesiastical authorities there, the court at Rome had to be consulted.

In the second volume of "Transactions of the Geographical and Historical Institute of Brazil" is a notice of Don Francisco de San Jeronimo, the founder of this convent. A holy man, he wrought miracles; two are cited: When coming over from Lisbon the ship took fire; he prayed to God and Our Lady, and instantly the flames went out. A favorite servant became diseased in his legs, and, after trying several methods of cure, the doctors proposed amputation. On hearing this, the saint prayed over the sickly members, and they became sound ere he rose from his knees.

CHAPTER XIV.

Candelaria Church.—Jacks of the Clock.—Peccary.—God's Stepfather.—Botanic Garden.—Snake.—Fences.—Dinner and its Cost.—Catalogue of Plants in the Garden.

March 16. Among the first objects which attract the eye on entering Rio Bay is a couple of light and handsome turrets, surmounted with glittering domes resembling inverted pears—pinnacles of "The Candelaria" Church. These turrets command an extended prospect, and to the top of one of them I ascended with some friends to-day. Here we contemplated the dingy red roofs beneath us, and the narrow threads of streets still lower down—the silver Bay, its shipping, verdant isles, and mountain boundaries, particularly the organ peaks at its head, shooting up in the blue ether in fantastic pinnacles, ranging from three to seven or eight thousand feet above the Bay. "The Serra," a term universally applied by Spaniards and Portuguese to mountain ranges, is peculiarly appropriate to these, for they resemble the jagged teeth of a saw, or the serrated vertebræ of a fish, quite as much as the pipes of an organ.

The Candelaria has no clock, and, if I mistake not, of the forty odd churches, that of St. Francis de Paula alone has one. Certainly no other has one that strikes the hours. Dials are in front of some which have no works behind them. Though Rio is thus poor in town horologes, she is rich in a race of artists long extinct in Europe. Before devices for measuring time were made to announce its divisions, men were employed for that purpose; and here "*Jacks of the Clock*," like ancient sacristans, grasp the clapper of church bells and proclaim the hours, sometimes by a corresponding number of strokes, but not always so. The Candelaria officer attends to the duty only three times a day—at 8 A.M., noon, and 6 P.M., and then generally gives a fancy flourish.

While sauntering along the Flamingo Beach, one of the numerous tailless quadrupeds of Brazil came out of a building near by—a peccary. Attempting to feel its speckled hair and hide, instead of avoiding me it settled on its haunches, and exposed a terrible set of fangs. A negro approached—probably one it knew—when it crouched at his feet playful as a kitten. These animals, when tamed, are infinitely more tractable than their domesticated relatives. A man passed up the Cattete a few evenings since leading a couple by a string; they trotted close to him like favorite dogs. In the woods they go in troops, and are dangerous to solitary travelers, whom they have been known to attack. They make nothing of killing dogs; and even the great ounce or tiger, when attempting to make a meal of one, often furnishes the herd with a repast.

19th. Festivals were formerly greatly more numerous than now, though not less than fifty, ecclesiastical and lay, are kept up, to the dissatisfaction of merchants. Add Sundays, and one fourth of the year is lost to commerce. This being the day of San José, the public offices are closed, that all may compliment him at his church in Dereita Street on the anniversary of his birth. His espousal is celebrated in January. "And, pray, who is San José?" I inquired of a devout old lady, the very counterpart of Gil Perez. Lifting her hands, and soliciting the Virgin's protection, she in amazement asked where I had been brought up, and if it were possible I did not know who that great saint is.

"I am not positive that I do, senhora."

"Alas! alas! be advised, then, that San José is God's stepfather!"

It was now my turn to stare. Besides strange expressions used by Romanists of the Old World, and sanctioned by heads of the sect in the United States, how few are consistent as Brazilians in carrying out the idea! With them, "God's grandmother," "husband of God's mother," "God's stepfather," are common as "the baby God," "the body of God," "the burial of God," and other authorized expressions equally exceptionable to Protestant ears.

The Botanic Garden is celebrated for its collection of exotic and indigenous plants. Located six miles from the city, it is an agreeable resort on holidays, and there it was arranged that we should pass the day. J—— hired a "gondola"—not a Venetian skiff, but a Brazilian omnibus—in which nine of us whirled through Boto Fogo, and at length came to a beautiful lake, exceeding two miles in diameter, and connecting with the ocean, on whose borders the garden fronts. We passed handsome cottage residences by the way: near the door of one was a king vulture chained on a post. As we drew near to the Corcovado, I was surprised, though aware of the cause, at the sensible diminution of its magnitude and grandeur.

The garden is situated behind the Corcovado, and between that mountain and the sea. A neat hedge of Brazilian thorn separates it from the road. Many of the trees present novel features to strangers, while among the plants amateur botanists might revel in enjoyment. Gravel-walks, and trellis-work with seats, surround a basin in which a jet d'eau plays. A fine stream, two feet wide, and three or four inches deep, intersects the grounds, rushing over a stone channel, and broken at one place into a miniature cascade. It is difficult to describe the grateful, the exquisite sensations which such a cooling streamlet in such a place produces.

Extensive plots are occupied with tea-plants. Cocoas, mangoes, cinnamon, cloves, figs, cacti, bamboos, palms, &c., spring up every where. An East Indian tree of the size of the peach produces abundance of an agreeably acidulous and cooling fruit resembling small cucumbers, but of a pale straw color, and whose section is star-shaped. Bread-trees abound, and so laden with their rough-skinned orbicular and spheroidal treasures, that on a lad laying hold of one branch, down it came crashing to the ground. The fruit is not unlike a green pineapple, but not so rough, and seldom so long. We met Senhor Brandaõ, the director, who told me he had received letters from the States proposing an exchange of plants. He presented me with a corrected copy of those in his charge. As a document interesting to botanists, it is subjoined. After cruising about, we rested in a house-like arbor, whose walls, roof, door and window frames, are composed of dense vines. Erected on a mound, it is approached by steps cut in the side, and carpeted with grass. Here we were again amused with little lizards darting up and down the trees—an interesting feature in the heavenly scene around us.

While standing with the director near a dense cluster of bamboos, a brilliant band was observed coiled round the boll of a sago-tree. I took it for a riband of scarlet and other variegated colors. It was a coral snake, the most beautiful, and reputed the most venomous of Brazilian serpents. It was disturbed and disabled on the gravel-walk. A negro was sent for a quart bottle of *cachaça*, into which the pretty cobra was put before it had ceased to writhe. [This bottle, on the voyage home, was dashed to pieces in a storm, and its tenant rendered valueless.]

To refresh ourselves and cattle, we now drove a mile to a tavern, a low and mean-looking building, without any indication of being a hostelry. After lunching, some of the party laid down to sleep; the rest of us strolled three or four miles toward the Irmaos Mountains. A species of black parrot hovered about; other birds darted out of the woods; and one low piece of ground was alive with small gray butterflies.

Here was the common Brazilian fence. Sticks, generally straight, and varying from one and a half to two inches in thickness, stand five feet out of the ground, and about the same distance apart. They are the posts. The rails are bamboos, averaging twenty-five feet in length, and one and a half inch at the thick end. Four, sometimes five rows of these, a foot apart, are lashed by a vegetable withe to the posts. Wherever bamboos grow, such is the planter's fence. It is cheap, light, and strong enough to confine cattle, and lasts for five or six years. A better kind occurred. The posts were five inches thick, and cut to a uniform height; the rails two inches thick, and both nailed and lashed. When the thorn fence is designed, an artificial one, to protect the young plants, is not required over two to three years, so rapid is the vegetation. Climbing parasites and vines soon render any such boundaries impenetrable to man, and beast, and even birds.

By 3 P.M. we returned, and found a dinner nearly ready that surprised me as much as any thing else. A slice of bread and cheese, with a handful of mandioca meal, I supposed the extreme limits of the hotel's bill of fare. We had soup; fish, resembling large striped bass, brought ashore alive, and prepared in three different ways; boiled beef; roast beef; fried eggs and greens served together; boiled chickens; roasted do.; do. fricaseed; curry sauce; salads; potatoes; mandioca, dry and made up like mush; rice; sweet puddings; sweetmeats (quince and citron); bananas; oranges; almonds; prunes; wine of two kinds; liqueurs for the ladies, and a dozen other things. Half an hour after, strong coffee was served. This repast for nine persons, another for the driver, the previous lunch for the party, and feed for four mules, cost only ten dollars. At 8 P.M. we rode home, after enjoying a day of unmixed pleasure.

CATALOGO DAS PLANTAS QUE SE CULTIVÃO NO JARDIM BOTANICO DA LAGÔA.

Arvores e Arbustos.

Acacia lophanta, *L.*
Acer saccharinum, *L.*
Achras sapota, *L.*
Acrocomia fusiformis, *Swt.*
Adansonia digitata, *L.*
Adenanthera pavonina, *L.*
Aleurites triloba, *Forst.*
Amygdalus Persica, *L.*
Anacardium Occidentale,*L.*
Anda Gomesii, *Juss.*
Anona muricata, *L.*
Anona palustris, *W.*
Anona squamosa, *L.*
Apeiba Tibourbou, *Aubl.*
Araucaria Brasiliana, *Lamb.*
Areca alba, *Bory.*
Artocarpus incisa, *L.* Var. nucifera.
Artocarpus integrifolia, *L.*
Astrocaryum airi, *Mart.*
Astronii spec.
Attalia funifera, *Mart.*
Averrhoa bilimbi, *L.*
Averrhoa carambola, *L.*
Bactris caryotæfolia, *Mart.*
Bactris setosa, *Mart.*
Bambusa arundinacea, *W.*
Bignonia chrysantha, *Jacq.*
Bixa orellana, *L.*
Bombax pentandrum, *Jacq.*
Cæsalpinea echinata, *Lamb.*
Calamus Rotang, *W.*
Carica spinosa, *W.*
Carolinea alba, *Lod.*
Caryophyllus aromaticus, *L.*
Castanea vesca, *Gae.*
Casuarina equisetifolia, *L.*
Cecropia palmata, *W.*
Ceratonia siliqua, *L.*
Cerbera thevetia, *L.*
Chrysobalanus icaco, *L.*
Cicca disticha, *L.*
Citrus aurantium, *Risso.*
Citrus decumana, *L.*

Citrus limeta, *Risso.*
Citrus limonum, *Risso.*
Citrus medica, *Risso.*
Citrus nobilis, *Lou.*
Citrus vulgaris, *Risso.*
Coffea Arabica, *L.*
Cookia punctata, *Sonner.*
Copaifera officinalis, *L.*
Corypha cerifera, *Mart.*
Crescentia cujete, *L.*
Croton sebifera, *L.*
Cupressus thyoides, *L.*
Diplothemium maritimum, *Mart.*
Elæis Guineensis, *Jacq.*
Erythrina corallodendrum, *L.*
Erythrina crista-galli, *L.*
Eucalyptus robusta, *Sm.*
Eugenia Brasiliana, *Lamb.*
Eugenia Jambos, *L.*
Eugenia Malaccensis, *L.*
Eugenia Michelii, *Lam.*
Eugeniæ, spec. 3.
Euphoria litchi, *Defs.*
Euphoria longana, *Lam.*
Euterpe oleracea, *Mart.*
Ficus carica, *L.*
Ficus elastica, *Roxb.*
Genipa Americana, *L.*
Gossipium arboreum, *L.*
Guarea trichilioides, *L.*
Guilandina moringa, *L.*
Hymenæa courbaril, *L.*
Ilex Paraguayensis, *Hil.*
Indigofera anil, *L.*
Inga vera, *W.*
Jacarandá Brasiliana, *Person.*
Jatropha elastica, *L.*
Juniperus Virginiana, *L.*
Laurus camphora, *L.*
Laurus cinnamomum, *L.*
Laurus nobilis, *W.*
Laurus Persea, *L.*
Laurus sassafras, *L.*

Lecythis lanceolata, *Poir.*
Liquidambar styraciflua, *L.*
Magnolia fuscata, *Andr.*
Magnolia grandiflora, *L.*
Magnolia pumilla, *Andr.*
Mammea Americana, *L.*
Magnifera Indica, *L.*
Melia azedarach, *L.*
Mespilus japonica, *Thunb.*
Mimosa Lebbek, *L.*
Mimusopsis spec.
Moquilea Guianensis.
Morus alba, *L.*
Morus multicaulis.
Morus nigra, *Poir.*
Myristica bicuhyba, *Schott.*
Myristica officinalis, *L.*
Nyctanthes arbor tristis, *L.*
Œnocarpus regius.
Olea Europæa, *L.*
Ormosia coccinea, *Jack.*
Pandanus utilis, *Bory.*
Phœnix dactylifera, *L.*
Prunus domestica, *L.*
Punica granatum, *L.*
Pyrus communis, *L.*
Psidium cattleianum, *Lindley.*
Psidium pyriferum, *L.*
Robinia pseudacacia, *L.*
Salix Babylonica, *L.*
Sambucus nigra, *L.*
Sapindus edulis.
Sapindus inæqualis, *DC.*
Spondias monbin, *L.*
Spondias tuberosa.
Sterculia acuminata, *Beauv.*
Sterculia fœtida, *L.*
Sterculia helicteres, *Pers.*
Swartzia Langsdorfii, *Raddi.*
Sideroxilon atrovirens.
Tamarindus Indica, *L.*
Tectona grandis, *L.*
Thea viridis, *L.*
Theobroma cacáo, *L.*

Plantas de Ornamento, Economicas e Medicinaes.

Abroma augusta, *L.*
Abrus precatorius, *L.*
Achillea millefolium, *L.*
　Var. alba.
Adiantum capillus Veneris, *L.*
Agapanthus umbellatus, *Herit.*
　Var. albus.
Agave vivipara, *L.*
Aloe vulgaris, *DC.*
Aloysia citriodora, *Ort.*
Alpinia nutans, *Rosc.*
Alstrœmeria ligtu, *L.*
Alstromeria salsilla, *L.*
Amarantus tricolor, *L.*
Amaryllis belladonna, *L.*
Amaryllis formosissima, *L.*
Amaryllis reticulata, *Ait.*
Ammobium alatum, *R. Br.*
Amorpha fruticosa, *L.*
Anchusæ spec.
Anethum fœniculum, *L.*
Apium graveolens, *L.*
Antirrhinum majus, *L.*
Antholyza Æthiopica, *L.*
Arachys hypogæa, *L.*
Argemone albiflora, *Sims.*
Aristolochia macrura, *Gomes.*
Aristolochia symbifera, *Mart.*
Artemisia absynthium, *L.*
Arundo donax, *W.*
Asclepias curassavica, *L.*
Asclepias fruticosa, *L.*
Asparagus officinalis, *L.*
Aster Chinensis, *L.*
Atropa belladonna, *L.*
Aucuba japonica, *L.*
Babiana villosa, *Ker.*
Baccharis genistelloides, *Pers.*
Barbacenia purpurea, *L.*
Basella alba, *L.*
Basella rubra, *L.*
Begonia argyrostigma, *Fis.*
Beta cicla, *L.*
Beta vulgaris, *L.*
Bignonia capensis, *H. K.*
Bignonia spectabilis, *Vahl.*
Bignonia stans, *L.*
Boerhaavia decumbens, *Vahl.*
Borrago officinalis, *L.*
Brionia racemosa.
Bromelia ananas, *L.*
Browallia elata, *L.*
Browallia demissa, *L.*

Buginvillea Brasiliensis.
Buginvillea spectabilis, *Juss.*
Buxus sempervirens, *L.*
Cactus cochinillifer, *L.*
Cactus ficus Indica, *Haw.*
Cactus hexagonus, *L.*
Cactus melocactus, *L.*
Cactus pendulus, *Swz.*
Cactus pentagonus, *Haw.*
Cactus pereskia, *L.*
Cactus tetragonus, *L.*
Cactus truncatus, *Link.*
Cajanus flavus, *DC.*
Caladium bicolor, *Vent.*
Caladium esculentum, *Vent.*
Calathea grandifolia, *Lindl.*
Calathea zebrina, *L.*
Calendula officinalis, *L.*
Calla Æthiopica, *L.*
Caliopsis bicolor *Rchb.*
Camellia japonica, *L.*
　Var. alba.
　" rubra.
　" versicolor.
Camellia oleifera, *Abel.*
Canna gigantea, *Desf.*
Canna glauca, *L.*
Canna Indica, *L.*
Carica papaya, *L.*
Carthamus tinctorius, *L.*
Cassiæ, spec. 6.
Centaureæ spec.
Celosia argentea.
Celosia cristata, *L.*
Centranthus ruber, *DC.*
Cestrum vespertinum, *L.*
Cheiranthus incanus, *L.*
Chenopodium graveolens, *W.*
Chrysanthemum carinatum, *Schous.*
Chrysanthemum grandiflora.
Chrysanthemum sinense, *Sab.*
Cleome heptaphylla, *L.*
Cleome rosea, *Vahl.*
Clerodendrum coccineum, *Hort.*
Clerodendrum fragrans, *Vent.*
Clitoria Plumieri turp.
Clitoria ternatea, *L.*
Cobæa scandens, *Cav.*
Coix lachryma, *L.*
Cichorium intybus, *L.*
Combretum secundum, *Jacq.*

Concuielina tuberosa.
Convolvulus batatas, *L.*
Cordia hircina, *Hil.*
Cosmea bipinnata, *W.*
Costus spiralis, *Roxb.*
Crinum Americanum, *L.*
Crinum longifolium, *Roxb.*
Crinum scabrum, *Herb.*
Croton picta, *Roxb.*
Cucumis anguria, *L.*
Cuscutæ spec.
Cycas revoluta, *Thunb.*
Cyperus esculentus, *L.*
Dahlia frustranea, *H. K.*
　Var. coccinea.
　" aurantia.
　" lutea.
Dalechampia pentaphylla, *Lam.*
Datura arborea, *Hort.*
Datura fastuosa, *L.*
Datura stramonium, *L.*
Daucus carota, *L.*
Delphinium consolida, *L.*
Desmoncus polyacanthus, *Mart.*
Dianthus caryophyllus, *L.*
Dianthus plumarius, *L.*
Dichorisandra thyrsiflora, *Mik.*
Dioscorea alata, *L.*
Dioscorea sativa, *L.*
Dolichos Lablab, *L.*
Dolichos urens, *L.*
Dorstenia Brasiliensis, *Lam.*
Dracæna arborea, *Lk.*
Dracæna ferrea, *L.*
Elephantopus scaber, *L.*
Eranthemum pulchellum, *B. R.*
Eryngium fœtidum, *L.*
Erysimum perowskianum.
Erythrina isopetala, *Lam.*
Eupatorium ayapana, *Vent.*
Fragarea vesca, *L.*
Francisca uniflora, *Pohl.*
Fuchsia coccinea, *L.*
Gardenia florida, *L.*
Gay-Lussacia buxifolia *Humb.*
Gesneriæ, spec. 2.
Gladioli, spec. 3.
Gloxinia speciosa, *Ker.*
Glycine precatoria, *Humb.*
Glycine subterranea, *L.*
Gomphrena globosa, *L.*
　Var. alba.
Gynerium saccharoides *Humb.*

LIFE IN BRAZIL. 175

Hæmanthus puniceus, *Jacq.*
Hedychium coronarium, *Roxb.*
Helianthus annuus, *L.*
Helicrysum bracteatum, *D. Don.*
Heliconiæ, spec. 3.
Heliotropium Peruvianum, *L.*
Hemerocallis flava, *L.*
Hemerocallis fulva, *L.*
Hibiscus esculentus, *L.*
Hibiscus mutabilis, *W.*
  Var. flore pleno.
Hibiscus Rosa sinensis, *W.*
  Var. rubro plena.
  " flavo plena.
  " albo plena.
Hibiscus trionum, *L.*
Hoya carnosa, *R. Br.*
Hydrangea hortensis, *Sm.*
Iberis saxatilis, *L.*
Iberis umbellata, *L.*
Impatiens balsamina, *L.*
Ipomœa quamoclit, *W.*
Ipomœa maritima, *R. Br.*
Ipomœa noctiluca, *Her.*
Jasminum flexille, *L.*
Jasminum grandiflorum, *L.*
Jasminum revolutum, *B. R.*
Jasminum sambac, *L.*
Jatropha curcas, *L.*
Jatropha multifida, *L.*
Jussieua villosa, *Lam.*
Justicia calycotricha, *Link.*
Justicia lucida, *Vahl.*
Justicea carnea, *Lindl.*
Lagerstrœmia Indica, *L.*
Lantana salviæfolia, *L.*
Lausonia alba, *Lam.*
Lavandula spica, *DC.*
Leonotis Leonurus, *R. Br.*
Lepidium sativum, *L.*
Leria nutans, *DC.*
Lilium japonicum, *Thunb.*
Lilium tigrinum, *Ker.*
Limnocharis Commersonii.
Limodorum Tankervilliæ, *Ait.*
Linaria genistæfolia, *Mill.*
Lobelia Surinamensis, *L.*
Lonicera periclymenum, *L.*
Lotus Jacobæus, *W.*
Lupinus albus, *L.*
Lychnis Chalcedonica, *L.*
Madia sativa, *Mol.*
Malva crispa, *L.*
Malva Mauritiana, *L.*
Malva rotundifolia, *L.*
Maranta arundinacea, *L.*
Maranta bicolor, *Ker.*

Marica semi-aperta, *Lod.*
Melealeuca ericæfolia, *Andr.*
Melampodium australe, *Lofl.* •
Melastoma velutina, *W.*
Melissa officinalis, *L.*
Mentha crispa, *L.*
Mentha odorata, *Sm.*
Mentha piperita, *L.*
Mentha pulegium, *L.*
Metrosideros salignus, *Sm.*
Mimosa Farnesiana, *L.*
Mimosa pudica, *L.*
Mimosa sensitiva, *L.*
Mirabilis jalapa, *L.*
Moræa vaginata, *Red.*
Murraya exotica, *L.*
Musa paradisiaca, *L.*
Musa sapientum, *L.*
Mutisia speciosa, *B. M.*
Myrrhinium atropurpureum, *Schott.*
Nepeta cataria, *L.*
Nerium oleander, *L.*
  Var. album.
Nicandra physaloides, *Pers.*
Nicotiana tabacum, *M.*
Nigella Damascena, *L.*
Nymphæa ampla, *DC.*
Ocymum basilicum, *L.*
Ocymum gratissimum, *L.*
Ocymum minimum, *L.*
Œnothera longiflora, *Jacq.*
Olea fragrans, *Thunb.*
Origanum majorana, *L.*
Oxalidis, spec. 2.
Pancratii, spec. 2.
Papaveris. spec. 3.
Parietaria officinalis, *L.*
Passiflora alata, *H. K.*
Passiflora albida, *Ker.*
Passiflora edulis, *B. M.*
Passiflora fœtida, *L.*
Passiflora racemosa, *Brot.*
Passiflora serratifolia, *L.*
Pedilanthus carinatus, *Spr.*
Pelargonium inquinans, *Aѧ.*
Pelargonium odoratissimum, *Ait.*
Pelargonium roseum, *Ait.*
Petiveria alliacea, *L.*
Petrea volubilis, *L.*
Putunia nyctaginiflora, *Juss.*
Petunia Phœɴicea, *D. Don.*
Phaseolus caracalla, *L.*
Phlox paniculata, *L.*
Phyllanthus niruri, *L.*
Physalis Barbadensis, *Jacq.*

Piper nigrum, *L.*
Piper umbellatum, *L.*
Plantago major, *L.*
Plumieria acuminata, *H. K.*
Poinciana pulcherima, *L.*
  Var. lutea.
Poinsettia pulcherrima, *W*
Polianthus tuberosa, *W.*
  Var. flore pleno.
Polygonum hydropiper, *L.*
Pontederia crassipes, *Mart.*
Pyrethrum Parthenium, *Sm.*
Quisqualis Indica, *L.*
Renanthera coccinea, *Lou.*
Reseda alba, *L.*
Reseda odorata, *W.*
Richardsonia scabra, *Kth.*
Ricinus lividus.
Ricinus communis, *L.*
Rosæ, spec. 22.
Rosmarinus officinalis, *L.*
Rubia tinctorum, *L.*
Rubus rosæ-folius, *Poir.*
Rubus urticæ-folius, *Poir.*
Rudbeckia amplexifolia, *Jacq.*
Rudbeckia-pinnata, *Vent.*
Rumex acetosa, *L.*
Rumex crispus, *L.*
Ruta graveolens, *L.*
Saccharum officinarum, *L.*
Saccharum sapé, *Hil.*
Salvia splendens, *Ker.*
Salviæ spec.
Saponaria officinalis, *L.*
Satureja hortensis, *L.*
Scabiosa atropurpurea, *L.*
  Var. alba.
  " rosea.
Schinus terebinthifolia, *Raddi.*
Sechium edule, *Br.*
Sidæ, spec. 3.
Sesamum Orientale, *W.*
Sesbania grandiflora, *Poir.*
Silene armeria, *L.*
  Var. alba.
Sinapis nigra, *L.*
Sisymbrium nasturtium, *L.*
Smilacis, spec. 3.
Solanum, *Giló Raddi.*
Solanum melongenum, *L.*
Solanum nigrum, *L.*
Sonchus Hispanicus, *Jacq.*
Sophora litoralis, *Schr.*
Spinacea oleracea, *L.*
Stifftia chrysantha, *Mik.*
Tagetes erecta, *W.*
Tagetes minuta, *L.*
Tagetes patula, *L.*
Tanacetum vulgare, *L.*

Tetracera volubilis, *L.*	Turnera cuneiformis, *J.*	Vinca rosea, *L.*
Tetragonia expansa, *H. K.*	Typha angustifolia, *L.*	Var. alba.
Thunbergia alata, *Lod.*	Urena lobata, *L.*	Viola tricolor, *L.*
Tigridia pavonia, *Jacq.*	Vanilla aromatica, *Swz.*	Vitis vinifera, *L.*
Tillandsia usneoides, *L.*	Vellosia candida, *Mikan.*	Yucca aloifolia, *L.*
Thymus serpyllum, *L.*	Verbascum virgatum, *W.*	Yucca filamentosa, *L.*
Tolpis barbata, *Gae.*	Verbena psuedo Gervão, *Hil.*	Yucca gloriosa, *L.*
Trachelium ceruleum, *L.*		Zingiber officinale, *Rosc.*
Tradescantia discolor, *H. K.*	Verbenæ, spec. 2.	Zinnia elegans, *Jacq.*
Tropæolum majus, *L.*	Verea crenata, *Andr.*	Zinnia multiflora, *L.*
	Veronica spicata, *L.*	

Mais uma grande collecção de orchideas indigenas, que fazem em muitas partes a belleza do interior das nossas florestas, muitas Bromelias, Tillandsias, Pitcairnias, Melastomas, Acacias, e diversas outras especies valiosas, indigenas e exoticas, que não achei descriptas.   B. J. DE SERPA BRANDAŌ, Director do Jardim.

CHAPTER XV.

Goddess of the Blind.—Her Church, Shrines, and Symbols.—A Slave consulting her.—Interview with her Sacristan.—Ex Votos.—Our Lady of the Cape of Good Hope.—Insuring Friars.—Other Professional and Competing Saints.—Street Images.

March 20. Wandering out early, I brought up, I know not how, on the beach or street of St. Luzia: a rua without houses, but not without a church—one dedicated to the lady just named. She is the patroness of the blind, and much celebrated for affording that relief for which we have recourse to oculists and eye infirmaries.

Stepping through the open door, I found no one within. Marble basins, in the form of shells, for holy water, are built in the wall on each side of the door, and near them esmola boxes. Besides Luzia, only two others have shrines here. Against the right wall is St. John, and opposite to him the Lady of Navigators. She stands on the deck of a ship, with its broadside to spectators. A strongly-bound box, secured by two padlocks, with her likeness on its front, and a slit at top, hangs by the wall close to her; reminding sailors that, while she confers favors on them, acknowledgments in the shape of vintems and milreis are expected.

At the farther end Luzia stands of natural size, holding two eyeballs on a plate or saucer. By the altar rails are four gilt candlesticks of wood, each six feet high, and on their triangular bases *eyes* are portrayed, besides a pair of colossal ones on the screen near the front door, looking very like an optician's sign. And why should not churchmen hang out symbols of good things they deal in as well as laymen, where numbers of their customers can read no other kind of writing? [Luzia's collectors carry with them a silver eye for contributors to kiss.]

In a corner the handsome movable pulpit stood, one of those fashioned apparently after table tumblers—gigantic goblets on fancy stems and bases. They are very light and picturesque in appearance, but, from inequalities of the floors, are liable to be unsteady. Indeed, I never could resist the idea that a gesticulating orator might, in a paroxysm of ardor, throw himself so far forward as to close his discourse with a peroration that would save the sacristan the trouble of bringing forth the portable step-ladder for him to dismount.

It is an old and a current trick of children to break the end of a black peascod, and turn the piece back to represent the cowl of a monk, while the exposed pea resembles his smooth-shaven crown : put one of these Liliputian preachers into a swelled wine-glass, and you have no bad picture of a friar in one of these perambulating pulpits.

A slave came to the door, removed a large basket from her head, sprinkled and crossed herself, and dropped on her knees within two feet of where I stood. With her eyes on Luzia, she muttered her wishes or her thanks, rose, put her mite into an alms-box, made another reverence to the saint, and went away. Poor creature! she feels relieved by pouring out her sorrows before the image of one who, she is told, has the power to mitigate them. I am almost ready to reverence superstition which can thus soothe the sorrows of the desolate, and reconcile them to a joyless existence. Perhaps not her own, but another's woes induced her to call in—some purblind mother, brother, friend. Whatever is the cause, blindness is exceedingly prevalent among the slaves. It is distressing to meet so often one or more bearing full "barils" on their heads, rolling their sightless eyeballs, and feeling their weary way with sticks.

I had now been half an hour in the place, and, except her, not a soul had appeared to break the stillness that reigned within, nor without but the surf. Within the altar rails were two

M

side doors, one partly open. What harm can there be in stepping up and looking in? So I reasoned, and so I acted. The left door opened into a passage in which were several votive tablets. Only two had eyes painted on them. I next crossed over to the other door. Pushing it gently open, a pair of eyes near the floor glistened on me, and the next moment came forth in a living head—the sacristan's! Here had he been seated all the morning, on the floor, with his back to the wall, repairing mule-harness, of which not less than two cart-loads lay near him. I learned subsequently that he was by trade a shoemaker, and had a family that required his awl to make ends meet.

I had some difficulty to make him comprehend my wish to learn something about a saint who repaired defective eyesight; but the instant he caught the idea he beckoned me in front of the altar; closed both eyes; inclined his head on one shoulder; moaned; raised his hands in supplication to Luzia; paused a moment; slowly opened the corner of one eye; then the other; then gradually disclosed the full orbs of both; gazed up, down, and around with well-feigned astonishment; clapped his hands in exultation, and kneeling, held them up in gratitude to the saint; rose, and smiling, turned to me. I exclaimed, "Bom! muito bom!" And so it was; it was capitally done; nothing could have better shown how little true eloquence needs exterior helps to set her off, for he was without a neckcloth, coat, or vest, and had neither shoes nor stockings on.

To illustrate the subject farther, he went to where the tablets were, and referred to them as proofs of the lady's power. I mentioned the "sacristia;" on which he opened a door at the end of the passage, and introduced me into a room behind the altar. Here was the great staple of vestries—a mammoth bureau (over twenty feet long) of wood, black as ebony, containing the plate, wardrobes, and regalia of the images. Its bronze furniture might be shown as antiques from Pompeii, so similar are the drawer-handles, key-holes, &c., to such things found there. From the walls were suspended, with votive eyes, other members of the human frame: proofs that the presiding patroness did not confine her practice to one class of diseases. Here were heads, arms, hands, feet, and a half-length portrait in alto

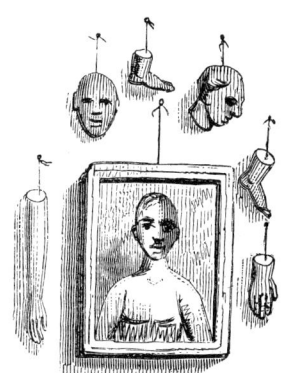
relievo, all of wax. They were apparently very old, for their color was something between that of the floor and the bureau. No explanatory labels were attached, each being left to tell its own story, and, with one exception, little could be drawn from them. The half-length had been colored, to represent the miserable condition the unhappy original was in before the saint relieved him — one side of the face purple, the eye destroyed, and its place marked with a horrid mass of black and livid matter.

There was no telling from the heads what their owners ailed —whether the seats of the complaints had been within or without—scald heads, broken heads, weak or deranged ones. The lineaments are disfigured and all but obliterated. Were it not pretty certain that this is the result of heat and age, one might infer the originals had belonged to pugilists. Of other wall-ornaments, the most characteristic was an old picture of a ship in distress, and the Lady of Navigators saving her.

The artist now resumed his labors on leather straps and panels, and I left in quest of other novelties. Two sailors were sunning themselves at full length on the steps outside, and watching vessels moving over the Bay. If theirs was a visit of devotion to the goddess of seamen—and it is not likely any thing else brought them to a place so lonely and so remote from the shipping—they might serve to remind one of Sidonian or Carthaginian mariners lounging in front of Neptune's temples after thanking him for a successful voyage.

The unpaved thoroughfare of St. Luzia has been made by cutting away the outskirt of Castle Hill, which here extended into the Bay. Men are still digging into the red, tenacious soil. I passed them, climbed the huge mount, descended into the city on the other side, and landed in Rua do Carmo, where I observed a street-image over the gateway of a handsome passage, leading to the Public Library and the Carmo Church. Upon a stone bracket stands a species of glass lantern, three feet high, with a large pane in front and a smaller one at each side. The glass wanted washing, for not till gazing a moment or two was it certain that the saint was within.

A tinman has his shop directly opposite. I tried to get information from him by pointing to the image, and naming every saint I could think of. I did not hit the right one, nor could I if I had been guessing still. Mr. W—— subsequently called with me on the artist, who told us the image was an old one of the Carmelites, and that he and other neighbors are at the cost of illuminating it every night.

"But who is the saint?"

"Nossa Senhora de Cabo da Boa Esperança."

"What! our Lady of the Cape of Good Hope?"

"Si, Senhor."

I stepped over the narrow pavement to an esmola box fixed to the left post of the gateway, which till then had escaped my notice. A full-length miniature of a lady, holding a nosegay in one hand and a baby in the other, was painted on the back, and, sure enough, on a scroll under her feet was inscribed, in minute letters, her name as he had given it.

This is another of the almost endless metamorphoses of the Virgin and child—an affair got up for the special accommodation of Portuguese seamen bound round the South African promontory. By calling here, they used to secure (and some yet secure) a fair passage by raising their eyes to the lady in the lantern and dropping something into her money-box.

The Portuguese were the first, and for a while the only navigators exposed to the dangers thus provided against. The frightened crews and shattered vessels of Bartholomew Diaz, its discoverer, prevented him from doubling Cape Tormentoso, as he named it. In the absence of a proper maritime god, the White Friars proposed a goddess—their "sister"—in the new character of "Our Lady of the Cape," and Heaven, by miracle, confirmed the proposition on this wise: A vessel was on the point of foundering off Table Bay. "Our Lady" appeared in *propria persona*, and saved her. On landing, the men were surprised to find an exact image of her as she appeared at the mast head. From this "milagroso imagem" all others were copied.

There can be no doubt that a shrine of the lady was as useful in Rio as in Lisbon. It was more profitable. Vessels called in here on going to and returning from the Indies. Passengers and crews bound round the Cape renewed their vows or made fresh offers for a fair passage, and those on their way home had an early opportunity to make their acknowledgments before a due sense of them vanished. But, passing such matters, certain it is that the Carmelites came in for a handsome share of this species of marine insurance; and though they did not issue general policies, like their brethren of Boa-Viagem, their business at one time was thought to have been not less profitable than endorsing all kinds of risks.

Insuring friars have peculiar privileges. Whatever risks they underwrite, they never return a premium or make good losses. There are so many strange things in the world, or this of beggars turning underwriters had attracted notice. The Carmelites are an order of mendicants.

Whatever happens to other professions, the resources of friars never fail. It is a maxim with all who trade under the name and style of a particular saint, that he or she can meet all human exigencies. At the same time, the managers do not hesitate to follow the practice of lay dealers in drawing custom from other establishments; leaving their own fields when in stubble to glean in their neighbors'.

St. Sebastian, like his brother Roque, was originally a plague-doctor, but the pest is rare; his practice has become general, and scores of holy competitors undertake epidemics. Anthony's forte once lay in protecting houses from thieves and recovering stolen goods. He now dips into every thing—interferes with St. Brass in curing sore throats; competes with St. Michael dos Santos, the prince of cancer eradicators; takes a large slice of the business and profits of the two lady protectors of seamen; has used up St. Gonçalo in marrying young folks; sends more rain to planters in dry times, and makes more poor land fruitful without manure than all other friends to farmers—a universal genius—a saint of all work.

Then here is the great Francis de Paula—who, when in the body, knew not the bottom of a breviary from the top, save where there was a picture—removing cataracts from the eye, tumors from the brain, water from the head, and even enlightening people's understandings, though, when alive, Heaven itself could not illumine his own. Yet his church records prove that in these things and many others, as driving away demons and calming tempests at sea, he is as successful as the most eminent of canonized practitioners. He is, I am often told, "a very miraculous saint."

To worldly-minded people there appears a lack of discrimination in the distribution of these avocations. Such would associate the Rio favorite with St. Gertrude, who, as a rat and mouse destroyer, was unprecedented. To Francis they would give in charge other vermin, and not have saints of more delicate and refined habits asked to extirpate the most loathsome. But this and other incongruities arise from the principle cultivated by the managers of every institution possessing a saint, namely, that whatever a devotee may want, *their* saint can give or get it for him, and that it is unnecessary to go farther. As a natural consequence, some become popular, and others lose caste and linger on by picking up chance customers; the Lady of the Cape, for example—her shipping business is dwindled almost to nothing, and she ekes out a bare subsistence by patronizing a few shoe and leather dealers and a tinshop; coming in collision with her brother Crispin at one hand, and at the other with ———, perhaps St. Goare, the pot-makers' patron.

Formerly there was no threading a street or turning a corner without having to compliment one of these diminutive divinities. To a devout population they were convenient, as every one could perform an act of devotion *en passant*—merchants at their doors could invoke a blessing on their speculations, tradesmen ask for better times and prices, and slaves for any thing they pleased except their freedom. To prevent disrespect through thoughtlessness, in the absence of the sun, lamps were lit before them, so that no gentleman in going by should neglect to raise his hat, nor lady to make a courtesy. To us, these venerated genii are but eighteen-inch dolls; to Romanists, they are acknowledged media by which prayers reach those they represent.

It is worth recording that the slaves have contributed to deprive their masters of these images—a minor retribution for robbing them of their homes and idols. Blacks never do any thing by halves except labor, and, under similar circumstances, every white race would imitate them. Give them any congenial subject to cultivate, and they become enthusiastic amateurs. They so thronged round the street images, and so annoyed the neighbors with their orisons, that, instead of a city blessing, the little genii verged toward a municipal nuisance, and became gradually removed. Last year several disappeared, and soon hardly one will be left. T—— kindly sketched for me a venerable one at the corner of Hospicio and Ourives Streets.

Most of them were perched up some ten or fifteen feet against private houses. It was and is deemed auspicious thus to put a dwelling or a store under the immediate protection of a saint. It would be less subject to fires and thieves, and its indwellers to the casualties of life. They would be more fortunate in business, have larger profits and fewer losses than others, better customers and more of them—the very ideas and practices of the heathen. That such buildings should have brought higher rents than others was reasonable.

CHAPTER XVI.

Rain.—Mechanical Professions.—Labor versus Respectability.—Effect on young Men.—Building.—Hammer-gamut.—Working Hours and Wages.—Rejoicings over Rafters.—Masons and Masonry.—Scaffolds.—Walls.—Antiquity of the Tools.—Plummet.—Hatchet or Adze.—Carpenter's Bench.—Saw and Planes.—Mode of laying Floors.—Doors, Shutters, Hardware.—Pavers.—Lithography.—Coppersmiths.—Lamp.—Slave Artisans.—Merchants.—Barbers.—Beggars.—Lawyers.—Lotteries.

March 21. I have now been nearly fifty days in Rio, and more or less rain has fallen on about thirty of them. Heavy showers are now descending, accompanied with lightning and rattling thunder. Last night I thought the windows were battered with hail, but on putting out a hand I caught no "stone-water." The opportunity is favorable for posting up notes on labor and mechanical professions.

The unavoidable tendency of slavery every where is to render labor disreputable—a result superlatively wicked, since it inverts the natural order and destroys the harmony of society. Black slavery is rife in Brazil, and Brazilians shrink with something allied to horror from manual employments. In the spirit of privileged classes of other lands, they say they are not born to labor, but to command. Ask a respectable native youth of a family in low circumstances why he does not learn a trade and earn an independent living; ten to one but he will tremble with indignation, and inquire if you mean to insult him! "Work! work!" screamed one; "we have blacks to do that." Yes, hundreds and hundreds of families have one or two slaves, on whose earnings alone they live.

Dr. C——, an old resident, says the young men will starve rather than become mechanics. He, some years ago, advised a poor widow, who had two boys (one 14, the other 16), to put them to trades. She rose, left the room, and never after spoke to him, although he had attended her family professionally for eight years without charge. He was recently accosted by a clerk in the Police Department, who made himself known as the widow's oldest son, and happy in a situation which brings him 300 milreis a year—150 dollars! To be employed under government in the police is honorable, but to descend from an emperor's service even to a merchant's is degrading. As an example of the general feeling, take the following: the parties are known to me. A gentleman of eighteen was induced to honor an importing house with his services at the desk. A parcel not larger than a double letter was handed him by one of the firm, with a request to take it to another house in the neighborhood. He looked at it; at the merchant; took it between a finger and thumb; gazed again at both; meditated a moment; stepped out, and, a few yards from the door, called a black, who carried it behind him to its destination!

This pride is, however, giving way, and the Legislature has taken measures which will tend to subdue it, by requiring foreign merchants to take a certain proportion of native clerks into their establishments.

Thus taught to shun honorable avenues to independence, it may be asked, How do they live? On the public, wherever they can. But the country is poor, and salaries, except the emperor's, are very low; still, the government is beset with applicants for every species of office by which a few hundred milreis a year can be got. Every department is full to overflowing. Broods of embryo diplomatists seek initiation in the various grades of *attachés.* Swarms solicit commissions in the army—in allusion to which, it is said the officers will in time outnumber the men. The Church is next besought for the means of genteelly soaring above the lower orders, but she has shaved more heads than she can shelter. Hundreds of tonsured gentry are without professional employment; obliged to seek out other ways of living, and fortunate are they who accumulate enough to buy a black or two, by whose wages their creature comforts are secured. Law and physic are the other inlets into which the hungry fry throng for food; but these are crowded, and little room left for new comers to squeeze in. The great mass have to turn disappointed aside. And what are they to do? Descend below physic they can not without dishonor. What then becomes of them? I know not; but this I know, that it is distressing to see so many talented young men without any settled plan or definite purpose before them, and unfitted by education for independent exertion in the industrial or commercial pursuits of life; lounging away years of their prime in vague expectation of public employment, living on friends little able to help them, incurring debts, and, from inability to meet their engagements, accused of verifying an old adage, "The day of obligation is the dawn of ingratitude."

These remarks sufficiently explain why it is that master mechanics and tradesmen, with the exception of a few French and other foreigners, are Portuguese. The richest men in the country, the most industrious artisans and assiduous of store-keepers, are Lusitanians. Brazilians dislike them, perhaps as much for the competence their diligence in business realizes as for any thing else. I shall devote this chapter to the mechanics of Rio. They have customs, processes, and tools, which, if on no other grounds than their antiquity, deserve a passing notice.

As two or three new houses are going up close by, I have had daily opportunities of observing the manœuvres of builders. At first I was puzzled by a species of melody, regularly executed, morning, noon, and night, with the hammer. It is the "call" of the men to work, and the signal to quit it. A man kneels on a scaffold plank, and strikes it, or the side of a beam, or any piece of sounding timber, in such a way that few but a practiced hand could well do. The sound reaches to a great distance; and woe to the slave that, ere the last blow is struck, is not at his post with his trowel, his hoe, or his saw in hand. The device is in general use.

Twenty times have I scored the notes as they were being struck off by as many musicians, without perceiving any material variation in the music or its duration. It was easy to represent the force and succession of the sounds by different-sized dots and the spaces left between them, thus:

● ● ● ● ● ● ●●●●●●●●●●●●●●————————●●●●●●●●●●●●●● ●

They exhibit what might be called the Hammer Gamut, or Builder's Tattoo. To read this metrical morceau aright, it should be considered as composed of four bars, corresponding to as many parts of a short address, namely: two, sometimes three, sonorous and startling knocks—a roll of raps tapering down to an inaudible rattle—the roll repeated in inverted order, and closing with a triple and emphatic menace. Put into words: "D'ye hear?—run, then—quick, or you'll catch—a thrashing."

Working hours are from dawn to dusk, *i. e.*, from half past five to half past six, very little twilight preceding sunrise or following sunset. From the rains and oft-recurring festivals, mechanics do not average over five working days to the week. The master mason of the large house going up next door works full hours. He is a Portuguese, and receives $1 a day for himself, from 40 to 70 cents for his men, and 25 to 30 for his laborers. His assistants are all slaves. The carpenter, also a Portuguese, has the same wages as the mason. Most of his men are white, and their pay varies from 40 to 80 cents—the latter is considered high wages. Here are no master builders, as with us; they are little more than foremen—owning tools, but provided with neither shops nor materials. Every thing is prepared on the premises of their employers.

When the walls of a house are ready for the rafters, the laying down of the first pair of these is announced by a concert of instrumental music, and other demonstrations of joy. Hearing an unusual noise one day, I went out, and found it came from a new building in Machado Place. Two rafters had just been raised on the second story. The Brazilian, Portuguese, and some other flags were flying over them. Black and white artists aloft were drumming *con gusto* on beams, planks, and crowbars, while hissing squibs and Chinese crackers contributed to the harmony. This was kept up till the owner appeared and made them a donation, when up rose a rocket in honor of his liberality, accompanied with an original fantastacio rattled off with hammers on girders.

The head carpenter and mason of J——'s new mansion, having got the first two rafters in their places, came yesterday, according to ancient custom, to inform the family of the fact, and to express the wishes of the workmen " that whoever shall dwell in that house may be happy."

Masons and Masonry.—Bricks are little used except for kitchen fire-places, rough arches over doors and windows, and as finishing courses to receive plates for rafters. (There is not a brick house in Rio.) In laying them, workmen are careful to run the mortar into the upright joints, for which purpose every man has water in an ox's horn. The water in the horn is called the " mason's *nail*," from the solidity it imparts to his work. Were a Brazilian artist to witness a Yankee brother carrying up a five-story building, laying the bricks as fast as they could be picked up, he would flee the place instanter, calling on the saints by the way to keep up the walls till he got clear of them. The bricks are not hard burned; they are ten inches by five, and two and a half inches thick.

The walls of houses in Rio are exceedingly thick; for two-story houses, seldom less than five feet below the surface. They are not in courses, but are faced with innumerable pieces, varying from two inches to half an inch, stuck in mortar between the large stones, so that before the stucco is laid on the structure appears as if composed almost wholly of these fragments.

The scaffolding is on the old plan, and secure. Putlocks pass through the work, and project equally on both sides, though supported by upright poles only on one. Every five feet of elevation, a fresh platform of planks on each side of a wall is laid down. They make miserable work of lifting the larger stones. A few days ago, eight negroes were yelling an African virelay for nearly half an hour on elevating one not over two hundred and fifty pounds' weight to a height of ten feet, under the direction of the master mason, who pulled too. It was hoisted by a chain passing over a *single block* lashed to one of the scaffold poles.

Hammers, trowels, hoe for mixing and lifting mortar, and round baskets for carrying it on the head, are precisely such as we see in illustrated works of the fifteenth and illuminated MSS. of preceding centuries; such, too, as are portrayed in Egyptian sculptures. The costume of the laborers, and their mounting ladders with bare feet, also accord with building-scenes in Pharaonic days. The shovel in place of the hoe is a modern acquisition; and the hod, of English or Irish origin, is not seen. The level is of course used, but not the plumb rule. In place of it, an implement equally efficient and of more extended application is in every man's hands. Strange that so old and valuable a device should have been neglected by British and American workmen. Here are sketches of a couple.

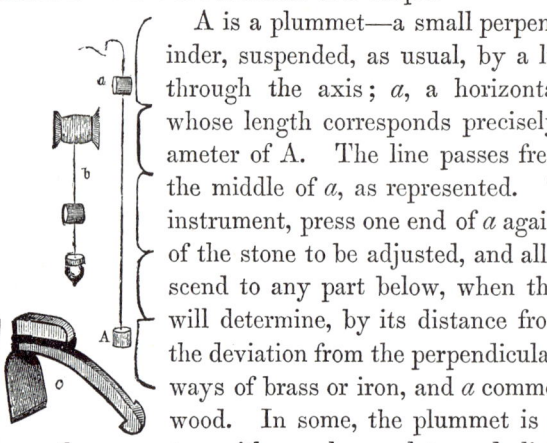

A is a plummet—a small perpendicular cylinder, suspended, as usual, by a line passing through the axis; *a*, a horizontal cylinder, whose length corresponds precisely to the diameter of A. The line passes freely through the middle of *a*, as represented. To use this instrument, press one end of *a* against the face of the stone to be adjusted, and allow A to descend to any part below, when the *side* of A will determine, by its distance from the wall, the deviation from the perpendicular. A is always of brass or iron, and *a* commonly of hard wood. In some, the plummet is pointed. *b* shows the apparatus, with a reel, complete, and slightly varied, as sold in the stores.

Carpenters.—That in Spain and Portugal Moorish customs are inherited with Moorish blood, and traceable in their colonies, is well understood. On going among wheelwrights, carpenters, joiners, carriage-makers, &c., I was struck with traits decidedly

Oriental in their tools and processes, such as I had not dreamed of witnessing. A hasty judgment might pronounce them peculiarly Asiatic, but in reality they were common to the old civilized world. The carpenter's art in Portugal and Brazil is very much what it was in Italy twenty centuries ago.

The first tool I took up I recognized at once as Roman and Egyptian. There was no resisting the striking resemblance between it and those in the hands of chariot-builders, wheelwrights, chair-makers, coffin and cabinet makers, &c., portrayed in Theban sculptures. It is here employed, as it was of old, by *all artists in wood*—their principal implement, and by the use of which an expert or inexpert workman is known. It is the *single-handed adze* to which I refer—the most popular tool of ancient carpenters, and the one by which their talents also were determined. Here it is at c, in the preceding cut, consisting of three parts: a blade, a strong oblong iron loop or ferrule, and the handle: the latter is slightly curved; the part next the blade, $3\frac{1}{2}$ inches deep; the part grasped by the hand, $5\frac{1}{2}$ inches long, $1\frac{1}{2}$ deep, and 1 in thickness, with the corners rounded. The end is enlarged to prevent its flying out of the hand. Except this part, the handle is of uniform thickness, but here is a projection to support the lower edge of the hand. The blade is five inches wide, and nearly six in length.

The shank is placed against the butt end of the handle, and the ferrule slipped over both, or it may be put on first and the shank passed in, when a few blows of the blade on a block brings up the shoulder (seen in the edge view) against the ferrule. Neither wedge nor any other fastening whatever is required. It is not possible for the blade to fly off. The harder the blows struck with it, the securer it becomes. The ferrule is made deeper and thicker where it grasps the shank.

The general outline approaches that of the adze of the South Sea Islanders, the difference being due to the substitution of metallic blades for those of stone, and a loop of iron for a lashing of sinews. To these primeval implements some Egyptian adzes are allied, but others have the blades secured to solid butments of the handle by ferrules, precisely as this modern one. (See Rosellini, or Wilkinson's "Ancient Egyptians," vol. i., p. 349.)

The adze is applied with much tact as a substitute for the axe in squaring beams, and for the plane in smoothing them. Wheelwrights dress spokes and felloes with it; chair and carriage makers can not do without it. It is a universal former, and next to the hammer in utility.

We recognize the same tool, and expertness in the use of it, in an ordinance of Lycurgus directed against sumptuous dwellings. The planks of doors were not to be planed. With the floors and ceilings, they were to receive no other finish than what was given them by the adze. We know from other sources that flooring-beams were left exposed, as in our ships and old Dutch houses, and that they were carved, colored, and polished. This the Spartan lawgiver denounced. The subject is farther and happily illustrated by an anecdote of Leotychides the elder, preserved by Plutarch. Being at Corinth, he observed the beams of the room in which his host entertained him curiously and richly wrought, and satirically inquired if trees grew square in that part of Greece. The inference is clear that in Laconia the beams were but little dressed. The exposure of rafters was a universal feature in the domestic architecture of the ancients. From their prominence in every room the Savior took occasion to illustrate one of his most memorable apophthegms.

In the antiquities of Herculaneum is a representation of a carpenter's shop, including the work-bench, a piece of wood secured on it by an iron clamp (the same as now used), a box for tools under it; a mallet lays on the floor, and a couple of young artists are cutting a plank, which one holds down on the bench with his left hand, and works a frame-saw with the other. His associate, seated on the floor, grasps the opposite side of the frame—[see Herculaneum and Pompeii, tome iii., Paris, 1840] —implements which correspond with those of Portuguese and Brazilian workmen. Their bench is a smooth, stout plank, supported on four diverging legs. It has no side screw or wooden vise, but is furnished with the device which preceded that; and which, as illustrating the progress of the arts, is worth noticing. Two stout slats, whose length exceeds the width of the bench, slide in dovetailed grooves (three or four feet apart), cut across its under surface; their front ends are enlarged into what may be called jaws. The slats are pulled out, and the piece of wood to be dressed placed upon them. They are then pushed in till the jaws press it against the side of the bench, when the workman, reaching over, drives in a wedge at the farther side between each slat and the groove it moves in. Sometimes the jaws are not pushed up close, but are purposely fixed to allow a wedge (which hangs by a string to the front of the bench) to be driven between one of them and the plank or other object which is to be held.

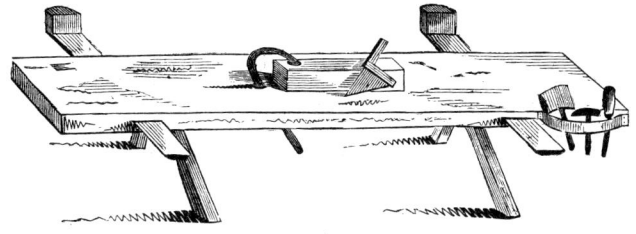

CARPENTER'S BENCH.

This contrivance is efficient, but clumsy, and requires more time than the vise to secure and release its object. It is, however, too refined to be the original of its type. It is an improvement on a rude predecessor that still competes with it, consisting of two stout blocks secured on the bench, one toward each end. A deep vertical notch is cut into each block, presenting fixed jaws some five or six inches wide and as many deep. Between these the article to be trimmed, or plank to be edged, is dropped, and made fast by a wedge. I noticed half a dozen of these benches at the public works on Castle Hill, and repeatedly met them elsewhere.

The hand-saw of England and the United States—the most valuable of the genus—is never found in the hands of workmen here. The little framed blade—the universal implement of antiquity—is indiscriminately employed. It is true that the Egyptians, like modern Hindoos and Asiatics generally, had an imperfect instrument for slitting boards, which they lashed upright to a fork or other fixed object, but it was little more than a large toothed knife. The old Latin saw is at present the saw of all the Latin nations. Planes are few and old-fashioned. Fancy moulding ones are comparatively unknown.

Flooring planks are never laid in single courses as with us, end joints being deemed eye-sores; hence they are made to run in one line entirely across the floor; and, when not concealed by a partition, a number of planks are interposed as at A—a plan that affords no bond to the walls at those places. Sometimes half a dozen planks are laid together end to end, and the joints broken by an equal number, as joints are crossed in a brick wall. Ordinary sized rooms are floored as at B. A plank border, more or less wide, runs round all.

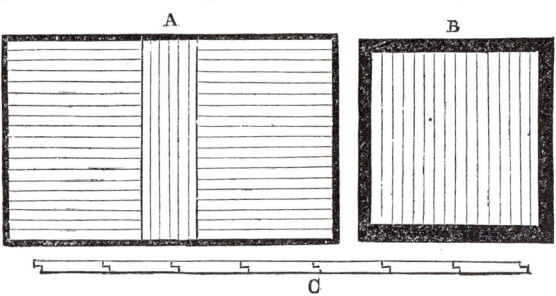

The planks are never plowed and tongued, but lap as at C, which represents the ends of a series.

I have been thus particular in a small matter, because we have unquestionably here the ancient system of flooring.

Window sashes are those of past centuries—small squares, and no moulding on the bars; few or none suspended by weights. The one in my bed-room is a fair specimen: the lower half is heavy, as if made of iron, and when raised, care is required to turn the cleat safe under the lower edge; for, were it to fall when one's head is out, we should never look out of windows more.

Interior doors are large, of the same heavy wood as the floors, and without relief. Even in the best rooms they are made of three or four perpendicular planks held together by dovetailed battens; nor are they enlivened by furniture, an iron lock and key being the only fastenings, and an iron escutcheon over the key-hole their only ornament.

Inside window-shutters are universal. The uniform mode of securing them is extraordinary. A perpendicular bolt, seldom less than five feet in length, is fixed on one leaf of a shutter, and at its lower part is a hasp, which drops over a catch or staple in the other leaf. The bolt neither rises nor falls, but the act of turning the hasp over its catch turns the curved end of the bolt into a staple fixed in the wall or window-frame overhead. A strong lock is attached to every hasp, and a key hangs by every keyhole. In one house I observed, in addition, a bell hung to each shutter! This excessive precaution against housebreakers is an ancient trait in Portuguese building. The material of the floors and doors, etc., is a dark red and heavy wood. With difficulty I raised from the floor a new inside door, its weight not being less than one hundred and fifty pounds.

Carpenters and joiners' hardware is chiefly imported from Portugal. Of wrought iron, it is well made, and far more durable than what English shops supply. It is very old-fashioned. There are keys, hinges, and bolts similar to those preserved in the museum at Naples. Some good smith work is done in Rio.

The tile roofs and gutter-spouts noticed in Chapter VIII. are purely classical.

No plans or sections are drawn for buildings. Generally the mason and carpenter are told to make the house a brother to Senhor Somebody's, and the windows sisters to those of some dwelling pointed out. The work progresses slowly.

The street-pavers use a short cylindrical rammer, larger and heavier than ours, and worked by three men—the "three-man beetle" of Shakspeare. The signal of the foreman to assemble his men is sounded by a hammer on an uplifted crowbar.

Cabinet wares are well made, chairs of rosewood included, but they are inconveniently heavy, and not so strong as veneered ones with us. Their legs are liable to snap.

The largest lithographic establishment in Brazil is that of Heaton and Rensburg, in Rio. Their pressmen are African helots. Mr. H—— was surprised to learn that lithographic printers have from $10 to $15 a week with us. "A milreis (fifty cents) a day," he remarked, "is good wages here, and slaves do not cost us a quarter of that."

In a coppersmith establishment I found fifteen men at work, every one a slave, including the foreman. The proprietor was a Portuguese.

Subsequently I spent part of another day among the braziers, and may as well insert the substance of my notes here. All the copper is imported from England. Of staple articles stills appeared the chief. I counted fifteen in one shop. Every sugar plantation requires one or more. Nests of pans, from two to three feet over, presented another article in great demand. Shallow and tinned, they resembled such as I had seen used by some lavandeiras. Piles of stew-pans stood in every shop. In these and the plate-stoves of the country we have fac-similes of the chief kitchen apparatus of the Greeks and Romans, and of remoter people. I thought it strange to find portable furnaces among braziers' wares, since handsome cast-iron ones are imported, and clay ones of domestic fabric are so common, but here are so many applications of copper and its alloys, where with us iron would be used (in clamping stones, *e. g.*), that one is irresistibly reminded of the profuse use of bronze by the Latin ancestors of this people.

Of smaller things few interested me more than a simple and cheap lamp, in universal use by the poorer classes, and of which immense quantities are in demand for the interior. Adapted 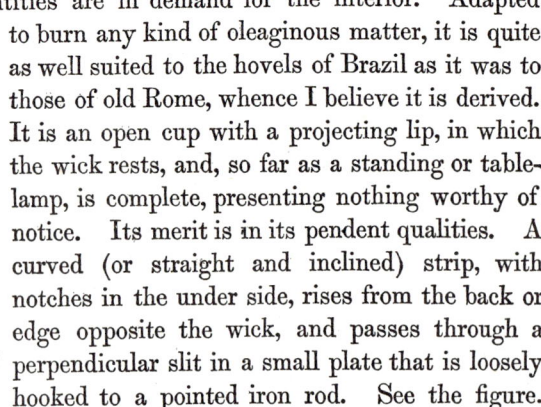 to burn any kind of oleaginous matter, it is quite as well suited to the hovels of Brazil as it was to those of old Rome, whence I believe it is derived. It is an open cup with a projecting lip, in which the wick rests, and, so far as a standing or table-lamp, is complete, presenting nothing worthy of notice. Its merit is in its pendent qualities. A curved (or straight and inclined) strip, with notches in the under side, rises from the back or edge opposite the wick, and passes through a perpendicular slit in a small plate that is loosely hooked to a pointed iron rod. See the figure. The sharp end of the rod is stuck into a beam, rafter, etc., in an upright, horizontal, or any other position or angle; and as the oil gets low, it is canted toward the wick by passing the strip, notch by notch, through the plate, till every drop is consumed. The barb, or sharp hook at the upper end of the rod, is to suspend the instrument from the edge of a shelf or table, and to pass over a nail, etc. Except the iron rod, the whole is of thin sheet copper. Instead of being worked up into the form represented, some are made by simply pinching a piece of metal at the corners. Nothing could be simpler, cheaper, or more durable, the cost is only five or six cents.

The modes of working copper are very similar to ours. Indeed, into none of the old standard professions have less changes been introduced than copper-smithing, as if the fathers of this art had perfected it. The tools in use are such as Mamurius employed on the Ancylia—such as have ever been common with the workmen of Egypt and Asia. In one shop twenty blacks were at work, and not a white face in the place except the clerks. Here I observed three or four marimbas hanging against the wall. With these instruments of their own land the artists amuse themselves after working hours.

Besides Capuchins and other sacerdotal artists that came over with or followed the empress, were a couple of Italian coppersmiths. They make out to buy a sheet or two of metal, and, working it into ladles, skillets, and colanders, start out and "cry" them through the streets. H—— and I once stopped in Theatre Square to observe one at work. Seated on the floor, he was bringing into form a couple of small coffee-pots. With no greater stock of materials and tools than are figured in a painting of a brazier's shop in Herculaneum, he was a lively representative of an ancient pagan craftsman.

I have now seen slaves working as carpenters, masons, pavers, printers, sign and ornamental painters, carriage and cabinet makers, fabricators of military ornaments, lamp-makers, silversmiths, jewelers, and lithographers. It is also a fact that sculptures in stone and saintly images in wood are often done admirably by slaves and free blacks. A little gray-headed fellow—an old African—begs in the Cattete who was once noted as an excellent sculptor, but now is an habitual drunkard. The vicar mentioned lately a slave who is a first-rate workman in sacred carving in Bahia. *All* kinds of trades are carried on by black journeymen and boys.

The foreign merchants of Rio struck me as forming something like an order of monks. Nearly all are bachelors of from thirty to sixty years' standing. Their homes, like monasteries, contain no females. Seeking to accumulate the means of enjoyment, they continue the chase till the powers of enjoyment are well-nigh gone.

Barbers.—Barbers here sharpen their razors on the cork-like pito-wood. The leech trade is in their hands. H—— and I occasionally stepped into one shop to look at the thick plank boxes, three feet long, filled with a fine soft clay, in which the worms are imported, and in which they burrow till drawn out for use. Some are of enormous dimensions. The usual price is twenty cents for each one a barber applies.

Beggars.—A good old custom is kept up by Portuguese and native merchants, and is imitated by some foreign houses. A pile of coppers is placed on the counter on the last day of every week for the clerks to give to the poor. When the pile is gone, the universal answer sends every applicant away: *Paciencia Deos lhe favoreta.* This asking God to favor them is understood as equivalent to "I can't" or "I won't." One gentleman gives out two dollars from his counter every Saturday morning. Beggars go their rounds on other days, but Saturday is their best one. An old Rio rascal got rich by mendicity, and, to the annoyance of his family, would not cease to follow the lucrative business. I was at first surprised at the prompt turning away of mendicants on receiving the above reply. It is the same, however, in Spain: *Perdone umd por Dios, Hermano.* A similar mode of denial is equally effective in the East. An Egyptian beggar is silenced at once by *Allah yeuzoock*, God will sustain, or *Allah yoateek*, God give thee.

Lawyers.—Of the administration of law, complaints loud and deep from both natives and foreigners are heard continually. Criminals are tried before juries, but civil suits are determined by judges alone; and from them, it is said openly, justice can scarcely ever be obtained, unless purchased for more than it is worth. It is, however, not to be doubted that there are men on the Brazilian bench as pure from the pollution of bribes as are to be found any where else. Judicial depravity is confined to no one country. Of numerous examples recently bruited, it is not necessary to quote any, nor would they have been alluded to but for the fact of their elucidating a marked feature in the ancestors of this people. "Approach the judge with feet in hand"—with a present of fowls and game—is a modern as well as ancient Peninsular aphorism. "Rather bribe than lose thy cause" is another. The rapacity of some judges is still likened to that of the Abbot of Corcuelo, who, having supped on a poor man's porridge, wanted the pot; and to another, who, after eating a widow's last egg, was not ashamed to ask for the hen. In all countries, the humorous Gallician's invocation may still be offered up, " God keep me from the strokes of a gander"— from a lawyer's goose-quill.

Lotteries.—Gambling in these is universal. Granted for all sorts of things, fresh ones are perpetually announced. Boys run about peddling tickets; they enter stores, visit the markets, and even stop you in the street; nay, women are sent out as agents by the dealers. This day two stopped at T——'s, and offered tickets to the clerks. The Diario of the 9th contained the plan of the *fifth* one granted for the " Beneficio do Obra da Nova Igreja do Senhor Bom Jesus de Iguape," and advertised another for the "Beneficio da Igreja Matriz do Ceará."

The papers contain notices of tickets purchased for distant customers. Thus: " No. 4395, of the Sixth Lottery in favor of the Theatre of Nictherohy, belongs to Senhor M. Pinheiro de Mendonça, of Pernambuco." " Senhor A. Airosa has purchased, by order of and for J. F. A., of Porto Alegre, the ticket 2318." Rio is, with respect to lotteries, what some parts of Europe and the United States were a few years ago. As in olden times, they elicit the passions and superstitions of the poor, and strip them to the skin. The lavandeira of J——'s family, a poor white woman, who attends regularly at the palace for alms, was in deep distress the other day. She had lost her all, and was in despair. Her ticket had come up a blank! She ran over a string of saints that she had invoked, vows made to them, amulets and talismans she had worn, divinations performed, in order to make the number a prize, and complained woefully that not one of them had done any thing for her!

She attended the late feast of St. Braz, has got one of his measures and medals, and has great faith in their curing her swelled throat. As she has lost the sight of an eye by gutta serena, it was suggested to her to exercise equal confidence in Luzia, who has been known to release immovable pupils.

CHAPTER XVII.

Maté and Cups.—Sunday Scenes.—Gloria Church.—Images, Vestry, Ex Votos, and Paintings.—Miracles in behalf of Pedro I. and one of his Daughters.—Lady of Gloria and a Larangeiras Absalom.—Chapel of the Ajuda grated like a Jail.—Its Shrines and Images.—A Penitent licking the Dust.—Public Notice of a Procession.—Images, Angels, and Pomp described.

MATÉ, or Paraguay tea, is not very much used in Rio. In the interior its consumption is great, as it is considered an indispensable preservative against climatic influences, besides bracing the stomach and invigorating the system. A staple article of commerce, vessels in the southern provinces are sometimes wholly laden with it. In the prices current of Montevideo and Buenos Ayres it is enumerated as regularly as coffee or flour.* It is shipped in tin chests covered with colored paper, somewhat after the manner of China. The aboriginal mode of preparing and taking the decoction universally prevails. A little of the leaves is put into a small gourd, sugar is added, and the vessel filled with boiling water: the whole is stirred, and a sucking tube—commonly a reed, with a miniature basket-strainer—is introduced, and the hot liquid imbibed through it. The two lower figures in the cut are gourds: the one on the left has been ornamented after the Indian fashion, by drawing a heated point of metal over it; the other is mounted in silver, with a tube or "bombillo" of the same. The upper figure is an ancient maté cup in terra cotta.

The first knowledge of tea-drinking in Europe was derived,

---

* *Yerba Maté.*—En octubre se introdujeron 3237 tercios de *Parnaguá*, 786 de *Rio Grande*: en Noviembre, 3275 tambien de Parnaguá, y 82 de *Rio Grande*, y en Diciembre, solo 89 de Parnaguá. Total, 7387 tercios.

LIFE IN BRAZIL. 199

not from China, but South America. More than half a century elapsed after maté had been imbibed before the Chinese infusion was introduced.

22d, *Sunday.* By 7 A.M. the streets were alive with human ants, with carts, ox-teams, and pannier mules. Met five gangs of chanting slaves, fifteen to twenty in each, bearing to new habitations the furniture of as many families. Pavers, carpenters, coopers, and tinmen were busy, smiths at their forges, tailors and tailors' boys seated as usual on stools, slabs of jerked beef hung out at some doors, and dry goods fluttered at others. By a stream which a cow might drink up as it oozes out of some rocks on the Gloria beach, a solitary lavandeira is scrubbing shirts and spreading them on a few handfuls of grass to dry. Men and mules are cooling their heated bodies just within the surf; one animal lies down with its head only above the surface, nor can the driver induce it to rise, so grateful is the bath—to every shout it returns a snort. A little farther a negro is coming ashore with the end of a seine, while three associates in a boat take a sweep outward and return; a naked black wades out to meet them, and, with his nude brother at the other end, slowly draws the net to land; lads watching in the street now run down, and passengers stop to look. That line of ripples is caused by the finny game, and now, like flashes of light, their white sides appear, leaping and struggling on the shelving shore.

On sultry mornings like this, the noisiest scenes are at the fountains. The gabbling crowds, pushing forward their "barils" to the spouts, remind one of litters of squealing porkers hustling each other in their eagerness for a breakfast.

I turned up to the Gloria church, and rested on a low wall put up to prevent the unwary from tumbling down the steep. Here, on a point jutting into the Bay, and several hundred feet above it, the prospect is delightful. Far down are seen crowds of mangoes and stately palms, and every where the broad-leafed banana. Evanescent rays of green and gold flash from the breasts of humming-birds, while butterflies flap lazily their wings, and tempt one to follow them. Two linnet-looking strangers keep hopping on the wall, and anon dart down the precipice to a tamarind-tree, and again and again return. Above are chacaras scattered here and there, recalling the Scripture idea of a city on a hill; but not "from the top of Hermon," or any other mount of old, was the scenery more enchanting.

The door of the temple stands open, and invites us to climb higher and look in. How different the plan of this venerable edifice from others! It is an octagon, fourteen paces in diameter. The main entrance faces the Bay, and the farther side opens into a smaller octagonal structure, in the centre of which is the high altar. Behind it is the vestry, very much in the shape of a horse-shoe. As we enter, two scalloped marble basins offer lustral water, and an alms-box of "Our Lady" solicits subscriptions. Continuing on to the middle of the floor, a pulpit projects from the wall on either hand; we advance, and two more esmola boxes present themselves; the one at your left has a sickly friar's portrait on it, and on the other is a still more moving appeal—a squalid monk holds up his gown to show you a wound in his right leg. Had I not learned that Ambrose was his name, I should have taken him for St. Roche, who is commonly painted with a boil on his thigh, and exposing it in like manner.

Farther on we stop between the two converging walls to look at a couple of shrines, with images large as life. He at the right is Gonçalo, the great patron of maids and bachelors. This on the left, draped as a monk, is Emygdio—he is celebrated for protecting people from earthquakes. A little farther the chief altar rises, and over it the lady of the place, Nossa Senhora da Gloria. She looks short, but is, I am told, of full stature. She is fashionably draped in silks and frills, and wears several finger-rings.

Now glancing around, the walls are observed to be lined for eight feet up with blue and white Dutch tiles, representing landscapes and mythologic characters. Actæon and others, with hunting-poles and dogs, are starting and coursing game. Cupid is out sporting too—obese, as he generally is when born and bred in Holland, he flies his arrows in a manner altogether unfit for such a place. The general impression of this ancient temple is pleasing. Columns, niches, altars, candlesticks, and carved work are white and gold, contrasting prettily with the blue pagan scenery on the walls.

The sacristan came in and led me into the vestry. Its walls are lined with tiles similar to those in the church. Portraits of some of the fathers hang on them, and two large and confused bundles of ex votos, enough to stock a chandler's store. All are stained with age. A fresh one is not among them. Here is a large painting, representing a man in a blue coat and white pants, on his knees, and a stout angel assisting him to rise; a lady is fast approaching him from below on horseback, and a female head is smiling through the clouds. I had heard of the picture and of its origin. The first wife of Pedro I. had much devotion to the Lady of Gloria, and named her daughter, the present Queen of Portugal, after her. Pedro came with her one morning to mass, both being mounted. On coming up the hill, his horse fell and threw him. His wife, in the rear, at once called on Nossa Senhora to save him harmless and cause him instantly to rise. This she did, and, to commemorate "the miracle," the picture was painted and put up here.*

The present emperor and his sisters were brought here soon after birth, that they might first open their eyes on the image of the family protectora. It is said the child was always placed in the arms of the image, but S——, who was once present, informed me the emperor, on that occasion, placed it on the altar only.

Every manifestation of the lady's favor is acknowledged by such presents as are deemed the most acceptable. Several sets of diamond necklaces and ear-rings have been given her, the sleeves of her gown are united at the wrists with diamond buttons. Doña Januaria (Joinville's wife), when sick a few years ago, vowed her "richest jewel" if Senhora da Gloria would restore her to health. Yon diamond brooch on her bosom is the gem earned and paid on that occasion.

This wooden deosa has a splendid head of hair. It is the last of a series of rapes of locks committed on her account. When the brother of Senhor P. L——a, a young gentleman of my acquaintance, was seven years old, his hair reached more

---

* "A igreja de Nossa Senhora da Gloria, muito visitado pila primeira imperatriz do Brazil, e muito da sua devoção, que buscou a sagrada imagem da Senhora da Gloria para protectora da sua filha primogenita."—*Universo Pittoresco*, tomo iii., 374. Lisboa, 1844.

than half way down his back. His mother, having great devotion to Nossa Senhora, sheared off the silken spoils, and offered them "as an act of faith" to her, little thinking how literally she was copying the practice of heathen dames. The locks were sent to a French hair-dresser, who wrought them into a wig. It was brought here, laid in due form before the lady, when the priest reverently removed her old wig and covered her with the flowing tresses of the Larangeiras Absalom.

On returning, I passed, as I do almost daily, the Ajuda Nunnery. Through one of the two heavy doors in the high dead wall we went on the 10th instant. The other opens into the chapel, and this is the first time I have seen the leaves thrown back. Let us step in. If we don't get a sight of the nuns, we may perhaps hear their voices, or at least learn how it is that, when present at mass, they are invisible.

Ascending a few steps above the pavement, we cross the sacred threshold. Few persons are within, and no priest in sight. The room is a long and high one; its arched ceiling can not be less than thirty feet above the stone floor. One end is, as usual, taken up with the altar dedicated to the presiding genius—the Lady of Ajuda. The opposite end is startling—a vertical wall of iron work, three stories high! The bars are inch-bolts passing through loops forged in cross ones, leaving spaces three inches square between them. The uppermost story seems of finer texture.

Behind this lattice-work the vestals attend mass, yet no one can behold them, nor can they steal a peep at people here. Between them and the grating hangs a black linen curtain that defies mortal vision. Here am I close to the bars, and can no more see through it than through a plate of metal, nor can it be pushed aside; for, besides being secured to the walls and floor, it is four feet from the grating; and I am told by one who knows that a similar screen of metal keeps the nuns at an equal distance. Tons of iron bars to prevent egress and ingress! Why, this is Newgate; if not, 'tis Bedlam, for who but monomaniacs could introduce such things into the house and church of Jesus!

Turning our backs, as we ought, to the grating, the whole interior of the chapel is before us. Here are six shrines besides the chief one, three against each side wall. This one close to us on the left is Tereza's, and there she stands, the stoutest lady saint I have yet met with. She is tall enough for wife to Saul. Her throat is covered, and her chin tied up, as nun's chins commonly are; but the rouge on her face, and her gown half covered with gold (leaf), are not in accordance with her vows. Several favorite male recluses attend her, among them Anthony and Francis de Paula—represented in statuettes. The next shrine to Tereza is St. Anne's, who is giving her young daughter a lesson in reading. A little St. Michael stands on one side, and St. Barbara on the other. This last lady is, according to the Compendio de Oraçoes, "a great protectress against thunderbolts." At the next shrine is a full-sized image of Christ, in a half stooping posture, crowned with thorns, the hands crossed and bound. Blood trickles over the pallid face, the knees are bruised, and the entire body more or less covered with gore. This image is carried in public processions.

The opposite shrine (on the right) is dedicated to "the sacred heart," which, with its auricles, veins, etc., is carved in high relief, and colored most sanguifluously. Two male attendants guard it—one who, of all the Church's heroes, put on the soldier most—her Suwaroff—Dominic. There he appears, with shaven crown, bare feet and neck, and armed with a rosary, from which a cross like a dagger hangs. He extirpated heresy and heretics together. The altar of José faces that of Anne. Besides "the Baby God" in his arms, he grasps a stick decorated with flowers and ribbons, because he had one which budded like Aaron's. "Of good days for confession, his anniversary is one of the best."

The next shrine faces Tereza's; it is that of John of Nepomuceno. A professor of divinity and canon law in the University of Prague, he flourished in the 14th century, and wrought so many miracles, "such as the wonderful preservation of the city of Nepomuc from the plague, and the cure of diseased persons given up by physicians," that he was canonized, and added to the host of heavenly solicitors which the Church retains to plead for her earthly clients. As usual, several small friends attend him. One is Apollonia, and another might be taken for "St. John the Dwarf." In the long catalogue of Johns, Butler has such a saint, and another whom these little folks still more resemble, "St. John the Silent."

Of the seven altars, only one was approached professionally, viz., the last. A well-dressed man of thirty-five or forty came in, dropped on his knees before the Bohemian doctor, to whom he raised his eyes for a minute or more, broke into a low murmur, and suddenly fell flat on his face. He was within eight feet of me, and supposing he had fainted, I sprang toward him, when lo! he was kissing the floor and whispering to it. I drew back, and he shortly crept on his hands and knees from one end of the altar to the other. Then addressing the saint, he brought his mouth to the ground a second time; he next wriggled himself on his knees to the centre of the altar, and once more saluted the floor. He rose, wiped his dusty lips, rubbed down his pants, picked up his hat, and bending his right knee nearly to the floor in reverence to the saint, drew sidelong to the door, and departed.

Mentioning what I had seen to a native lady, she observed that he had probably been required thus to humble himself by way of penance. But why kiss the dust at the feet of the Bohemian in preference to more ancient intercessors? She could not say, except that St. John of Nepomuceno is a powerful advocate, and has many devotees among the respectable classes.

My surprise was great at the beginning of the man's devotions, but it was heightened at their close. While they were progressing, I felt for him as for one whose heart was torn with anguish, and his face pale and suffused with tears. I was dreaming. He rose from his knees as if he had never been on them, wiped his mouth as if he had just taken a drink, and dusted his clothes as if shaking off crumbs of a lunch.

27th. This is the first of the Setanaria—seven days dedicated to the seven griefs of Our Lady. The papers announce processions. One comes off to-day from the Church of Bom Jesus in Soap Street. The official advertisement, after requesting the occupants of dwellings in certain streets to remove obstructions, concludes thus: "It is recommended with much solicitude to our beloved sisters, and other devout persons, to be punctual in preparing and sending their angels, in order to impart greater splendor to the procession.

"M. A. Picanço, Secretary."

At 4 P.M.—the hour announced—I reached the church in the long and narrow lane, now covered with mango leaves. The doors were closed, but a couple of soldiers, with bayonets, stood by the vestry door. I passed in. I found the place crowded with brothers, busy as artists in a theatre just before the curtain rises. In an inner passage were rows of votive tablets and waxen offerings. A troop of cavalry arrived, and presently a long line of infantry, with music and banners. I secured a stand in a private entry facing the church door, which at length was thrown open, and showed the interior a blaze of waxen lights. Above the shoal of heads a swallow-tailed crimson banner came forth, accompanied by tassel-holders, and having on it the initials of the senate and people of pagan Rome— S. P. Q. R. A company in albs, with five-feet candles (unlit), issued, and formed in line ; a silver crucifix, between two superb mourning bouquets, followed, and then more candle-bearers. Now something fills the door, and for a moment hides the light. It is a platform on six men's shoulders, and upon it a man bending forward on one knee. Dressed in a russet gown, his pale face contrasts with his black locks. Bearing an enormous cross, he personates Christ on the way to Calvary. He has reached the street, and stops within five feet of me. Why! the figure is an image, which till this moment I had no idea of, so naturally it appears.* The military present arms, and receive it with a flourish of music. It passes on, and see! how natural the sole of the right foot and portion of the leg uncovered by the skirts of the gown!

Now smaller figures appear, and certainly not automatons —a troop of fluttering, smiling, black-eyed *angels*, whose cupid-formed and papilio-painted wings open and close behind them. Some are enveloped in purple clouds! No two are alike in dress and ornaments. Each is led by a brother, and carries a symbol of the crucifixion ; one a reed, another a spear, a third a cup, a fourth a scourge, a fifth dice, etc. They walk two abreast, and every couple is preceded by candle-bearers.

Another image issues—a female, full seven feet in height. " Nossa Senhora" is whispered about. They have got her safe-

* In this and other processions living characters perform various parts in the drama.

ly into the street, and for a while she stands close to me, receiving the salutations of the soldiers. Her handsome face is bent down, her hands are folded on her bosom, from which project the handle and part of a sword-blade. A deep purple robe thrown over her shoulders reaches to her feet. The platform is richer than the other; its panels are gilt, cypress plants rise at the corners, and the green mound she stands on is set off with flowers. Silver lanterns are borne aloft; more tiny celestials skip down; two tall negroes, bare-legged, with bandboxes on their heads, now fall in, and become conspicuous members of the pageant.

A flourish of trumpets and a swarm of alb'd men come forth, followed by a rectangular canopy, beneath which are newly-shaven monks and priests—one carrying before him a vase containing the Host. As it draws near, the people kneel; the troops to a man are down, and dare not rise till it gets past them. More angels, brothers, and candles appear, and finally the troops wheel in and close the rear. The whole is now in motion. The band strikes up, and to the tune the soldiers march, and rock their bodies to and fro as if they were in liquor. The motion is one enforced upon them.

An hour later I met the procession in Dereita Street. The images were coming out of the church of San José. I was not aware that they were to visit it, or I would have witnessed the part assigned to Joseph. As it drew near, it was headed by a character, who had escaped my notice in the throng in Soap Street, enveloped in a dull brown gown, secured round his waist with a common rope; a hood, or cowl, concealed both head and face, openings being cut in it for the mouth and eyes. With folded arms and stooping gait he strode on, a very suspicious-looking fellow. He represents a Roman officer—a masked executioner. The monk (I am told he is one) performed the part well.

Twilight had now set in, and soon every wax torch would be kindled as by magic; but I was tired, and turned homeward, gratified at having witnessed a specimen, though a meagre one, of those ecclesiastico-histrionic entertainments which in dark ages won over heathens to the faith. From the beginning to the close, the soldiers, officers, and men sling their caps by their sides, and the numerous brotherhoods leave their hats at home. I counted fifty angels. Some carried censer boxes and some purple flowers. They are girls from six to eight years old, and the prettiest that can be procured. Their parents vie with one another in furnishing the richest dresses. Their faces are painted, and supplemental tresses added where wanting. Some are prepared by professional costumers. On their heads were crowns, coronets, plumes, wreaths, etc. One resembled a young Minerva, wearing a glistening helmet, a red boddice with blue skirts, scarlet boots, and crimson stockings. Some few were draped in white, and wholly free from tawdry. Their frocks, exceedingly short, are expanded by fine wire, and have quite an airy motion, such as is imparted by the same means to their wings and clouds. The latter are of colored gauze stretched over shapeless frames that spring from and return to the back part of the dress. In a word, these little misses are fitted for the parts they play in much the same way and with equal artistic skill as theatrical fairies.

The bearers of the images carry staves in manner of walking-sticks, each having a metallic fork at the top resembling the letter U. Whenever the procession stops, these are slipped under the bearing-poles, and thus relieve the bearers. Not till I observed this did I fairly comprehend the bier-scene in Don Quixote.

ANGELS.

CHAPTER XVIII.

All Fools' Day.—Streets flooded.—Breaking down Mountains.—Notices of Festivals.—Flying Visit to Francis Paula, St. Anne, Joaquim, St. Rita, Bom Jesus, and the Candelaria.—No Animal Oils burned in Churches.—Carmelite Procession with full-grown Images.—The Nimbus and its curious Origin.

April 1. "All fools' day" is kept up with some of the spirit of past times, but not comparable to the frolics of the old "feast of fools"—the parent institution; itself derived from a Roman, and more remotely from a Hindoo saturnalia.

Rain pouring down last night has cooled the air to 78°. After breakfast, indications of fine weather tempted mé out, but ere noon three several showers flooded the streets. Men and boys, with umbrellas, rode upright on negroes' shoulders, and in the rear of the Paula Church a horse was employed to transfer passengers across the street: to keep their legs out of the stream, they rested them on him in a kneeling posture.

It is worth a ducking to be abroad in such weather, if only to observe pedestrians run the gauntlet between balcony-spouts and roof-gutters! Shot at right and left from single and double tiers of copper guns pointed from window-sills, and when, to get out of their range by springing into the middle of the street, to be instantly driven back by douches from the roofs which none but hydropathic men can stand. When Rio was built the Pluvian god must have been architect in disguise, and contrived these liquid muskets to exercise his troops in gunnery. They vary as in old armories: some flaring at their mouths, like blunderbusses, scattering wide the shot; others are contracted, and project the missiles more compact and rifle-fashion.

A few years ago several houses at the base of Castle Hill were destroyed by the rain loosing an impending mass of the tenacious soil, which fell and buried them. I may as well mention here a simple and philosophical mode of breaking down mountains of similar material in some of the mining districts of Brazil. Wells are dug into them, and, during the rainy season, filled with water by means of gutters. By this device the hydrostatic pressure of the liquid columns forces off masses from the faces of mountains which would require hundreds of men for months to accomplish with the mattock and shovel.

2*d*. The season for ecclesiastical performances has set in in earnest. The papers are charged with advertisements; *e. g.* : The Paula committee inform the public that the anniversary of their saint will be celebrated this evening. Another notice runs thus: "On Friday of Triumph, April 3, will be celebrated, with all pomp and decency, the festival of our Lady of Griefs before her miraculous image, which the holy father, Pope Pius VI., consecrated, and which is preserved and venerated in the Church of the Candelaria. . . . . On the day of the feast, the brethren who serve the holy image and implore its aid [implorar o seu auxilio] will find the books at the entrance of the church." The Bom Jesus committee offer the following rich bill at their establishment: "The solemnity of our Lady of Pains on the 3d instant, procession of Palms on the 5th, a procession on the 9th, the burial of God on the 10th, allelulia and blessing the great paschal candle on the 11th, and on the 12th the most religious and devout act of the coronation of Our Lady."

A gloomy, threatening day; I did not care to repeat the splashing travels of yesterday, but the rain held off, and the Paula fête was celebrated with much eclat. Illumined with over a thousand waxen lights, and fitted up with new silk and damask tapestry, the saint's residence was crowded. In his best robes he stood forth, and complacently received the compliments of his visitors. Like the reverence paid to the Pope, multitudes kissed his feet. A sermon was delivered detailing the miracles he wrought and still works. After sunset the front of his house was made luminous with lamps, while serpents, crackers, rockets, and other pyrotechnics proclaimed to earth and heaven the rejoicings at the saint's soirée.

3*d*. There has been much talk and no little feeling manifested about the vicar of St. Anne's parish having brought some sacred bones from Rome, and waiting the emperor's return to have their advent into the New World duly honored. We may as well make his church one of the objects of this day's visit. In going down the Cattete, a gang of freshly-imported slaves came along: their tribal marks, cut in their cheeks, reminded one of scores of the knife in the crisped skin of roasted pork. They stared at a smart young fellow bearing a baril of water jauntily inclined on his head, and twanging the keys of his marimba to a waltzing tune. A little farther, and a meagre old man in an alb leans over a hatch, waiting to know whether any indweller wishes to secure the friendship of Antonio dos Pobres by adding a few vintems to his dish.

But here is the Campo and the little village-looking temple of St. Anne. The floor is sanded, and the pulpit, like a swallow's nest, projects from the wall. The place has a poor, worn-out appearance, according with an unusual number of begging saints painted on alms-boxes. One I can not make out—a stout figure in a tunic and kilt, or short petticoat, and plaided stockings —apparently a Celtic chieftain. The five shrines are all concealed. The "covering of the saints" began on the 29th ultimo, and ends on the 11th instant. In a side passage are very old-looking votive tablets, and only one cereous offering. The passage opens into a small cemetery. Into the few empty niches swallows are flying and twittering as if they were the souls of the departed occupants asking where their bodies are.

A short distance from this house of "God's grandmother" is that of her husband, Joaquim, who is not honored with the title of "grandfather," but simply the "father of Our Lady." His church is surmounted with two chanticleers. Such favorites were these symbols of holy vigilance in the Middle Ages that the clergy called themselves "the Cocks of the Almighty."

The doors being closed, I passed on to the small triangular largo of Santa Rita, with its octagonal fount and small church. As the bells kept ringing a general welcome, I pushed the crimson screen aside and was in another world—one where a mellow artificial light rivaled the sun, and where people were as busy as without. On a pinnacle formed of alternate rows of flowers and lights the lady stood and smiled on the mortals at her feet; among them were slaves of both sexes, and all apparently striving to catch her eye. The place was crowded. A committee had not a moment's breathing-time from taking dues and making change for her little paper portraits. Negro assistants were running to and fro among ladders, planks, and paint-pots, as if the doors had been thrown prematurely open. No priest was present, nor is any required when the festival is once opened. It was Santa Rita to whom was given the power "to make impossible things possible."

In the "Bom Jesus" the altar was the basis of one grand bouquet that reached the ceiling, and as the feast here was in honor of " the Lady of Pains," her image was unveiled. Exquisitely carved and draped, she captivated all eyes. Rows of old and young ladies were seated on the floor gazing at her. In an adjoining apartment, white and black workmen were seen preparing machinery for new attractions. I can see little difference between these and theatrical entertainments. The managers of both are applicants for public favor on the express ground of the " brilliancy and splendor" of their spectacles. A contest in the papers is going on between those of the buskin and the scapulary. The latter insist that the former shall not interfere with them during Holy Week, and they ask the authorities to prohibit a masked ball just announced.

We have time before dinner to visit the Candelaria, and see the famous image which Pope Pius blessed. Here is the church, facing a narrow lane in the mercantile part of the city. Slaves are generally found sleeping on the steps, as some are now, and noisy coffee-carriers waiting to be employed. A committee sit at a table, with a silver dish piled up with money received for portraits of the Lady of Griefs, most grievously cut in wood or copper. This temple, for chasteness and richness of decoration, eclipses every other. No smutched-faced saint in shabby apparel resides here. The side altars are laden with flowers and flaming tapers, but the chief one surpasses all. A double row of seven-feet candlesticks, of classical beauty, form a passage to it, and terminate at a couple of porcelain vases four feet high, holding bouquets of equal altitude. The front of the altar is a plate of embossed silver, fourteen feet by five, wrought into five equal panels with gold borders and rosettes. There is no sham in this plate. It is used only on great occasions.

Upon the altar candlesticks and vases of flowers alternate, and from it rises a tapered tower some thirty feet high, composed of series of vases, bouquets, and candles. Upon this pedestal the miraculous lady stands. She is of the natural size, and superbly dressed. After gazing a while, I imagined she inclined her head and answered my salutations with a smile, and thus I again perceived how such miracles have arisen, and how easy it is for certain souls to be favored with them. Not less than a thousand perfumed tapers were burning, amid vases holding flowers sufficient for a state floral exhibition. The effect was really enchanting.

There is something pleasing in the idea which excludes animal substances from materials for illuminating churches—that suffering and death may not be elements in the worship of the Author of mercy and life. Hence neither whale, sperm, nor lard oils must be introduced into lamps, nor tallow into candles. Next to olive, cocoa oil is deemed the best: it gives out in burning an agreeable odor. Palm oil is also used. None but bees' and vegetable wax must be used for candles, the former because it is not obtained by killing its producers. It is also deemed improper for crucifixes, amulets, ex votos, praying-beads, etc., to be of bone or ivory.

As the procession of the Carmelites to-day will equal any thing of the kind during the rest of my stay in Rio, I was in Dereita Street by 4 P.M. The balconies were filled by ladies in full dress, and the side-walks occupied by waiting spectators. A finer evening could not have been selected for the spectacle. Soldiers fell into ranks, the crowd thickened, and soon the first image of the series was seen emerging from the Carmo Temple. The brotherhood extended from the church, some three hundred feet, to where I stood. In their uniform of cream-colored albs, and armed with waxen staffs, they presented a fine sample of the Church's troops. Here and there one hurried to and fro, giving orders, and wielding his candle as a marshal's baton. Others clutched winged cherubs by the hand, and dragged them onward, as if they had just captured or brought them down with their truncheons to ornament the fête.

The particulars were briefly these: Infantry troops formed two walls between which the procession was to pass. It was headed by horse soldiers with drawn swords, three abreast; then a banner, inscribed S. P. Q. R.; next, brothers and candles; a crimson bag on a silver pole, with a mourning candle on either hand, the wax being painted with black spiral stripes. Brothers and candles; three angels abreast—the middle one, with a banner, personated St. Michael the Archangel. She wore a shining helmet, a silver breast-plate, nankeen pantalettes, and scarlet boots. Her wings were spotted prettily, and the cloud behind her was bordered with (paper) lace. Her arms were naked. I wished her mamma had kept her large ear-rings, bracelets, finger-rings, and necklace at home.

1. As the first image now was drawing near, the soldiers fixed bayonets and shouldered muskets to do it honor. It represented *The Passion*. A large statue of Christ in a kneeling posture, with the hands clasped as in prayer. Drops of blood rolled down the pallid cheeks. An angel, between three and four feet high, stoops and presents the cup. Three silver lanterns were borne on each side, and a file of soldiers, with drawn swords, attends.

2. A long line of brothers follow, who are followed by the second stage, on which stands *Christ before Pilate*, pale, emaciated, and submissive.

Brothers and angels three abreast.

3. *Christ scourged.* This image is naked, except a fillet round the loins. It is tied by ropes to a pillar, and the face, breast, back, thighs, arms, and legs are painted streaming with gore—vividly horrible.

Crowd of brothers and angels.

4. *Christ mocked.* Seated, a reed in his hand, and a short purple robe thrown over his lacerated shoulders. He is bruised and bleeding all over.

Brothers and angels.

5. On this stage Christ appears standing, and holds a stalk of Indian-corn or sugar-cane in one hand. A similar spare robe to the last covers a small part of the naked body. (The incident represented I did not perceive; perhaps the scene *before Herod* is intended.)

Brothers and angels.

6. *Bearing the Cross.* The figure is similar to, or the same as the one noticed in the procession of 27th ult. Great numbers of devout Brazilians, and the blacks generally, knelt as it passed them. The attending angels were quite numerous. Of

the symbols, one had the sponge of vinegar on a rod, another the spear that pierced him.

7. *Christ on the Cross.* The top of the latter is, I should think, nearly twenty feet from the ground. The shaft rises from a greeen hillock on the stage, and springs considerably. As it drew nigh, the cause of this was apparent. The cross is of plank, and the weight of the image causes it to bend to and fro, for it has no support except at the foot. I surmised that the large image might be of papier-maché, but I subsequently learned that it is of hard, heavy wood, and nearly 200 years old. A crimson stream flowing from the wound in the side contrasted strongly with the chalk-like hue of the face and body.

Brothers and angels followed, and behind the latter two negroes with boxes of bon-bons, to refresh them during pauses in the procession.

8. The managers under a long canopy. Of the sea of heads in sight, theirs only are covered (by skull-caps, rochets, and mitres), besides being screened by the golden drapery over them. Every spectator in front falls at their feet, not excepting the soldiers. Among the young smirking monks is my confessor friend of the Lapa. They are passed, and now the drums, bugles, and French horns burst forth and do their best. The air is not Yankee Doodle, but it is quite as lively. The foot-soldiers wheel in, a guard of honor to the fathers, and sway their bodies as in ecstasy. Finally, the national banner brings up the rear, and closes the Pomp.

I afterward met it in Quitanda Street, through whose entire length people were waiting. As the image bearing the cross came up, many knelt and most stooped, but some young fellows got into a squabble and fight with three or four blacks for looking over their shoulders.

The images rather exceeded the natural stature. As works of art they are pretty good, and some are very good. At the ordinary distance as seen by spectators, their expression is all that carving and colors can impart. But there is no avoiding a painful feeling induced by their stiff, unnatural gaits—now pitched forward, and anon inclined backward.

It was here I first saw what is supposed to have been the

original figure and position of the Nimbus, viz., a flat, circular plate, notched all round like a circular saw, and suspended horizontally a short distance above the head of each image. Of remote devices, none is more singular in its origin and change of purposes than this.

Roman emperors assumed the nimbus as a mark of divinity, and under this respectable patronage it passed, like other pagan customs, into the Church. Among Pompeian paintings illustrating scenes in Homer is one of Ulysses and Circe. The glory over the head of the sorceress represents a portion of a vertical disc or ring, but nothing like rays or pencils of light appear. Lucian refers to the latter in his Timon: "A golden statue of the hero was ordered to be put up in the Acropolis, with a thunderbolt in his right hand, and 'rays on his head.'" But the origin of the nimbus is the most curious trait about it; and, strange to say, on this point enlightened Romanists coincide with archæologists. In a late number of The Tablet, the organ of the English Catholics, is a paper on "The Meaning of the Nimbus." A century ago the author would hardly have escaped expiring in a halo of flame.

"It appears to me," he observes, "that in our zeal for symbolism and mystical meanings, we are peculiarly apt to overlook the origin of certain details and usages which never had any mystical or conventional sense attached to them until centuries after their adoption in the Christian Church, and not even then necessarily or invariably. This observation is illustrated in a remarkable manner by the history of the 'nimbus' or 'glory' which is universally seen in medieval paintings of saints; for this is, in reality, one of the customs which was perpetuated from pagan antiquity, and consecrated by its applications to the purposes of the Church.

"It is nothing new to state that the nimbus was in its origin a metallic disc of copper or silver, placed upon and around the heads of those statues which stood in the open air, in order to prevent birds from alighting on them and defiling their faces with dirt. This custom is first mentioned in a passage of Aristophanes, written more than four centuries before Christ. The chorus of birds, addressing the judges of the rival dramas, then present in the theatre, thus speaks: 'If you do not decide in our favor, forthwith make yourselves *plates of copper, like statues;* for otherwise every one of you who has not a *disc* round [upon?] his head shall be punished by us birds, being dirtied with our dung whenever he has a clean white garment on him.'

.... In process of time, the original use, as applied to statuary, was forgotten, and the nimbus was believed, and perhaps conventionally intended, to represent rays of light emanating from a divine or saintly countenance; and hence, by a farther development, a frequent and ecstatic contemplation of these pictures gave rise to a belief (recorded in many legends) that a lambent light was actually seen to play around the heads and visages of living and departed saints. I hope that I am not offending against orthodoxy in maintaining that even this supernatural light was of pagan invention, as Virgil's *Lambere flamma caput* will show.

"The engrailed border which the nimbus so frequently exhibits, especially in stained glass, is undoubtedly borrowed from the patterns engraved on the metal laminæ, and is a curious instance of the detention of a conventional detail for many centuries after its real meaning had been lost.

"The early school of Italian painters changed the position of the nimbus from vertical to oblique; and sometimes the nimbus is very awkwardly placed nearly flat, like a trencher, or even a straw hat, on the crown of the head. The latest debasement was to paint a thin wiry line of light around the brows, by which all assimilation to the form of the original metallic disc was lost."

This writer justly remarks that the nimbus ought not to be regarded as an essential mark nor a certain indication of a saintly effigy. It has, in fact, been applied, in Christian as well as in heathen times, to characters of very doubtful morality. Even the Devil himself has been portrayed with it. The horizontal position of the plate here denounced was certainly the original and most effective one. How a vertical disc on the head of a statue could prevent birds from defiling the latter is impossible to imagine. It would foster the evil that was sought to be avoided. Placed flat on the crown, or supported a short distance above, and projecting sufficiently, it would perfectly shield the head, face, shoulders, etc., from pollution. Cases doubtless often occurred where a position more or less oblique was admissible. Thus, when contemplated from certain points of view, the edges only of the plates would be visible; hence probably arose the *wiry line* around the brows in paintings. There is reason to conclude that the under sides of these plates were highly polished and otherwise ornamented, and frequently the names of the persons represented engraved upon them; and farther, that the diversity of forms, triangular, polygonal, radiated, etc., arose from efforts to guard protruding portions of the figure and drapery without an unseemly and unnecessary enlargement of every part of the primitive circular disc. (For farther information on this curious subject, see Hope's Historical Essay on Architecture, and the first volume of the Archæological Journal.)

CHAPTER XIX.

Palm Sunday: Ceremonies and Customs.—Eunuch Singers.—Specimens of Ecclesiastical Advertisements.—Benedictine Chapel.—Dark Wednesday.—A Merçëeiro.—Juno Lucina of Rio.—Lady of Civilities.—Holy Thursday.—Matracas.—Silver Plate in the Carmo Church.—Kissing a dead Christ in the Candelaria.—Appearance of the Interior.—Kissing the Floor and Steps in the Bom Jesus.—Plate in the Paula.—Mine-finders.

April 5. Palm Sunday was never ushered in by a more inspiring morning. Not a patch of curtain hides an object on earth or heaven. Nature has thrown aside her shuttle, and refused to weave a single yard of floating gauze. Every mountain rears its sides and crests in brightness, and there is a bracing, balmy influence in the atmosphere that makes the soul tingle with pleasure. At breakfast, Doña B——, Miss C——, and old Senhora P—— came in from confession, and I could not but again admire the system by which impressible natures are relieved by empiric formulas from present anxieties and future fears. They laughed and chatted with such a juvenile lightness that St. Anthony himself might have joined them in a coranto.

I walked out to observe the customs of the day. The streets were alive with peddlers, and tradesmen as busy in their shops as yesterday. Overtook a lady on her way to church, accompanied by a slave in livery, with a tall, tufted stem of palm, adorned with ribbons, in either hand. Kindred offerings were going up Castle Hill to the Capuchins. A gorgeous bouquet, large as a bushel measure, was beautifully arranged around the upper end of a straight palm stem. At either side, on separate stems, and borne by separate slaves, were two diamond-shaped fields of velvet green, with nosegays in the centres, and flowers and ribbons at the angles—the offerings of three young ladies who preceded them.

In Rua da Gloria strange sounds came from an alley, as if a host of innocents were being murdered. On nearing the Lapa Church, I first saw what produced them. Here were two negroes making, and a negra selling palm trumpets—pretty toys, that vary in length from eight to eighteen inches; some plain and straight, others decorated and curved like the rams' horns of the tabernacle. They are made by coiling palm-leaf ribbons upon themselves. Their music is surprisingly imitative of agitated geese and goslings, and of sucking-pigs in search of lost mothers.

I peeped into the Lapa vestry, where four monks sat at a table amid piles of palm branches, which they aspersed with holy water. One gentleman counted down a dozen vintems and received six leaves in exchange. Both sexes crowded round the merchants and kept them busy. "Blessed" palms are reputed "good for keeping demons out of dwellings."

Soldiers at the door of the Imperial Chapel induced me to step in. Two rows of halberdiers formed a passage along the middle of the floor, and presently the vestry door (near the street) was opened, and out came the bishop and a dozen padres, one bearing his train, and swept up to the altar, where they took their turns at courtesying and other strange posture-making. They finish, and a chant of females breaks forth; so any stranger would have thought who was not in a position to see them, and so I thought till I got a view of them. They were Italian eunuchs—presents from Mother Church at Rome to her Brazilian daughter.

The bishop sprinkled and prayed over bundles of plain and ornamental palms; then he and a score of priests, each with a branch in hand, came, in slow procession, to the door, and passed out. Taking a short turn on the platform in front, they returned to the door, which had in the mean time been closed, and, knocking, were readmitted, when they passed up to the altar chanting appropriate verses. Their re-entry symbolizes the triumphant entrance of Jesus into Jerusalem. The ceremony is the same in all the churches. When the emperor is present, he goes out with the bishop and raps for readmission. The affair was rather flat, and the attendance meagre. A low bench was prepared for twelve poor men to sit on while the bishop washes their feet. The operation took place while I was next door in the Carmo temple, whose interior might have been taken for a London or Paris ball-room. Tall boards, with angels painted on them, were fitted up at the entrance, precisely like the side-scenes in theatres. It is an old custom to show up at this festival all the sacred plate, and hence the front of the long counter-looking altar was covered with panel-work of embossed silver; tripod candelabra alternated with silver-gilt vases, and eight massive lamps of the same metal were pendent from the ceiling. The Lady of Carmo shone in a blaze of silver.

I had been advised to look into the Benedictine monastery, but the ceremonies were over and the congregation coming down the hill as I began to climb it—a crowd of handsome, smiling, black-eyed ladies and their children, and such a display of chains, frontlets, ear and finger rings as I have seldom seen. Having got so far, I went up. By closely observing the chapel walls, angels are perceived peeping out of the forest of old gilt scroll-work. This elaborate carving is dated "1694." The cherubs are in legions, from ten to twelve inches in height, in every imaginable position, flesh-colored, and four fifths in relief —probably of Dutch origin, for every one has the anasarca in his body and the elephantiasis in his limbs.

Passing into the interior area, noticed on my first visit, there was a singular sight, considering the day and place. Besides friars and other lookers on, some fifty carpenters, designers, carvers, painters, and machinists were busy among lumber, ladders, benches, canvas, and paint-pots. A negro, with chalk and compasses, was making fancy ornaments, another sawing out similar ones. Here were skeleton columns, and there men, with brushes three feet long, coloring scrolls and flowers upon canvas stretched on the ground—stage-scenery in every stage of progress.

Surely these monks might be mistaken for venerators of an English saint whose image is in Stratford Church.

6*th*. Rain from morn to night—no going out. None but ecclesiastical spectacles are sanctioned this week. Marriages are not allowed; balls and kindred entertainments are forbidden; table delicacies suppressed, and macerated saints invoked: hence, if this and following chapters are heavy, the reader may suppose it would have been improper to make them *alegré*.

Church advertisements abound. " The brotherhood, and all who venerate the Disaffronted Image, are informed that the Church of the Cross will be open on Holy Thursday from sunset to midnight." " The brotherhood of our Lady of Lampadoza will celebrate the Passion on Friday, and the coronation of Our Lady on Saturday."

" In the Church of St. Sebastian, Holy Week will be celebrated with all the rites prescribed by Holy Mother Church. On Holy Friday will be a devout exercise at noon, celebrated in this city for the first time. . . This sublime exercise, so becoming the Christian, has merited the attention of all, especially that of the holy pontiff, Pius VII., who granted a plenary indulgence to the faithful that confess on Holy Thursday, take the communion, and practice this holy exercise according to the intentions of the holy father. The faithful must not neglect to profit by this treasure of heaven that is offered with such liberality," etc.

The last is a specimen of Capuchin announcements. Much feeling exists in the native clergy against the order, but they are, notwithstanding, operating successfully in town and country, chiefly, it is said, by the novelties they have brought over. A couple of their images have, to my knowledge, got, within a few weeks, necklaces of votive heads, feet, necks, hearts, etc.— proofs of miraculous cures just wrought by them. It is a common remark that " three things are making the women mad— masked balls, polka, and the Capuchins."

8*th*. Dark Wednesday, when lights are extinguished in the churches, and mischievous youngsters play tricks with female worshipers. In the evening I scaled·the Benedictine Hill after tacking to and fro, without which none but agile goats or other natural climbers can get up. The ceremonies had just begun. For an hour the organ played and the monks behind it chanted. The chapel was gloomily lit up by a theologic candelabrum peculiar to the day. It consisted of a strip of bar iron bent into a large equilateral triangle, the interior filled with open scrollwork. The base was supported on a pedestal or stand, and on each of the two converging sides were seven sockets, and one at the apex. In these were fifteen candles, forming a pyramidal light. At length one of the lowest was put out, then, in a little while, the one opposite to it, and so on till the whole were extinguished except the top one; finally it shared the fate of those below it, and the place was in utter darkness. There was, of course, an increase of bustling and tittering; but scarcely a minute elapsed before a few lights were kindled.

The affair went off quieter than I expected, but on coming out a band struck up whose music was enough to awaken the seven sleepers and throw a dozen Mozarts into apoplexy. The rattling, deafening clatter of matracas, mingled with the squealing of palm bugles, might have defied any Sus concert in Kentucky. Thus ended Dark Wednesday.

This putting out of lights in churches — an old medieval practice—is in imitation of the sun being darkened at the Crucifixion.

The Ajuda chapel door being open as I passed this morning, I stepped in for a moment. No one present except a lad in a roundabout jacket, and a young man of very stunted growth, with large head, coarse, dark features, and splay feet, reminding one of Bertholde the Lombard. Dressed as a priest in a russet surplice, he was rehearsing at one of the side shrines. He said nothing — all was pantomimic. He bowed, courtesied, moved back, stepped forward, and mixed quite a number of other motions with these. Now he seemed to read, anon pushed the book aside, turned to the lad behind him and received something out of a cloth—a cup. He raises it, sets it down, wipes it with a napkin, folds and places the latter on it, elevates it again, brings it down, steps back and courtesies to it, etc.

Poor fellow! He is, I am told, a *merçeeiro* (which the dictionaries tell us means "a person hired to say prayers for the souls of the dead"), and was earning a couple of patacas by going through a mass for a soul lately departed, whose friends had no more to give. He had got permission to perform it here, had borrowed the requisite apparatus, and picked up the lad to render the necessary assistance. His tonsure and official drapery heightened rather than diminished the oddness of his appearance. The alb had surely been loaned him or bought at second-hand, being half worn out, and any thing but a fit, while the buckles on his shoes might have served Goliah, had they been in fashion in King David's time.

I had supposed such persons were excluded from serving at altars. To say the least, the prohibition would be politic where so much dumb show is executed, and by performers with their backs to spectators—an undesirable frontage to have every the minutest motion and posture scanned. Public worship addressed to the sight must, like less reverent pantomime, be judged of by the eye.

On reaching the end of the street (Ajuda), an old red cloth hanging in the doorway of the *Lady do Parto* induced me to step in. With little, except being perceptibly enceinte, to distinguish her from other Pão Senhoras, she is the Juno Lucina of Rio, to whom applications and acknowledgments are made, and precisely such as were addressed to her pagan prototype. Her apartments consist of this small and dark room, with no ornaments but its images; the walls are bare, and the floor level with the narrow and dirty street. Here are but two other images—both females. One, tall and stout, is attended by two full-grown monks (de pão) in white gowns. The other is Nossa Senhora das Mercês. "Mercê is a term of civility: it means courtesy, favor, kindness." The lady personifies one or more of these. Brazilians are remarkably ceremonious, having great devotion, as the expression is, to "Our Lady of Civilities."

Some twenty ladies were within, apparently waiting for a confessor.

9th, Holy Thursday. Matracas have been named; they are instruments which probably date from as remote times as any thing employed in the Church, and, as such, are worth noticing.

They are never used but during Passion Week. For several days I have met boys with them, and this morning a negro sent out by the Candelaria sexton came along announcing the parish festival with one. I took the opportunity to examine this venerable sacerdotal rattle. Here it is, and the genius playing on

it—a piece of hard board, twelve inches long and six wide, with an oblong opening at the upper end for the fingers that grasp it, and a vertical clapper of bronze jointed in the middle. It is carried suspended by the right hand, and by twisting and turning it to and fro, the knocker hits the board at every movement. Some have a knocker at each side, by which the number of blows and amount of clattering are doubled.

Others are made wholly of wood. I met a couple of these

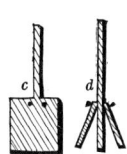

to-day. A piece of rose-wood board, three inches square, with a handle, as at c. Two flapping pieces nearly the size of the blade are attached loosely by a cord, as at the cross section, d. They make a loud, snapping noise.

In the Middle Ages bells were not rung during Passion Week, because the apostles deserted Christ.

The Candelaria being within a stone's throw, I found it thronged. The front of the altar, beneath the shrine of Our Lady, was removed, exposing a "dead Christ" extended within. As I got up, a gentleman who had been adoring it arose and drew back; a negro girl then falls on her hands and knees, creeps to the exposed hand and kisses it, showing the muddied soles of her bare feet to every eye. She rises, drops a vintem into a mammoth salver, courtesies, and retires. Two white lads, ragged and dirty as clam-boys, speak a few words to each other, cross themselves, fall on their knees, and creep forward together; one waits till the other salutes the hand, and then wriggles himself forward and takes his turn: each drops in a vintem. Next comes a lady, with a female slave behind her; drops on her knees, and for half a minute prays and crosses herself, rises, drops some vintems, and goes away. She won't kiss the hand on which so many black mouths have been already rubbed, and she is right, for I've seen enough diseases on black faces here to justify her.

I was about to leave, when a feeble and purblind negra crept forward to the *feet;* putting in her head, she pressed her lips to them a dozen times. Then turning to the hand, she fondled it, kissed it, laid her left cheek on it, then her right one; then drew both sides of her face over it, and again rested them on the open palm. She seemed unwillingly to give place to others waiting. I think some one gave her a hint, for she reluctantly rose, put a copper acknowledgment in the salver, courtesied three times down to the floor, and went her way. She was succeeded while I remained by a score of devotees of both sexes, of whom half were whites. On mentioning her case to a devout lady, I was told she most likely had some troublesome disease in her face, which she, in common with thousands, believed would be expelled by placing it in contact with the Holy Image.

Formerly no white person performed this act of devotion without first taking off their shoes. This is not now required, though some practice it. The great majority, however, are barefooted worshipers, viz., slaves.

The train of serious thought which the performance might induce is dissipated by the chattering and bustling about of alb'd brethren, arranging candles and flowers at one place, giving instructions to decorating artists at another. But, however annoying this might be to some people, worshipers are not troubled by it here. I stood for some time beside a man on his knees: every now and then he looked about—his eyes now on the sacristan, and now turned behind to watch some one that swept past him; then taking a general gaze, and finding nothing particular to see, he hawked, spat on the floor, and began again to finger his beads. A gray-headed slave, with a large basket on his head, came within the door, made a leg to the altar, scooped up almost a gill of holy water and discharged it on his head; again making a cup of his hand, he poured an equal quantity on the contents of the basket, stood a moment, and gave his vegetables a second dash.

But night is the best time to witness Church festivals. I called in here this evening, and after counting seven hundred waxen lights about the altar, gave up the task. There were ten or eleven hundred burning in the place, all in costly candlesticks. Whites and blacks thronged about the prone image: three ladies knelt and kissed the wooden hand immediately after it had been touched by negro lips.

The enterprising brethren of "Bom Jesus" hold their reunion not far off. We may as well look in. Here's the place. Those half dozen mustached, bare-headed soldiers parading before the door, handling and puffing cigars, might be taken for old matchlock heroes blowing their lints preparatory to firing off their pieces. But let's push by the crimson screen and enter. Well! this would be a sight if one had not just seen greater. The tapestry is showy, but much worn; the flowers, in vases, are pretty and in plenty, but the candlesticks are wood, and the best ones gone—no, not all; for at the railing gate stand two that might be compared with the richest in the Candelaria or Carmo. They are alb'd brothers holding five-foot torches, reminding one of similar candelabra in the halls of feudal barons.

Here was more bowing, kneeling, courtesying, kissing, and leg-making going on than in the Candelaria, though no image is placed within reach of the worshipers. For want of one, they kissed the floor, steps, carpeting, and penny pictures on the walls. A gentleman (I was told he was a dry-goods' merchant) rose from his knees near me, went directly to the right wall, and put his mouth to something on it; next, crossed himself, went to the railing, then knelt and kissed the step (not the altar-step, but one where the nave is separated from the choir or chancel); getting up, he made a leg and crossed over to the opposite wall, and kissed something there, four or five feet above the floor; and yonder he is, again standing on his toes, his neck stretched to the uttermost, trying to reach a higher object with his lips. It was not till after three trials that he succeeded and withdrew. The first object of his devotion was an engraving of the Virgin, the oldest and coarsest thing of the kind I have yet seen. A piece of glass was before it, so that he kissed it and not the picture. The frame, print, and glass could not have cost five cents. The second object was a saint on an alms-box, and the third a framed print similar to the first in style and finish.

Next, two negroes drew up through the middle of the audience and kissed the floor, then the step. Three white men and one woman followed them. The filthy condition of the soles of the negroes contrasted strangely with a pair of new pumps a dandy of a man turned up a little way from them. At one time five men and two women were before me with their mouths on the floor. Not feeling much edified by these groveling scenes, I turned toward the Paula. The steps in front swarmed with negras, selling fruit and doces to exhausted worshipers. The altar was gorgeous as that of the Carmo; but the greatest novelty was the contents of two silversmiths'-shops, piled on tables at each side of the altar, and guarded by musketeers. Here were trays, ewers, basins, pitchers, and other things, besides some large caldron-looking vessels whose use was not apparent. Of trays alone I counted over forty, most of which were not less than three feet long, and of proportional width. What this meant I could not imagine, not dreaming that the whole could belong to one church, but it was even so. The Paula brotherhood is very wealthy, and surpasses others in this branch of devotion.

After visiting two or three smaller temples without observing any thing special, I turned home. Near the door of the Lapa the monks had got a piano, on which a lay professor was playing to the chanting of two young friars.

According to the old philosophy, children born between noon to-day and twelve o'clock to-morrow will be natural mine-finders, endowed with the faculty of seeing seven yards through solid earth.

All holy wafers and water are used up to-day; none must be left over till to-morrow.

CHAPTER XX.

Good Friday.—Capuchins preaching.—Burial of God.—Dresses and Jewels of the Angels.—Allelulia Saturday.—Blessing Fire and Water.—Paschal Candle.—Killing Judas.—Church Machinery.—Cinerary Urns and Commemoration of the Dead.—Symbols carried by Angels.—Boy Monk.—Little Prospect of Protestant Missions succeeding in Brazil.—Mary of Nazareth.

April 10, *Good Friday.* The morning light at six o'clock is not sufficient to read by, and soon after that hour in the evening darkness sets in.

Four great processions are announced for to-day, if the weather prove favorable. At 10 A.M. rain came down heavily; at 1 P.M. it ceased.

I strolled up Castle Hill to witness some new performances announced by the Capuchins. Seventy or eighty persons, mostly women and children, were waiting for the service to begin. Suddenly the profound silence was broken by a loud hammering that knocked all meditation on the head—carpenters fitting up a scaffold for musicians, six of whom soon came in, with a bass-viol, two violins, a couple of flutes, and a clarionet. One of the preachers emerged from the vestry. Bless me! I exclaimed to myself, how like the pictures of his class I have seen! There is something unpleasant in his appearance, independent of a coarseness that of itself is any thing but agreeable. A shaven crown, a reddish peaked and matted beard, uncovered neck and exposed sternum, bare legs, and feet pushed into slip-shod wooden slippers, large and hairy hands, and his only garment a brown serge gown, tied round his middle with a cord, from which hangs a string of beads. Then there is the ugly hood or cowl flapping behind, turned back like the hinged cover of a coffee-pot or tankard.

The music struck up, and two monks began a chant, during which the people knelt, and the friar just described got into a box pulpit, which, like all pulpits here, is so placed that the speaker does not lose sight of the images, or turn his back to them or the altar. As the chanting ceased he rose to speak, and every now and then broke into long wailing ejaculations of "*Madonna!*" "*Nossa Senhora!*" "*Sangue!*" "*Mizericordia!*" "*Feridas!*" etc.; turning occasionally and pointing to the images. As he warmed, his gesticulations became energetic. He leaned over the edge of the box till his wide-spread hands nearly touched the shoulders of devotees below him; then stepping back, he threw his head, his eyes, and, to the utmost, his arms, up to the ceiling—the very action of a nurse lifting an infant from the floor, and holding it at arms' length above her. There was one novelty in his manner which struck me rather favorably. As he finished each telling passage, he sunk, and not ungracefully, into his seat, where he remained half, and sometimes a whole minute, till fresh ideas rose in him. He rarely spoke five minutes without sitting down; occasionally he gave out a sentence in that position, with one hand on the edge of the pulpit, and the other applying a handkerchief to his perspiring face; but the instant a new view of the subject, or a touching thought occurred, he started up, and put it into glowing language, *i. e.*, if one might judge by his excitement. I suppose his hearers were affected, though they gave no visible sign of being so. Possibly the indifferent Portuguese in which these Italian apostles are said to deliver themselves diminishes the effect of their elocution. He had no book nor notes about him.

I began to tire, and thought of leaving, but another friar stepped into the speaking-box, older and stouter than his predecessor, with a darker beard and fairer skin. His action was confined chiefly to his head, combined with a singular power of drawing down his neck into his body, and suddenly pushing it up again. Seated or standing, his head rose with his ideas and his voice— now buried beneath his cowl, now half a foot above it, and still rising.

A slight rain was falling, which I preferred encountering to remaining longer. As I came in sight of Dereita Street, the sound of music came up, and shortly after appeared, some two hundred feet below, the Mizericordia Procession of the Burial. I reached the Hospital in time to witness its order and arrival. The unpleasant weather had reduced the number of spectators. The performers were drabbled, and seemed anxious to get indoors.

LIFE IN BRAZIL.

First came a man with a powerful matraca; then a young monk in a white hood and tippet, both in one: the latter went all round him, and reached to his elbows; the former was bound round his head with a new hempen rope. He carried before him a black wooden cross, over the transverse bar of which a white cloth was thrown in the form of the letter M, to signify death—*Morte*. The cloth is supposed to be the one in which the body of Christ was enveloped by Joseph of Arimathea. A number of monks, draped like the cross-bearer, follow. Then came brothers in white gowns, bearing candles; and after them *angels*, with wings and a colored gauze cloud attached by wire to the shoulders of each. Next three women (or men disguised as such), representing "the three Marys." They were concealed in gowns and hoods, with their faces bent toward the ground, and had a mournful appearance. A large ring of silver was attached to the head of each, to represent a halo.

The bier, more like a French bedstead, came next. On a mattress lay a "dead Christ"—one of those exposed in churches. The whole was borne by four monks on two staves, whose ends rested on their shoulders. Each carried a pronged stick to support the load, at intervals, when all stand to hear an angel-chant. They wore hoods, and tippets, and hempen cords by way of ribbons.

More angels, led by brothers, came next, followed by the tallest of their number, a girl of fourteen, who mounted a pair of steps, and, chanting, opened a white cloth, the handkerchief of Veronica, whom she represented. She performed the part exceedingly well, notwithstanding the thick drizzling rain. Stepping down, the brother took up the steps, and all went forward again. Now came brothers, monks, and candles; angels, monks,

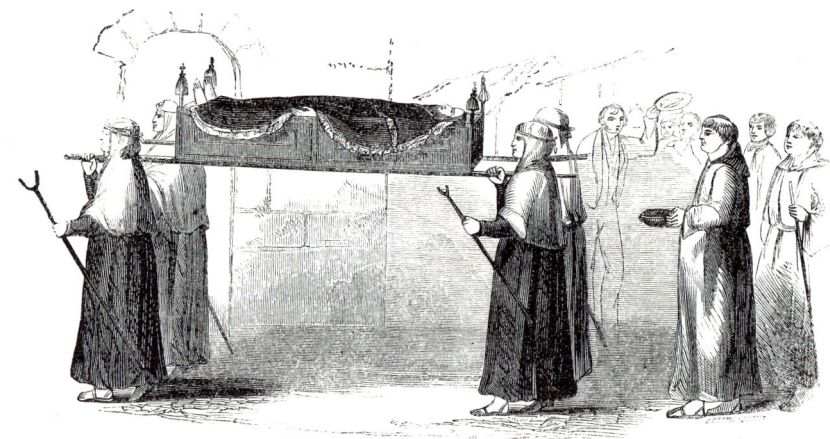

and brothers; and then "Nossa Senhora," erect, large as life, in purple dress, silver rays on her forehead, and standing on a stage richly paneled, and set off with cypress, but no flowers. Borne, as the bier was, on men's shoulders, she might be seen over the heads of the people a mile off.

The band of music, more brothers in white albs, and bearing candles, came next, and last of all the soldiery. In the hurry to get out of the rain, Nossa Senhora was nearly knocked off her base. Her head came slap against the door-jamb, in consequence of the bearers on one side not lowering her from their shoulders in concert with their comrades. After the doors were closed, the leader once more worked his matraca, whose sounds died gradually away in the extensive interior. The soldiers now put on their caps, and, with reversed arms, were marched to their barracks.

The rain so increased that no one supposed any other pageant would take place. The Carmo one did not; but the Paula brotherhood, who excel in these things, after waiting in vain till six o'clock for clear weather, determined not wholly to disappoint the public, the angels, and themselves. Arranging matters as well as they could, in large apartments connected with the church, the Pomp emerged from the side passage, where the waxen ex votos were, on the front stoop or platform, and pacing slowly along it to the main entrance, turned in, proceeded toward the high altar, and thence, through a side door, into the interior again. The last spectacle of the kind I ever expect to see, I shall preserve a few particulars, although, excepting the superior style in which it was got up, it differed little from that of the Mizericordia. The managers being wealthy and ambitious of outshining other establishments, their angels are allowed to be the handsomest, and, with their saints, to have the best fit-outs. While others can hardly draw an audience, they command full houses.

The church was darkened, the glimmering of a solitary candle barely preventing persons from running against each other. Only when a new-comer, or one whose patience in waiting was worn out, pushed the crimson screen in the door-way momentarily aside, did sufficient light flash in to enable us to distinguish the faces of those close by us. The place was three fourths full of people (no females), all moving and muttering like so many discontented phantoms.

At last the sound of a distant rattle came from the interior; it drew nearer, ceased, and soon after was heard as if in the street, when those with umbrellas rushed forth and met the bareheaded musicians and soldiers stepping out of the side passage upon the platform or long stoop, along which the troops formed a passage to the church door. There came forth a swarm of candle-bearers, who, with undignified speed, hastened in again through the front door. They were followed by a monk in a white long gown and hood—the latter bound round his temples with a half-inch rope—bearing a black cross, on which a towel formed the letter M. More candle-bearers, then brothers and a legion of angels; over the heads of several their guardians held umbrellas. Next, a neat pedestal was brought forth and placed on the flagging. An angel came, and, being lifted up, chanted a strain on the sufferings of the Savior, unfolding from a roller, as she sung, a piece of white muslin full six feet long, on which was depicted a full-length figure of Christ. This she turned gracefully round that all might see. Her voice was sweet and plaintive, and the little performance quite affecting. Veronica's handkerchief took a likeness only of the Savior's face, but the cloth his body was laid in received an impression of the whole. It was a copy of the latter that the little songstress unrolled before us.

She passed in and made way for the bier, or Golden Bed, upheld by monks in white hoods and cassocks. A "dead Christ" lay on it, partially covered by a rich counterpane. "The three Marys" followed weeping, dressed in long russet gowns and close hoods, and handkerchiefs in their hands. Their halos seemed made of bobbin wire, and might any where else have been taken for the frames of caps or bonnets. Next came Saint John and Mary Magdalene: she is one of the preceding trio, being twice represented. In the Carmo procession the *Prophets* attend as mourners.

Next three suspicious-looking, bare-armed chaps in steel caps drew up—Roman executioners. Behind them walked the centurion in gorgeous array—golden helmet, scarlet tunic, a staff surmounted by an eagle, and all the insignia of an ancient military officer. The character was well conceived, but spoiled by attempts to make it gigantic. The person of this actor was swelled by stuffing, and, from the vibration of the upper part, his head was clearly within the breast of the figure; the face was a mask. The helmet and metal ornaments were too heavy to be controlled by the artificial neck and shoulders. He passed on quickly, but stumbled on ascending the only step at the front door, and would have fallen but for St. John, against whose back he staggered.

Flocks of angels now flitted past us. Ere they had disappeared, the image of "Our Lady" was out on the stoop and exposed to the rain. Similar in size and outline with her sister of the Mizericordia, between the rays of her crown were seven stars. The most attractive person in the Pomp, the managers allowed her to remain full five minutes in the storm. Nothing common is put on her, her dress and jewels being of the most costly material.

Parents commonly send a confidential person with their angels, who is careful not to lose sight of them, on account of the jewels on their persons and dresses. The breast-piece of one was almost covered with diamonds. A doctor last year decked out his daughter so gorgeously, and chiefly with borrowed gems, that he would not trust her even in the vestry without an attendant. If a father belongs to the brotherhood, he can accompany his child in the procession; if not, no. It is a rule that none but a Church brother must lead an angel.

11*th*. Allelulia Saturday—the end of Lent: the day when the saints throw off their mourning, and the screens before the images are withdrawn—when bells begin to ring again, and matracas, their substitutes during Passion Week, are put away for another year—when scores of Judases are torn to pieces, and when the annual consecration of fire and water takes place.

At noon I went to the Paula Church to witness the performances, but found it so dark within and crowded, that I was glad to get into the vestry, where people with bunches of rosemary were waiting to have them aspersed with the new holy water. I subsequently procured a seat in the music-gallery, where, besides the old organ, there were one bass and two kettle-drums, violins, clarionets, French-horns, trumpets, &c., waiting to strike up the moment the ceremonies ended. The process of consecration was as follows: The baptismal font being filled, the officiating padre put his hand into or on it, making the sign of the cross in the action. Next he waved three crosses over the surface, in the name of each person in the Trinity, saying, " By this [sign] I bless thee creature water—By the living God [a cross]—By God [a cross] most true—By God [a cross] most holy—By God who in the beginning of the world divided thee from earth." Then he breathed three times upon it, making the sign of the cross in the act of blowing, and exclaimed each time, " The virtue of the Holy Ghost descend upon this water." He dropped oil from a minute vial cross-wise on it, and dipped the vial itself in, saying, " The infusion of our Lord Jesus Christ and of the Holy Ghost is made in the name of the most Holy Trinity." He then took a portion of the water up and threw it toward the four quarters of the earth. When he got through, the attending officials sprinkled themselves and the spectators near them.

Water being thus made holy, it was employed in the consecration of fire. The *Cirio*, or " Great Paschal Candle," a very large and elaborately ornamented one, is the principal object in this ceremony. I wonder the Church on these occasions does not follow the universal practice of antiquity in both hemispheres, and introduce new fire—draw it direct from the sun by lenses, from wood by the friction of two sticks, or produce it afresh from flint and steel. Instead of this, the custom is

to prepare three *triune* candles, each consisting of three tapers longitudinally united, to represent the unity of the Godhead in a trinity of persons. One is placed near the entrance, another half way to, and the third at the altar. They are lit, and all others carefully extinguished.

The priest takes the *Cirio*, and with the usual ceremonies baptizes it at the font. He drops chrism and baptismal oil from vials on the water; breathes three times over it, not cross-wise now, but as if forming with his breath the letter Y. He dips the lower end of the *Cirio* a little in, raises it, and plunges it farther down a third time, and it reaches the bottom of the font. Each movement is accompanied with similar expressions to those used in sanctifying the water. It now is lit at one of the triune tapers, placed on the high altar, and the other lights kindled at its flame.

After baptism the Litany of the Saints was said, and then mass, as on Palm Sunday. When the officiating padre came to the words "Allelulia, allelulia, allelulia," the bells struck up a merry peal, music in the gallery burst forth, screens before the images dropped, and the building, hitherto almost dark, is instantly illuminated, and resounds with chants of "God is risen from the dead." Every face is radiant with smiles, and the day is spent in pleasure. Now the *agoa-benta* basins are replenished, and families send bottles and tumblers to be filled to sprinkle their children and friends. Some

LIFE IN BRAZIL.   235

preserve the fresh liquid as a preservative against many complaints.

The padres of the various city churches wait for a signal from the Imperial Chapel where the bishop officiates. As soon as he arrives at the "Allelulia," rockets are sent up. Priests contrive to be near that part of the service, and ready, on hearing the guns, to utter the joyful words.

On returning, I stepped into the Imperial Chapel. The *cirio* was standing in an antique-fashioned candlestick of silver, four feet or more high. The candle was about the same length, four inches in diameter, and beautifully painted over its entire surface. The figure given is from a sketch taken at the time.* Upon leaving, I fell in with half a dozen negroes carrying live turkeys with blue ribbons on their necks. They were "Allelulia presents," gobbling innocents being as much in demand now as in New England on Thanksgiving Day. Next I overtook a band of youthful devotees—blacks and whites—hoarse

* In olden times the Paschal taper at Westminster Abbey was three hundred pounds' weight. Sometimes a wax-light called a serpent was used; the name derived from its spiral form, being wound round a rod. To light it, fire was *struck from a flint* consecrated by the abbot. In the cathedrals every taper was extinguished, in order that new fire might kindle a parent torch at which the rest were ignited.

with uttering comminations on the fallen apostle, perspiring and exhausted with punishing him. These young zealots were "killing Judas." The preceding illustration conveys a correct idea of this "act of devotion."

One, after being dragged through mud and mire, and thrashed and stoned till little like a human form remained, was stuck up in Hospicio Street. Another I saw hanging from a lamp-post, and before reaching home I passed the limbs of several more. Some practical joking is occasionally played off by dressing the figure after an obnoxious character. A few years ago, a British minister, on account of his opposition to the slave-trade, was stoned, and thrashed, and hanged in effigy.

In the upper floors and passages of the Paula temple were various kinds of ecclesiastical machinery. Painted boards like side scenes of a theatre; images and angels—two of the latter damaged in their wings; ladders, tressels, brackets, benches, tablets, and a pile of waxen ex votos in a corner. Here were some cart-loads of cinerary urns—I counted over a hundred—mostly of rosewood, highly polished, locked, and labeled. Some are fixed on short pedestals, with inverted torches, winged hour-glasses, or other emblems of mortality. These receptacles of the bones and ashes of the dead called up one of the most honorable and affecting customs of the Roman Church. On the 2d of November, these little chests are taken down and ranged before the high altar, when mass is celebrated over them. That day is the annual "Commemoration of the Dead." Friends come and sprinkle flowers on the vases, and weep over the ashes of their kindred.

A kindred custom was common with every classical and cultivated people of old. With the Chinese it is known as the "Worship of Ancestors," at which offerings are made to the manes of the dead, and masses performed for their repose. The tombs are repaired and ornamented; candles and incense are burned on them.

The practice accords with the best impulses of our nature—is congenial to the tenderest and purest feelings. Like other primeval rites, traces of it are found among all people. The Indians of both Americas indulged it. The burial-grounds of their ancestors were the last spots they would yield.

An officer led H—— and me into a spacious apartment, occupied from floor to ceiling with drawers and cases. Here were locked up the most select of the pageant apparatus. Banners, tapestries, plate, jewels, and dresses of the images, etc. Among other matters, he showed us the symbols carried by angels in

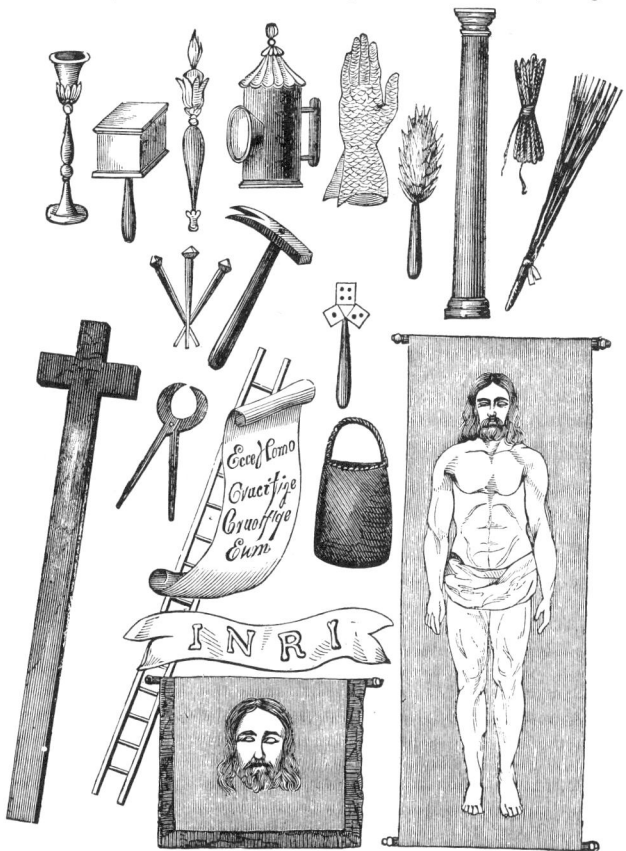

processions. I sketched each as he held it up, and noted his descriptions verbatim, thus:

1. The cup God drank out of.
2. The cold stone he sat on.
3. The torch they sought him with.
4. The lantern by which they found him.
5. The mailed hand that smote him.
6. The club that felled him.

7. The pillar he was tied to.
8. The cords that bound him.
9. The rod that beat him.
10. The cross he was nailed to.
11. The nails that fastened him on it.
12. The hammer that drove them in, and,
13. The pincers that drew them out.
14. The dice they threw lots with for his garments.
15. The bag containing the thirty pieces of silver.
16 and 17. Inscriptions.
18. The ladder by which he was taken down.
19. St. Veronica's handkerchief.
20. Santo Sudario—the holy towel he was folded in.

I met with another novelty. Three or four boys were playing about, and one, not over six years old, dressed as a monk— a black gown, white scapulary, buckles on his shoes, and an enormous white beaver, with the wide rim pressed close to his ears. He raised it, and showed me the shaven spot on his crown. On naming the circumstance, I was told such sights were formerly very common, but that now there are not over a dozen lads in Rio thus costumed. They are such as have been devoted by one or both parents (often before they were born) to certain saints, in acknowledgment of special favors received in answer to anxious longings. St. Anthony had befriended this lad's mother, and to him the youngster has been made over and put into his livery.

The more I see of this people, the more distant appears the success of any Protestant missions among them. Festivals are obstacles that can not easily be got rid of. The masses are too fond of them, and the national pulse beats in unison with them; moreover, there are powerful classes interested in maintaining them. Sundays, too, are universal seasons of recreation. Ladies laugh outright at the seriousness and alleged long faces of English families passing to church as to a funeral. To see them is enough to make one pity them! Protestants, it is said, degenerate here. The British chapel never received a native convert, while monks have drawn members from it. The Episcopal Methodists have had a mission here for some years, and have abandoned it. There is no ground on which a missionary can meet the people. They avoid him as one with whom association is disreputable, and they entertain a feeling toward him bordering on contempt, arising from a rooted belief in his ignorance and presumption. In their estimation, he and his employers are no wiser in Church matters than the people of Zago, who manured the foot of their steeple to make it grow. Then the climate is against the severities of northern sects. Neither stringent Methodism nor Puritanism can ever flourish in the tropics. The commerce of the country and its internal trade are opposed to the overthrow of Romanism. Civil and social relationships would be broken up, and thousands upon thousands lose the means by which they live. No sudden conversion of a city ever occurred.

To preach against Romanism is as much treason against the state as attempting to introduce the republican form of government, but the greatest of obstacles would probably be found in the reverence paid to the Virgin.

Mary of Nazareth is the great goddess of Romanists. Her deification was no chance matter, but the deliberate adoption of a principle, which was too closely interwoven with the habits, thoughts, and feelings of ancient nations to be at once torn away. The most refined and the most illiterate of the heathen were steeped in Polytheism. Every system of worship had its goddesses as well as gods, the one being held as essential as the other. It was deemed the dictate of reason and of nature that females should have *deosas*, to whom they could prefer petitions peculiar to themselves, and such as they could not be induced to make known to male deities, and here was found a prime hinderance to the reception of Christianity. We can imagine how the high-minded Lucretias and Virginias of Athens and Rome would be shocked at the proposition to transfer their petitions in the most delicate matters from the mother of the gods to one whom they could at first only view as a Jewish bachelor. A Madonna was therefore held necessary by the early fathers of the Church, in order to overcome the scruples of the sex, and she was realized in the exaltation of Mary. Moreover, in making her "Queen of Heaven," the way was opened to associate with her other lady celestials, and to rival in that feature also the court of Jove.

As "Our Lady"—her generic title—she is invoked by all, because, as "the mother of God," she has unlimited influence over her son, and, as "the mother of men," sympathizes with mortals with feminine tenderness. Hence she is honored at festivals by having her statues carried in triumph, precisely as were those of her prototype, the Magna deorum mater.

To make the most of her, she is represented in an indefinite number of characters, and named after the prominent attributes of each; *e. g.*, as N. S. da Saude, she occupies the place of Salus in Rome and of Hygeia in Greece; as N. S. do Bom Successo, she is pestered by the same class of worshipers that thronged the old shrines of Fortune; as N. S. de Cabeça, she has succeeded Minerva; as the goddess dos Remedios and do Succoro, she is consulted by the sick and those in distress; as N. S. da Conceição and do Parto, by those of her own sex only, and on special occasions. Even as the Lady of Navigators she was anticipated by early marine people. The Chinese still have their ancient protectoress of seamen, and have prudently associated with her two able assistants—the demigods of long sight and large ears—"the thousand-mile-eyer" and "the favorable-wind-hearer."

This remarkable multiplication of one person seems to be peculiar to Mary. I suppose it is but imperfectly understood by Protestants; for one, I had no clear perception of it till I arrived in Rio, and then it became interesting from furnishing additional evidence of the fact that, when heathenism was overthrown politically throughout the Roman empire, the old deities were retained under new appellations, and with them the cardinal principle of adding to their numbers.

In Rio, Mary is held in the same enthusiastic reverence as was the great Madonna of the Ephesians, nor could the city be sooner thrown into an uproar than by a Protestant missionary publicly attempting to diminish her reputation. Silver shrine-makers would, with one accord, rush out of Ourives Street and address their fellow-workmen in the very words and spirit of Demetrius, for the craft by which they live would verily be in danger if the great goddess should be despised and her magnificence destroyed, whom all Asia and the world worshipeth. Then the armadors, costumers, carvers, painters, gilders, image-makers, and wax-chandlers, equally inflamed with wrath, would add to the commotion, and render it next to impossible for any town clerk to wrest the blaspheming babbler alive out of their hands.

CHAPTER XXI.

Amulets: the Church a Mart for them.—Measures of Saints.—Royal Touches and metallic Tractors.—Bentinhos.—Pictures of Saints.—Indulgences.—Hindoo Pictures. — Portable Images. — Medals of Saints. — Bedini.—Symbols of the Cross. — Crossing Manual. — Pieces of holy Rock.—Hippocanthus.—Figa.—Ashes of Palm.—Rue.—Love Powder. — Sieve and Shears.—Curing the Bewitched.—Negro Witches. — Cures for Whitlows and Toothache.—The Evil Eye.—Rio Poulterers troubled with it.—Horns quench it.

April 13. Worn by both sexes and all ages, charms and Church amulets keep off the evil eye, hold demons at bay, and arrest the natural course of events when unfavorable to the wearers, just as they did when ignorance and credulity had the world to themselves. The variety in vogue includes several that did not fall in my way. I shall confine myself to such as did. They might be divided into lay and religious, but both are in a manner held sacred, those of heathen origin being "blessed." The Church, with the best intentions, but from a mistaken policy, early sanctioned these things, and has added a long list to the number. Her temples are marts for, and her ministers the great dealers in them. A powerful and not unprofitable means of maintaining her hold over the unthinking and simple, she has continued them till grown obsolete around her, exposing herself to the charge of fostering delusions she was ordained to eradicate. At every festival they constitute a prominent item of sacerdotal merchandise.

Measures of Saints.—These are ribbons, cut by priests to the exact length or height of their images, with the names wrought or printed on them. Worn round the waist next to the body, they remove pains, diseases, and otherwise promote the wishes of their wearers. Females commonly wear those of saints of their own sex, though those of Anthony, Braz, and Gonçalo are sometimes relied on. They are provided of all qualities, to meet the wordly circumstances of all. Some are

Q

of velvet, with portraits of the saints wrought on them, and some are strips of common tape. I received one—a present from a priest—a blue and white ribbon, four feet long, with the following inscription stamped on it: "M. de N. S. da G^a"— that is, Medida de Nossa Senhora da Gloria—not the lady on Gloria Hill; she is a foot taller. The color varies with the saint.

I had an opportunity of examining a smaller one, of narrow red ribbon, blessed and sent by a priest to its fair owner the day after the saint's festival. It was used to remove headache, toothache, and other pains, by being wound round the parts affected, and, as was said, really did remove them. Of this there is little room to doubt. Charms act on a principle recognized from the earliest times—one which, by exciting the hopes, fears, and faith of the impressible, has wrought wonders in all ages, and will continue to work them.

I was not a little surprised a few evenings ago in hearing ladies speak of "measures of the Holy Ghost." In reply to the inquiry by what standards the lengths were determined, it was said, "They are cut to no particular lengths, but are stamped with the triangle and dove, and are found good for many complaints." When E——a was about to sail to Rio Grande, Doña C—— gave her one, and told her to use it if attacked with sea-sickness.

Having taken cold, accompanied with hoarseness, S—— offered to procure for me one of St. Braz's specifics; "but then you must have full faith in it, or it may do you harm." This medical saint is celebrated for the successful treatment of bronchial affections. A few days before the 3d of February, a priest takes his measure with fine *wire*. A number of these medidas are provided, also pictures of him, and little green tapers. At his festival these are distributed to those who contribute to the fête—a print to one, a candle to another, a measure to a third, and, it may be, one of each to a liberal donor. The directions are, Fold the wire round the neck as often as it will go, and make the ends fast; place an image or picture of the physician on a table, light a bougie, place it before him, and—you will get well.

I think faith in these fooleries is propped up in many minds simply by habit; in others by the idea that, if erroneous, it is complimentary to God and the saints, and, on that account, not altogether unacceptable. Had Plutarch written yesterday, he could not have hit off this people better than he has done in his life of Nicias: "The people had a dislike to natural philosophers, supposing that they detracted from the divine power and providence by ascribing things to insensible causes, unintelligible powers, and inevitable necessity."

That persons with nervous ailments, and constitutionally impressible, have been benefited by royal touches, metallic tractors, and mesmerizers' fingers, is unquestionable. They establish the fact that strong faith in fictions, united with certain temperaments, can cure all that is curable by means of the imagination. The virtue of touch in King Pyrrhus lay in the great toe of his right foot. Pliny and Plutarch have recorded its cures. Its nature was so divine that the funeral pyre had no power over it; hence it was, after the death of its owner, preserved in the temple, and the sick had recourse to it there.

Bentinhos.—I suppose there is hardly a Roman Catholic female in Brazil, from the empress to a negress, who does not guard against invisible foes by wearing, in contact with her person, a couple of these diminutive shields. A friend procured for me a pair from the most esteemed fabrica, the convent of Tereza. Two embroidered pads, an inch and a half square, are connected by a double silk cord. On one is the Lady of Carmo and child, on the other a fanciful figure or flower. Passing the cords over the shoulders, one pad rests on the bosom and the other at the back, thus protecting the wearer before and behind. Large numbers are imported from Rome.

Pictures of Saints.—At the anniversary of a popular saint, vast numbers of his portrait are, as has already been perceived, exchanged in the Church for money or wax at an average profit of one or two thousand per cent. I never saw one handed out until the applicant dropped one or more vintems into the dish, or laid down a candle. As specimens of the fine arts, there is nothing remarkable about them. Commonly carried about the person, they are worn out before the feast comes round again. Besides some procured at festivals, I purchased an assortment at a print-seller's, in which were John of Malta, Ursala, Luiz,

Crispin, also "N. S. da Immaculada Conceição, copied from two pictures revealed from heaven, and conformable to the miraculous medal of Jesus, Mary, and Joseph."

Besides preserving them in books, pinning them to bed-curtains and chamber-walls, slipping them under pillows, etc., etc., they constitute a large class of amulets called "*breves*." Each is folded into a small compass, commonly an inch square, sewed up in minute bags, and worn next the body, like Bentinhos. I understand Old Senhora P—— has one of the Lady Conceição on her heart, and another of Anthony at her back.

To several the following is appended: "His Excellency the most Reverend Bishop, Grand Chaplain to the Emperor, Don Manoel do Monte Rodriques Araujo, on visiting the church whose patron saint this image represents, conceded to all who pray before this image one Paternoster and one Ave Maria forty days of indulgence." In answer to inquiries, it was said the indulged might eat meat on fast days, would be pardoned for little sins they might commit, and if they died within the time, would go direct to heaven, escaping Purgatory altogether.

Even for pictures of their deities Romanists are indebted to the pagans. Thus the Poojarees, a sect of Hindoo priests, worshipers of the goddess MARIETTA, celebrate her praises with chanting, and accompany their songs with a hand-bell, while their wives keep time with castanets. "They also carry with them pictures representing the goddess in various characters."

Portable Images.—These are occasionally of wood, but many, if not most, are of plaster of Paris. H—— and I met, a few days ago, a *girl* in a black iron mask, and shortly after stopped at a smith's open window, where slave-collars and chains were hanging up for sale. Close by, our attention was called to a fabricator of things typical of other fetters—a sacred image-maker. Seated on the floor, with paint-pots beside him, the little man was surrounded with a regiment of six and seven inch genii, to whose faces, cloaks, and cowls he was giving the last finish. The Antonios were the most numerous. The street in pagan Rome where such things were made was named Sigiliaria.

Medals of Saints and of the Pope.—Little elliptical plates of silver, brass, and tin. One of silver before me is so thin that, though an inch and a half by an inch, the value does not exceed ten cents. On the approach of feasts, dealers advertise them. As long as they have not been consecrated they can be offered at public sale, but when they have undergone aspersion they can only be "exchanged."

By a judicious disposal of these trifles the clergy strengthen no little their hold on the affections of the people. Bedini, the new nuncio, has brought over a package. One of six, placed by him at the disposal of a certain padre, is now before me. It is of the size and value of a five-cent piece, and has on it the effigies of Gregory XVI. Having been blessed by the Pope, they are invaluable. The nuncio is unpopular, but he is adroit. At Praya Grande, the other day, he met a child which he was told belonged to Senhor B———, an influential lawyer, to whom he had not been introduced. He put into its hands one of these precious medals. The delighted parents are all his own.

Symbols of the Cross.—Nothing is more potent than these; neither witches nor wizards can bear the sight of them. Besides the ordinary figures, a very popular form of this class of amulets is represented in the margin. By it we learn that every person, in the absence of an artificial cross, has a potent one at his finger ends. It shows the last movement in the crossing manual, or self-blessing exercise, which consists of five distinct acts when properly performed, thus: With the tip of the right thumb—on no account must the left be used—you touch the forehead, point of the nose, then the left, and next the right temple. (This is the first act or cross.) Touch again the nose, next the chin, and finish with the left and right sides of the mouth. (The second.) Return your thumb to the chin, remove it to the breast, and pass to each shoulder. (The third.) With the open palm retouch the forehead, heart, and both shoulders. (The fourth.) Lastly, turn the forefinger behind the thumb, and press the latter to your lips.

Pieces of Holy Rock.—Soldiers, and particularly those of the interior, protect themselves with amulets. I heard an officer recount, with edifying fervor, how one saved his life, in direct violation of a natural law. He was ascending the River d'Aldea Velha, in Espirito Santo, with government dispatches, in a canoe paddled by Indians. The current was strong against them, and the water rough. They were upset, one or both Indians were drowned, but the relator, who could not swim, after floating half an hour with the tide, reached the shore, he knew not how. On drying his garments, he found a paper parcel in his coat pocket—slipped in unknown to him by his wife—containing a small fragment of the "Penha," a mountain rock consecrated to the Virgin under the name of "Our Lady of the Rock." "That stone," said he, "kept me from sinking."

The *Cavallo Marinho*—hippocampus—is a favorite with many. This curious-looking little fish, when dried, is worn next the skin, and is powerful in driving off the headache as well as devils. Some have it in gold and silver.

The Figa.—One day I hinted that Chica, our little old African cook, had no amulet about her, as, from her spare dress, I could not imagine where it could be. It was said she certainly must wear one. To settle the matter, she was called in, and, to my surprise, drew from her bosom a bone figa. She said she wore a tooth in the same way in her own country. The first money a slave gets is expended on a figa, which is sometimes carved out of rosemary root.

Ashes of Palms, consecrated on Palm Sunday, carried about the person, protect the wearers from thunder and lightning. The smoke arising from the combustion of the leaves expels evil spirits from dwellings.

Rue retains its ancient property of keeping houses clear of witches. Whites and blacks have great faith in it as a bane to sorcery and enchantments. Occasionally persons may be noticed kneeling before altars on which they have placed sprigs, with the view of rendering them doubly efficacious. It is often seen peeping out between the hair and head-gear of colored women. A slip of rowan-tree or mountain ash was an old European charm.

Love Powders.—Some harmless dust, chiefly furnished by blacks to slaves, who secretly drop it into their owners' or employers' food to procure better treatment. Indians in the northern provinces employ the milky juice of herbs with the same intent.

Sieve and Shears.—Recovering lost goods by these is in vogue, and with an addition that makes apostles abettors of wizards. When the cutting instruments are laid on the inverted sieve, and the conjurer has finished his imprecations, he calls aloud, in a rhyming couplet, on

<blockquote>
San Pedro and Paulo,
Phillippe and Diego,
</blockquote>

to detect the thief and show where the stolen things are.

Process of curing the Bewitched.—It is a mercy that old women in compact with the wicked one are not so numerous in Rio as they once were. In the interior they are reported as mischievous as ever. When a person imagines him or herself possessed, he commonly gets a priest to make the sign of the cross over him with a sprig of rosemary dipped in holy water. Friars are preferred for this business; those of St. Anthony are reputed the most successful. If possible, the afflicted must go to the monastery, and enter the chapel with two or more monks. After certain rites they converse with him, and judge from his replies respecting the character of the demon and the place of its expulsion. They are careful not to drive it out at the mouth, lest the victim become dumb; nor at the ears or eyes, lest he lose his sight or hearing; nor at an arm, hand, or leg, lest they become disabled; but, if possible, at the soles of the feet.

Negro Witches cure Patients given up by Friars.—My friend the vicar had a lad long troubled with a bruised leg. The sore resisted all his attempts to heal it. As a last resource, a colored "wise woman" was consulted. She raised a smoke of dried herbs, muttered over the wound, made motions as if stitching its lips up, put on a cataplasm of herbs, sent him home, and in a week he was well. Another young slave had a diseased foot; nothing seemed to do it good; and at length his owner gave him leave to visit a dark sorceress, who talked to it, made signs over it, rubbed it with oil, covered it with a plaster, and in a few days he was sound too.

Ancient cures—worthy of Pliny—are still in vogue. Earthworms fried alive in olive oil, and applied warm as a poultice, remove *whitlows*, which are common among blacks and whites. Senhora Peres tells me she thus cured one of her slaves. The same thing has been done in J——'s family.

A popular remedy for the toothache is thus prepared: A living chameleon is put into an earthen pot with a close-luted cover, and baked to a cinder. A portion of this is crushed between the finger and thumb, rubbed over the gums, and put into the carious cavity. Senhor H—— L——, a senator from St. Catharine's, found this efficient. His lady preserves the remaining cinder for future use.

The blacks have very similar recipes brought by them from Africa.

The Evil Eye.—People in Brazil still suffer from it. Handsome children have fits and other complaints, induced by earthly and unearthly beings envying their innocence and beauty; and not hags and ogres only, but spruce ladies possess the unamiable organ. When the hair of a female becomes prematurely gray or drops off by disease, in nine cases out of ten the look of some envious fair one has done it. A young lady in our neighborhood had recently tresses equaling Eve's in length and softness. She has lost them, and says she knows too well which of her acquaintances it was whose malicious glances have compelled her to wear a cap.

When a stranger pats a child on the head, calls it pretty and fair, etc., both nurse and parents would be troubled if he did not conclude by asking God or the saints to bless it, *that* being the proof that he meant it no harm—that he had not been observing it with the evil eye. The withering power is said to be allied to that by which serpents draw fluttering birds into their mouths; and that human victims, when once struck, sicken, languish, and, if not relieved, must sink into death's jaws.

Besides the numerous preservatives figured and described in preceding chapters, there are others, and among them

Horns are not uncommon. I first noticed them in Barbonnos Street, at a place where fruit, vegetables, and other edibles were exposed for sale. A loose pair of sheep's horns, painted with alternate bands of blue, red, white, and yellow, hung against the side of the door-post. Inquiring for what purpose they were there exposed, the colored proprietress laughingly exclaimed, "To keep away the evil eye." H―― asked if she would sell them, to which she gave a decided negative.

There is a cluster of dirty shanties and apologies for tents near the Moura Fountain, in the vicinity of the landing-place at Palace Square, at which fowls are always on sale, and commonly a monkey or two. One of them is kept by Antoine, an active Portuguese in middle life. As I commissioned him to procure a sloth, I was in the habit of looking into his den. He had two pair of horns suspended over his coops. For my satisfaction, H―― one day pointed to them, and asked what good they did. With animation and immoderate gesticulation, he told us how his neighbors of adjoining shanties used to envy him for doing a greater business than they could get—how they looked on him and his fowls with an evil eye, and caused many to pine and die.

"How do they protect me! Why, when any one now looks in to injure me, he *sees them*, and his envy is *quenched*. He recollects himself, and walks off fearful of chastisement—that is, he is afraid of having a fit, of tripping himself up while walking and breaking a leg, of being choked when eating, or of some other misfortune." It need hardly be said that Antoine's neighbors guard themselves and the health of their capons against his glances by similar means.

Horns are also to be seen in Vendas. Faith in them seems pretty general, except with those who have become disenchanted by contact with foreigners.

Antoine could recognize the wicked organ in a stranger or any one else. Had he read Byron, he would oft exclaim,

> "I know him by his pallid brow;
> I know him by the evil eye
> That aids his envious treachery."

CHAPTER XXII.

Begging for the Holy Ghost.—The Symbols.—Mr. Barboza.—An afflicted Mother.—The City agitated through Mistake.—San Jorge.—Market.—Church of Peddlers.—Burying-ground of Heretics.—Small Water-craft.—Beeves of the Sun.—Lady of Navigators.—Mozambique tribal Marks.—Church of Boa Viagem.—Ex Votos and Miracles.—Curious Lavatory.—View of the Harbor and Mountains.—Alms-box.—Ships' Sails vowed to Our Lady, and sold on her Account.—Indian Boy.—Wax offered to Marine Deities by old Pagans.—Other Heathen Types of Romish Customs.

April 17. Forty days after Lent the most popular of Brazilian festivals takes place—that of the Holy Ghost. It is celebrated for several days in the Lapa, Rita, and Santa Anna churches, three competing establishments. Each has sent out a band of collectors, who for five weeks will canvass and recanvass the city, suburbs, and surrounding country. They have already visited the shipping in the Bay with their cry, "*Esmolas para Espirito Santo!*" Musicians always attend them, commonly negroes. The Lapa troop is composed of white barbers, who to a man are reputed as expert handlers of violins and bugles as of lancets and razors. They are hired at a higher rate than their sable brethren. While engaged this morning in writing, Doña H—— came running up stairs to urge me to descend. "Quick! Here's the Holy Ghost coming up the Cattete. Don't you want to see him?" I am sure no one could be more startled at such an announcement than I was, nor at the unaffected simplicity with which it was made. I went down, and, looking out of the open window, asked "Where?" "Gone into that venda" (a grocery half a block off), "but will be out directly," replied half a dozen voices. In a little while a negro band, consisting of two French horns, three drums, a clarionet, and a fife, emerged, and recommenced a waltzing air in the middle of the street. Next appeared four white men, in albs over their ordinary dress. Two had small crimson banners, on each of which was a figure of a dove in a triangle. Another bore a little silver bird on a stand resembling a chamber candlestick. Like the banner-men, he also carried an almsdish. The fourth bore a capacious bag.

The minstrels, except when they leave it—as just now—to take a drink, keep the middle of the street, and regulate their steps to the progress of the alb-men on the side-walks; now creeping, anon standing, and then dashing onward, the music rising with their motions. The collectors call at every house, but have occasion to knock at few, as the music draws the inmates out. Yonder a lady is throwing back a pair of latticed blinds; a banner-man flies over, and burying for a moment her face in the flag, she adds a contribution to his dish. Next door a cluster of girls have got the little bird among them, and return it with vintems. A neighbor now takes a flag in, that every member of his family may perform an act of devotion by kissing it; and there, a Mozambique fruit-woman bathes her face in its folds; her offering, two oranges, is dropped into the bag, the receptacle of donations other than money—no, not for all such, for the musicians have now come up, and, as I live, the clarionet-player carries a live rooster under his arm, the gift, probably, of some dealer in poultry. Of course it would not do to put it among eggs, bread, fruit, and kindred quiet things. Nothing is refused, from bank bills to a banana, or half a yard of ribbon as a streamer for a banner-staff.

It is our turn now: one of the embroidered treasures comes in at the window; all the ladies save one shrink from it. Senhora P—— gives it the kiss of reverence. In her zeal, poor soul, and under the popular belief that it is a powerful charm, she used it far too much like a pocket-handkerchief, rubbing her eyes, face, neck, and bosom with it. I now perceived that every Romanist does not care to become too intimate with such things. Some decline even to touch them. I think I saw and felt the cause, but shall not mention it at present. Opportunities will occur for verifying or dissipating my convictions. Pompey took the holy ensign to the kitchen to comfort Chica, the old black cook; and, ere she got through with it, the polite bearer cast anxious glances after it, as he had received pressing signals from across the way.

The troop now passed on. The minstrels struck up a fresh air that set young feet a tripping. The rooster actually crowed an accompaniment. Independent of the exhilarating fife and drum, and rousing trumpets, the scene is a stirring one. The collectors, with their banners fluttering over their heads, and their albs streaming behind them, are running hither and thither, crossing and recrossing the street as devotees appear at windows and door-hatches, while their brethren with the little bird and bag are as busy answering calls made on them.

I have heard much about the doings at the strange festa, but it is useless to speculate on what we shall soon have opportunities to see for ourselves.

18*th*. Walked with H—— to Rua Marecas, and turned into a private entry near the Duck Fountain. My companion clapped his hands—an Oriental summons common in the Levant—an Ethiopian appeared at the stairhead. Being told who we were, he returned with an invitation to step up and take seats in Senhor Barboza's parlor.

After resting a while, the Senhora came in, saying she expected her husband every minute. Her sprightly conversation made me regret the inability to commune directly with her. A native of Montevideo, she ought to be half Republican, and perhaps is so. She laughingly remarked, "Ah! you North Americans don't love monarchs nor the splendors of royalty." To this pretty fillip it was replied that, though we had no very marked regard for kings of diamonds, we admired queens of hearts, and that every lady with us was one. It was conceded at once that if our taste was defective as respects one class of governors, it was unexceptionable as regards another. The conversation was here interrupted by the arrival of Senhor B——, who led us into his sanctum, a room actually crammed with curiosities. Besides collections of Brazilian relics, here was a rare one of Peruvian antiquities, in earthenware, stone, and metals. These I begged permission to sketch. For his prompt acquiescence I made my best acknowledgments, and when the reader comes to the Appendix in which they are described, he will feel equally obliged to this enlightened Brazilian gentleman.

19*th*. J——'s birth-day, and kept in Brazilian fashion. His brother-in-law, H——, vice-president of a neighboring province, and member of the National Legislature, arrived with his family. The lady of this gentleman has endured an amount of affliction which falls to the lot of few of her sex, and, though now resigned to the severe dispensation of Providence, its effects are visible in her calm but plaintive face. Like Niobe and Rachel, she weeps for her children because they are not. A few years ago, returning by sea from Rio to Rio Grande to join her husband, a storm arose—the vessel became unmanageable—broke in two—all on board perished except herself and a seaman. After being in the water twelve hours, she was washed ashore insensible. With returning consciousness, the shrieks of her offspring ere the billows dashed them from her were recalled. She asked for them, called them by name as though they still were clinging to her, and the youngest in her arms. Alas! the whole *seven* were ingulfed in the watery abyss.

20*th*. The emperor has been expected every hour for the last three or four days. Preparations have been going on for months to compliment him with a triumphal pomp. A stately and massive arch has been erected in Dereita Street, surmounted by an equestrian statue of him of colossal dimensions. The entrance by the public garden is prettily set off with an elevated pediment and emblematic paintings, while within, colored lanterns, ready for lighting, are pendent from the trees. These joyful proceedings were met to-day by a contretemps. At 1 P.M. the fort signaled the imperial frigates in the offing. The National

Guards assembled, guns were fired, church bells rung, a little steamer started down the Bay with officers of the palace, the schools were dismissed, and at length the vessels hove in sight —the United States frigate Columbia and the Saratoga corvette! The unlucky signal-man at the outer fort is to be dismissed for thus bringing the whole city together. Had the American commodore appeared an hour later, the city had certainly been illuminated.

23*d.* Anniversary of "San Jorge, Defensor do Imperio." This mighty warrior appears in public only once a year, on which occasions, armed cap-a-pie, a baton in his hand and a falchion by his side, he leads the emperor and court, the national troops, the Church's staff, and an army of lay people through the streets in triumph. I supposed this was the pageant-day, but it occurs in June, so that not till then can we pay our respects to the hero.

J—— and I took a boat early at the Flamingo Praya to go up the Bay, but the mist over the water became so thick that we were liable to lose ourselves. No object, not even a ship, was visible at a distance of a hundred feet. Veiled in the gloom, and without a compass, we sought the shore, till the great Cloud Creator and Disperser should gather up the dark one that involved us, and through which, with much uncertainty, we were driving.

Landing at Palace Square, some four miles from where we started, we found the market crowded with buyers and sellers of fish, fruits, earthen and wooden wares, live turkeys, sucking pigs, Guinea and common fowls. No dressed poultry or pigs are seen. In one cage were pigs differing from any I had seen —longer legged, of a dullish gray color, and long, pendent tails, with a tuft of hair at the end of each. Of fish, besides five-feet sharks waiting for purchasers, here were streaked bass and mackerel three feet long, if bass and mackerel they were.

To pass the time till the fog cleared up, I strolled to the lower end of Ouvidor, where stands an ancient temple of the peddlers—dos Mascas. The body of the little place is circular, and fitted up with two shrines of Ann and Joaquim. The figures are of natural size, and accompanied with minikin attendants, fresh painted, that looked quite comfortable. One is a friar. Little angels also, hovering about the niches, are genuine soaring ones, not like obese things modeled after penguins, and no more able to rise above the ground. No one was present but myself. At length a negro came in, dropped on his knees, and, instead of addressing the saint, kept watching my every movement. A boy, not over six or seven years old, entered from a side door with a cruet, small bell, and a napkin, which he placed on Joaquim's table. In a friar's gown, the hood hanging down his back, a white tasseled cord round his waist, slip-shod and bare-legged, he was the youngest acting monk I met with.

"After rain comes sunshine." By nine the haze had vanished, when a boat, propelled by four African oarsmen, took me two miles up the Bay to the British burying-ground—an irregular plot, part of a mountain slope, opposite the little Bay of Gamboa, and the last resting-place of heretics that die here. The broad path leading through it is necessarily steep and crooked. Half way up, a spot has been leveled for a little structure in which the burial-service is read. The graves are generally level with the surface, and marked by narrow plates of cast iron thrust into the ground and numbered. The prevailing monuments are horizontal slabs. Foreign officers lie here, who might at this moment have been the pride of their parents and ornaments of their country—victims of a false sentiment of honor, that has consigned them to corruption and oblivion in their bloom.

One monumental souvenir above all others engaged my attention. A low stucco fence incloses it, leaving room for lilies, rose bushes, saudades, and purple flowering vines, while at the corners young cypresses shoot up. It is the grave of Alfred ———, an affectionate and precocious child, whose departure has torn his parents' heart-strings.

A more auspicious resting-place for the dead can hardly be found on earth. Located on the declivity of a tropical mount, clothed in perpetual verdure, its walks and tombs bordered with flowers, and its area dotted with Indian walnut-trees, mangoes, cinnamon, African corn, and the sweet mandioca; with araças, cajus, and the cardamoma, with its rose-colored clusters; pinheiros, pitangas, and calabash-trees with both rounded and elongated fruit—what Christian could desire a fitter sepulchre, or where find one more abounding with emblems of innocence and immortality! The blights of winter invade it not; ranges of everlasting hills surround it, and earth's brightest skies smile over it.

On returning, I could not but observe the variety of water-craft in motion—handsome-shaped canoes, with elevated bows and sterns, and their rapid propulsion in right lines by a single paddle. The faluas appear to me identical in form and rig with Egyptian Nile-boats.

But the day was favorable for observing bodies floating in another medium. In few parts of the earth are the phenomena of clouds — their formation, attraction by mountains, and absorption—more visible than here. If Homer derived not his "Beeves of the sun" from cumuli, he might have done so if Sicilian skies resemble those of Rio. The feeblest imagination can not fail of being struck with the analogy and of realizing the imagery.

Regularly almost as evening comes do these celestial flocks collect about the highest peaks, and descend among the lowest, to empty their chargéd udders. See! at this moment, while some are stationary half way down the Corcovado range, others are moving along the Tejucan valleys as if to meet water-nymphs waiting, like mortal dairy-maids, with empty pails. Thus are they seen at eventide approaching, and in the morning hieing away to distant pastures. Such are the kine that diurnally furnish the Flumenensians with life's richest, sweetest fluid. Yonder, far as the eye can reach, a herd is coming in a right line. How steadily they approach, and how beautifully their snow-white sides are relieved by the azure of their ethereal meadows! I think these sights are equal to any in Brazil. The evening dews are dense as if showers fell. A few mornings ago, after sketching a fountain, I scrambled up a mount, and my dress was as thoroughly soaked as if it had been dragged through a stream.

24*th*. A friend and I agreed to devote a day to a mountain isle on the opposite side of the Bay, and close in with the shore, between San Domingo and the fort of Santa Cruz. From the city it looks no larger than a good-sized haystack, which it resembles. It is sacred to the protectress of seamen, having been dedicated, with the church that crowns it—yon small white patch on its summit—some two hundred years ago, to " Nossa Senhora da Boa Viagem," a lady to whose providence Brazilian and Portuguese sailors committed and commit themselves, make vows to and call upon her when in peril, just as ancient navigators dealt with Neptune and Oceanus. Having had a prosperous voyage from the States, a pious relative says I ought to go.

We crossed the Bay in a small steamer, whose pilot was a Mozambique slave, and landed at San Domingo, where the gatekeeper or ferry-master was, or had been, another. Both were tall, middle-aged, and as finely-formed men as I ever saw, the latter particularly. He had no more of the negro lineaments than had Mark Antony or Cato, but both had indelible marks of their barbaric origin—one a double, the other a single row of pimples, the size of peas, down the middle of the forehead, and along the ridge of the nose to its very tip—the signs of their native tribes. The Mozambiques are among the best of slaves. Equally intelligent and more pacific than the Minas (from the Gold Coast), faithful and trustworthy, they bring a high price. A gentleman who crossed the Bay with us had witnessed, while on a visit to the eastern coast of South Africa, the process of producing the fleshy beads. At one time he saw forty or fifty lads and young men lying on the ground suffering from the operation. A minute incision is made through the skin for each pimple; the lips of the wound then are pulled up and tied by a thread, and in time the protuberances become permanently globose, smooth, and shining.

After skirting round a mountain, and following a narrow pathway darkened with dense foliage towering over us, with coffee, orange, and banana trees, and chacaras concealed among the exuberant vegetation, we came plump on the beach in the rear of the Sacred Isle, which was now between us and the city, as represented in the cut on p. 62. A strip of sand connects it at low tides with the opposite shore, and on it a stone causeway has been built; but the whole is broken down and dispersed by the surf, save part of an arch projecting from the precipitous face of the isle. The tide was coming in, and we had to retreat.

My companion hallooed, and presently a naked yellow boy came over in a leaky canoe, which could only take one of us across at a time. The only craft belonging to the place, it was hardly creditable to the patroness of watermen.

While my companion was being paddled over, I had an opportunity of observing a very interesting fact in physics. The ridge of sand just mentioned is formed by waves rolling in from opposite directions and meeting there. While reclining on a stone at a spot where their force was reduced almost to nothing, the tiny surges crossed each other, and continued on their way without having their forms or movements apparently the least affected. One swept over the other, while each preserved its outline and progress as if no such contact had taken place. The shallow, transparent fluid, and the almost snow-white sand below, rendered their movements distinctly visible.

Young Charon returned, and I joined H—— on a rock, in which notches were cut for the feet and hands to mount it. By careful climbing, we got into a zigzag path, at places too steep for any biped to ascend, had not the soil been cut into steps, with stakes driven in for risers. The only passage up, it presents one of those cases where a few determined spirits could keep an army at bay, or children put bold men to flight. As we rose, we found preparations made to test the latter. We came to a stone door-way. To pass by it without wings was impossible, and within it stood a sentinel with musket and fixed bayonet. He was supported by a comrade in a military cap, blue roundabout, a cartridge-box at his side, and a brass-handled sword in his hand. Neither of these warriors exceeded four feet in height nor ten years of age! One I perceived was an Indian. What all this meant I could not divine, nor find breath to ask. They made way for us, and we passed through —two sweating, panting, broken-winded pilgrims, pressing onward to the shrine above.

Tacking this way and that, we at length stopped to rest, when H—— told me that the place had been little visited by devotees of late years, and that the government had established a school on it for a hundred boys, to be educated for marines. The governor was his old army acquaintance. Starting again, we approached the top of this immense rock, came to a low dwelling, and observed the church a little farther up. The governor and his amiable family received us both as old acquaintances. Being a widower, his mother takes charge of his children. The old lady, with spectacles on nose, but no cap on her gray head, was busy with her needle. The house, of one story, is cool, comfortable, and wholly void of ornament. After taking a draught of sugar and water, H—— entered into conversation with our venerable hostess in native style. As his tongue rattled on, his arms were here, there, and every where; he frowned, smiled, and grinned successively; his voice, now a whisper, next a shout; his eyeballs rolling, and his whole system in commotion. He wound up with placidly drawing forth his *caixa de rapé*, and begging his smiling auditress to take a pinch. He had merely been relating some commonplace city news.

We found the little church open. A contemporary of that on Gloria Hill, every thing about it reminds one of former times. Almost the entire structure, as well as its images and ornaments, came from Portugal. For want of repairs, both stone and wood work are going to decay. The lady patroness is neglected too. No priest lives here to wait on her, and only at long intervals does one appear. Her glory is waning with her walls. The "noble brotherhood" once devoted to her service has been long extinct. Even the records of her former greatness are no more.

The low walls support a rather high roof, whose converging sides are truncated, leaving the interior like the lower half of the letter A. Entering the old-fashioned door, the hat of a tall man would touch the ceiling of a little gallery stretching overhead. Here were marine subjects—ships tossing on the ocean, and Our Lady in the clouds watching them. Advancing, we found the side walls set off with Dutch tiles, and the ceiling covered with paintings of shipwrecks and the miraculous rescue of drowning sailors; of Portuguese in conflict with Mohammedans; the marriage of the Virgin; the mother of the mother of God and her husband teaching the mother of God to read; an emblematic fountain, in which the Virgin holds the infant Christ, from whose toes and fingers issue streams of water into an overflowing vase, while men gaze and crowd to catch the falling drops. Here are three altars, with their appurtenances. Over the chief one "Our Lady of the Good Voyage" presides. She is only thirty inches high, yet far too large for the ship she stands on. Though inclosed in glass, her garments and the Baby's are faded and colorless. Of the candles before her none are lit; all look yellow, as if they had been years on duty, that tall one in front excepted. It is white, clean, and distinguished farther by a red ribbon tied round the middle. "That," said the governor, "was sent here yesterday from a woman whose husband is at sea—an offering on his behalf." A few days since, another female sent over eight pounds of wax to secure the safe return of her son from Pernambuco.

One of the lesser shrines is dedicated to Santa Rita, the other to Santa Clara. Neither of these ladies are over twenty inches in stature, and not being inclosed, are left to take their chance with less sacred wood-work. They are destitute and perishing. Every thing is on a small scale as well as the images. A preacher in the box-pulpit could, with an ordinary coach-whip, administer discipline to every sinner in the congregation.

Now let us, in passing out, take a glance at the collection of old *ex votos* at the right and left of the entrance. Here hang bunches of waxen legs, arms, feet, hands, paps, breasts, heads, eyes, entire abdomens, etc., all of natural dimensions. A votive tablet records that Justina de Araujo Silva had a cancer no one eye, and was miraculously cured by N. S. da Boa Viagem. A monstrous tumor is represented in lively colors bleeding on a waxen neck—another great cure wrought by her. A tablet has a foundering ship portrayed on it, and tells us she was overtaken by a hurricane, when the crew called on the lady of this church, and she saved all. The vessel was trebly guarded from evil in her name: "Santa Anna, San Antonio, and E Almas!" This small board declares that the female who offered it was long afflicted with a pain in her side, and she was in danger of making a voyage to the other world. She came here to consult Our Lady, and was healed. One more, dated 1756, has a painting on it of a man sick in bed, and Our Lady in a corner of the room, telling him to rub the diseased parts with oil taken from the lamp then burning before her, in this very place. He followed the advice, rose a sound man, and hung up this tablet as a testimony of his gratitude and of the miracle.*

We passed into the sacristy. Two lads came in and opened drawers of the old bureau to look for something. In one lay loose leaves of an early volume in manuscript on the "Nobre Irmanda de N. S. da Boa Viagem." Some entries were dated in 1719. The only existing volume begins with 1769, and closes, without being filled, in 1818. In other drawers were the lady's linen and holiday dresses, two purple silk gowns, embroidered stomachers, and frocks and frills for the infant; a pill-box held their crowns and three or four *splendores*—i. e., silver or tin rays attached to wires to stick them on the head. Quite a number of old pictures hang on the walls. One, three feet by two, represents the birth of the Virgin. St. Anna is in bed, her husband in an arm-chair near her, and half a dozen women washing the new-born child, making posset, etc. Every canvas is ready to drop from its frame, nearly eaten out by ants. Strange, that one who can rescue sinking ships and seamen, cure colics, cancers, and other ills, should not, by a small miracle, keep her own place here in better order—save it, as well as souls, from perishing.

As characteristic a thing as any is the Lavatory. In city vestries this is generally of sculptured marble; here it is of Chinaware, and exhibits in a striking light the piety of ancient mariners voyaging from the Indies. Every piece was a gift to the lady of the place. The ewer has been a soup tureen; the wash-basin an octagonal salad-bowl. Auxiliary ornaments are from tea-sets. The manner of arranging and combining them is curious, and the whole affair is unique: against the wall arises from a step a conical fancy slab, its scalloped sides terminating with a trefoil at the apex some six feet high. It is not of stone, but stucco. Four feet up is the tureen, of which one third nearly has been buried in the mortar to sustain the two thirds projecting from it. The plaster has been scooped out to

---

* A strictly parallel case may as well be given from Gruter: One Lucius was sick of a pleurisy, and applied to Esculapius, to whom he had great devotion. The god appeared to him in a dream, and told him to take ashes from his altar, mingle them with wine, and apply them to his side. He obeyed, got well, and hung up in the temple an acknowledgment of the miraculous cure.

allow the cover to be removed. In front of the vessel a hole is drilled to receive a faucet—at present filled with a cork. Below is the basin, fixed in the same way. Then all over the remaining parts of the slab are imbedded tea and coffee-cups, saucers, tea-pot lids, plates, preserve-dishes, etc., of porcelain, with the painted sides outward. Parts of vessels are stuck in where whole ones could not be. I counted a dozen cups, four plates, between thirty and forty saucers, all whole, besides full as many broken pieces. Placed outside of a building, it would be taken as the sign of crockery on sale within.

The little cinerary vase at the foot is modern, of polished rosewood; it contains the ashes of a child, with the touching inscription, "T. d'Amor P."—" Testimonial of a Father's Love."

By a flag-staff near the church a couple of Liliputian sentries paraded. Others were sweeping paths with bunches of leaves. Several Indians are among them, chiefly tamed ones from Jesuit settlements. The authorities pick them up wherever they can, and send them down to the marine and naval schools here. They are said to make good seamen. It was asserted that the aborigines, wild and tame, have little regard for their children, often selling them for cachaça rum; and that their offspring care nothing for their parents. To illustrate this, the governor called, at my suggestion, a little fellow from the vicinity of the Amazon. In reply to interrogatories, he told us his father was dead, and he wanted to go to his mother.

We ascended the roof to get an uninterrupted view of the bay and ocean—of the city and surrounding scenery—and such a prospect! The sea, a sheet of silver; not a ruffle on the glistening bay to divert attention from its emerald isles and verdant shores, nor a cloud on the smiling face of heaven. It was like a scene in Eden. I shall not attempt to describe it, nor to portray the buoyancy of mind and feeling it inspired.

Not till now did I perceive the relative positions of the famous peaks in the vicinity of Rio: the Sugar-loaf, Two Brothers, Gavia, Corcovado, and Tejuco. But here they rose before us in such bold outlines that I could not resist the impulse to sketch

them; and the rather, as no such view, I understand, has been taken, notwithstanding its conveying so clear an idea of the physical features of the country, including even a large portion of Brazil. Instead of hills and dales, plains and valleys, it presents an endless succession of mountains, rocks, and ravines.

The point on the extreme left is the site of the Fort of Santa Cruz. Outside of the harbor's mouth are Razee and Rond Islands. In the range are seen the Sugar-loaf, Two Brothers, Gavia, Corcovado, Tejuco, the Isle of Villegagnon, and part of the city, about five miles off.

In a garret over the vestry, used as a school-room, were, among obsolete apparatus, two wooden friars, two feet high, fixed on a base, and pointing to a perpendicular slit in a board between them. A short tin tube proceeds from the breast of each. The governor thought it was an ancient weather-indicator, and that, when fair, the shaven crowns were exposed; when wet, the cowls, which moved on joints, were raised to shield them from the rain. Probably a modification of the old popular toy of a man and woman in a box: when the sun is out she appears, but when a storm is brewing she goes in and sends her partner forth.

Here was also an alms-box, worn out in service. It is of an oval form, made of tin plate, provided with a lock, ornamented with a picture of the Lady of the Good Voyage, and with a strap to pass over the neck of the collector when he started forth to receive contributions from her friends among the shipping, and from others on the city shore. It is rusted through and through.

After dining with our excellent host we took our leave. On our way down, we found the Indian child who longed for his mother on guard. At one spot the granite seemed stratified, the seams inclining at an angle of 40°. At the water's edge it resembled an artificial pavement, the white quartz projecting half an inch to an inch and a half from the dark matrix like so many pebbles. Having to wait for the steamer, we noticed theatrical and other bills posted on the ferry-house walls, esmola boxes to receive contributions for the saints, etc. It was near dark ere we reached the city, and concluded this delightful pilgrimage of a day.

The church of Boa Viagem is, in some respects, well located. No vessel can enter or leave the harbor without passing it. No votary comes in without being reminded of his promised offerings, or goes out without a hint of the value of the lady's protection. Still, it is too distant from the city and anchorage-ground, and too difficult of approach. To accommodate all who do not like to cross the Bay, or from other causes find it inconvenient to go so far, an office is opened in the city, in Saint Luzia's Church, where, as we have seen, the Lady of Navigators has an altar and a cash-box. In other churches, also, she is invoked by those who wish to secure safe passages over seas for themselves or friends, and receives the acknowledgments of such as she has saved from hurricanes and lee shores. Many a ton of wax and the sails of hundreds of vessels have been offered to her on the island, but the business is now almost entirely done in the city.

Doña S—— told me that she came from Rio Grande in 1816 in one of her father's vessels. The passage was pleasant till within a day's sail of the Sugar-loaf. A small cloud then rose rapidly from the horizon, darkness gathered over them, the sea began to swell, and other indications of a storm so alarmed the captain, that he called the men aft and asked them to join him in offering the mainsail to Francis de Paula on condition of his carrying them safe in. They agreed. Doña S—— remembers them standing round the commander, and with loud voices calling on the saint, reminding him of what they had promised, each man confirming the gift so far as his proportion of the cost went. On arriving safe, they paid for a mass, and a few days afterward went to the saint's quarters in procession, barefoot, bearing the sail through the streets, with the captain at their head. The offering was deposited in front of the church. A fair value was put upon it in presence of the priest; the captain laid down the money, and was handed a receipt stating the amount which the pious commander, Antonio Martines Bezerra, had paid into the treasury of the saint, the value of his mainsail, in fulfillment of a vow made at the approach of a storm on such a day, as an acknowledgment of the saint's miraculous interposition in behalf of himself, his ship, and crew.

Auctions of ships' sails vowed to saints in stormy weather were, till recently, quite common, and are not yet obsolete. The captains always bought them in, and not unfrequently the priests had some one to run them up, to prevent their being knocked down too low.

A regular receipt was always given. Similar scenes occasionally take place at St. Anthony's Convent, in front of the churches of Sts. José, Sebastian, Luzia, and others; but the priests of St. Francis have the greatest run, though this holy man probably never knew the difference between a barnacle and a binnacle.

In coming down from Pernambuco in 1831, my informant says they had unusually bad weather near the Abrolhos. Three water-spouts were in sight, and one so near that the noise of the ascending fluid was quite audible. Instead of depending on his own energies, and stimulating those of the crew, the captain had recourse to the Lady of the Good Voyage, promising her a large amount of wax if she would run them in alongside her island by the following day, the 4th of April. They did not get in till the 5th, and the lady lost her reward, the captain having no idea of paying her, *pro rata*, for what she had done—illustrating the ancient saying, "When the danger is over the saint is neglected."

It is an old custom of popish mariners (and pagan ones too) to scourge their patron saints when praying to them fails. Whether the practice is enforced upon the Lady of Boa Viagem I know not. It is probably confined to the other sex. Anthony comes in for many a thrashing at sea as well as on shore, *i. e.*, in ordinarily rough weather, for, when storms rage, recourse is had to entreaty and to vows, according to the proverb, "When the pilot promiseth wax and mass, it is going ill with the ship." As a tempest increases, the inducements held out increase also; officers and men, by a natural as well as devotional impulse, bidding higher and higher. Thus one or two of the smaller sails are first offered the saint; if they do not soften him, more are promised, till the main sheet is added, and, as a last resource, its weight in wax has been given.*

* The custom of offering *wax*—that is, candles, or the material to make them—

The identity between institutions, doctrines, and ceremonies of Romanists and pagans was a sore puzzle to the Jesuits on their first reaching China, Thibet, and India. There they found monks and nuns, and hierarchies from begging friars up to abbots, cardinals, and popes, with the usual appurtenances to altars and images, but confession, extreme unction, and, what was still more perplexing, a virgin represented with a child, and adored as the Queen of Heaven, Holy Mother, and the Madonna. So, also, on board of Oriental craft, they found little genii set up in cabins, with lights and other offerings before them, as in their own country shipping.

CHAPTER XXIII.

People of Color.—Twilight and Climate.—Barbonos Monks.—The Ex-Nuncio.—Henry A. Wise recalled.—Arrival of the Emperor and Anxieties of Courtiers.—A new Saint.—Mask.—Market Incident.—St. Peter's Church.—N. S. Conceição.—Plaster Images proposed.—Collecting-days and Collectors.—Church of the Mother of Men.—Fat Ladies and Gentlemen.—Unctuous Worship of N. S's. Shoe-sole.—Bedini, the new Nuncio.

April 25. Here are many wealthy people of color. I have passed black ladies in silks and jewelry, with male slaves in livery behind them. To-day one rode past in her carriage, accompanied by a liveried footman and a coachman. Several have white husbands. The first doctor in the city is a colored man, so is the President of the province. The Viscountess C——a, and scores of the first families, are tinged.

This morning the brief duration of twilight was very observable. Within half an hour the heavens changed from black to gray, and from gray to blue. Dark at half past five—at six, sunrise. Thus abruptly the business of life is ushered in and closed.

---

by seamen is of unknown antiquity. It is mentioned by Pitts, in the 17th century, as practiced by the Moors, in storms to allay, and in calms to secure a wind. When one of their vessels was about to pass the Straits, the sailors were accustomed " to make a gathering of small wax candles, which they usually carry with them, and bind them in a bundle, and then, together with a pot of oil, throw them overboard, as a present to the marabout or saint who lies entombed there on the Barbary shore, not in the least doubting but the present will come safe to the marabout's hands."—*A Faithful Account of the Religion and Manners of the Mohammedans.* London, 1731.

The heat, so uniform, and the lassitude it induces, make people seek repose at early hours. Here is nothing like our social gossipings over winter's fires. Verily, the pleasures of perpetual summer, of flowers ever blooming, and of weather ever warm, are not all that poets make them. They become monotonous, and cease to charm. The body languishes, and the mind itself begins to lose its vigor. At any rate, a feeling of the kind makes me long for the elasticity that attends a northern spring, which makes the blood, like that of plants, leap through the veins. Not insensible to the glories of the tropics, I prefer the alternations of the temperate zones—snow, and ice, and summer's sun.

In going to town, I overtook three of the monks recently returned in a Genoese vessel from a mission to the Holy Land. They have brought home select articles of vertu: scraps of the Virgin's veil and of Peter's scapulary, chaplets in great variety, pieces of the true cross, etc. To my fancy, they are, as they shuffle on before me, with fresh-shaven crowns and newly-washed legs, enormous white beaver hats, pinched up like canoes, and carried in their hands, flapping cowls and knotted belts, from which large beads, like strings of onions, hang, as great curiosities as any imported from the Old World into the new one. They belong to the "Barbonos" or Bearded Friars. Their house or monastery is in Barbonos Street, and the greater part of it sacrilegiously occupied as a blacksmithing establishment; and, worse than all, by one of the monks who threw aside his cassock at the epoch of independence, and who, maugre the denunciations of his brethren and their efforts to eject him, keeps four forges going.

There is not a fountain in Rio but presents, with the landscape of which it makes the foreground, the elements of a picture, and some are eminently picturesque. For several days I have been endeavoring to secure their outlines. After visiting one this morning in Engenho Velha, I continued along the avenue to the residence of the Hon. Henry A. Wise, and spent the day with him and his amiable lady.

The ex-nuncio, an old gentleman in a three-cornered hat and red stockings, called to take leave of Mr. Wise, having been superseded, and, as report goes, by a deep-designing Jesuit. He is reputed to have been too liberal to suit the views of the Vatican, and too enlightened to sanction the popular superstitions. He says the people here have no religion; they worship images, and delight only in the grossest of Church usages, while the clergy are notorious for the worst of vices. He was once asked why the Pope did not send a legate to preside over the Romanists in the United States. His reply was, "There is no need of one. The clergy there are more spiritual than any where else. Their conflicts with Protestant sects keep them pure."

[Mr. Wise was subsequently recalled. If the published accounts of the first interview of one of his successors with the court are to be relied on, there is a passage in Plutarch respecting two Theban embassadors to the Persian monarch worth transcribing: "Pelopidas submitted to nothing unworthy of his country or his character, but Ismenias, when commanded to adore the king, dropped his ring, that, stooping to pick it up, he might make the required prostration." There are Republicans without even the virtue of Ismenias—who pander to royalty to an extent that, in an Athenian or Spartan embassador, would have been punished with death.]

26*th*. The morning papers announced the probable arrival of the emperor from his southern tour, and by noon the expected frigate entered the Bay. Guns at the fort and flags on Castle Hill proclaimed the news. Hackney-carriages and liveries are in fierce demand—flowers too, to shower on the monarch and his queen. Ladies for some time back have been preparing their dresses, and gentlemen also—men of fifty, ex-councilors and senators, consulting about costumes in which to join the procession; whether to dress like the courtiers of Francis I., Henry IV., or to imitate those of Louis XIV.! studying, moreover, in what drapery their youngest sons should, by waiting on their imperial majesties to-day, "take the first step in nobility," for such is the expression.

It is amusing to hear, as we have heard for the last two hours, of gentlemen at their wits' end in consequence of the dilatoriness of the artists on whose skill their hopes have been placed; but the delay, in one or more instances, is known to be due to alterations ordered after the last cut and finish had been repeatedly given. On this account, and because some public decorations are not quite complete, a deputation has been off to ask the emperor to remain on board till to-morrow, when every thing will be ready to receive him. He is said to have given an emphatic refusal.

He landed at 4 P.M. A light rain fell, but a procession was formed from the Bay to the palace, consisting of officers of the army, navy, and the Church, ministers of state, gentlemen of the bed-chamber, and a fair bevy of maids of honor. Pedro walked under a canopy. Six feet three inches tall, his wife with difficulty reached his arm. Some of the officers of the household had their sons with them—lads of eight, ten, and twelve, dressed in court costume. Several had the *right* to attend, from having rendered personal service to the emperor, and becoming thereby ex officio members of the household. Inquiring what the nature of the service was, I was told such as picking up his handkerchief, presenting him a towel after dinner, a tooth-pick, or a snuff-box, for which their fathers or friends contrive to give them an opportunity. They are named "the emperor's young and noble servants," a title, with the privileges, much sought after. At the christening of the little prince, four of them climbed the first rung of glory's ladder by carrying a cloth to wipe the child after being anointed.

As a fact indicative of republican feeling, a young Brazilian of my acquaintance refused to succeed his father as "a gentleman of the bed-chamber," saying he would perform no such services for any man.

The bishop informs the public through the "Jornal" that he has designated the 10th proximo for the inauguration of the *new saint* brought from the catacombs at Rome, to which day we will postpone our notice of her.

27*th*. Met a negro with an iron mask in his hand, probably to put on one of his fellow-slaves, or possibly himself; he looked sorrowful enough for either contingency.

An exciting scene to a stranger was the unloading of several faluas. Laughing and yelling slaves came wading through the muddy surf with crockery-ware, coffee, and other inland produce on their heads. A cargo of the former they spread out on clean spots of Palace Square.

Stepping into the market, an old man at the doorway offered

me a little framed picture. "My friend," quoth I, "I don't want it;" but he so persisted in holding it up before me by a loop, that, to satisfy him, I took it in hand, and lo! it was a thin rectangular alms-box, having a dirty engraving of some saint pasted on one side. A negro, crippled and awfully disfigured by elephantiasis, seated on the steps, watched us closely, and when I handed back the box, burst into such a shriek of laughter as I suppose is seldom heard out of Africa. On receiving it, the man seemed all but transfixed. He wore a withered alb, and was taking up collections for the saint figured on the box. I am told his amazement probably arose as much from my neglecting to kiss the portrait as from not contributing, no one taking in hand such holy things without carrying them to the lips. Were the Savior to revisit the earth and walk through this market, would he drop alms into the receptacle of sacerdotal mendicants, or into the hands of poor black Lazaruses at their feet?

In Rua San Pedro I found the dark and little church dedicated to him open, and went in. It is slightly elliptical, with a domed roof, divided into panels, in which mitres, crooks, and kindred symbols figure. Here are two side shrines, at one of which a priest and lad were performing mass. Not a worshiper present except an old negress and myself. In a few minutes the priest finished, folded something up in a cloth, and, with his assistant, retired. Among a group of little statues at one shrine was *Becket*, with a knife sticking in his skull. While trying to make out the others, a dark shadow swept over the floor, accompanied with a slam. I turned; the old black woman had vanished, and a half naked negro was staring at me with the church keys in his hand. Here are some good old carvings, but the names of the images, large and small, I could not extract from the grinning sacristan. The only intelligent replies as I pointed to each were "San Pedro" and "San Gonsalves."

I next toiled up Mount Conceição to the bishop's palace—a plain two-story structure, with nothing observable about it but its location and pompous name. I have already remarked that here the constituted servants of the Lord are lords of the hills, and own no small part of the city valleys too, while in the interior some ecclesiastical orders can exclaim with God himself, "Every beast of the forest is ours, and the cattle upon a thousand hills."

Turning into Violas Street, I came to a very mean-looking church. The door was closed, but a side passage led into the vestry, where were huge collections of ex votos, and among them quite a number of babies—and properly so, since this is the temple of the Lady da Conceição. Masons were replastering the niches in the cemetery, of which there are ninety. An open door showed a negro taking up an old carpet near the altar. Stepping in, I found myself close to the goddess of the place, and was greatly disappointed in finding the most popular of Brazilian patronesses—the lady par excellence—she to whom the emperor's mother cried for a boy, and had him sent her—in so wretched a home, and so sooty and shabbily dressed! And who could have expected that this lady, of all others, should be represented in a four-foot doll, with garments stained and tarnished as if from standing years in a toy-shop window?

Were I familiar with ecclesiastical managers, I would suggest the replacing of the legions of their wooden ladies and gentlemen with saints cast in Paris plaster. Such, from their snowy whiteness, their freedom from spots and stains, would harmonize with, and even suggest ideas of moral purity, and consequently be contemplated with more advantage than images which irresistibly lead one to associate those they represent with sluttery or with rakes, who, having spent their fortunes, have nothing left but shabby finery. To keep these fading characters in fit condition to edify the devout, the services of a host of artists are constantly required, and are secured when funds are provided, but when these are wanting, a coat of paint and varnish, to improve the complexion of their faces and cleanse their hands, is about all that is done for them, and that only once, or, it may be, twice in a generation. Now saints in plaster can have new suits for nothing. They would always be "at home," and dressed in character—never denied to visiting friends for being in an undress, and unfit to receive company. In the murkiest churches, the most they could require would be a dipping in lime and water once or twice a year.

Images are peculiar to and essential to Polytheism. Originating in low stages of mental development, it is difficult to imagine how, without them, any thing like uniformity of views respecting the persons, attributes, and functions of legions of invisible beings invoked could have been established in the minds of the ignorant masses. What confusion if every imagination had been left to conjure up figures of the gods for itself! Standard patterns removed the difficulty; being greatly multiplied and met with every where, in public grounds, gardens, temples, and private dwellings, they circulated like modern tracts, and kept alive a knowledge of the chief characteristics of each divinity. They were books that were never closed, and such as all could peruse and comprehend. What they were to the heathen they are to the untutored Romanists—indispensable. Independent of the part they have played in human history, they are not without interest when viewed simply as an invention by which sensible media were made to convey definite ideas on spiritual things.

Every church has services somewhat peculiar to itself, in consequence of the special divinity to whom it is dedicated. But there are weekly masses, exclusive of those on Sundays, common to all parish churches, and on the days they are celebrated collectors go forth to ask alms to meet the expense. Thus, in the Cattete, every Monday a man knocks at our door for a donation to release imprisoned souls; on Thursdays, "for the sacrament;" on Saturdays the cry is, "Wax for Our Lady." For some purposes these men do not go beyond their parish boundaries, while for others they canvass the city at large. Every day more or less are out. On Thursdays they are so numerous as to be met with every where. They call at every door, and enter every store, no matter what number of customers are within, nor how much proprietors are engaged.

Tuesdays are appropriated to replenish the purse of the treasurers of Nossa Senhora da Conceição. Friday is the day for the friends of the Lady of Pains to do what they can for her. Every few weeks an old gentleman appeals to us for the Lady of Lampadoza, and another gives us frequent opportunities of securing the good will of Luzia. Every saint that holds a feast has a collector. Once a month an agent of Antonio's Convent comes round; hence these fathers canvass the city twelve times a year. Wearing a primitive Quaker's hat, a coarse black gown, be-

S

neath the skirts of which his bare legs are seen, with a dark, long bag in his hand or slung over his shoulder, he draws up at the door or window. His cry is, "For the friars of St. Anthony." Under a vow of poverty, these mendicants originally asked only for bread; hence the bag is still carried, and occasionally charged with victuals, but the collections generally are in coin. When money is given him, the rule now is to pull out a loaf from the bag, to intimate that for bread it will be expended.

Impressions derived from accounts of the old barefooted friars are hardly sustained by a personal acquaintance with their modern representatives. The romance of the character is very much dissipated. Formerly the duty of asking alms was performed by respectable members of the brotherhoods from religious motives, but of late years they have begun to decline it. The collectors, being poor men, are often charged with defrauding the saints whose agents they are. Doña B—— says the old chap in her district pockets considerable! It is, however, an old popish sentiment that he who begs for God collects for *two*. The amount yearly taken up must be a large one; and were it expended for educational purposes, illuminating the minds of the living instead of attempting to alter the condition of the dead, and stocking churches with toys and bawbles, it would prove a public blessing. It is a poor compliment to patron saints to suppose they can be gratified with the puerile honors paid them. If they *are* tickled with such things, they are not worth tickling.

The little church of Mai dos Homens—mother of men—in Alfandega Street, being open, I stepped in. Black and white upholsterers had sole possession, preparing it for a festival. Some, on bamboo ladders, were tacking up hangings and borders; others covering skeleton columns with red cloth and gimp edging. There are only two auxiliary shrines. The glass before the images was so much in want of washing that I could not make out who they were.

29*th*. The public walk or garden was illuminated this evening in compliment to the emperor. For the first time since I have been here there was in it quite a throng. Some of the handsomest and some of the fattest ladies and gentlemen I ever saw were among the promenaders.

I was on my way to H———'s, who agreed to accompany me to the house of Senhor Barboza. He had gone to visit the Capuchins, so we strolled up and found him in the vestry. While we stood facing the framed pattern of Mary's shoe-sole, a colored  man came between it and us, and, putting his hands against the whitewashed wall, pressed his mouth and rubbed his nose against it. Shortly after, a respectable white man came in, and saluting it three separate times, passed into the chapel, where I found him with his colored predecessor, half an hour after, both on their knees. Two cloud-like patches were on the wall right and left of the frame—stains left by the hands of the worshipers. These unctuous proofs of devotion had accumulated since my previous visit. The central parts were dark as umber. A long bench beneath the picture rendered it necessary to use the hands in this act of piety.

Coming down, we met the new nuncio—or nounce, as the word is pronounced—with a white youth in flaming livery behind him. M. Bedini is said to be the confidential adviser of his countrymen, the unpopular Capuchins, whom he was climbing and panting to visit.

CHAPTER XXIV.

Pluvial Deity. — Aqueduct Records. — Pope John. — Ecclesiastical "Cries." — Slaves. — Army Recruits. — The Emperor opens the Legislature. — Fires and Fire-engines. — Slaves. — Suicide. — Begging for the Holy Ghost. — Auction of Slaves

May 1. This morning every black peak pulled down its cloud. A milk-white one hung like an apron on the hunchback's breast, leaving his rough head alone exposed, as if the freak was to imitate a negro in the barber's hands. Surely the Pluvial deity and the nymphs his daughters have few locations more congenial than this. The glens and glades, the leaping streams and gurgling eddies, seem expressly made for wood and water goddesses to sport and splash in. There are seasons, however, when the gushing rivulets are reduced to broken threads, trickling feebly on, and scarcely able to prevent evaporation taking all: then the Corcovado driads mourn, and the Tejucan naiads lean pensive over their empty pitchers, then the city fountains begin to fail, and anxious mortals entreat the showery deity to incline his vase and let the rain come down in earnest. As elsewhere, when they have got enough, they beg him to turn the talha up.

Spent part of the day in the Office of Public Works, and was greatly surprised at learning that no document is extant relating to the origin and history of the great Carioco aqueduct.

H—— and I passed through the new buildings erecting for the Mizericordia. On a pile of stones lay a marble slab belonging to the old burying-ground. An inscription signified that Pope John XXII. had granted to all the faithful who repeated a subjoined prayer "as many days' indulgence *as bodies are buried here.*" It begins with " God bless you, Christian souls." Such prayers have, it is said, virtue in them yet, and that, too, in a land not heard of till more than a century after John himself had been buried.

We met an alms collector quite cast down at his poor success. He told H—— the priest had detained him so long that other esmoleiros had been round and left him nothing to glean. His dish was an old article of silver, six inches over, and three deep. On the flaring rim was engraved, "Frequezia do Santissimo Sacramento do Sé." Here are a few ecclesiastical cries with which I have become somewhat familiar:

Para a cera de Nossa Senhora da Gloria.
Esmola para O Divino.
Para Santa Luzia Milagraza.
Para a Propagação da Fé (Capuchin's cry).
Para a Santissimo Coração do Jesus.
Para a Frades de San Antonio.
Para a cera do Santissimo Sacramento.
Para a Missa das Almas.

And so on for Joseph, Joaquim, Anne, the ladies Piedade, Conceição, do Parto, Dores, Terco, and many more.

The friars of Anthony are candid—their cry is openly for *themselves;* at the same time, they are prohibited from touching money; but *no quiero mas echadmelo en la capilla* is not a proverb of yesterday.

2*d.* While waiting for Colonel F——, whose office is not far from the Matadoura, a dozen at least of butchers' slaves went past in the course of an hour with crushing loads of fresh-killed beef. The flesh was warm; it smoked, and all but quivered.

One poor fellow had a collar, and a chain extending from it to an ankle; he belonged to a meat-shop in the Cattete. Two hindquarters are a common load. Other slaves went by, awfully crippled in their feet and legs; among them two women, lame with elephantiasis, with light loads. The right leg of one was really almost as large as her waist. A purblind man, with a talha of water on his head, crept along, feeling his way with a stick.

Some Minas girls, dealers in fowls, smartly dressed, and with tribal scars on their faces, passed on laughing. Each had a wide basket and a supplemental chicken in her hand, holding it, as the custom is here, by the wings. Of about one hundred and fifty blacks who thus passed by, all were slaves save one. His feet were thrust into a pair of old shoes or slippers—the badge of freedom. Proud of wearing the same covering to their feet as white people wear, some pay dear for the gratification. When men are wanted for the army, a keen look-out is kept up for them. Those aware of their danger go barefoot, and sometimes throw the recruiting officers off their guard, as slaves can not be impressed.

I met, a few days ago, a hundred recruits just coming in from a northern province. They were nearly all colored; one third were Indians. "How long do they enlist for?" I asked. "They don't enlist at all," was the answer. They are caught and made to serve. Governors have orders to send down all disorderly fellows, and such Indians as they can catch.

3d. As the emperor opens the legislative session to-day, H—— and I walked over to the senate-chamber—a plain room, forty feet square, with an internal arrangement similar to that of most of our state chambers. The throne is a high-backed chair, placed against the wall behind the presiding officer's seat, and set off with drapery. The hour had arrived, and not over fifty spectators in the gallery, although admittance was free. With the exception of four priests, both senators and deputies were in official costume—white pants with laced seams, green coats buttoned up to the chin and half covered with lace, swords, and chapeaux. Most were of middle stature and corpulent—not a Cassius among them.

Brazilians do not lack the elements of greatness, but a patriot in homespun—a Franklin, Phocion, or Dentatus—would hardly be appreciated.

An aerial looking personage, powdered and uniquely draped, tripped in and out. I took him for master of ceremonies, but he was Speaker of the Chamber of Deputies. The President of the Senate now rang his bell. The secretary read the roll, and about twenty answered to their names. A committee was detailed to wait on the emperor, and presently he entered, with long but very deliberate steps, resting the forward foot till the rear one got up and halted, precisely as players tread the stage. He carried a long gilt staff in manner of a walking-stick, grasping it two feet below the top, as hermits are sometimes painted. From where I sat, I might have touched the finial that crowned it. He had nearly reached the throne, when a gentleman came in, holding up with both hands the continuation of his train or mantle. He had necessarily to remain with his back to us till this long piece of drapery was gathered up, as he could not turn till this was done without being tripped up.

At last the troublesome appendage is coiled up and laid on the floor by his chair, he leans the staff against the wall, turns, inclines his head right and left, and, dropping into the chair, begs the senators to be seated. An officer hands him "the speech." He reads it well—I should say very well. His enunciation is rapid, but distinct, and agreeably diversified with emphasis. His voice is rather feminine. It is musical, but slightly nasal, as if he indulged in snuff. Running down three pages of the foolscap sheet, he handed it back to the officer, arose, slightly nodded to the empress in the gallery, took the staff, gave a glance behind, where the train-bearer—a marquis—was shaking it out, bows to the senators, and goes out as he entered. The performance lasted about twelve minutes.

His dress was in imitation of some ancient monarch's. (He was married in the costume of Francis I.) His throat was naked, and surrounded like a school-boy's by his shirt-frill, whose triple row of edging rested on an ermine tippet that reached to his elbows. His arms were in close white satin sleeves, that met gloves of the same material, with ribbons and ruffles at the wrists. From the tippet to his toes he was in white satin; his very shoes and roses on them were of it, and the whole so closely fitted to the upper and nether limbs that, divested of the train and tippet, he might have been taken any where else for a pantaloon, or, judging from the long pole he leaned on, for a rope-dancer about to turn a somerset.

So excessively punctilious in trifles as Brazilians are, there was one part of the performance not quite the thing. The chair was either too low or the legs of Pedro too long. It seemed as if, on sitting down, he became aware that he could not keep them upright without some part of his dress giving way; and as it would have been undignified to throw them out in front, he was compelled to coil them under the seat, where, judging from their restlessness, they were very unhappy. (Like other histrionic gentlemen, royal actors must submit to theatrical criticism.) The crown worn by this modern cacique is a large spheroidal, ungraceful mass, which at a distance might be taken for a head preternaturally enlarged with hydrocephalus. It seems to have been made after the pattern of an orange or melon. The orbicular sections meet at the top, support a globe—the earth—and over it—the church's emblem—a cross shoots up conspicuously.

Nothing of interest occurring, we left, and found the emperor waiting for the empress in a low, old-fashioned, and open carriage, said to have belonged to Sebastian, who lost his life warring with the Moors. Here he remained five or six minutes longer. Besides the guards, not over twenty persons were about, and hardly a moiety of them paid more attention to him than to his coachman. Not a hat was raised, nor a viva uttered; nor did he court any thing of the kind. Pertinaciously looking up, none could catch his eye. He was evidently acting—putting in practice the royal aphorism, "Avoid familiarity with the masses." He finally was whirled off with no more eclat than attends the departure of a common stage. The gilt staff, I am told, is the *sceptre*—an ensign that I supposed never exceeded one third of its length.

5th. The bell of the Antonio Convent rang an alarm of fire. It was in a store near by. Desirous of witnessing the management in such cases, I arrived before the engine. Dense smoke was issuing from the doorway and windows. Two negroes came along, screaming and dragging an engine, accompanied by an officer in a blue roundabout and a brass-handled sword in hand. The machine consisted of an open copper cistern on wheels, containing two pump cylinders, the pistons of which were connected to a lever, and worked fore and aft by a man at each end. The apparatus was identical with those of Europe in the seventeenth century. To feed it, a water-cart was brought up, and the contents drawn into buckets and poured into the cistern. A small hose conveyed the water to the flames.

In a couple of hours all was over, and but little damage done. In New York, an entire block had been consumed under the circumstances, for the little garden pump—it was no larger—would have been all but useless. It might be suspected that conflagrations in tropical cities like Rio would be frequent and extensive. The reverse is the fact. They seldom occur, and rarely is a house destroyed—not one, I am told, in many years. The cause is partly to be ascribed to the little use made of fire except for cooking, but chiefly to the comparative incombustibility of woods employed in building. It is not easy to kindle the beams of a dwelling. Pine joists are prohibited.

On returning, I passed in the same street a short, spare, and feeble old woman, creeping along the pavement with a baril of water on her head. An iron collar grasped her shriveled throat, and from its prong a chain ran up and was secured to the handle of the vessel by a padlock—about as cruel a sight as I have seen yet.

"Is it a cause of wonder that so many of your slaves emancipate themselves by death rather than endure life on such conditions?" "To treat them in that way," replied my friend, "or to put masks on them, is forbidden, but laws respecting them are disregarded." Every day or two suicides are announced in the police reports, yet it is affirmed that not half are officially noticed. Those who plunge into the Bay and float ashore come under the cognizance of the authorities. Of such as sink and never rise, and all that pass out to sea, or are devoured by sharks before they reach it, no account is or can be kept, nor yet of those who destroy themselves in the secret places of the city or dark recesses of the neighboring forests. Many are advertised as runaways who have reached the spirit land. Suicides, it is said, have greatly increased during the last three years.

Yesterday I met in Ajuda Street the Santa Rita collectors for the Holy Ghost, flying to and fro, and screaming "Esmolas para O Divino." Instead of a silver bird, they had its picture in a little tin frame for contributors to kiss. The two banners, a yard square, were of faded crimson, with a white dove in the centre, or rather it had once been white, for, saluted by hundreds of perspiring faces, it could not long retain the color of snow. Both musicians and collectors were meanly and not over-cleanly dressed. They had a shabby, and, in truth, a rakish appearance. To-day the music of the Campo troop returning from the country drew us to the windows. One of the drummers and the player on a triangle had each a live fowl—donations, probably, of rural devotees. While E—— dropped some coppers into a dish, I relieved the bearer of the holy emblem, and bore it to an inner room, he imagining, of course, for the family to salute. It consisted of a small piece of thin metal struck up in a die, and resembled the spread eagle on some of our soldiers' caps. It was fastened in a tin case, little larger than a blacking-box, with a piece of glass in front, and a handle at the back for holding it to the lips of worshipers. One of the banners I also took in. The central part was of the color of snuff, and thickened and stiffened with grease, apparently the accumulation of years from sweating faces, black and white, and which time had hardened to the consistence of wax.

H—— was employed this forenoon in releasing from the press-gang a slave who slipped out last night in tamancos. Another, belonging to the same family, was taken sick, when one of his associates cupped him—a favorite African remedy; many negroes are not less expert in applying than in removing disease by it. The process and apparatus are of extreme antiquity. The operator scratches the skin with a flint, places the wide end of a sheep's horn over it, and sucks out the air. Negro chirurgeons uniformly prefer bleeding their patients in sunshine, insisting that the effect is then most beneficial.

8th. I have repeatedly passed an auction store at the corner of Ourives and Ouvidor. To-day printed bills were hanging by the door. I took one and stepped in. A long table extended from near the entrance to the low box pulpit of the salesman. Behind it, a light iron railing cut off a portion of the store. The place was filled with new and second-hand furniture, old pictures, Dutch cheeses, Yankee clocks, kitchen utensils, crockery-ware, old books, shoes, pickles, etc.—the very kind of shop which a young Athenian once stopped a plain-looking citizen in an alley to inquire after—that is, when Xenophon and Socrates first met.

Vendues of these things are held here daily, and once or twice a week another variety of merchandise is offered. This was the case to-day—an assorted invoice of colored goods, arranged on benches behind the railing. The catalogue contained eighty-nine lots, and each lot had a corresponding number pinned to it, that purchasers, on running over the list, might compare the articles with their description. These goods were living beings. Every lot was a man or woman, a boy or girl. There were fifty-three males, most of whom ranged between eighteen and thirty years of age—carpenters, masons, smiths, and country hands. One was a sailor, another a caulker and boatman. There were two tailors, a coachman, a saddler, a sawyer, a squarer of timber (one expert with the adze), a shoemaker, cooks, a coffee-carrier, and a barber surgeon, who, like most of his profession, was a musician—" No. 19, 1 Rapaz, Barbeiro, bom sangrador e musico."

Of females, the oldest was twenty-six, and the youngest between seven and eight—washers, sewers, cooks, two dress-makers " muito prendada" — very accomplished. Others made shirts, dressed ladies' hair, etc. A couple were wet-nurses, with much good milk, and each with a colt or filly, thus: " No. 61, 1 Rapariga, com muito bom leite, com cria." Cria signifies the young of horses, and is applied to negro offspring.

They were of every shade, from deep Angola jet to white or nearly white, as one young woman facing me appeared. She was certainly superior in mental organization to some of the buyers. The anguish with which she watched the proceedings, and waited her turn to be brought out, exposed, examined, and disposed of, was distressing. A little girl, I suppose her own, stood by her weeping, with one hand in her lap, obviously dreading to be torn away. This child did not cry out—that is not allowed—but tears chased each other down her cheeks, her little bosom panted violently, and such a look of alarm marked her face as she turned her large eyes on the proceedings, that I thought at one time she would have dropped.

"Purchasers of pots and pot-lids," said Diogenes, "ring them lest they should carry cracked ones home, but men they buy on sight." If such was the practice of old, it is not so now: the head, eyes, mouth, teeth, arms, hands, trunks, legs, feet—every limb and ligament without are scrutinized, while, to ascertain if aught within be ruptured, the breast and other parts are sounded.

The auctioneer, a tall, black-whiskered man of thirty-five, was a master of his profession, if one might judge from his fluency and fervor. A hammer in his right hand, the forefinger of his left pointing to a plantation hand standing confused at his side, he pours out a flood of words. The poor fellow had on a canvas shirt, with sleeves ending at the elbows and trowsers of the same, the legs of which he is told to roll above his knees. A bidder steps up, examines his lower limbs, then his mouth, breast, and other parts. He is now told to walk toward the door and back, to show his gait. As he was returning, the hammer fell, and he was pushed back within the railing. Another, who had but four toes on one foot, was quickly disposed of.

The clerk next went behind the rails and brought forward a

woman—a field-hand. She was stout, and seemed older than reported in the catalogue. Dressed as sparely and plainly as the men, she too was examined, and told to walk to and fro. When near the door, a bidder interrogated her, but on what l could not comprehend. His last remark was translated plainly by her raising her skirt to expose her legs. They were much swollen. Two hundred and fifty milreis was the sum she brought.

The sale, half over when I entered, was adjourned for an hour. What became of the white woman and child I did not learn. One fact was most palpable—no more regard was paid to the feelings of the victims than if they had been so many horses.

Thus have I seen, for the first time in my life, the bones and muscles of a man, with every thing appertaining to him, put up for sale, and his body, soul, and spirit struck off to the highest bidder—God's automata knocked down for less than Maelzell's wooden puppets. They brought higher rates than bodies at surgeons' halls; but, if negroes were worth more dead than living, the supply, it is said, would equal the demand. That, however, I do not believe; yet, from what I have seen, I should say it were better—yes, unspeakably better—for many to be knocked on the head in their youth, have their skins converted into glue and their bones into ivory black, than endure through life what some endure.

CHAPTER XXV.

Winter.—New Saint.—Lady do Parto.—An English Monk.—Black and white Infants in Purgatory.—Auction at a private Dwelling: its Furniture, Garden, Lares, Oratorio, and Slaves.—Barber's Basin and Shaving-cloth.—Mass and Capuchins.—Church of the Rosary, its Images and Ex Votos.—A sick Man.—Old Slave.—Uncertain Origin of the Negro Saint.—Ramble through Nictherohy.

May 10. Winter is coming on apace. Ladies are occasionally seen chilled and shivering as in an ague-fit, from the humidity of the air and absence of fires. Rain has depressed the thermometer to 72°. The little Cattete stream has again swollen, till barils, pans, and talhas are borne away, and dashed together in its whirling eddies—a scene like that from which the ancient fabulist derived the story of the iron and the earthen pot.

The new saint was to make her *début* to-day, but the wet condition of the streets has induced the managers to postpone it for a week. When it does take place, the Sugar-loaf, Corcovado, Tejuca, and Organ peaks will witness a piece of folly unequaled on the hemisphere since they raised their everlasting heads.

"Leilao extraordinario, hoje Domingo, 10 de Maio, na rua Novo do Conde, No. 167, Catumby." This was a favorable opportunity to look over the interior of a wealthy native establishment. Passing, on my way, the Lady do Parto's church, a red cloth hanging in the doorway intimated that she was "at home." A fine-looking Mozambique, with a row of artificial pimples down his nose and forehead, and perpendicular lines cut in each cheek, was making a leg and otherwise complimenting her. The only worshiper present, he turned his head, glanced at me, and resumed his address. What on earth he could want with her I could not imagine, nor what she could possibly do for him.

I overtook the short and plump English monk, Father T——y. Holding up the skirts of his cassock with his left hand, his right swung to and fro quick as an eight-inch pendulum. His skullcap, like an inverted saucer made of sticking-plaster, covered the shaven circle of his crown, and stuck so close that, had he been a Preto de Nação, it might have been taken for the natural cuticle. I was about crossing the pavement to address him, but a lady was approaching. As she drew near, she quickened her steps, snatched his hand, and in a twinkling her lips had met it and left it with a chirp. It would not do for priests and friars to wear gloves here.

Near the door of a low venda (in Novo Conde) was a wooden cross, four feet high, secured in the pavement, and to it was attached an alms-box, which presented the best piece of picture-writing I have met with. As the box was for soliciting contributions for souls, what form of words could so vividly portray the torments of the sufferers, and show that all races and ages are exposed to them, as an official representation of two *infants* in perdition, and one of them a negro! There is not

a colored mother in the neighborhood mourning a lost child but here beholds it crying to her for relief. What can she withhold to mitigate its pains or snatch it from them? Nothing that she has or can procure. The box is a sermon written in characters possessing perpetual Pentecostal properties. To the men and women assembled in this city from almost every nation under heaven, it speaks in their own tongues —dark strangers from Congo, Angola, Cabinda, the Gold Coast, and remoter regions of Ethiopia, red aborigines, fair children of Japhet, and dusky descendants of Shem, and to all is equally explicit, if not equally effective.

Passing travelers can hardly refuse a trifle to innocents thus beseeching them, with screeches, tears, and uplifted hands, to drop some vintems in, and the rather when so small a sum as a pataca has been known to get one out. Children whom death has deprived of a brother, sister, or a playmate, often thus dedicate to affection presents they receive. Indeed, who of the faith can withstand invitations to shorten the purgation of departed friends, or fail in this way to show the sincerity of their regard; and then, where the finer feelings are not, self-interest steps in and induces many to give, from a consciousness that when their turn comes their sufferings will be thereby lightened.

The auction was at the adjoining premises. The front half of the ground floor was paved, and served for entrance and coach-house. Dark stairs led to the principal floor. The arrangement of the rooms and their finish reminded one of old Dutch dwellings; two only were papered, the rest stenciled three feet from the floor, and all above whitewashed. No carpet concealed the dark flooring-plank in room, passage, or stairs. The paraphernalia of our luxurious parlors would be out of place. The furniture of the Cozinha was simple, and evidently allied to the appurtenances of Greek and Roman kitchens The usual cooking plate, with openings for pans, and a place beneath for charcoal or a few sticks, a dresser and shelves over it, and a marble slab for pastry, constituted the whole. Not a stool or seat of any kind. The walls, for three feet up, were lined with tiles, the floor paved; the window-frame, occupied by iron scroll-work in place of glass, opened into a fine and large garden. Half of it was divided off for kitchen vegetables, the other cut up into fancy plots and fountain basins. Vases filled with flowers stood on pedestals amid statues of the seasons and of floral deities; and if gods or mortals got tired, sofas of stone and shell work were every where at hand. The flowers were richer than Chloris ever wove in a wreath, but the trees, laden with golden fruit, took my fancy most.

The plate, exceeding two thousand ounces, was the richest part of the catalogue. The auctioneer, an elderly man, with white and shaggy eyebrows, beard, and whiskers, surpassed in volubility—" hum milreis, dous milreis, tres milreis," and slap his ivory hammer came down, giving for a moment rest to his tongue and hirsute chin. The whole affair was managed precisely as with us, differing only in language and the absence of females, who never attend.

The oratorio had an antique table for an altar, and on it the lares that presided over the house and family—Our Lady, Antonio, and Jeronimo—three coarse wooden figures whose stature was a span. Minds accustomed to worship through images require something before the bodily eye to exercise the mental. Even those who, from intellectual culture, might be supposed free from the infirmity, have their traveling apparatus. Here was one which I took for a clothes-press, but, on opening the door, an altar and images were carved in half relief against the back. The article is catalogued a " rico oratorio portatile."

But for its adjoining the kitchen, an angel might seek to worship in this room, opening, as it does, on scenes of unusual natural grandeur, as well as on the loveliest of the Creator's works that a tropical flower-garden and its winged visitants can display. Here are incitements to devotion which, if contemplated at all, must purify the coarsest souls, and throw torpid ones into paroxysms of adoration.

While admiring the grounds, a man came rushing down stairs bawling João—José—José—João. Presently two half-naked negroes threw down their hoes. He addressed three or four words to them as they approached, and pushed both into the passage, up which he hurried them. "What did he say?" I inquired. "*Come in to be sold*," was the reply. There was something in the order and manner of it, its suddenness, and the silent acquiescence of the poor fellows as they were driven in, that at the moment thrilled through me. In form and spirit it resembled an old sheriff's address on the morning of an execution to a prisoner, "Come out to be hanged."

We returned up stairs. The salesman was expatiating on a dinner-set. Another bid, and down it went. While applying his glass to a catalogue for the next article, it was forced into the crowded room close to him: "1 preto de roça de nome José, de nação Congo." Eyeing the lot a moment, he ordered it to mount on a stool, and there, utterly abashed, the poor kidnapped negro stands. Apparently of dullish intellect, short, stout, and about thirty years of age, a canvas shirt and pantaloons complete his dress. No scars are visible on him, but he is shockingly disfigured with hydrocele. He is told to pull up the longer leg of his trousers, then the other, next to turn round, and, within a minute, to get down and follow his new owner—a thin, meagre, wedge-faced old man, who bought him for 420 milreis. José, from his age and build, was deemed a prime plantation hand. The watery hernia did not reduce his value ten dollars. As a horse, when sold, is transferred to the purchaser in the cheapest kind of halter, so José could hardly have been turned over to a new owner with a poorer fit-out.

Lot 124, "1 dito de nome João," was, with as little ceremony and loss of time, put on the stand, told to bare his legs, breasts, etc., turn this way and that. He appeared more intelligent than José, and was described as possessing various qualities—he could "cook with stove and furnace"—brought 520 milreis. A Mozambique next stepped up—a melancholy man of middle life. Little was said of his acquirements. I understood he had not been long imported. He was struck off at 400 milreis to the buyer of João—a speculator.

The salesman next offered "Uma Cuya para maté com pé e guarnição de prata." The next article drove us off—a paliteiro.

The conflicting deeds and creeds of men who can reconcile? Here, in one house, were Christians selling, and on the Lord's day, into mortal thraldom, the bodies of living men, and next door taking in subscriptions to redeem the souls of dead ones!

11*th*. A smart young barber passes the window daily, with a fac-simile of Mambrino's helmet under his arm—the bright brass, wide-rimmed and scalloped basin being as common here as in Spain when Cervantes wrote. While speaking of this, singular enough, a present came in from my afflicted friend, Doña F——a; a piece of delicate cambric, not larger than this page. It had a margin of flowers in needle-work, and, outside of that, a border of lace. Ignorant of the use of this tiny mouchoir, I turned to E——a for information. "Ladies," she observed, "in the United States and England, present male relatives and friends with wrought slippers; here and in Portugal it is an ancient custom to send them *embroidered shaving-cloths.* The present is to wipe your razor on."

12*th*. The bishop, assisted by the Capuchins, celebrated mass, on account of the empress being again in an interesting way. More packages of worshiping machinery have come in from Italy. Two of the uncomely fakirs attended yesterday at the custom-house to receive them.

H—— having, according to appointment, joined me in Dereita Street, we turned up an old and narrow lane named, after the Praying Abacus, Rua do Rozario. At the head of it stands the ancient metropolitan temple, now a negro church, and the only one conceded to the colored population. Here are genii not met with in other temples, and to them our visit was intended.

At the door were three alms-boxes; on one the African's own patron, curly-headed Benedicto, was painted; on the second, Luzia, with a pair of eye-balls in her hand, appealed to us; and on the third, pointing to the slit in the cover, stood the Lady da Cabeça, holding a human head suspended by a twine or lock of hair, reminding one of Judith bearing off that of Holofernes. A timid stranger, ignorant of the character of these female beggars, might be led to imagine one a tigress that tore out the eyes of non-contributors, and the other revenging herself by spinning round the decapitated heads of those who gave her nothing.

Entering, we found the place a picture of desolation; nothing
T

visible but bare walls, ceilings, and decayed floors. The principal image, and those of the six side shrines we had come to see, had vanished. The sacristan appeared, and led us into the vestry, a large room, on one side of which an altar and apparatus were fitted up. Every thing looked old, mean, and worn out, for want of soap and paint. Being asked where the saints were, he said four were put away in the garret till the church is re-edified, and the other three are there, pointing to the altar. We drew near, and contemplated the Lady of the Rosary, or "Do Terço," as she is sometimes named, of the natural size. On one palm a naked infant sits, and from the other a string of beads —her emblem—hangs. Near her stands the popular goddess da Conceição, five and a half feet high. Her child is in a frock and sash, which once were white and red, but now are neither. From her arm is suspended by a ribbon a fresh wax votive head—a female's, and differing from any yet seen. Its ear-lappets remind one of an Egyptian head-dress. In front of these ladies is Benedict himself, black as jet, and rather low in stature, the baby in his arms being any thing but a white one.

Here are by far the best-shaped wax votos to be found in Rio. Of seventeen heads, not one had blunted or inexpressive features. Five had been taken from a bust of Demosthenes; part of the females were also from classic models; and two, judging from their bull necks, were Neros or gladiators. There were three breasts, several abdomens, and a couple of hands. Inquiring why there were no legs, arms, eyes, and feet, our informant said there had been many, but they fell and were crushed.

While making memoranda in front of the altar, I was startled by a groan at my elbow. I turned, and lo! a white man, of forty-five or fifty, on his knees, almost in contact with me. He had come in "on woolen feet." One arm was bandaged and in a sling. He was cadaverous and evidently very sick. His languid eyes were fastened on one of the images, to which he began to pour out his sorrows in a suppressed voice. I withdrew, and, joining H——, pointed to the supplicant. "Yes," said H——, with a shrug, "he told me yesterday he was coming to see if Nossa Senhora do Rozario would stop the running sore in his arm." "But why come to a black church?" I asked.

"Because during the last eighteen months he has been to every white one, without being able to interest a saint in his behalf. The lady he is now consulting has her shrine in this place, and saints, like physicians, must be called on at their residences. Many whites come here for assistance, and some make vows even to that blackamoor."

Our presence and talking, and the noise made by two romping colored boys, disturbed not in the least the poor man's devotions. In seven or eight minutes he crossed himself, rose, bowed to the lady, dipped a finger in the lustral basin, and went noiselessly away, giving H—— a sign of recognition as he passed.

We were about to follow, when an extremely old and infirm female came tottering in, barefooted, with the aid of a staff. She was nearly blind, had lost her teeth, and was the oldest slave I ever saw. She stood a while to disengage from her skirts a rosary composed of beans. A few coppers were put into her hands; she rolled her yellow eyeballs, gasped and gurgled her thanks, approached the altar, and knelt close to the patron and kinsman of her race. We left her communing with him, probably the only consolation left her.

The cemetery of this church is large. The niches for the dead are four deep, and all tenanted except two.

"Black Benedict" is generally considered an imaginary saint, got up by the Portuguese with the view of more effectually keeping slaves in subjection. I have interrogated several priests on the subject, including Father Tilbury, but not one could say who he was, where he dwelt, nor how and when he became canonized.

The portrait of him is a fac-simile of his "blessed picture" given out to his devotees, and worn in their bosoms. As a specimen of art, it is a fair sample of those of other saints.

16*th*. A fruit-woman who brought in vegetables for dinner had bunches of "witch-expelling rue" for sale.

I went over to Nictherohy. When on the Bay, the land before us appeared in gigantic heaps crowded together as if it had once been overrun with monster moles or other hill-builders. As we drew nearer, some which from the Rio side appeared inland, were in advance, as if they had waded out to meet us. Low white houses skirt the Bay, and are rural rather than city dwellings. Like country seats, they stand apart, have gardens in front, and garden walls of brick and stone, plastered and perforated with fancy apertures. Some are composed of panels

filled with inverted tiles piled on each other, their semicircular ends, and cusped openings left by them, producing an agreeable net-like appearance. Some are arranged to produce circles. As they cost little and endure for centuries, I do not see why they might not be introduced in fences with us. In form and dimensions they might be varied to meet every exigence. Between the water and these walls Rua da Praya extends — an unpaved avenue, bordered next the Bay with mango and other trees, beneath the shade of which, or even on the white, sandy beach, a glorious promenade might be laid out.

I turned to the left on landing, and strolled along the beach till a wall of rocks met the roaring surf. Cactus plants, common as thistles and docks with us, spring out of the crevices; a row of palms varied the scene, and pitos here and there reared their graceful boles. The pito is a species of aloe. Its light, spongy wood is the Pāo do fogo—tinder-wood—of the natives.

Retracing my steps, I walked in the opposite direction, where things were more lively. Stores occurred, a small market-place, and, farther on, a kind of ship-yard for repairing small craft. Ferry faluas were coming in, plowing a path through the sand till a plank answered as a bridge for their passengers. These vessels are to Rio and Nictherohy what periaguas were thirty years ago to New York and Jersey City. Hundreds prefer crossing in them than in steamers since the explosion of a boiler a few years ago, when a great number of lives were lost.

A sign-board here recalled one of Le Sage's best characters: "B——, Sangrador, Barbeiro, Dentista; vendemse e aplicāose bichas;" that is, bleeder, barber, dentist; sells and applies leeches. Piles of fire-wood were for sale; the bundles two feet long, and each containing eight or ten sticks, whose section scarcely exceeded a square inch.

Most of the streets are at right angles to the beach. In few are the houses continuous. A splendid park has just been laid out, inclosing the old church dedicated to the patron of the city, San Joāo. The population borders on three thousand. Rua da Imperatriz is the last one toward San Domingo, and has but one side built on. A large house, with wide door and two open flights of stairs, I took for the chamber of the Provincial Assembly, and passed up to a low gallery. No one was present, and, being fatigued, I took a seat. It was the theatre, as the drop-curtain and side-scenes testified. After a while there arose a burst of singing, then a measured dialogue, next came forth an exclamation as of rage, and anon a stamp followed by a shriek. The players were rehearsing.

I walked down the beach to San Domingo, passing a dog four fifths buried in the sand by the action of the surf. The next tide will wholly cover it, and there it may possibly remain, and furnish a fossil relic to geologists of the remote future.

CHAPTER XXVI.

Inauguration of a new Saint: how the alleged Bones were procured.—Buried in a waxen Figure.—The Bishop's Letter.—The Affair generally condemned.—Bedini and Miranda. — The Emperor declines joining the Procession. — The Pomp.—The "Arca" and Saint within.—Official Account.—Newspaper Puff.—A Visit to Priscilliana.—Miranda's Circular.—A French Tribunal on Religious Impositions.

May 17. The imported saint is to be added to-day to the Brazilian calendar, and her bones to the Church's treasure. Had I been three centuries in the country I could not have witnessed such an act, since nothing of the kind has heretofore occurred on this half of the globe. Not a shrine in North or South America is enriched with so much as a sacred leg, arm, or foot brought from abroad. The introduction of a new saint into the New World, in the middle of the nineteenth century, is therefore a fact of some significance in Church history. I shall give the particulars a little in detail, and quote official documents.

Let it be premised, then, that the spruce vicar of St. Anne's parish, a man of enterprise, versatility of genius, and address, took a trip to Europe, and so won on the late Pope, that his holiness conferred on him the titular dignity of "Monsenhor," and gave him access to the Catacombs. Whether his great feat was conceived before he left home is uncertain; the general opinion is that it flashed on him when abroad. Be this as it may, the idea of procuring the bones of a saint, having them officially verified, duly prepared, and set up in his own church, was a brilliant one, since, if carried out, he would have a shrine unique in Brazil. Creditable to his sagacity and taste, instead of rummaging for a modern or medieval monk, he sought for an ancient martyr; and as the sex in his country is distinguished by the title of "devout," he preferred a heroine to a hero. Of innocents butchered in early persecutions, Priscilliana was one, and her alleged bones were found and given to him.

The world is not so coarse and uncouth as it used to be. Ornate arts are acting the part of smooth files in reducing asperities left by old hatchets and rasps. The people of Rio are attached to the refinements of modern life, hence ghastly remains of mortality are not so attractive to them as to their ancestors and ours in less polished times. Relics, to be revered, must not be repulsive. Miranda, therefore, employed an artist in Rome to bury them in a waxen figure of a beautiful girl, and another to furnish her with appropriate costume; a third, also, to make an "arca," or chest, in which he brought her over, and in which she is, and is to remain.

He arrived in January or February. On the 30th of March the "Jornal" contained a notice of the saint, furnished, as generally understood, by him. It states that she was the daughter of Priscillia, who devoted herself and child to the Church—succoring the persecuted members, visiting those in prison, collecting relics of the martyrs, etc. Priscilliana, when sixteen, was arrested, confessed the religion of the cross, was tortured, wounded in the neck by a sword, and eventually put to death. She was buried in the Catacombs, and providentially found by his eminence the Cardinal Patricio, vicar-general of Rome, and, by the special grace of his holiness, given to Dr. M. J. de Miranda Rego. Near the body was a vase, containing her blood mixed with sand, which was also given him.

It states farther, that the bones have been united and covered with wax, to represent the holy maid as she appeared before her death; and farther, that the crown of her head has been left uncovered, to show the cranium of the virgin; that the solemn exposure and translation to the church of St. Anne of these precious monuments of religion, which the city of St. Sebastian has the good fortune to possess, will take place as soon as their imperial majesties arrive, and in the form and manner prescribed by his reverend excellency the bishop.

On the same day there will be installed a new brotherhood of St. Priscilliana. Their duties will be to take charge of the place where the holy relics will be deposited, assist in the celebration of a mass on the day of her feast, and to award to poor maids, on their marriage, six hundred milreis, to the honor and glory of the said virgin martyr. (See Appendix B.)

On the 14th of April the bishop's Pastoral Letter on the subject came out. It is characteristic; says much about Chrysostom, early piety, and general virtue, but little about the bones, how discovered, how authenticated, and not a word about the blood, or how it was obtained and verified. (See Appendix C.)

Before proceeding, it may as well be stated here that the affair is condemned by a large portion of the people. I have not met with an individual who does not shrug up his shoulders and pull down the corners of his mouth at the mention of it. The idea has been scouted by the better classes of the government endorsing it, nor are the clergy of one mind. Many bitterly but privately oppose it. My old friend the vicar has been invited to assist in the translation. He declines. The feeling against it is strengthened by the reputed character of the projector. Pious ladies have said in my presence that the bones of the saint had better have been left where they were than that he should have any thing to do with them. Others doubt their genuineness; to which it is replied, " If they are the true ones, they will work miracles."

In the face of this opposition, the managers, with the nuncio at their head, have not been inactive. Invitations to the numerous brotherhoods occupy the papers. Albs are offered to poor members. There was a talk of having " eleven thousand virgins" in the pomp, or as near that number as possible, but too many parents refused to send their daughters. It was also in contemplation to issue a general invitation to the ladies of the city, and that idea was abandoned, so many viewing the affair with cold suspicion. The schools have been applied to. Miranda begs the " Imperial Society of the Lovers of Instruction" to permit their pupils to walk in the procession, and offers to supply twenty with appropriate attire at his own cost.

On the 8th of the present month the " Jornal" published this official notice: "*Procession of Saint Priscilliana.*—On Sunday, 10th instant, at four in the afternoon, the procession of the holy relics of the virgin martyr St. Priscilliana will start from the church of St. Francisco da Prainha, passing through the streets of Prainha, Imperatriz, and Largo Joaquim, to the church of St. Anne. Their reverend excellencies, the bishops who are in Rio, will bear the *arca* at the commencement. As soon as the relics of the holy virgin are placed on the altar, a solemn Te Deum will be chanted, and a sermon will be preached by the Reverend Monsenhor Doctor Manoel Joaquim de Miranda Rego. *Their imperial majesties will honor this religious solemnity with their presence.*"

The announcement, as may readily be supposed, moved scores of native breasts with deep chagrin. Not till now did they believe it possible that the emperor could so far " disgrace himself and the country." But, while some glow with indignation, others think it his duty to attend, irrespective of the genuineness or spuriousness of the relics ; that neither he nor the Legislature can interfere, as both have sworn to support the Church, and she is sole judge of her own matters. Such, in fact, is the case. The Constitution binds government and people to the papal chair; accordingly, the Church has put her crest or cipher on every public establishment; it surmounts the crown, and is stamped on every coin. To oppose her is treason, literally. Editors dare not come out against the imposition, however convinced they may be that it is one. It is rumored that the late bishop would never have given it his sanction, and that the scruples of the present one have been with difficulty overcome by Bedini.

To allay the feeling elicited by the notice of the 8th, another was issued on the 9th, stating that the emperor will *not* join the procession, but will witness it from a window in the War Department, a building close to St. Anne's church. This, it was rumored, was a damper to the nuncio and his associates.

As we have already seen, the long-expected 10th of May came at last, and disappointment with it, but to-day all looks favorable. The air is cool and bracing, and the heavens are neither in sackcloth nor tears. The pomp is to move at 4 P.M. Determined to witness the apotheosis, I took a turn after dinner through the Campo to Rua da Prainha, the Water Street or Wapping of Rio. The intervening avenues had been swept and strewed with beach-sand and leaves. About one third of the stores and dwellings were in gala dress. Strange-looking ensigns, apparently priests' vestments, with crosses wrought on them, and what looked like silk bed-quilts with lace borders, were hung out of second-story windows, while national and sacerdotal banners waved from lines stretched across the streets. The Prainha church stands amid timber and boat-builders' yards, ship-chandlers and blacksmiths' shops, vendas and slop-stores, all set off with strips of colored calico. Built on a precipitous rock, the pathway up rises twenty feet in almost as many paces on the bare, unbroken granite. It will be a ticklish business for the nuncio and other reverend dignitaries to get the saint and themselves down safely. One false step, and the "arca" will descend of its own accord. While climbing with caution the smooth surface, a negro lad slipped above and rolled some distance past me, and but for a low wall that serves as a balustrade, he had been whirled into the street and killed.

The door, with crimson strips tacked to its posts and lintel, was closed, and I passed up an alley to the vestry, where, amid a busy crowd of officers arranging bouquets, I observed two lots of old votive wax-work. On the left of the door there hung a foot, a head, a female's diseased breast, and parts of members I could not make out. On the opposite wall, two distorted hands, a leg, and part of a thigh were pendent from a single nail.

It was now past four. The street by the church was jammed, but I procured a good stand at the door of a venda, four feet above the pavement, that commanded a full view of all that passed. For an hour and a half official personages and brotherhoods kept arriving and marshaling themselves in the ranks. Such a numerous turn-out of the latter I have not seen. All are bare-headed, and in albs and gowns so varied as to distinguish every company — black, with white cords; blue, with white sleeves; black, with white capes; slate-colored gowns, with cream-colored sleeves [these last were all colored men]. Here are some in white albs and light blue tippets; yonder, in orange and white; some in green, and some in cream-color wholly.

Every company has in front a crimson triangular bag or banner, between two imposing bouquets, on fancy ten-feet staves, and every brother carries a five-foot candle, as yet unlit. It was now near six, and I began to tire, and to wonder how reverend managers can tell such fibs, like profane proprietors of public spectacles.

At a signal the soldiers ranged themselves along the apologies for side-walks, compelling spectators to get out of the way, or fall in behind where they could. The hero in front of and in contact with me (so straitened the place) was a black, and his right-hand brother a white. They talked, joked, and laughed together as freely as if of one color. A dozen torches now descend from the church, followed by the "arca." Off go spectators' hats! The military, having slung theirs to their belts, present arms to the saint now resting in the street, and fire a feu de joie! A second! A third! My colored neighbor, the carbinier, amused me greatly. He wished to save his ammunition. Without dropping a grain in barrel or pan, three times has he gone furiously through the manual of priming, loading, ramming hard the wadding, pulling the trigger, and rubbing his hand over his perspiring forehead at the end of every shot; so that if the officer's eye chanced this way, he will be at no loss whom to promote.

The vanguard of brothers is now out of sight, so far does the procession extend. The company now passing us is followed by two hundred girls, dressed in white to their very shoes. They wear low-skirted and long-sleeved frocks, with gauze veils hanging behind, with a portion secured on the head in manner of a hood by circlets of white roses. They carry banners, censers, incense-boxes of an antique pattern, bouquets, and branches of palms. Few appear over ten years of age. They are the most interesting feature in the spectacle.

Next come older innocents in more variegated garbs. 1. The friars of the three monasteries of Anthony, Benedict, and the Carmo. Their newly-shaven crowns, and the diversity in size and color of their tonsures, irresistibly attract a stranger's eyes. While the sacred spot is white and glistening in some, it is of a leaden gray, and then of a bluish tint in others. The back of every head, beneath a line drawn from the tip of one ear to the other, is shorn and shaven smooth as their cheeks. The young monks seem to pride themselves on showing as full and fair a surface there as in front. I never saw human crania so strangely treated with lathers, razors, tweezers, and depilatories. 2. Hosts of priests in new skull-caps, in crimson, black, and other colored gowns and tippets. 3. The Capuchins, their heads farther out of their cowls than ever; their coarse garb and squalor contrasting well with the fat and delicately-trimmed ranks whose rear they bring up. The sanguine, hirsute one should have staid away. His red neck looks raw—a sight reminding one of any thing but the beauty of holiness.

They were succeeded by the ARCA or chest, under a canopy held up by silver staves, three on each side. Bedini carries one of the foremost; that abreast of it was designed for the emperor.

The arca is five feet long, two deep, and eighteen inches wide. [I subsequently measured and sketched it.] The front and both ends are of glass.

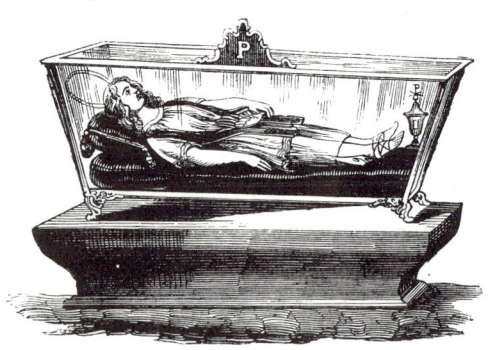

The figure within is that of a girl of twelve years reposing on a light blue silk mattress, her head slightly elevated by two fringed pillows, and turned to the spectators. The coronal region is left bare. The halo is a ring of wire, the ends buried in the cranium. Her black tresses are gracefully gathered on one shoulder, partly covering a gash in her neck, where a streak and a few drops of blood are portrayed. The eyelids have a bluish tint, said to have been caused by attempts to destroy her sight. She wears a white silk tunic with pink sleeves. Skirts of the same are continued below the laced border of the tunic. On her feet are sandals of yellow leather. Her left hand grasps a green parrot's wing—a fan; the other, half open, with the palm upward, rests by her side. A scarlet scarf heightens the effect, and, as I heard a lady say, "makes her look very pretty." The small vase, said to contain a portion of her blood, and of the sand that mingled with it at her martyrdom, is at her feet.

The Bishop of Rio, with a group of attendants, followed the saint, his train, attached to his neck and shoulders, being held up by three men some distance in his rear. Music came next, then more troops, and finally the national banner. The whole being now in motion, bombs were exploded, ordnance fired, squibs and rockets kept flying overhead, and the bands playing a swelling air. St. Anne's Church, in front, was emblazoned with a cross of light, the bells chimed a welcome, and when the arca reached the door, scores of projectiles hurried off to heaven to bear the tidings of the saint's arrival. The emperor and empress passed in from the adjoining building to receive her.

What then took place is recorded in subjoined articles from the daily papers, with some particulars that escaped me.

"*Santa Priscilliana, Virgem Martyr.*—The most holy father, Gregory XVI., has been pleased to distinguish this bishopric with the precious relic of St. Priscilliana, which was yesterday solemnly deposited in the Church of St. Anne. The most excellent and most reverend senhor, bishop, count, and grand chaplain, published a pastoral letter establishing the ceremonies to be observed in translating the relic, conformably to the instructions of St. Charles Borromea, the rubric of the Roman ritual, and precepts of the Liturgy. His most reverend excellency recapitulates the life of the saint thus: [Here follows the eighth paragraph of the pastoral—Appendix C].

" At 3 P.M. yesterday, in the Chapel of St. Francis da Prainha, in presence of his most reverend excellency, of the most excellent Internuncio, the most reverend Bishop of Chrisopolis, Monsenhor the Vicar-general, the most illustrious and reverend chapter, the reverend canon notary, the vicar and clergy of St. Anne, the holy relic was verified and authenticated, the box containing it was opened, and the pontifical brief read. Minutes of the examination were made, and signed by all present.

" After this ceremony the relic was incensed and exposed to the veneration of the clergy and others present. Then followed the procession, in which his most reverend excellency had invited all the brotherhoods and third orders, the reverend and secular of the city, the most illustrious and reverend Cabido, to join. They walked in the same order as in the processions of the body of God and St. Sebastian. Between the ranks formed by the third order of Our Lady of Carmo were two hundred and fifty young girls, dressed in virginal vestments, with chaplets of white flowers, holding in their left hands bouquets of natural flowers, and in the right small wax candles. From space to space they chanted a hymn, which charmed the hearts of spectators in whom the light of the Catholic religion is not obscured by philosophic luminaries of the age. Toward the close came the box containing the body of the holy virgin beneath a canopy, and incensed by two acolytes. In coming out of the chapel, and for some distance from it, the body was borne by his most reverend excellency, the most excellent Senhor Bedini, the Senhor Bishop of Chrisopolis, and the Monsenhor Vicar-general. Afterward the illustrious chapter took up the holy burden, and were relieved at intervals by other priests.

"The procession went through Rua do Imperatriz, Largo de St. Joaquim, and thence to the Church of Sta. Anna. In the passage were chanted the Litanies of the Saints, with invocations of St. Priscilliana, the Canticles, *Benedictus, Magnificat,* etc. Entering the church at half past 6 P.M., the arca was incensed and placed on the high altar. A Te Deum was chanted, then an antiphony, verses and prayers from the 'Commune das Virgems,' and a sermon by the vicar.

"The relic was then open to public veneration. His most reverend excellency gives indulgence for eight days to the faithful of both sexes who are truly penitent, and have confessed and communed, and who will visit the Church of St. Anne in any of the eight days, and pray there for some time, following the instructions of his holiness. These indulgences can be applied to the souls of the dead.

"The act of verification and translation will be recorded in proper form and place; a copy will be framed and hung up near the arca of the virgin martyr. His most reverend excellency has designated the 30th of August as the annual festival of St. Priscilliana. On that day the mass *Loquebar pro Virgine et Martyre* is to be chanted, and from the evening of that to sunset of the following day, the same indulgences will be conceded as those granted by his reverend excellency on the eight days of translation.

"A great multitude concurred in the solemn and pious act of translation. The people crowded the streets through which the procession had to pass; the windows were filled with the beautiful and devout sex, who threw flowers upon the virgin and the canopy. Satisfaction was evident on every face, and obviously emanated from true Christian sentiment."—*Sentinella da Monarchia of the* 18*th inst.*

The presence of the emperor is not here noticed. The omission is said to have been intended as a slight, for this paper is owned by V——s, whose gross immoralities, though an influential senator, young Pedro, to his honor, will not sanction.

From the Diario.

"MR. EDITOR,—As an obedient son that I am of the Roman Catholic Apostolic Church, I could not refrain from assisting at the translation of the virgin martyr, St. Priscilliana, to the church of Sta. Anna, where she now is, nor from admiring the magnificence, pomp, and decency with which the scene was celebrated—fruits of the efforts of the worthy minister of that parish, the Reverend Monsenhor Dr. Manoel Joaquim de Miranda Rego, who filled [or conferred on] the translation with much glory, and concluded that religious act by delivering an oration, after *Te Deum,* in the august presence of their imperial majesties. His eloquence and his logic imparted the highest satisfaction to all who heard him. The theme was brilliant; the opening of the subject still more superior from the force of his arguments—dignified, lucid, worthy of a Brazilian preacher who is an honor to his country and to the ecclesiastical tribunes. May it please the heavens to continue his brilliant career, and that he may leave to posterity a name to be recorded by his countrymen and impartial foreigners! Blessed mother! that has brought up such a son for the glory of divine worship! Praises to the Brazilian nation who endows her with a son so useful in the pulpit! And praises to the Church who enjoys a minister with such talents, and a pastor so respectable!

"A BRAZILIAN WHO HEARD HIM."

A few days after I called on Priscilliana. Three soldiers with bayonets stood on each side of the door, and more armed centurions at the altar rails. An oval silver dish, such as graced of yore barons' tables, was at her feet, piled to overflowing with money.

The china vase containing the blood, palpably modern, is like a coffee-cup with a cover. Several donations of 100 milreis each have been handed in to Dr. Miranda, and so have contributions of another kind—abusive letters, squibs, and pasquinades. Some of the latter were in print, and circulated to a limited extent *during the procession*. I obtained one, but it will not bear translating.

As a whole, nothing could have been better got up than this waxen figure to attract a superstitious people. Such as it is, it is officially recognized as "the sacred *body* of the virgin martyr St. Priscilliana."

The reader has now seen how, in modern as in pagan days, tutelary deities are made and miracles produced. A month did not elapse before some wrought by the new saint were proclaimed.*

A French tribunal recently condemned a printer and a print-publisher for issuing an engraving of "the apparition of the Holy Virgin to two children on a mountain of Sallette," as a criminal attempt to foster superstition and to prey upon the vul-

---

* A letter from a friend, dated August, 1848, informs me that he had "just called at the temple of Priscilliana, and was shown a closet full of miracles."

A printed circular of Miranda to the clergy is now before me. After stating that divine Providence had made use of him, a weak instrument, as the bearer to Brazil of the mortal remains of the glorious St. Priscilliana, and that, to improve the special favor of God, "the Brotherhood of the Holy Virgin Martyr Priscilliana" has been instituted, he continues:

"Confiding in the piety and zeal that pervade the heart of your reverence, I invite you, in the name of the same virgin martyr, to take a part in this religious and charitable work; giving it your valuable aid; inviting devout parishioners and friends of your reverence to enroll themselves among the brothers of the holy virgin martyr Priscilliana; and for that end I fully authorize your reverence to receive the names of new members, and from time to time to remit me a return of the same, to be registered in the proper books, and also to receive the sums that may be given on their admission. You are advertised that the initiation fee is not a fixed one, the amount being left to the inclination and devotion of each individual. The annual dues are fixed at one milrea. All persons, of every age, sex, condition, or state, can be admitted into the order of St. Priscilliana, who will specially take your reverence under her protection for all services rendered to her order."

gar. And are not the authors of this Brazilian tragedy—for, viewed aright, it is one—worthy of the galleys for attempting, at this day, still farther to dwarfen and stifle God's image in their countrymen? With the masses, the sickly imagination already sits, an incubus, on the prostrate judgment, and visions of insanity are reckoned as realities.

CHAPTER XXVII.

A Day for getting Souls out of Purgatory.—Trip to the Falls of Tejuca.—Character of the Country.—Anacharsis and Charcoal.—Fat Pigs and Morphea.—Mills.—Cotton-tree.—Coffee Plantation.—Tailless Dogs and Fowls.—Process of preparing Coffee for the Market.—Early Notice of Cauphe.—The Falls.—Dinner and Dessert at them.—Inscriptions on the Gavia.

May 21. A general holiday. In Minas the Ascension is celebrated in the church of Our Lady of Ampora, and indulgences granted for seven years and eight months. Souls can be drawn out of Purgatory to-day.* Without attempting any thing of that kind, I was one of a party who withdrew from the heat and turmoil of the city, and sought coolness and comfort at the Falls of Tejuca. Mounted, and buoyant in spirits, we cantered at an early hour through Engenho Velho, where I almost envied the owners of paradisiacal chacaras. On the walls of one a huge black monkey skipped and grinned. As we proceeded, dense forests walled us in at either hand. A beautiful mount, perfectly isolated and covered with foliage, rose up, and farther on, a granite pyramid, regular in outline in the distance as any in Egypt. The road becomes more and more rugged as we enter the gorges. Solitary habitations appear half way up horrible precipices, and are overshadowed by protruding rocks one or two thousand feet above them. How men reach and leave such places without wings I can not perceive.

A short level spot occurs, and we gallop two abreast; anon our animals, in single file, are picking their way amid boulders down break-neck descents. In five minutes we are climbing similar paths, and every mile drawing up to allow a string of

---

* Numerous days are marked in the calendar with the word "Alma." The explanation is invariably given: "A palavra 'Alma' indica que se tira uma alma do Purgatorio."

charcoal-mules to rub past us, each carrying three bushels, worth sixty cents in the city. The compliment Anacharsis paid the Greeks for *thus* carrying wood into the cities and leaving the horrid smoke in the mountains is equally applicable to the citizens of Rio.

At a venda, perched on a bluff by the road, a peon with refreshments was to have met us. He had not got up, and we breakfasted on eggs, bread, and coffee. The laughing sky, excitement of the ride, and sharpened appetites it had given us, with the cheerfulness and gayety that animated all, made this, I think, one of the most delightful meals I ever partook of.

The store was a dark little hole, with a stock of goods that I should have hesitated at purchasing for ten dollars, and the building for ten more. Stepping in, I stumbled over a black yielding mass close by the counter—a sleeping pig—one that more completely filled the rectangle of symmetry in farmers' stock than any animal I ever saw. Of the common breed of the country, it was said not to be unusually fat, yet its eyes were half buried by its swelled-up chops. I don't know that the race possesses qualities superior to those in the United States, but the short nose, sharp ears, small bones, thin skin, its corpulence, "ready disposition to fatten," with other good points familiar to cattle physiologists, made an admiring contrast with the tall, gaunt, coarse, flap-eared, long-faced specimens that perambulate some of our cities. Their flesh is pretty nearly all lean, while Brazilian pigs are literally "all lard." Pork-growers here reap richer, if not larger crops than are raised in our Western States.

Droves of these animals are brought over the mountains from Minas, in which province people live chiefly on pork, and are consequently subject to *morphea*, a species of leprosy, for the cure of which guano is used. The patient is laid on a bed of that substance, and his body covered with it, or a hole dug, and all but his head interred.

Upon a fence close by, a three-foot cross, of hoop iron, told us that some one's spirit had been disembodied there by a bullet, knife, or bludgeon. We came to a Moinho de Papel, driven by a foaming streamlet. The paper, whity brown, was spread over an acre of ground to dry. Next we stopped at the Fonte

D'Aqua, Ferrea de Andarahy, a tiny rill of iron-water, to which a pretty fountain structure has been dedicated.

Not far off, the very rheumatic undershot wheel of a clattering grist-mill was painfully whirling round, impelled by a furious torrent that danced and laughed at its groanings, and pushed and kicked it on.

The road presented as varied a succession of ascents and descents as a section of the ocean in a storm. At times it reminded one of traversing the ruins of some mighty Babylon, where, at every step, fallen masses interrupted progress, and awful structures were ready to tumble down. Tedious, and to timid travelers somewhat dangerous, to thread the broken, abrupt, and tortuous tracks, no sooner was a moderately level spot attained than most of the party, to make up for previous creeping, scampered off like flying Camanches.

The pervading material is bare white granite, that soars up to heaven and descends into glens deep down below us, while insulated masses, large as our largest mansions, lie tossed about in all directions, as if the wars of the giants had been waged here. But wild and awful as the scene is, it is occasionally diversified with floral and horticultural gems, the ever-recurring plantain and banana, clusters of pendent mamãos, air-plants, creeping vines, graceful pitos, and stately palms. Young coffee-plants cover one mountain slope, full-grown ones another, and, farther on, forests are being cut down to make room for more. We paused a moment by a tree, large and wide-spreading as an oak, conspicuous for being without leaves — the only one, I think, that loses them in winter; but its fruit arrested my attention: hundreds of cucumber-shaped husks, some open at their lower ends, and showing a white substance within. In a week or two they will split wide open and fall, leaving compact balls of snow-white cotton, which soon swell out large as human heads. This is the cotton-tree of old travelers. The fibre is soft, short, and silky; it is used to stuff pillows, and has this singular property, that when one of them is crushed or flattened, by simply exposing it to the sun, the contents swell it out to its original form and volume.

Mr. O—— led us aside to one of the best-conducted coffee plantations in the province. The low mansion is seated in a valley that angels might love to dwell in. A dozen times to-day, and now again, I have mentally exclaimed, "Oh, but this is a glorious world, if we would view it through some other medium than dollars!" The proprietor had gone to the city, but his amiable lady received us politely. She was followed about by two parrots, which, from jealousy, chased each other from her. Perfectly free, they take excursions abroad to scream and chatter with their untutored kindred.

Familiar with the place, Mr. O—— led us first into a long barn, fitted up throughout with stalls. At the head of each, in place of a manger, was a wide board on trestles. "What are these?" I asked. "Beds and bedsteads of the slaves." Had we passed through in silence, I should not have suspected the place was any thing but a stable; still, it was clean swept, and is said to be superior to the general run of slave accommodations. Against some stalls leaned bundles of torches, used by travelers after dark, and kept for sale at vendas. They are long splints of a resinous cedar, and are made by industrious slaves on Sundays for their own benefit. Mats and coarse straw hats are also fabrics by which they earn a few coppers.

Here were two goats confined, the only milch cows on the estate; and here were domestic fowls without tails, known as the *Sura* breed. A couple of large dogs also, belonging to a race that have no caudal members. In one place stood the popular mandioca mill [described in a subsequent chapter].

We next witnessed the processes by which coffee on this estate is prepared for market. I think I have remarked that the ripe fruit is not unlike a cherry in shape or color. The skin, rather thick and tough, incloses *two* of the grains or seeds known as coffee. The old procedure, still the prevailing one, is this: When the berries have acquired a deep red, they are picked into bags, thrown into heaps, and spread out on level spots of ground to dry in the sun. In front of a chacara, on the face of a mountain full seven hundred feet above us, I observed, as we came along, the entire surface of a detached table-rock, presenting several thousand superficial feet, covered with them. When the skins become shriveled, hard, and almost black, they are pounded in wooden mortars. The blows break the skins without injuring the tough grains. By sifting, the latter are separated and again laid out to dry, till a pellicle enveloping each grain is deprived of moisture, when a fresh appeal to the mortar and winnowing-fan leaves them ready for sale or consumption.

The improved mode consists in drying the grains on wooden trays or beds of slate, by which an earthy flavor, acquired when dried on the soil, is avoided; and in the introduction of two mills for removing the outer and inner envelopes. The chief feature of the first mill is a horizontal copper cylinder, whose surface is roughened after the manner of a rasp. It revolves against a board, between which and the teeth space is left for the grains to pass, but not the husk. The grains drop into water, and are left to soak twelve hours, by which a mucilaginous matter is removed, and the thin parchment film inclosing each grain softened. They are spread out in trays to dry. I counted 200 of these in one row, covering a space 700 feet by 15.

When completely dry, the grains are taken to a mill resembling those used for grinding plaster, except that the two vertical rolling discs are wood, six feet in diameter, and five inches thick. Their light weight suffices to break and abrade the pellicles without injuring the grains. After being subjected to a fanner, they are put up in bags for exportation.*

Resuming our journey, we overtook four slaves conveying lumber from the city. Each bore on his head two or more planks. Another advance, and we hear the Tejuca stream tumbling among rocks at our left, but concealed below among shrubbery and crags. More precipices covered with coffee-plants occur, and men like midges picking the fruit. How they retain foothold, especially when working the soil, is wonderful. Plows

---

* Of the decoction of coffee, which was not introduced into Paris till 1667, nor into London till a few years after, Henry Blount, in his Voyage to the Levant in 1634, thus quaintly speaks:

"They have another drinke not good at meat, called *Cauphe*, made of a berry as bigge as a small beane, dryed in a furnace and beat to powder, of a soote colour, in taste a little bitterish, that they seethe and drinke hote as may be endured: it is goode at all houres of the day, but especially morning and evening, when to that purpose they entertaine themselves two or three hours in *Cauphe-houses*, which in all Turkey abound more than innes and ale-houses with us. *It is thought to be the old black broth used so much by the Lacedæmonians* (!). It dryeth ill humors in the stomacke, comforteth the braine, never causeth drunkennesse or any surfeit, and is a harmelesse entertainment of good fellowship."

are wholly out of the question in these regions, unless drawn by goats, and Pan himself turns plowman. The scene grows wilder; we are surrounded by stupendous peaks, and before us the mighty Gavia towers, quite altered from its city aspect. Here are rocks scattered in profusion, and varying in dimensions from hogsheads to ten-story houses. The road winds among them, and at one place but eighteen inches are left for us to pass through. A singular variety of granite appears in two or three immense blocks of a bluish slate color and close grain, differing in toto from all around. A patch of the ocean becomes for a moment visible at the extremity of the glen, through which the Tejucan River is hastening to the universal reservoir.

We reached a woody cliff, on the edge of which a miserable venda stands. Fastening our cattle to protruding roots of trees, we climbed the ascent, passed through a banana orchard, went down a winding foot-path for one fourth of a mile, and emerged from the forest upon the glistening floor of our selected dining-hall, at the foot of the falls of the Tejuca. Here our peon had arrived with a basket charged to the brim with refreshments.

A rather small body of water comes tumbling down some sixty feet upon a broad and broken descent, inclining 25° from the perpendicular. The thin sheet pouring over the top is divided as it falls, so that not half the precipice is covered by it. Collecting below us at the edge of the enormous table-rock on which our repast was laid, and gliding by, only a few inches beneath our feet, it expands again, dances down short rapids to another fall of a narrow shute, and soon is in the arms of Oceanus. In this secluded retreat the Bishop of Rio lay concealed during the troubles with the French Protestants in Coligny's time. Remains of a wall built by him were pointed out.

But the *jantar* now, more than aught else, attracted us. It included a condiment, not put in the basket, that surpassed anchovy and curry sauce in heightening the flavor of every thing mixed with it—" St. Bernard's mustard," an essence distilled from abstinence and activity. Our table extended into the channel, and there we reclined and banqueted among scenery far excelling that which Pliny's Laurentinum dining-chamber opened on. Shielded from the sun by nature's parasols, far from the busy scenes of artificial life, not a carking care to trouble us,

LIFE IN BRAZIL. 311

and our spirits airy as our dresses, we laughed, and talked, and dipped our cups in the crystal stream as people did in the Golden Age. Flora adorned the hanging shrubbery; Pomona, from the distance, looked on; zephyrs played round us; and naiads—if naiads there be—frisked in the falls, and threw spray at us as they glided by.

Had the gods of Olympus and their ladies been on a visit to the gigantic Gavia, which now overshadowed us, they would not have waited for an invitation to our luncheon. They did not make their appearance, but other guests, as little expected, did—a couple of black hunters. Not daring to approach nearer than thirty feet without permission, they held up their game, the principal item being a black opossum. After waiting a while, they consulted together and vanished. In half an hour they re-appeared with branches of orange-trees laden with ripe fruit. These they brought, and in silence laid them at our feet. The appeal was not in vain.

Half way up the cataract a protruding rock protects a tuft of vegetation. Messrs. C—— and O—— challenged the rest of the party to reach it with a stone. Stones, however, were not at hand, but oranges were, and three dozen were sent flying at the mark, while only one attained it. The rest came leaping back, and, swimming past us, were soon tossing on the ocean.

Close to and immediately facing us, the highest peak of the Gavia soared in the blue vault. It has long puzzled the learned with its inscriptions. With a good telescope we made out several marks, something like I H × A I7II. Though to the eye these appeared of no unusual dimensions, they were probably thirty feet in length. It need hardly be said that they are natural sculptures. No mortal stone-cutter ever reached them, nor could any now stand to carve them except on a platform raised on balloons. If, as has been suggested of other characters on the opposite face of the peak (in the Journal of the Geographical Institute), they are to be referred to people of the primitive world, they will go far to prove that Roman letters and numerals were taught in schools myriads of ages before the flood, and that scientific navigators, in those early days, were cruising on these shores.

CHURCH OF SANTA RITA.

CHAPTER XXVIII.

Church Advertisements.—Auction and Fire-works at St. Rita's Church.—Articles sold.—Official Puff.—Horse-racing in honor of the Holy Ghost.—St. Gonçalo the Friend of the unmarried.—Capuchin preaching.—Two Slaves given to the Friars, and their Baptism by Bedini.—Chief Capuchin.—Priscilliana.—Famine in Ceara.—Indians bought and sold.

May 23. Church advertisements again abound. Specimens may be serviceable when a general history of religious vagaries is undertaken.

"The Board of the Brotherhood of the Divine Holy Ghost of the Parish of Sta. Anna participates to the respectable public that the Feast of the Divine Holy Ghost will begin on the 31st inst.; St. Bartholomew's on the 1st proximo; and that of Jesus, Mary, and Joseph, on the 2d, with all splendor compatible with the means and zeal of the administrators. On the third day of the Feast of the Holy Ghost there will be fire-works, such as have never before been exhibited, and superior from their magnitude and novelty of their mechanism. On Sunday, June 7, the Emperor elect of the Holy Ghost will take possession, which act will be followed with a Te Deum and sermon. At night there will be the Empire and the Auction. We beg the brethren and the pious to concur, with their alms and their presence, to make more brilliant acts so worthy of our religious regard.

"JOSE J. G. FERREIRA, Sec'y."

The emperor is a boy elected annually, and crowned in the church. His "empire" is a portion of ground adjoining the church, and fenced in for spectators, including the stage erected against the church, on which he sits enthroned, to preside over the auction and amusements. Formerly an Empress of the Holy Ghost sat by the Emperor, with little maids of honor to wait on her. Such is still the practice in the interior.

"The Brotherhood of the Divine Holy Ghost of the Convent of Friars of the Carmo, in the Lapa do Desterro, inform the public and devout persons that on the 22d inst. begins the *Novena* of the Ritual, and on the 31st the Feast of the Holy Ghost. On the 1st proximo the Feast of our Lord of the Paces; and on the 22d, that of Sta. Anna and St. Joaquim—all of which will be celebrated with appropriate magnificence. Every night there will be music and an auction. On the last one, beautiful fireworks."

"The Chairman and Directors of the Divine Holy Ghost of the parish of St. Rita inform the respectable public that to-day, 22d inst., will begin, with much pomp and decency, the Novena and Auction. They hope the brethren and the pious will contribute, by their presence and their alms, to the brilliancy of the Feast."

I thought of accepting this last invitation, but F—— said, "It is a long way to go, and there will be a poor sale to-night. Wait till the great day of the feast; then almost every person sends a present to the Holy Ghost, and there will be a Bom Leilão." After tea, however, I felt inclined for a walk, and bent my steps to the city by lamplight. Calling at T——'s, Messrs. C—— and M—— readily joined with me in a visit to the neighboring shrine of Santa Rita. A day view of this old structure and the adjoining fountain is shown on page 312. To be in character with our visit, it should have been a night scene.

As we drew near, the church tower was seen decked with colored lamps, and the white front red as blood with the glare of flambeaus in the little triangular largo. The scene which then burst on us was more suited to the suburbs of Tartarus than the court-yard of a heavenly lady. Nine young negro-heads, soaked in tar and tallow, and stuck on poles let into the pavement, were blazing before the church, amid the shouts and laughter of a crowd of men and boys, both black and white. The air was suffused with smoke, whose dense curling volumes appeared white in the universal darkness overhead—the sickening odor, hissings and spurtings of bursting blisters, the grinning visages of the restless throng—now lost to sight, and anon lit up with fire, as the wind affected the flames. There is but one place which such a scene could call to mind. But, lest the reader should denounce the goddess of the place a she-Moloch, delighting in roasted skulls, he is informed that the festival torches—"*Cabeças de Moleques*"—are spherical masses of oakum saturated with pitch and kindred matters.

We passed into the fane between two armed centurions at the door. Hung round with showy tapestry, it was brilliantly lit up. The lady's altar was a sheet of light. At a table on the floor sat a committee bartering "blessed pictures" for vintems and patacas. There were three qualities and sizes—quarto, octavo, and duodecimo. When a contribution was laid down, the chairman, eyeing it, spoke to the brother at his right, who then drew from a drawer a print of the proper value, while the treasurer, at his left, added the money to a pile on a silver tray. As usual at festivals, two soldiers, with fixed bayonets, stood by to guard the treasure. Senhor M—— procured for me one

LIFE IN BRAZIL. 315

of the paper gems; printed in red ink, it represents a dove and triangle within a nimbus, and over them an old man, with a long beard, looking out of a cloud.

After looking round a while, we crossed the floor and passed, as did most of the visitors, through an open door into an adjoining apartment, and found ourselves in a crowd. The room was long and narrow, and the benches on both sides jammed with men and boys. Against the left wall sat three brethren in official robes, and before them a table, upon which stood, between three-branched candlesticks, one of the portable symbols of the Holy Ghost carried by street collectors. Between the benches, a short brother, in an alb, was walking to and fro, and addressing the congregation with perspiring fervor. Every moment he kept applying a handkerchief to his streaming forehead. As he drew near, I perceived that he was descanting on a sugared cake which he held up on a salver. We were in Santa Rita's auction-room, and this gentleman was her salesman. The cake was knocked down; the purchaser handed a bill to the auctioneer, who hurried to the table, and returned with the change and a

AUCTION IN SANTA RITA'S CHURCH.

small print—such as were being disposed of in the church—every purchaser at the auction receiving one gratis.

Several large frosted cakes were put up, but the sale dragged heavily. The salesman was far from being an expert; he lacked volubility and wit. A laugh was now and then elicited, but seldom by his own jokes. He was much annoyed by young fellows predisposed to fun, and determined to enjoy it: they tried his temper severely. There was, in truth, something about him that whetted humorous appetites, as he came puffing along, holding up the salver to every face that looked like a buying one, and repeating, with a supplicatory tone and look, "*Hum milreis—hum milreis—hum milreis, Senhor.*" His head, half isolated from his body by the alb, and nearly denuded of hair, with his glistening face, was incessantly drawn this way and that by bids which he could find none to acknowledge. At length a quiet-looking young man made an offer, and was declared the purchaser. The article was handed to him, and, lo! he had no money! The enraged knight of the hammer seized him by the collar, and led him to the managers at the table amid roars of laughter. As he had no means of payment, nothing could be done but to reprove him and let him go. A gentleman took the lot and paid for it—or, rather, exchanged money for it. Nothing sacred is *sold*, only exchanged. We, of course, would consider these transactions cash sales; for the terms are cash on delivery, and delivery immediately.

Every eye was again turned to the recess or niche behind the managers, to see what next would be brought out. An officer, in a black gown and white tippet, who seemed to have charge of the goods, handed forth something, which the chairman no sooner passed across the table than there arose such a clucking! It was a live hen. Grasped by the thighs, it appeared to sit quite comfortably on the auctioneer's hand. It was struck off at fifty cents—double its market value. Next came a superb white chanticleer—the signal of a general crowing and clapping of elbows in imitation of wings. One or two young men were natural ventriloquists; the cock-a-doodle-do-o-o-ing came in at the street door, then out of the church, and anon was under the managers' table. The merriment was universal. The fluttering bird brought 1260 reis—62 cents.

A large custard was now tried, and the buyer turned out to be the one that had no money: he said he would call to-morrow for it! This gave rise to a general screech, and led to a scuffle between the bidder and the bantered salesman. The dispute was ended by a higher bid; but when the article was offered to the new bidder, he said it was too hard baked, and would not take it! The vender became furious; but, recovering himself, he said it was too hard for such a fellow's teeth —meaning too costly for his pocket. The fillip was applauded, and the little man, tickled with the hit, threw back his head, and laughed louder and longer than any one else.

He next brought round a folded paper, contents unknown. He refused to break the envelope, or say what was within. It brought 300 reis, and proved to be cold roast chicken. Three "*Macaàs Americanas*" (Newtown pippins) brought thirteen cents each. A lady informs me she has known fifty milreis, or twenty-five dollars, given for an apple at this feast, the competitors showing in this way their attachment to the Church. Other matters were put up; but I got tired, and left the auctioneer trying a large plum-cake, over the frosted top of which he kept drawing his hand, as if stroking the back of a pet bird or rabbit.

Most of the articles sold at these ecclesiastical auctions are purchased at wholesale prices by the managers, and thus retailed at profits varying from 50 to 500 per cent., the donations brought in by collectors not being sufficient, nor always suitable. One of the best specimens of the salesman's eloquence is the following scrap, translated by an accompanying friend:

"Twenty-five—thirty—thirty-five vintems for this blessed cake; blessed by the Holy Father Xavier Maria Luiz Oliveiro. Who bids more? Thirty—ah! the good-will of Our Lady be with you, my friend. Forty are bid!—only forty vintems for food which will purge all diseases lurking in him that eats it. The saints befriend you, Senhor. Forty-five! Who is the next bidder? Who? Forty-five! Allelulia! Fifty vintems are bid—it is enough—and," taking the money, "may your victuals be always as sweet as you'll find this, Senhor!"

No females were present. Though respectable families are

invited; it was obviously no place for ladies. One of my companions belonged to the Church, and, in answer to my inquiries, said the place was wholly unfit for respectable females to appear in. Of the evening's entertainments the following puff was inserted in one of the daily papers:

"Mr. Editor,—The auction of the Divine Holy Ghost, in Santa Rita, to be continued to the 3d proximo, is very interesting. The select company that assembles there, the order and decorum with which the auction is conducted, reflect credit on the providor and managers. Permit me to invite, through your columns, all devotees of the Miraculous Holy Ghost to attend, with their families, in order to increase the brilliancy of this devotional exercise. Um Devoto."

The same paper had the following notice to sporting devotees:

"The Brotherhood of the Divine Holy Ghost of San Gonçalo (a small village across the Bay) will hold the Feast of the Holy Ghost on the 31st instant with all possible splendor. Devout persons are invited to attend, to give greater pomp to this act of religion. On the 1st proximo the Feast of the Most Holy Sacrament, with a procession in the evening, a Te Deum, and sermon. On the 2d, the feast of the patron San Gonçalo; at three P.M. there will be *brilliant horse-racing*, after which a Te Deum and magnificent fire-works."

As I shall not have an opportunity to pay a visit to Gonçalo, I may as well remark here that he is a popular friend of Portuguese and Brazilian elderly single ladies. Young ones invoke him too, but in a petulant spirit. Their staple address is:

"San Gonçalo of Amarante,
Match-maker for old women!
Why don't you marry young ones?
What harm have they done you?"

The Carmelites at the Lapa Church surpass St. Rita's managers in external display. The front is covered with festoons of colored lamps, cords stretch from the roof bearing flags and tapestries. A handsomely draped stage for the auction is fitted up at one side of the doorway, and at the other a band of musicians sit. The fire-works are not confined to blazing skulls of negroes, for on high poles stand men and women waiting to be consumed. But, after all, the festival is not very attractive during day or night. The auctioneer has neither tact nor wit, so that his sales drag heavily. The poorest of artists he is, to use a native proverb, "a John Lopez—neither vinegar, honey, nor Malmsey wine—nothing."

Pyrotechnists notify the churches of new and cheap fogos, heading their advertisements with vivas for the saints, particularly Anthony and John.

The Capuchins announce for public veneration a relic just arrived from Rome. Another notice runs thus:

"On Sunday, 24th, will be celebrated the Feast of *St. Fidelis de Sigmaringa*, proto-martyr Capuchinho, with a solemn mass by the excellentissimo senhor, the Internuncio Monsenhor Bedini. Preaching by the Brother John Baptist de Caserta, Capuchin missionary. The feast will begin at 9 A.M. In the evening a sermon, and the Litany of Our Lady, with other devotions; to conclude with the presentation of the relic of the holy martyr to be kissed. We all must imitate the examples of those who, faithful to God, confessed with an apostolic bosom the faith of Jesus Christ, and sealed it with their proper blood. Behold the true age of light!"

A lusty brother preached. His voice was small for so large a man, weak and soft as a woman's. His theme was Fidelis, whose image stood before him. The pathetic is his forte. Dilating on the sufferings of the saint, he rose from smothered groans to thrilling wails, pressed his hands to his breast, threw them toward Fidelis, and sunk every five minutes on his seat to suffer his emotions to subside. About 200 persons were present, the greater part females. During the sermon a brother was dealing out pictures of Fidelis. The little temple was improved in appearance. A series of oil paintings of Capuchin worthies occupied the walls; among them, "Crispim de Viterbo." The main altar has been touched up, and the wax votos suspended by fresh ribbons. An additional female saint, of full stature, was there; a naked baby plays at her feet, and a smaller sits on the palm of her hand, reminding one of the Pompeian picture of Leda.

The preacher being through, the nuncio entered on the part advertised for him, and subsequently performed another not mentioned in the papers. In an embroidered gown, assisted by two priests, he perfumed the altar, candlesticks, and images by shaking a censer among them. A country bishop, with a five-inch cross on his breast and a skull-cap on, stood at one side, and to him the nuncio swung the smoking vessel, receiving a smiling inclination of the head in acknowledgment of the official compliment.

At one part of the performance two men stepped behind Bedini, and stooping, raised his skirts to the small of his back, then, after a pause, threw them over his head, and bore the garment away. He then stood in a cream-tinted gown, gathered round his waist with a cord. By-and-by the disrobers reappeared, stood by him till he untied the ends, tucked up the skirts, and whisked them in like manner away, leaving him in a cambric camisa. A little while, and the spoilers came and stripped him of that also! I almost expected to see him in buff, but he now shone forth in a crimson tight cloak or coat that would have given his valets some trouble to get off. The place was not suitable for equestrian exercises, but those changes of apparel were very suggestive of a popular performance of circus-riders.

The performances ended, many left, but I learned that two young slaves, given a few days ago to the Italian friars, were to be baptized, and their transfer formally ratified. Capuchin names were given them—Bernard and Bernardine. Till matters were ready, the nuncio, as if desirous of continuing his devotions, came and knelt near the front bench by the spectators. He had no book, but closed his hands and looked on them. Meanwhile, the sacristan, a brisk old man, got into a spicy dispute with one of the monks about the proper passages to be read on the occasion. First one took the book, then the other, and to end the matter they rushed to Bedini. The eyes of the friar glistened apparently with anger, the sacristan drew down the corners of his mouth, and both, as the still kneeling nuncio turned over the leaves, rolled out their arguments. He seemed himself at a nonplus, when the zealous sacristan fairly snatched the book and pointed to the appropriate captions. Familiar with all usages respecting slaves, the inexperienced foreigners had to yield to him.

The defeated friar went out and returned, leading two lads, about ten and eleven years of age, accompanied with their owner, whose head was of a singular conformation. The occipital region descended down his neck, and being bare, appeared like a tumor overhanging his vest collar. After conversing again with the friar, the nuncio rose from his knees; the sacristan brought in a scarf, the nuncio kissed it, stooped his head, and the friar threw it over his neck. The helots were now placed before him, when it became evident that he did not comprehend the formula, for twice the sacristan took the volume and turned to the appropriate pages. Bedini now crossed the air over the boys' heads, read, then put his face to theirs, and breathed three times on each; read again, stopped, and, putting out his tongue, brushed off a portion of its moisture with his thumb, ordered Bernard to thrust forth his organ of taste, and transferred to it, by a dab, a portion of his own saliva. Bernardine was told to expose his flexile member, but the lad was confounded, and kept it concealed within his teeth. Not till the angry sacristan shook him could a portion of the fluid secreted by his excellency's salivary glands be got into the little fellow's mouth. With the same holy spittle were their breasts, necks, and collar-bones anointed.

Entirely novel to me, the ceremonies increased in interest. The nuncio changed his scarf for one of another color, took from a saucer a pinch of salt, and rubbed it on the lads' foreheads, upper lips, and, to remove the insipidness of the saliva, as I supposed, their tongues also. A friar next produced a small morocco case, containing three minute oil-bottles, with stoppers, to the under sides of which minikin spoons were attached. With a piece of cotton wool, on which the sacristan emptied one of the spoons, his excellency rubbed the neophytes' foreheads, lips, breast-bones, and napes of their necks. To facilitate the last operation, the sacristan roughly bent down their heads, and, with a promptitude that must have caused them

X

pain, a spoonful from another vial and another sponge was transferred to the same places and by the same processes.

The lads were next led to a table, brought in for the occasion, on which were a large tray and a long-necked vase, both of silver. A Capuchin took Bernard, and called on his owner to lay his hand on the lad's shoulder while the nuncio read some particular passage. This was done, and the boy's head bent over the tray for his eminence to pour water from the pitcher on it. The liquid rolled off in drops like rain from ducks' feathers, but the inexorable sacristan was not to be thus defeated. Holding the head down on the tray with one hand, he took the end of a towel, rubbed the fluid *in*, and so energetically as to draw smiles from other faces besides mine. As soon as Bernardine was served the same way, the performance was complete.

Seeing nothing of the relic that had been advertised, I made out to ask the picture-man, who still sat at the receipt of custom. His reply was, "Quatros horas da tarde." As I could not return at four in the afternoon, I never learned what it was —whether a bone, lock of hair, a toe, a finger, or a foot.

On leaving, I stepped for a moment into the vestry. The clouds on either side of the Virgin's shoe-sole were enlarged, and the central parts tinted as with bistre. The chief of the Capuchins was busy, as on a former visit, selecting linen out of drawers, holding the pieces up to the light, rejecting some, tucking others under his arm, and then vanishing toward the images, his bare feet in slip-shod, clattering tamancos.

28*th*. Yesterday an old lady, long confined by a painful disorder, insisted on being taken to Priscilliana's shrine, having wrought herself into the belief of the saint's ability and willingness to help her. The exertion and excitement were too much for her. She was carried from the church exceedingly ill, and H——, who knows her, says her recovery from the shock is doubtful.

A deputy from Ceara spent the evening with us. The famine now raging in that province, he says, is worse than as described in the papers—too horrible, he says, to be described. As with previous calamities of the kind, the drought has killed all vegetation. Cattle, the great staple of the province, have perished, and next, men, women, and children. In extensive districts not a pint of water was to be had. Rivers were dried up, and in towns where it was usually in plenty near the surface, wells had to be deepened from twenty to thirty feet. All who could flew to the coast for relief, and thousands perished by the way. Before he left the capital, twenty-six thousand persons had applied for bread. In dealing forth small measures of mandioca, maize, and beans, a hundred hands would be stretched out to snatch at them. Indians—even Indian mothers—brought in their boys and sold them to the navy for food. Previously it was difficult to get an Indian lad under seventy milreis, but now their parents, having nothing for them or themselves to eat, freely offered them for ten. The drought was followed by locusts that consumed every particle of remaining vegetation. Pestilence succeeded the locusts, and now yellow fever is sweeping off its victims at a fearful rate.

Private charity had become exhausted, the government had done nothing or next to nothing, and no sister province except Maranham had sent them aid. A subscription was begun in Rio, but it fell through. Their representative is disgusted with the apathy manifested by the Chambers. "There are plenty to talk, but none to act. Words are women, *deeds* are men. The only thing to bring them to their senses is to get up a revolution." There is a bitter feeling at the north against the government for spending two or three hundred thousand milreis on illuminations and trumpery pageants here to flatter the young emperor and his wife on their return, and millions on his junketing down south, while so many are perishing for lack of life's first necessaries.

The people of Ceara, he admits, are improvident as Indians —not one whit better. Granaries stored with one or two years' provisions would prevent these recurring famines, but the people have no thought of, and no care for, to-morrow.

Indians appear to be enslaved as much almost as negroes, and are bought and sold like them. In Rio a large number are thus made merchandise of. Of this fact I was not aware till this evening.

CHAPTER XXIX.

Winter and Western Islanders.—Brazilian Names: their Derivation and Import.—Primitive Patronymics.—Combinations.—Names in connection with Professions.—Names of Ships.—Pigs and Pig-stealing.—Invitation to Tea.

May 28. Heavy rains and streets impassable except to quadrupeds and colored bipeds, who happily use no nether garments. There they go! a troop of mules bound up the mountains. See! their ears are not now erect, for in that position the falling floods would fill them. Turned back and pendent, all is dry within as the contents of the two hairy sacks each beast is laden with. Yon dark nymph crying oranges and bananas, with a bunch of rosemary in one hand, is coming over to this side. Her wide and shallow basket is a colander, and under it she a fountain goddess in the midst of falling jets—an Ethiopian Venus in a shower-bath. Though lithe and well formed, she is not a Minas—her garments had not then been so brief nor few. The left half of her bust is wholly nude, and the jagged skirts of her only vestment are short as a figurante's. Look! or rather don't, for she raises them as she comes wading through the torrent in the gutter. There, on the side-walk, now she splashing treads—an itinerant priestess of Pomona! Her spirits are not drowned at any rate, for that shriek of mirth is hers. She is bantering the muleteer as he stolidly paces in the rear of his charge.

Here come again those eternal sand-carts, and now doubly laden, one half with water. How the poor overwrought and lacerated animals strain to keep, and hardly keep, the wheels in motion. These Western Islanders, industrious as they are, should have, or be made to have, compassion on their beasts. Digging down hills by contract, they labor every day and half of every night. Neither rains, nor heat, nor even darkness stops them; no, nor saints nor Sabbath-days, so anxious are they to make up the number of milreis their moderate wishes centre on. Observe, they go without shoes, stockings, coat, or vest, and this is winter too. Winter! how like glorious summer in our latitudes! Forests and fields in bloom, silver streams meandering among natural bowers, and birds and butterflies as busy as at this season in the North.

But we must find something else to do than gazing through the window. Here is the Orçamento, or Brazilian Budget for 1847–8, just issued from the government press, exhibiting the receipts and expenditures of the empire, salaries of the emperor, officers of state, and a list of about 2000 pensioners. On turning over the leaves, names occur remarkable for their literal import, others for their deep religious hue, and some for their singular combinations. As there is no going out to-day, suppose we devote an hour to this collection, for names every where supply material for curious speculations.

As in olden times, alphabetical lists are those of individual, not of family appellations. Thus letters in the post-office are advertised as with us, but, like this pension-list, the names begin with Agathas and Annas, proceed to Claras, Floras, Henriques, Manoels, and so on to Pedros, Theresas, Veronicas, and Zepharinas.

Names derived from personal qualities, occupations, implements, animals, trees, plants, etc., are common to most people. None retain finer traces of them, and none have more disfigured them by legendary trash than the Portuguese. As it is the belief that beatified saints are gratified by naming children after them, Pedros and Josés prevail among boys, while Annas and Marys carry the day with the girls. Then, as the mother of Christ is worshiped in many characters, nearly all Marias have agnomens expressive of popular personations of the Madonna. Another custom is to fasten a cluster of names on a child in the hope that it will attain the virtues of each celestial sponsor. With this view masculine prenomens and agnomens are conferred on females, and feminine names not withheld from males.

Of *primitive patronymics*, chiefly drawn from nature, the following are but a tithe of examples that might be given. The prenomens, mostly religious, are for the sake of brevity dropped, save one: Angelica Dead Branch, Amelia Quiet, Imogine Pilchard, Anne of the Willow-tree Remedy, Rose Lamprey, Frances the Stammerer, Clara of the Fire-pans, Flora Scourge of the House, Claudine Little Fish, Emilia of the Saucer, Maria of the Fountains, Charlotte House-leek, Louisa Emancipated of France, Louisa of the Pen, Good Shepherdess of the Coast of Navarre, Joaquim the Sucking-pig of Almeida, Mary of the Olive-tree Beautiful, Maria Crow of Almeida, Isabella of the Great Beard, Isabella Milfoil, Barbara of the Door-bolt, John of the Axe, Florence of the Caldron, Anthony Hawk of Merchantmen, Innocencia the Torch of Arruda, Joaquina of the White Castle.

Combinations of Primitive Surnames.—Lewis Egg Chicken Thick, Catharine of the Wolf and Bramble, Mary of Bouquets and Saucer, John of Apple-tree Wedge, Jane of Gentility and Snows, Mary of the Partridge and Brook, Chicken of Mori and Falcon, Barbara of the Latch and Spider, Frances Cockles and Snow, José Leather-strap and Quarry, Manoel Sucking-pig and Banner, Anne Woe to Alençar. A lady at my elbow is Maria Saucer Rabbit, and a doctor writes himself Fortegato—Strong Cat.

Lay and Religious combined.—Pine-tree of Jesus, Conception and Rabbit, Assumption and Thorn-bush, Purification and Male Partridge, Purity and Sparrow-hawk, Jesus Flowering Pink, Blacksmith of the Trinity, Garden Nun of Macedon, Justus of the Saints of Portugal, Cross-bowman of the Saints.

Wholly Religious.—Mary of Holy Love, Rose of Conception, Rose of the Holy Ghost, Catharine of the White Saints, John of the Holy Rock, Joaquina of the Brave Jesus, Anne of Placidity of the Heart of Jesus, Mary of Light, of the Maternity, etc., etc. The washerwoman of our family is Maria Rose of Jesus and of the Holy Ghost.

We must not forget that this mania for Scripture names has not always been confined to one sect. A Protestant type of the disease was rather prevalent in England during the Commonwealth; and of lay patronymics, there are doubtless those current among ourselves curious as any given here. It is only when they present themselves in a foreign dress that they excite surprise; strip them, and most will turn out old acquaintances, if not near relatives.

Names in connection with Professions—examples from the Rio Directory.—José Maria of the See is a soap-boiler; José Jesus makes spurs and amulets; Sabina of the Wood of Nazareth is a silversmith; St. Francis Anthony Cæsar sells paliterros; John of Jesus and the Olive keeps a liquor-shop; John Baptist is a gilder; Francis Stream of Holy Pork [or sausage] a pyrotechnist; Michael of the Nativity a currier; Manuel Jesus a hatter; Joseph Mary of the Trinity a carpenter; Widow Lizard sells tobacco; Matthew of Light sells washing-blocks; Joseph of the Pine-tree Saints is a coppersmith; Louis Sylvan Milk sells city wines; Joaquim of the Saints deals in jerked beef; Baron of Good Venture is a shipping-merchant; José Mother of Gods sells cigars; Benjamin Country Sheep is a second lieutenant; Simon of Nazareth is a gunsmith; Antonio of the Sacred Paces keeps a livery-stable; Michael Archangel of Miranda is a paper-hanger; Vicente Dresser of Forest-trees is a barber; José Bookworm of the Saints makes combs; Augustus Cæsar Orange is a custom-house clerk, and Antonio José of the Holy Plow-tail Handle a secretary.

In the principal theatre we find Antonio Thomas the Palmer, *manager;* John Araujo of the Holy Spirit, *box-keeper;* Maria José Nunes, *prompter;* Antonio of the Olive, *bill-poster;* Joseph of the Nativity, and Joaquim Observer of Santa Rita, *scene-shifters;* Joana Rose of Jesus, *figurante*, etc., etc. Most of the performers, and among them B. J. Ferdinand Caqueirada—literally, a blow from a broken pot—have rooms in Ruas do Espirito Santo, Conceição, and Sacramento.

If there were morals in words and virtue in names, occupants of the Southern Continent would be superlatively happy; but neither earthly nor heavenly appellations make men wise or good. The police reports expose daily the association of sacred names with the vilest passions.

Esmeria Maria da Conceição and Anna de Jesus were imprisoned yesterday for street brawling, and Saturnina Maria da Conceição for being drunk. The other day, Monica Maria da Paixão, Luisa Teresa Rosa, Zepharino do Espirito Santo, José Maria dos Anjos, and Antonio Luiz dos Santos, were arrested for physical offenses; and again: Generous Louiza of the Conception, Maria of do., and José of the Saints, were committed for fighting, José Dionysius of the Mercies for wounding, and the mulattoes Lawrence José Alves and Jacintho Joseph of the Holy Ghost for necromancy.

Names of Ships.—By running over the marine columns of newspapers, the piety of ship-builders and owners is apparent in the names of their vessels. Political and moral appellations occur, but the bulk are named from the calendar and monkish records. A few specimens must suffice:

Triumph of Brazil, Temptation, Good Jesus of Alem [common], Conceição [very common], Holy Cross, Great Courage, New St. Francis, Holy Martyrs, Our Lady of the Birth, Segunda Conceição de Maria, The Pleasure of God, Protector of Angels, The Holy Ghost, Allclulia, Shining St. Anthony, Protectress of Angels, Asylum of Virtue, Conception of the Queen of Angels.

Change of Names.—Nuns and monks cast their old ones away, and every cardinal, when elected to the papacy, assumes a fresh one. This custom begun with Sergius, and with some reason, for *Os Porci*—pig's face—was any thing but a suitable appellation for the holy father.

Many Portuguese patronymics indicate not simply a remote, but an Oriental origin, especially some of those derived from animals, fowls, fruits, domestic implements, hunting, the bow, etc. Of later names, Sylvan Silversmith may be one, but it can hardly be posterior to the epoch of the Iliad. Good Venture and Good Success are of high antiquity. The latter was the name of Aristotle, which in Greek signifies the same thing. Some, that appear of monkish origin, are of anterior dates. Silva is probably one. It signifies a shirt or cloth of wire worn by penitents; but self-torture goes back into the earliest times. Baal's priests encouraged it. So with Romeiro, a palmer. It probably dates from times long preceding the Crusades, as pilgrimages to saints and holy places were made by the ancient heathen.

The original Senhor Sucking Pig may have received his name from resembling in infancy one of those younglings in vigorously draining his mother's breasts, or from an eagerness to devour them in after life. The families of Sausages are clearly derived from one with carnivorous appetites. The great ancestor of Joaquim and Joaquina Holy Pork was possibly convicted of feeding his family at the expense of a monastery. Hogs were common presents to ancient friars, and were then considered sacred, but that stealing them was not a rare sin there is abundant proof. Some convents had not less than two thousand, the feeding of which cost them nothing, "as they were privileged to range through the streets, markets, and even private houses, scarcely any person daring to check them, because they were considered *the Lord's swine.*" To save their pigs, woes were denounced by monks on those that stole them, and examples are given of men dying raving mad after dining on stolen pork. Let us hope that the first Senhor Holy Pork sanctified his theft according to the proverb, "Steal a pig and give the feet in alms"—an instructive saying, for which we are indebted to his or some other pig-purloiner's piety.

With the reader's leave we will close the subject of names, and the rather as Senhor Pompilio, a young gentleman from Congo, has for some moments been bowing before us, and smiling as his countrymen only can smile. A Para fly-flap in his left hand, he points the forefinger of the other over his shoulder, anon brings it point blank at our mouth, and then whisks it back into his own. Next he makes a species of courtesy, waves the scarlet feathers toward an inner door, and seeing us at length drop the pen, his eyes swim in joy at the success of his invitation for us to join the ladies at tea.

CHAPTER XXX.

St. Anthony of Padua: his Monastery and Miracles.—His Rank and Salary as a Soldier.—Shameful Treatment of his Images.—Feast of the Holy Ghost.—Auctions and Fire-works, etc.

WE spent the best part of two days in an irregular pile of three-story buildings, located on one side of a hill, dedicated to and owned by the most popular of Brazilian minor divinities. The ascent, wide and paved, winds up at the rear of the Carioco Fountain. Here and there a slave was asleep, reclining against the dead wall on either hand, while almost every where were revolting nuisances committed by them.

There are several Antonios in the calendar, and one is often mistaken for the other. He who had such amusing personal conflicts with Satan was of Egypt, and not a few of his acts and powers have been ascribed to his namesakes. It was he who, centuries after his death, began to cure people of a disease not heard of while he lived—one that, from his success in treating, still bears his name. He only should be pictured with fire and a pig—not, as the wicked might surmise, to indicate a favorite monastic dish. The early appearance of erysipelas in Europe, association of the saint and pigs with it, etc., will be found accounted for in the subjoined extract from Gabriel d'Emilliane's History of the Monastical Orders, 1693:

"In the year 1089, a contagious sickness, called the Sacred Fire, a kind of very dangerous leprosie, having spread itself into several parts of Europe, those of the Province of Vienna, in France, had, at last, recourse to the Relics of St. Antony the Egyptian. They say that whoever did call upon him was delivered from the Sacred Fire; and contrariwise, those who blasphemed or took the name of St. Antony in vain, were immediately, by the saint's unmerciful vengeance, delivered up to it. This gave occasion to Gaston Frank, in company with some other persons, to institute, in the year 1095, the Religion [Order] of St. Antony, whose principal care it was to serve those who were tormented with the Sacred Fire. They represent St. Antony with a fire kindled at his side to signifie that he delivers people from the Sacred Fire. They paint a hog near him as a sign that he cures beasts of all diseases; and to honor him in several places, a hog is kept at common charges, and called St. Antony's Hog, for which they [the people] have great veneration. Many will have St. Antony's picture on the walls of their houses, hoping by that to be preserved from the Plague. And the Italians, who did not know the true signification of the fire painted at his side, thought that he preserved houses also from being burnt, and they call upon him on such occasions. As for the Fryars, they know so well how to make use of the power of their St. Antony, that, when they go a begging, if one does refuse what they ask for, they threaten immediately to make the Sacred Fire to fall upon him; therefore the poor country people, to avoid the menaces and witchcrafts of these monks, present them every year with a good fat hog apiece. Some Cardinals and Prelates endeavored to persuade Pope Paul III. to abolish these wretched Begging Fryars, but they could not compass their good design; and these Monks do subsist yet to this day in several places, though the sickness of St. Antony's Fire be now very rare."

This old establishment contains good specimens of carving; and the chapel, without a tithe of the gilt that glistens in others, is a gallery of paintings, which, if not miracles of art, are exemplifications of the miraculous. They may not equal the best productions of Raphael, or of Annibal Carracci of Bologna, but they are attested copies of the works of an individual deemed vastly more gifted than either, viz., Anthony of Padua.

The plan of the chapel is two parallelograms of unequal width (the smaller one the chancel) joined end to end. The entrance is at the wide part, only half of which is appropriated to the audience. We are standing at the door, and see! yonder at the opposite extremity is Anthony over the high altar facing us.

ST. ANTHONY OF PADUA.

Two minor shrines are near the junction of the chancel with the chapel. One is occupied by a female, and opposite to her the original image of Black Benedict stands. Large as life, good looking, his crisp hair shorn *à la tonsure,* he bends over the prone baby in his arms, and is hushing it to sleep.

For half an hour we were alone. No person entered except a slave belonging to the monastery, and he merely peeped in. I endeavored to take a full-length portrait of the patron of the place—a stout-built gentleman, rising five feet, and draped in a black gown, braced round his waist by a tasseled cord. No other article of his proper dress is visible, but he is loaded with accessories. Curving outward his left arm, he grasps with the hand a closed book, the cover of which constitutes a pedestal for his baby, without which he is never seen. It is a pretty thing, resting with one foot on the volume, the other in the air. Its stature is fifteen inches. It wears pantalettes, a white silk frock with sash, and gold-laced tucks; tiny frills go round its neck, a crown is on its head, a ball in one hand, and in the other an artificial nosegay. Between Anthony's right arm and breast a cross-headed staff shoots upward, and with it a bouquet. Thus far there is nothing very remarkable. But in his right hand is, what I first took for a walking-cane, a marshal's baton, over his shoulders a broad red military sash, on his breast the star or cross of some militant order, and, as if to mark still more emphatically the hero, his brows are encircled with a wreath, in the manner of a Roman conqueror.

"What does that mean?" I exclaimed. "Mean?" replied H——; "why, that he is a Knight Commander of the Military Order of Portugal and Brazil, belongs to the regular army, is commissioned as lieutenant colonel, and receives his pay monthly the same as every other officer." "Come," said I, "no poetry. Anthony a soldier and commander of a living regiment! It won't—" At this moment a monk came in suddenly through a side door close to where we stood. Making a reverence to the saint by bringing one knee nearly to the floor, he turned inquiringly to us. Under thirty, fat, rather short, but of a handsome mien—a fair specimen of a Brazilian—my companion spoke, and told him I was a stranger desirous of going over the saint's establishment. With a dubious glance at the memorandum-book and pencil in my hand, and then at myself, he asked, "Is he pious?" The answer was satisfactory; and, sure enough, what H—— had said of the martial offices, dignities, and salary of the saint was all true. The monk spoke of him in the character of a general, and I asked, "Why give him that title if he is but a colonel?" The answer was ready: according to Brazilian etiquette, every Knight of the Grand Cross is entitled to the insignia and honors of the highest rank; hence, in common with his brother knights, Lieutenant-colonel Anthony, though wearing neither stockings nor shoes, is complimented with the badges and dignities of a general.

We now turned to the paintings. While gazing on one rather intently, I risked my reputation with the monk by inadvertently turning my back on the general, a piece of forgetfulness deemed incompatible with true devotion. I ought to have been on my guard, inasmuch as at another church I had been reproved for a similar offense. The subjects are incidents from the life and deeds of Anthony. I shall notice a few only.

1. At the mouth of a well, over which a chain and pulley are suspended, stands an enraptured monk. He has just raised the bucket, and with it a small image of the saint. The story is this: The brother of a monastery, whose duty it was to draw water, lost the bucket from the chain. Distressed, and not knowing what to do, for the well was very deep, the saint at length inspired him. Drawing from his bosom an image of the general, he sent it down. On reaching the water, it caught hold of the floating bucket, properly hooked it to the chain, and rose with it, to the delight of the lay brother and the edification of the brotherhood.

2. The saint, acting the part of a surgeon, is fixing the foot of a living person to the limb from which it had been severed. A young man, said our cicerone, once kicked his mother. He went out and met a stranger, who startled him by saying, "He that kicks his mother should lose his foot." Conviction seized the culprit; he returned home and chopped off the offending member. His injured mother came in, began to cry, and before he bled to death, picked up the foot and took her son with her in search of the stranger. He was close by, and recognized as St. Anthony. Seeing the youth repentant, he immediately healed him. The foot, in drawing nigh to its proper place, sprung out of the saint's hands like the keeper to a magnet, and the line of separation was not visible

3. Meeting some Turks, they reviled him. One, more violently wicked than the rest, was strangely punished. Both his eyes flew out of their sockets into Anthony's hands. The saint is painted with one between each finger and thumb, and the screaming sinner kneeling before him. This was evidence too awful for Mohammedans to resist; they were converted, and the saint returned the balls to their gaping voids, where all became right again.

4. "What of those horses kneeling before the saint, and Turks standing near?" I asked. One day Anthony was raising the Host as Mohammedans were passing. They derided and refused to kneel. To convince them of their error, he told them to bring their cattle near. They complied, and, to their amazement, the brutes set them an example of devotion by bowing down before the good man and the wafer. I observed that this miracle had been explained by saying grain had been put into a cavity which the hungry beasts could not reach without stooping. "That," said he, "is a lie."

5. Two of the largest paintings are *chefs d'œuvre*. Preaching in Pavia, he stopped suddenly, and, agreeably to ancient practice, requested his congregation to repeat a short prayer. He appeared to his audience to be leaning over the pulpit, but in reality he had left the church. Our Lady had whispered to him that his father had been arrested in Portugal for murder, and was at that moment on his way to the gallows. By her aid he arrived before the rope was passed round his parent's neck, and, as the pictures show him, stopped the posse, consisting of the judge, sheriff, hangman, and crowd. The murdered man was in his coffin close by, and on him the saint called. The corpse obeyed the mandate, threw off the cover of the shell, sat up in it, and proclaimed aloud the innocence of the accused. Anthony saluted his father and returned to Pavia, arriving as the congregation finished the prayer, and concluded his discourse without his absence having been suspected.

6. I next pointed to a female at a counter behind which a man was busy weighing money. That young woman, we were told, was friendless and destitute. Nothing but dishonorable means of living were before her. Anthony fell in with her, and gave her a scrap of thin paper, with directions to take it to a

certain merchant, and ask him, in the saint's name, to give her its weight in gold. The son of Mercury laughed as he dropped the feather-like slip into his scales, but when one—two—three—four piles of gold did not make it rise, he became dumb with reverence and fear. A few more pieces brought the scales to a level, and the now happy girl had the means of continuing in a virtuous course of life.

7. The way in which he helped a married lady is the subject of another. This woman was abandoned by her husband. Anthony met him, and told him to go home to his virtuous wife, who was daily praying for him. He refused. "Then," quoth the saint, "send her a letter and some money." To this he agreed. As the holy man would not touch the money of so bad a husband, he told him to drop it, with the letter, into his sleeve. As usual, the distressed lady was next morning praying to her favorite patron. A letter addressed to her dropped on the altar, and while reading it, money rained down from the sleeve of the image, as the painting represents.

One more.: The saint met a man in low spirits, and asked what ailed him. He had been in business, had acquired wealth, but was now ruined by the death of a dishonest partner, whose heirs claimed the property, and he had no evidence to show his right to it. "Never mind," quoth Anthony, "come with me." They entered a wood, and near a cavern the saint called on the devil to bring out the roguish partner. In the midst of fire and smoke, Satan appears with his victim. The saint commanded the latter to sign an order on his relatives to give up their ill-gotten riches. This he did, and the cheated merchant got his own again. The parties are pictured at the mouth of hell, and Satan holds the sinner by the neck while he signs the document.

Our reverend commentator was in his element. He dwelt with pleasing unction on a dozen or two more. Several had an irresistible influence over the muscles of our mouths; and the negro, who had come in again, exposed every molar and incisor in his head, nor could the father himself always keep his own eye-teeth out of sight. With charming naïveté he said to H——, "These stories can do no harm. If all are not true. most of them are."

We had now crept down to the junction of the chancel with

the main body of the temple, where two spirited angels, tall as I am, stood, as if to guard the passage into the holiest place. They are highly colored and gilded. Each holds a cornucopia, the mouth of which has been scooped out to receive a large cylindrical lamp, in which a lighted wick was floating. The angel near me wore a conical black cap without a rim, that contrasted strangely with the uncovered golden locks of the other. The mystagogue was filling my companion to repletion with picture stories, and I drew near and touched the cone. It was loose; I raised it, and, without a moment's delay, replaced it. It was neither more nor less than an extinguisher for the lamps, and, when not in use, dropped on the seraph's head as a convenient and the nearest pin to hang it on. Of necessity, the head was copiously anointed with soot and grease. This piece of desecration, at such a place, was remarkable, because it is deemed wrong to put figures of celestials to any low use. Conversing one evening about the various designs for paliteiros, a suggestion to make them after the figures of saints or angels, the picks to form the rays or halos, was declared inadmissible, because it would be wicked to stick tooth-picks in holy beings' heads.

When we reached the negro's shrine, the father was interrogated about his origin. Some persons, he said, suppose the saint was a Spanish slave in a convent, and, becoming eminently pious, was elected abbot, but where and when he could not say.

The vestry is a splendid room, paved with red and white mosaics. The ceiling is paneled, and covered with rich paintings by an old *slave*. The walls, for four or five feet up, are cased with painted blue and white tiles, illustrating the life of the saint, and the rest with paintings on the same fruitful subject. The carvings of bureaus, and round the doors, in high relief, are very superior. The lavatory occupies an adjoining room. In the centre is a marble basin, shell-shaped, eight feet over, and from it rises a column, at whose angles dolphins deliver the water, the whole surmounted by a draped female statue of "Puritas" some twelve feet from the floor.

We went up stairs into a wide passage opening into the monks' cells. Out of one there came the strangest substitute for a chamber-maid I ever saw—an old and miserable-looking negro, with nothing whatever on his person but a tattered slip of bagging round his middle. He and another were busy with the morning chores. Resting a while in one of the rooms, we beheld the Carioco Aqueduct winding like a low, whitewashed wall along the hill side; in one place half sunk in the ground, at another wholly out, while close to the monastery it passes under the road we came up, and enters the Carioco Fountain at the foot of the ascent.

Our cicerone led us up stairs to a large room overlooking a great part of the city and the Bay—the library. When the door was unlocked and thrown open, what a blast of damp and mildew came out! Pausing till fresh air could stream in, we spent an hour or two among the books. Here are between five and six thousand volumes—heavy tomes on Canon Law, Monastic Orders, Miracles of Saints, History of Byzantium, Works of the Fathers, etc. The only English book was a Life of Milton. With the exception of a work on magic, I did not see a volume of special interest, nor did I open one whose leaves were not glued together by damp, and of which large portions had not been devoured by ants. In a few years the whole will have perished.

The Saint as a Soldier.—When the royal family arrived from Portugal in 1808, Anthony was only captain of infantry, but before returning to Europe, John VI. raised him to a lieutenant colonelcy on the staff, to the great displeasure of older officers. Besides his salary of 960 milreis as lieutenant colonel, he appears in other grades in the army list, and receives pay and rations accordingly. I extract the following from the national budget for the present year:

		Milreis
San Antonio de Goyas	Granted November 18, 1750,	192
" de Minas, by royal mandate	" February 26, 1799,	480
" do Mouraria	" September 5, 1800,	120
" da Parahiba	" December 13, 1809,	75

Besides these army pensions, I am told that he figures in other characters as a creditor on the public ledgers. As the whole affair was strange to me, I inquired how the money was paid, to whom, and how disposed of. The answer was, that here, in Rio, the abbot of his monastery receives it, and expends it on the saint's person, on his clothes, washing, and ornaments,

Y

wages for his servants, and other expenses of his establishment. I was furnished with a copy of the receipt for his last month's salary:

 Pay this, Bastos.   Lieutenant Colonel, No. 363.
 Received from the illustrious Lieutenant-colonel Manoel José Alvas da Fonseca, treasurer and paymaster-general of the troops of this capital, the sum of eighty milreis, being the amount of pay due for the month of May last to the glorious St. Anthony, as lieutenant colonel in the army.
 To manifest the same, I sign this receipt.
 Noted Folio 6, Lira.   Father Miguel de Santa Rita, Superior.
                Rio de Janeiro, June 15, 1846.
 Paid, Alves. Joao Caetano d'Almeida França, Ex Syndic Procurator.

In times of peace his active services are not required, but in war he is expected to accompany the troops, and perhaps even now the enunciation of his presence might make some invading enemies pause, as in ancient times armies quailed when the gods of their opponents were brought into the field.

Anthony as a Saint.—To impress me with his manifold virtues, a lady loaned me a small volume, "Compendio de Oracões." In the "Week of Love to St. Anthony," the form of address on Mondays is, "Oh, my St. Anthony! Wonder of wonders! Credit to Omnipotence! Model of humility! Mystic doctor!" On other days: "Oh, St. Anthony! Treasurer of Italy! Precious Stone of Poverty! Human Angel! Prince of Heaven! Sun of the World! Atlantes of Virtue! Star of Spain and Portugal! Wonder of Nature! Brilliant Sun of Padua! Doctor of Truth! Trumpet of Heaven! Hammerer of Heretics! Abyss of Sanctity! Rule of Perfection! Column of the Catholic Church! Honor of the Seraphic Religion, and most Beloved of Glory! I offer thee thirty-six Ave Marias in honor of the thirty-six years during which thou practiced so many miracles!"

Again: "Do we look for miracles? St. Anthony makes death, sin, sorrow, error, and devils flee away. He is a prompt medicine for every disease. He takes us out of prison, delivers us from pains, and *all lost things he finds.* Perils he banishes, and to every one gives succor. Padua confesses all this. Pray for us, good Anthony!" Another passage—if the reader is not out of breath—explains why he is represented with a child. "Oh, glorious St. Anthony, who merited to receive from the hands of the Mother of God her only baby into thine arms!"

This was the highest of honors. No other saint received such a mark of favor. There was much trouble to get the infant from him; hence it is the common practice of his worshipers here, when they get out of patience with him for delaying to comply with their wishes, to threaten to take the baby from him. Nothing, a devout lady says, is more effectual than such a threat. Intimating that Nossa Senhora, at the time Anthony lived, had no baby to put into his arms, I was told she, by miracle, made one for the purpose!

As the restorer of lost things, Anthony is constantly appealed to in cases of runaway slaves, stray horses, mules, and stolen furniture. Senhora P—— carries his picture in her bosom, and, like thousands, keeps an image of him in her house. Not a day passes without her addressing him. To convince me that he was " a very miraculous saint," she mentioned that he had sent one of her mother's slaves back after a long absence, and how a valuable one of her own had run off, and been forced to return. This last confessed that the tortured image of the saint used to appear and tell him he must return.

When other saints do not comply with requests preferred to them, resignation is a duty; while, in such cases, Anthony is scourged, bruised, and tormented in every imaginable manner; and, what is strange, this is said to be agreeable to him! The measures adopted by Senhora P—— were such as her mother had recourse to. She took Anthony, a figure about the length of one's hand, of pottery, but more commonly of plaster of Paris —placed a lighted candle before him, asked him to send the fugitive home, and to mind and give him no rest till he returned. A week elapsed, and he came not; another and another passed away, and still no tidings of him. She then took the saint, laid him, with his face downward, on the floor behind the door, and put a heavy stone upon him, that there might be no intermission of his pain. I asked, " Why treat him so severely ?" Then came the stereotyped story : " St. Anthony wished to be a martyr, but as Our Lady did not permit him to have that honor, he loves to be afflicted in his representatives, and very often will not listen to his friends until they are tormented." As soon as the fugitive was recovered, the load was removed from the back of the little sufferer; he was washed, put on a covered table, two candles lit before him, and the best thanks of the lady presented with a courtesy.

It is common with some to put the uncomplying saint into ovens, and throw him into ash-pits, and never to take him out except to thank him or to chastise him; but the most general punishment is consignment to a dark and wet prison. Every house in Rio has a shallow well or cistern in the yard of brackish water rising within a few feet of the surface. In these the saint is immured. So common is it "*to put St. Anthony into the well*," that the expression is proverbial for having lost something. H—— says he had a slave who ran off, and was caught and returned in a few weeks. On communicating the news of the recovery of the fugitive to his family, his wife led him to the small well in the yard, and, opening the cover, showed him Anthony suspended by a cord just over the water. She had placed him there soon after the slave was missing. Of course he was drawn up, like Jeremiah out of the pit, and complimented with thanks and a couple of candles, and the slave reminded how useless were attempts to escape the vigilance of this heavenly negro-catcher. There is no doubt whatever that many slaves are recovered by means of the saint. The tortured image, like one of their native idols, haunts their imaginations, and constant dread of evil befalling them compels them to return.

Vast numbers of six and seven inch Anthonys are destroyed by angry devotees. I heard of disappointed lottery speculators hewing them, like Agag, in pieces; others throwing them into the fire during the prevalence of rage; so that if the saint did not seal the truth with his blood as he desired, scarcely one of his representatives escapes being martyred.

A few days ago an advertisement of a lost ass appeared in a daily paper. The animal had been taken from a garden belonging to the monastery of Saint Anthony, and a reward was offered for its recovery; so that while he recovers other people's lost cattle, he can not find his own—at all events, his friars have more faith in newspapers than in him.

The monks are unpopular. Of several recent lawsuits they have not succeeded in one. A house is being erected by a private individual on ground claimed by them. They have protested against the intrusion, but that is all. Some time ago, a similar outrage induced the abbot to appeal to the government. Carneiro Leon, an enlightened statesman, was Secretary of State. After hearing the complainant, he replied, "Well, we don't want monks, and the government itself wants the convent grounds." The frighted father fled—perhaps to appeal to Anthony? "No, no," said a native friend, "friars know better; they tell simpletons to do that."

Besides real estate, their means are swelled by bequests, proceeds of "blessed" prints, scapularies, medals, money for masses, and for consecrated habits for those who desire to be buried in them—a superstition quite common; men, women, children, and youths being frequently entombed in the garbs of monks and nuns, the wealthy paying high prices for them.

May 31. All concede that the brotherhood of Santa Anna bears off the palm in the current festival. This church stands on one side of the Campo, and is here represented; the flag-

FEAST OF THE HOLY GHOST AT SANTA ANNA'S CHURCH.

staff and flag of the Holy Ghost in front, a portion of the pyrotechnic poles with figures mounted on them, the auctioneer and empire fenced in, etc. Before noticing them, let us glance at the establishments of lay showmen, who are always welcomed here by their ecclesiastical brethren, both parties being mutual aids to each other. Here are, in the immediate vicinity of the church,

1. "*The beautiful Dog of the North*—the Phœnix of Europe. Madame Neif has the honor of requesting ladies and gentlemen to attend early to enjoy the brilliant spectacle of 'The beautiful Dog of the North,' as she can remain only a short time. The exhibition is in one of the tents in the Campo of Santa Anna, every evening during the Feast of the Holy Ghost."

2. "*Theatro Magico.*" (Phantasmagoria and natural magic.)

3. "*Theatro de Bom Gusto.*" (Posture-making, tumbling, lifting weights.)

4. "*Tourinhos Mechanicos.*" (Punch and Judy, and other puppets.)

5. "*Trabalhos* (feats) *do Senhor Otto Motti.*"

The precocious poodle of the advertisement is a canine *roué ;* "he plays at cards, spells out ladies' names, and does other wonderful things."

There were three more booths, in one of which sword-swallowing and drawing ribbons from the mouth were the chief feats, except that the performers rinsed their parched throats with fire. In another were ground and lofty tumbling, with rope-dancing.

The feast opened on Sunday, the last day of May. It was dark before I reached the place. The illuminated tower and steeple of the church sparkled in the distance as with strings and wreaths of diamonds. Bengola and other lights were streaming upward, and inverted cones of rockets—a dozen from one stick—were every few moments sent aloft, while bombs exploded with reports loud as the heaviest ordnance; the church bells pealed away, the drums, cymbals, and trumpets of the showmen helped them. Opposite the show-booths were others for the sale of wines, cigars, pies, and other refreshments. One poetical proprietor informed visitors, in the following verse, that his place contained every thing that could be wished for by those who love to taste and suck good things:

> "Quem bons potiscos
> Quizar chucar,
> Pessa que tudo
> Selhe ha de dar."

Avenues were formed by colored women seated on the grass, each with a basket of fruit, cakes, or doces, lit up with a paper lantern. Here were "Holy Ghost rusks," gingerbread, and scores of other articles thus designated, being stamped with a dove in honor of the festival. The noise, bustle, and excitement of the scene made a perfect Bartholomew Fair. The ground was alive with people, who kept moving like a colony of ants in commotion.

But let us turn to the church, and try to get through the crowds in front of the stage, which is very artistically got up. At each end an angel holds a lamp, while chandeliers, vases, blue and crimson tapestry, enlighten and decorate the whole. "The Emperor of the Holy Ghost," seated on a throne, presides, and really acts the part to admiration. The little fellow is ten years old; he wears a crown; a wide frill adorns his neck and rests on an ermine tippet; his coat, vest, small-clothes with strings at the knees, white stockings, and buckled shoes are those of adults two centuries ago. The managers and a number of ladies are sitting near him: the band is playing a lively air, and see! the little monarch points with his gilt sceptre to a side-stand—a signal for one of his secretaries to hand him a paper of sugar-plums. He wears "the sash of the Order of Christ." There is probably some alliance between these juvenile monarchs and the "boy bishops" of the Middle Ages.

Soon as the music ceased, out sprung the auctioneer, dressed in motley!—a young man of twenty-five or six—a Brazilian Grimaldi. In disposing of a large rusk, his antics elicited shrieks of approbation. After disposing of several more, and handing to each purchaser, with the change, a sacred print, he disappeared, and in a twinkling reappeared in a striped close-fitting dress like Harlequin's, with bells sewed on the front and side seams. Making a profound reverence to the emperor, he introduced, in a comic dance, a large white rooster to the audi-

ence. Holding it in a natural position by its legs, he made it scream by pulling down the tail feathers, and soon knocked it down to a laughing buyer, with a woodcut of a dove in a triangle thrown in. A quick broker, he put the first bid on himself, and struck off the lots at the first or second advance. He kept the company in the best of tempers, and there was no putting a joke upon him. Some one attempted this, when he took hold of what he called his "silver quizzing-glass," which hung by a ribbon low as his knees, and applying it to his eye, thrust his whole face through it. It was an open ring cut out of a sheet of tin. His manner of using it was irresistible.

Retiring, he came out next in the worn-out dress of a general, with enormous epaulets, and performed a comic dance, the music accompanying him. With every change of the step he changed the figure of his magic hat: one moment a regular *chapeau de bras*, the next a bishop's mitre, now a Phrygian bonnet, now a Quaker's castor, anon an inverted, and last of all a perfect cone with asses' ears, in which form he fell to business, and disposed of fowls, pigeons, pies, custards, and confectionery. After disposing of a dozen pigeons, the musicians played a popular overture, and, thinking I had seen enough, I turned to leave, when a sudden shout announced his reappearance. He was in a white and scarlet dress, mounted on high stilts, and danced a polka on them to perfection. With a hen in one hand and his eye-glass in the other, he placed his arms akimbo, and without hesitation came down eight or ten steps into the "empire," and traversed it for bids, stalking among the crowd like a heron or flamingo among penguins. For fun and drollery no actor among the showmen could surpass him. He had one drawback—his voice was hoarse and cracked.

Before I left he appeared in a night-gown and night-cap, which last he changed into various standard coverings for the head, and generally by hitting some one with it. The worst thing about him was his treatment of the fowls and pigeons, which he whirled and jerked about without the least regard to their sufferings. The latter bore their pains in silence, while the screechings of the former added to the general merriment. He is a professional buffoon.

Fire-works.—In pyrotechnics Brazilian artists are, I suppose, equal to those of any country. While they excel in staple "*fogos*," they have a variety which, though of ancient date, I have seen nowhere else. Admitting of endless applications, and opening a new field for our artists, a few specimens may as well be given. But first let us read the official announcement from the *Diario:*

"*Espirito Santo de Santa Anna.*—This evening, June 2, will be given, if the weather permits, a grand display of artificial fire-works, of every variety and color, all made by the famous artist, Bernardino José da Cunha. The attention of the respectable public is solicited. All are invited to enjoy the spectacle, and at the same time view the empire, which is fitted up in a style surpassing that of previous years."

Here were forty poles, varying from twenty-five to fifty feet in height. Against some were fixed wheels, wheels within wheels, suns, moons, stars, cones, polygons, vases, baskets, and forms various as produced by a kaleidoscope. A row of splendid archways of fire arose, and over them, in words of flame, "*Louvoures ao Divino Espirito Santo.*" But these are more or less akin to similar things with us. It was the human figures on the top of the poles, and the movements imparted to them, that constituted the novelty.

Large as life, and dressed in character, they were so well got up, that at a short distance all might be taken for living persons—a few feet off the illusion was strong. They represented barbers, razor-grinders, wood-sawyers, tumblers, rope-dancers, ladies, and ladies' maids, etc. The ablest tailors and mantua-makers could not have dressed them better. Workmen wore roundabouts and caps; gentlemen were in blue coats, striped pants, and black neckcloths. The barber's shirt-bosom was figured, the collars projected fashionably, and his cravat was tied *à la mode;* he wore a white jacket and pants, an apron, and highly-polished shoes, with a razor in his hand, and a comb behind his ear. One lady is dressed in spotted pink, with frills, sash, kid gloves, and every thing else to correspond. She is ready for a pirouette when the general dance begins. Had I not previously examined one or two, I could hardly have believed that their silk hats and bonnets, coats, vests, polished boots, linen, leather caps, veils, and muslin de laines, were nothing more than *colored paper*, supported on delicate wire frames: the faces were masks.

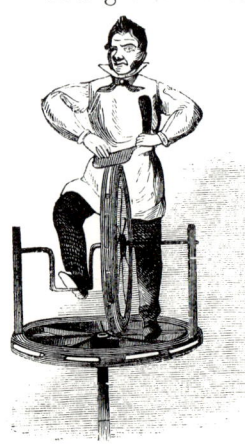

A slight reference to the mechanism by which motion is imparted to them will be sufficient. The base on which each figure stands is a horizontal wheel, some ten feet over. Its axis coincides with that of the pole, upon which it is made slowly to turn by a band of small rockets going round its periphery. Suppose on the upper side of one of these wheels two upright posts, supporting the ends of a horizontal crank-shaft, on which is a small vertical wheel. Imagine a man standing on one foot on the larger wheel and the other foot on the crank, and you have one form of the popular razor-grinder. He appears to turn the wheel with his foot, and, holding the instrument to the surface, a stream of fire flies from it as from a dry grindstone.

The movements of the wood-sawyer and the rest were produced in the same or in a similar way. At ten P.M. the display began, and continued till twelve. The place was as light as day with artificial flames. On one pole two gentlemen raised their hats and bowed to each other; close by them, a chambermaid waited with a candle in her hand to show them to their apartments. A lady on another moved her hands, as if to join them to a neighboring dandy, and whirled away in a cotillion. A tumbler stuck fast in a somerset, and remained in an inverted position to the close, when, with the rest, he vanished in a flash. The wood-sawyer and his African assistants worked away; the razor-grinder's wheel flew round, and his foot rose and fell with the treddle at a preternatural rate. Occasionally his grindstone lacked moisture, and then he spat jets of liquid fire on it, his face glistening with sweat or varnish. While admiring his ardor, I felt a slight movement at my coat pocket. It was picked. Five seconds had not elapsed since I felt my pocket-book in it. Turning quickly round, my eyes met those of two young fellows looking innocent as doves. One of them had it. They had, I presume, seen me take it out repeatedly. It contained only memoranda and sketches, chiefly of the auctioneer and empire. I had been reminded of pickpockets at the feast, and had no money or watch about me.

Having a long walk before me, I left ere more than half the figures on the poles were in motion. In passing the Lapa Church, I observed windlasses and wheel-work in motion on a few poles. Over an illumined doorway an angel unfolds a scroll, exposing the words "*Gloria ao Divino Espirito Santo.*" The auctioneer was inviting bids for a fowl; his audience were chiefly negroes and low fellows. T—— told me he stopped a moment in passing, and that the language of the brute was abominably indecent.

Thus ended the month of May and the first day of the feast of the Holy Ghost. In their general aspects and influences festas are certainly akin to operas and theatres, but it would be wrong to consider them specimens of papal worship. They are, I believe, just what their pagan prototypes were, reunions in honor of patron divinities, and not occasions for invoking them so much as for social rejoicings.

The fête was kept up by the Santa Anna managers for eight days. On the last day the emperor for the next year was elected. The same boy was chosen. He is the son of an apothecary, who is fond of the honor, which costs him, it is said, five hundred dollars a year.

The concluding official advertisements were as follows:

"It is communicated to the respectable public, and to the Brotherhood of the Divine Holy Ghost of Santa Anna, that on Sunday, 7th instant, there will be celebrated a *Te Deum* and sermon, when the re-elected emperor will take possession. At night the auction and empire.

"J. J. GOMES FERREIRA, *Secretary.*"

"*Divino Espirito Santo de Santa Anna.*—On Sunday, 7th, the ceremony of the Emperor of the Holy Ghost taking possession will occur in the afternoon, with a *Te Deum* and music. Signorina Cardiani [an Italian cantatrice] and other artists will perform gratis. The empire will be illuminated at night. There will be an auction, music, and splendid fireworks."

In the same paper the booth and show men advertise their attractions. On the evening of the 7th the Campo was in my way home from Mataporcos. The auctioneer wore a court dress, his hair powdered, a long queue, etc. He was in high glee— sold a basket of fowls and pigeons in no time. I left him dancing a polka on stilts. The Italian performers had got through their parts before I arrived. The showmen were doing a good business. The wide steps to one booth, where "the diverting scene of the monkey in a sack" was announced, gave way under the crowds waiting for admission.

Of tradesmen's advertisements relating to this festival the annexed is a sample:

"*Notice to the Illustrious Preparers of the Festival of the*

Holy Spirit.—In Silversmith Street, No. 78, may be found a beautiful assortment of Holy Ghosts, in gold, with glories, at 80 cents each; smaller sizes, without glories, at 40 cents. Silver Holy Ghosts, with glories, at $6\frac{1}{2}$ dollars per hundred; do., without glories, $3\frac{1}{2}$ dollars. Holy Ghosts of tin, resembling silver, at 75 cents per hundred."

CHAPTER XXXI.

Vicar and Vintems.—Theatricals.—Barbonos Monks and the troublesome Blacksmith.—Priscilliana.—Host and drunken Bellman.—Proceedings of the National Senate arrested.—Slave-trader's Office.—Anthony of the Poor: his Festival and Tablets.—Mosquitoes and Lizards.—Corpus Christi and St. George.—Showmen and the Burial.

June 1. Besides half-holidays, there are six full ones this month, exclusive of Sundays. The vicar got through mass early, and came in to breakfast and bisca. He mentioned an old lady in good circumstances, who plagued him for two vintems. As he had none about him, to get rid of her importunities he gave her a couple out of the alms-box. This was just what she wanted. As they were consecrated, they would act as a charm against poverty, and while she retained them she would never lack the means of living. Under a similar persuasion, a poor woman requests him, once a year, to fold up, for a few moments, a vintem in the altar-cloth.

3*d.* The great day of the feast; the performers in the Campo, and other artists also, are on the *qui vive*, thus: the play to-night at one theatre is "*The Jealous Woman :* a comedy, in five acts, with other entertainments, for the benefit of Nossa Senhora da Conceição, in Soap Street." In another, "*The Man of the Black Mask,* in five acts, with the comedy of *The Brothers of Souls ;*" the latter a satire on the collectors, who are represented as pocketing the alms they collect. To-morrow, "*The Scholars of St. Cyro,* in five acts; a *Mazurka Dance,* and the farce of *Judas on Allelulia.*" "*The Feast of the Holy Ghost in the Country*" is another popular comedy of the kind.

We fell in to-day with one of the Barbonos monks, recently returned from a visit to the Holy Land. B——, who is a wag, asked him how it was that they allowed Brother Leonardo to hold possession of property belonging to the order, and to carry on blacksmithing to the disgrace of the Church. How can the people venerate the Barbonos?

Monk. "Piani. Be advised that I have brought an order from Rome to call him to account and take away his credentials as a friar. The business requires caution, but with time and patience we will remove the stain from our order and recover the property. For several years he has received the alms collected for the poor saints at Jerusalem, and has sent neither money nor accounts to Rome; and, besides seizing buildings and land belonging to the society, he has made some of its slaves work for him, and now claims them as his own; but piani, piani" (softly, softly).

B——. "Let me tell you that he has strong friends under the present government, as he had under that of Pedro I. Several members of the Chamber of Deputies board with him."

Monk. "We know it. It is his influence with the Chambers and part of the ministry that makes us pause. He does not know the powers I have brought over respecting him. Were he to discover my thoughts, he would try to get rid of me, or perhaps induce the government to order me to leave."

B——, whispering in his ear. "Not so, padre, while the empress, your countrywoman, befriends you, and the nuncio is with you."

Monk. "Amigo, I will tell you. The nuncio and I are agreed on what is to be done." Here he placed his two forefingers side by side, and rubbed one along the other—an expressive sign of two parties drawing together in one business.

It was a treat to see the two confabulating, so rapidly did their features change and their tongues and fingers move; one moment aghast, the next bland and smiling; now a scream, next a whisper, anon the tongue lies still, and the hands take up the story. The monk was a young man, under thirty, and I could not but think him indiscreet to speak so freely on the subject. The chief of the Capuchins approached, called him from us, and, whispering to him, eyed us significantly. He was undoubtedly rebuking him for conversing with us, for, though we often fell in with him afterward, he avoided us.

As for the backsliding friar, he is said to care not the value of a nail-rod for all the tonsured tribe, and that, if he had the power, he would not hesitate to make his late brethren blow the bellows and wield sledge-hammers in his forge. On returning, we called to see him, but he had just stepped out. He enters his shop in his gown, takes orders for shoes for both mules and men (having slaves shoemakers), and almost any thing in the iron and leather trade.*

4th. In this morning's ramble H—— and I found Priscilliana holding a levee. Her portrait committee were doing as brisk a business as the adjoining Baracas gentlemen. As we were about to leave, a wretched-looking negro, with a small bell in his hand, came up and stood by us at the door. His only garments were the relics of a filthy shirt, and of more foul and tattered pants. He muttered to himself, and was so fragrant with cachaça that H——, after interrogating him, threatened to knock him down if he did not move farther off. "What is he going to do with that bell?" "Wait a moment," said my companion, "and you will see." The words were scarcely spoken when two mules drew a carro up. A man came out of the church with a lantern, and lit the carriage-lamps. A priest next came forth, with an attendant holding a red, flat canopy over him. Both got into the chaise, the half-drunken negro stepped ahead of the mules, the postillion laid his whip across their backs, and the cortège started for the house of some sick person with the Host; the bellman, in a jog-trot, keeping in advance, and causing people to move their hats, and some to kneel, till he and his followers passed by.

As the National Senate was in session, we stepped in and took seats in the gallery, which contained but four other spectators. Twenty members were present, two with skull-caps, and the secretary also had a tonsure. A senator was fervently discussing a project for distributing property of deceased parents equally between legitimate and illegitimate offspring. He wished the law to be more explicit; he alluded to the facility of ob-

---

* His enemies did not succeed in displacing him. In a late almanac he appears as usual, under the head of *Hospicio de Jerusalem:* "Fr. Leonardo de Encarnação Santa Anna, Commissario Geral da Terra Santa." However suitable in other respects his name may be, the Incarnation of the Virgin Mother is surely an unfit appellative for a modern Vulcan.

taining fraudulent testimony, and referred to a class of men, who, as in Lisbon, swear, he said, to any thing for a pataca, or at most for a milreis. From our seats we saw the drunken negro and carriage returning. Presently his bell was heard within, when the speaker paused, and every senator arose, and stood in silence till the sound died away!

We called at a slave-dealer's office. On the walls were penny daubs of the Madonna and other characters. One was a black saint, with Hottentot cherubs floating in the air, and two ebony mortals at his feet. There would have been no occasion to ask his name had it not been printed on the sheet—" The miraculous San Bento, Protector of Angola." There were no slaves about the premises, and nothing except these wallflowers to indicate the nature of the business transacted in them.

Antonio des Pobres was holding a festival in honor of " Our Lady of Pleasures," accompanied with an auction. We looked in on our way home. Beneath a shabby transparency sat four musicians on a small stage by the church door. The auctioneer had no stand, but hunted for bids inside and out. The images had been washed and otherwise improved. Anthony had on a clean gown, and his baby a new frock. Among waxen offerings in the vestry were numerous old tablets. H—— translated a few. On one a man's leg and thigh were painted, all red and sore with wounds; the owner had applied to Anthony and was healed. Another represents Graciana Maria da Conceição on a sinking ship off Rio Grande; she, too, called on him, and he saved her. One board certifies that a man, severely afflicted with spasms, was cured in a moment by Our Lady of Pleasures, to whom he offered the votive acknowledgment. On a large tablet a wild man is crouching in the woods, like another Orson, and gazing at a white man and three negroes. The writing below tells us that the poor fellow had become insane, and, flying to the forest, lived like a beast; but his wife, Paulina Maria da Conceição, had great devotion to the Holy Ghost, by whose miraculous interference the maniac crept out of his lair, and went quietly home with the four messengers sent for him. The painting represents him at the moment when they first came in sight of him.

June 11. Annoyed last night by musquitoes. The little

house lizards are a blessing, since they hunt these pests without ceasing. I found one on the wall near my pillow, and secured it in a glass shade. Though they dart up and down the sides of rooms, I have not yet detected one moving across the ceiling. The prisoner climbed the sides of the glass quite readily when they were dry, but when wetted it could not keep itself from sliding down. The sucker-apparatus by which they are supposed to suspend themselves against gravity I could not detect through the glass. Their feet are furnished with minute claws. They have their enemies, for our noble cat, allied to the wild species, has a hoarse cough, the effect of having lunched too freely on them this morning.

This is Corpus Christi, a great day with Romanists every where. Here, the emperor, his court, senators, and soldiers join in the procession. It is the only occasion on which *St. George* appears in public. Mounted on his charger, he, in his official character of Defender of the Empire, takes the precedence. Prince and people walk behind him. As the Church's champion, he heads her squadrons too. Not having been so fortunate as to find his residence once open during repeated calls, I must attend, if only to become acquainted with a character so popular with Protestants and papists as this chief of dragon-killers.

The morning papers announce that "the Board of Directors of the Brotherhood of the glorious St. George invite the brethren to attend at his chapel at 9 A.M., to accompany him in the Procession of the Body of God. The image will pass through Theatre Square, Piolho, and Cadeia Streets, to the Imperial Chapel, and return through Dereita, Alfandega, and Fogo Streets, to his chapel in Rua do Lampadoza."

As George is the only saint that goes on horseback, I determined to call upon him. The streets were thronged with people hoping against hope, for the sky was lowering. The early morning promised a splendid day. The Corcovado, in verdant vesture, and set off with the bright ethereal ground behind him, reared his head in glorious relief, as if he, too, had donned his best in honor of the festival, and was waiting for it to begin. Within an hour he shrunk out of sight, for the smiling heavens put on a face of sorrow, and at length burst into tears. I found a troop of cavalry in front of his shabby quarters waiting to escort him to the Imperial Chapel, where the emperor, ministers of state, the Legislature, judges, provincial governors, and the *élite* of the army and Church were ready to receive him. A native of the East, his fane reminds one of Arabian palaces with exteriors indicative of poverty's abodes. Here is neither steeple, tower, nor clock; no vestibule, railings, steps, nor even flagging, to separate its precincts from the common carriage-way. The front elevation resembles the gable end of a barn—no higher, wider, and hardly more tasteful. The sill is, of any thing, below the wet and clammy pavement. All things look mean about it—even the curtain that hangs between the door-jambs is faded, worn out, and borrowed from "Luzia," whose name is wrought on it.

We push it aside, and find the walls rough, and rafters bare, the damp floor giving way under one's feet, while bits of old carpet cover the worst spots. Passing by the committee on portraits, we discover the saint standing in full dress against the wall, waiting for the weather to clear up. Females crowd to kiss his hand, courtesy to him, and some sit down in front to admire him. He wears a plumed helmet, a cambric tippet frilled round his neck, a crimson tunic with skirts reaching to his knees, black leggins with large spurs; his feet are already in the stirrups, which are attached to his thighs instead of the saddle. He grasps a shield in one hand, and a baton in the other. A mantle lies ready to throw over him when mounted. A short sword is at his waist, and muslin frills at his wrists. His stature is that of an ordinary-sized soldier, but his ruddy, smooth face, without beard, whiskers, or mustache, is not like a warrior's. His horse is in a neighboring stable. His helmet, corslet, and armlets are of pasteboard, colored in imitation of steel; the shield is of tin plate. At 2 P.M., no signs of the weather improving, the troops were dismissed and the procession given up.

ST. GEORGE.

LIFE IN BRAZIL.

I called at the Imperial Chapel on my way home, and found it crowded. Two rows of halberdiers, extending from the entrance to the altar, had just formed a passage for a miniature procession. The organ was playing and eunuchs singing, and so foul was the air that two negroes dropped and were borne out as dead. I found it impossible to remain in five minutes without approaching the door for fresh air. The programme was at length arranged: first came chanting eunuchs, the brotherhood with candles, priests, and canons; the body of God under a canopy, the emperor with a lighted candle, ministers of state and others, with their sons in court costumes, reminding one of Tom Thumbs in morris dances. Then followed the guard with their burnished spears. In this order the whole passed three times up and down the floor, and so wound up the official ceremonies of the day.

I subsequently called with a friend on the "Defender of the Brazilian Empire," and was not a little surprised to find him stowed away in a dark closet, and stripped as clean as if a troop of Ishmaelites or Camanches had met him. He had not a rag to his back. As his equestrian attitudes required something more than a stiff statue, I now saw how the positions of his limbs were varied. He was sitting on a trestle, and is made in all respects like a jointed doll. His charger, a present from the emperor, the sacristan denounces as "a wicked beast," for dishonoring the saint last year by kicking and shying, so that but for Our Lady's aid he would have been thrown to the ground! The image is an old one, of hard and heavy wood. One horse was trained to kneel till it was properly adjusted to the saddle.

ST. GEORGE IN UNDRESS.

In reply to a remark about the saint's nudity, the zealous sacristan almost shed tears while telling us that the Church was too poor to buy him any clothing. "We contract with an armador to dress him on his festival, and that is all we can do. In Lisbon the saint receives the salary of a lieutenant colonel, and his chapel there is very rich."

Showmen in the Campo offer the following attractions:

"In the Barraca of Good Taste there will be an extraordinary divertisement on the day of the Body of God.

"In the Theatro Magico, a Representation in Three Parts: Part 1. *The Passion of our Lord*, viz., The Birth—St. Joseph—Garden of Olives—Holy Magdalen—The Tortures—St. Peter—Our Lord of the Paces—St. George—The Crucifixion—St. John Baptist—The Resurrection—The Holy Virgin. Part 2. *Cosmoramic Views*. Part 3. *Diverting Phantasmagoria*: The Sorcerer—Flying Death's Head—The Parisian Galatea—The Changed Head—Don Quixote—Walking Woman—Garden of Love and the Monster. To conclude with

"Three Cats Dancing the Polka."

Of religious plays and interludes by which the day was celebrated in the Middle Ages, The Passion of our Lord was one; The Creation, Deluge, Susannah, Dives and Lazarus, Burial of Christ, and scores taken neither from the Old Testament nor the New, were others. Even the whiskered artists are not modern, though the part assigned them may be. At Aix, on this festival, the finest cat of the country, wrapped in swaddling-clothes like a child, was exhibited in a shrine to public admiration.

The burial was performed in two or three parishes, but I did not attend. Passing by the Candelaria, I stepped in for a moment. The panel in front of an altar was removed, exposing a dead Christ, as represented below.

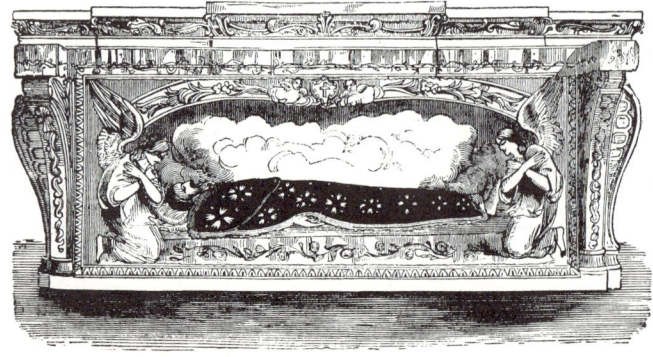

CHAPTER XXXII.

Crockery-wares: Talhas.—Monkey.—Moringues.—Furnaces, Flower-pots, etc.—
Water-baril.—Scrubbing-brush.—Mortars.—Fuel.

AN element of domestic life, and a chief item of household furniture, Brazilian crockery-ware is interesting to a stranger. The articles bear little resemblance to those in our kitchens, and some are obvious modifications of aboriginal patterns. With the exception of portable furnaces (Fig. 8 in the above group) and a few garden-pots (6), the entire cargoes of boats often consist of talhas and moringues—that is, of vessels to hold, and others from which to drink water. The material is a light red, porous clay, slightly baked, and unglazed. A penknife will readily drill a hole through it. The wares made in the neighborhood of Rio are not to be compared with the fabrics of Bahia, so much superior are the latter. A fine white clay is found there.

Every house has a talha (Fig. 1 of the group) standing in the corner of a room or passage, and holding from ten to fifteen gallons. A slave keeps it filled from the street fountains. Frequently the bottom is rounded, and then it rests in a wooden stand or table, half of it passing through an opening cut in the top. 2, 3, 4, 5 are variations. In the latter the neck is shaped like a human bust, and the hat-crown is the lid. No. 7 is the figure of a vase occasionally seen at the fountains.

I have not seen a European pitcher, or any thing like one, in a native dwelling. Home-made substitutes are cheaper, keep their contents cooler, and on other grounds are preferred. They form the class of water-pots next to talhas, and among them the "monkey" is pre-eminent. Met with every where, it is emphatically the "pitcher of Brazil." See figure *a*, page 359. Two sizes are in general use—one holding a gallon and a half, and the other two and a half. The monkey is an ancient moringue enlarged; I think it is the only vessel used in Rio with two spouts, an attribute common to old South American pottery, and not confined to it.* The larger orifice or tube is an inch bore, the other a quarter of an inch. On filling the vessel at the former, the air within escapes through the latter, and vice versa when the contents are discharging. Instead of using a tumbler, the old Portuguese and country people slip the small tube into their mouths, and slake their thirst as we do when we salute the lips of pitchers. Corks or wooden plugs to close the orifices are often seen attached by strings to the bale or handle (the curved strip between the two spouts). They serve to exclude ants, air, dust, etc. The monkey, independent of its water-cooling properties, deserves the attention of North American potters. It has advantages sufficient to justify its general introduction among us.

The figures *b, c, d, e* are specimens of table moringues, containing two to three pints. Smaller ones are figured at *i, i;* with their covers, these are made in imitation of pine-apples and other fruit. Earthenware decanters (*h*) are common. These porous vessels, by promoting evaporation, keep their contents cooler than glass ones; hence the preference to drink water at dinner, as the expression is, "from the clay." All have covers, which are removed and replaced at every sip.

"Gurgling moringues" are such as have the openings into the bodies made intentionally small. Like similar toys in vogue in the Middle Ages, they embarrass no little those who

* See a Grecian vase on plate 33, Traité des Arts Céramiques, Paris, 1844.

LIFE IN BRAZIL. 359

unsuspectingly attempt to quench thirst from them. A section of one is seen at *j*.

A view of an Indian moringue is shown at *r*—an interesting variety of conceits of red-skinned potters. A hunter's flask, it has loops by which to sling it over the shoulder. Its capacity is about a quart. It has two external openings, both quite small: one in the breast of the bird, the other in the bottom, through which it is filled. A tube, as seen by the dotted lines, extends from each opening to nearly the opposite extremity of the interior. To charge this vessel, it is inverted, and water poured into the hollow base, which serves as a funnel. When the liquid rises till it begins to enter the orifice of the other tube, the vessel then is turned to its first position. By applying the mouth to the breast of the bird, the contents are sucked up—an operation simple and easy. The orifice terminates sometimes in the mouths of birds and animals. These vessels are on sale in shops, and come from the northern provinces, where most of the potters are Indians.

The only apologies for mugs that came under my notice were

very rough affairs. (See *v.*) They are probably designed for slaves, being used to heat water in as well as to drink out of. A wash-bowl and basin from Bahia are seen at *f, g*. They are highly painted, but poorly burned.

Figure 9 of the first group, and figure *k* of the second, are the common censers. Placed on the floor, a few dried leaves of alecrim, a native species of rosemary, are dropped on the coals, when a strong acrid vapor rises and pervades every crevice. Seeds of alfazema, or lavender, are imported for the purpose. French pastiles are employed by the wealthy.

With the foregoing, the reader has not only fair samples, but a compend of the pottery fabrics of Brazil.

T is the universal, omnipresent "baril," with which the head of every slave is familiar. A natural and durable, as well as cheap scrubbing-brush, is shown at *m, n*—two halves of the husk of a cocoa-nut. This article is much used for scouring floors, as fibrous threads are developed by use, and continue to project about a quarter of an inch from the face as long as the shell lasts.

The god Pilumnus reigns as powerful here as in the East. *R, S* show the common wooden mortar and pestle of the country, the former standing about three feet high, and the latter nearly as long as the slave that wields it. In material and dimensions they are fac-similes of those found portrayed in old Egyptian kitchens, are identical with those of classical nations, and such as are still common in India, China, and, in fact, throughout the Oriental world. Not till I saw them did I perceive the appositeness of the aphorism of Solomon about the braying of fools. Some are large enough to squeeze a man into them.

Fuel.—The native fuel of Rio is charcoal and wood. The latter is quite small, the sticks seldom running two feet in length, and over an inch and a half thick. Bundles consisting of ten of these are sold by the quantity at two cents each. The Bay steamers raise steam with similar bundles, except that the sticks are somewhat thicker; but of vast piles on the steamers' docks, hardly a stick could be found four inches thick.

CHAPTER XXXIII.

A Trip to Macacu.—Steam up the Bay.—Prospects.—Slaves.—Sambayratiba.—Dense Mist.—Bed-chamber.—Attacked by Rats.—Extent of the Pest.—Sugar-house.—Stingless Bees.—Sheep.—Dogs without Tails.—Visit other Estates.—Wasps' and Ants' Nests.—The Rats again.—Scenes in the Forest.—Sipos.—Spoon Wheels.—Female Slaves making Brick.—Chigres.—Muleteers camping.—Estate of the Carmelites.—Mules.

June 13. The anniversary of Anthony of Padua, a ceaseless racket was kept up all last night to his honor; and now, rockets, Roman candles, bonfires, music, vivas, bells, guns, bombs, and every noise-making device, are the order of the day. Were he the god of fire and brimstone, they could not treat him to a greater variety of sulphurous compounds. I am well-nigh tired of the holy clatter of the city, its sacred shows and ecclesiastic toy-shops; and if the reader prefer a week's jaunt into the country, he will join a party of us bound this morning for Macacu.

In a diminutive steamer we pushed through a crowd of faluas and canoes, passed the foreign shipping, and sought the upper waters of the Bay. Among the passengers were a couple of planters, in scarlet vests and ponchos, tight-fitting white pants ending in yellow, sagging boots, to which enormous and far-projecting spurs were strapped, suggesting the idea of human roosters prepared for battle in a cock-pit; and with this their volubility and gesticulations accorded, for one moment they would start back as if each took the other for an adder, the next the shorter one whispers in the long one's ear, and a mutual distortion of mouths and shrugging of shoulders follow.

The scenes around us were exhilarating, and the air delicious in temperature and freshness. We passed Governor's Island, and numerous insulated rocks, one standing like a column on a larger one for its base, all bleached like chalk, and as bare of vegetation. Boats were at anchor among them fishing up shells for lime-kilns. We swept past Paqueta, the Capri of Rio, and the favorite island retreat of the old king. At 3 P.M. we were aground within a mile of the mouth of the Macacu River. The boat drew but thirty inches, and for some time the wheels had been working in mud. One or two sailing-boats now passed us, and played off jokes common on the Hudson in the early days of steam—offering to report us, to take our mail, etc. In half an hour the tide rose and we ran in. White herons, stalking along the shores, tempted some sportsmen aboard, but after each shot the birds arose, and threw their long legs behind them as if in derision of the gunners. Half a mile wide at its mouth, the stream rapidly narrows, and becomes crooked as a moving serpent. The water is turbid, and the banks but little above it. Dense shrubbery extends at the left over an impenetrable swamp for forty or fifty miles, and at the right for five or six, with occasional cultivated patches. Here are said to be two hundred leagues of morass, ever pregnant with malaria, and solely occupied by wild beasts.

We passed four boats laden with slaves, part of a cargo just landed east of Rio, and now being smuggled—if the term can be used where next to no secresy is affected—down to Christoval, to the depôt near the palace. Before morning they will be dispersed, and in a few days all at work. There were fifty in each boat, all young men. They stood up on passing us, surprised, probably, at a steamer. It was dark when we landed at Porto de Sampaio, a small town, where there was not room for the little steamer to turn, so narrow was the channel. We had now seventeen miles to go by land. Out of a troop of mules ready saddled we selected four, had spurs strapped to our heels, and in a little while were wending our way through a woody and wild-looking country. At a late hour we arrived at Sambayratiba, the hospitable fazenda of our friends J. and A. B——a, a property that has been in the family for several generations.

14*th*. The morning opened on us with a mist, exceeding in density any thing of the kind I ever saw or felt. The atmosphere was a sea of aqueous globules. Two small birds lighted on a tree in front of the house, and instantly a drenching shower fell from the leaves. Even humming-birds shook spray from the shrubbery. Before quitting our sleeping-apartments, a slave brought in strong coffee without milk, a universal custom, except in provinces where the berry is not grown, and there maté is taken instead. One or the other is deemed essential to health, and perhaps is so, in consequence of the morning fogs. The venerable dwelling of our hosts is a low one of stone, with the usual central court. At one end of the wide stoop or corridor was a small room containing two cot bedsteads, and on a table the family patrona, the Lady Conceição, in a glass case, with three candles, unlit, before her. Another shade inclosed what I took for a fancy Swiss figure, as it was draped in a roundabout jacket, trowsers, sash, and a wide straw hat. It represented the Baptist, to whose providence and that of "Our Lady" the old proprietors had committed the estate. This favored dormitory was appropriated to H—— and me; and here, I thought, as I wrote on the table, is something very like ancient penetralia with their penates, for Greek and Roman farmers had wax and wooden images of tutelary deities in their private chambers.

H—— had been in bed some time, and begged me to retire and put out the light. I complied, and laid down, excessively fatigued. A few moments after the room had been darkened, there fell what I took for a storm of hail, as severe as any in our Northern winters. The pattering fairly shook the low roof. The noise for an instant ceased, and in another was renewed upon the floor! Alarmed, I spoke to H——, but his reply was an unmeaning monosyllable. In the act of calling again, some half dozen objects fell on my bed. With a convulsive shudder, I kicked off the sheet—the only covering—and sent one against the ceiling, whence I heard it fall on the table, spring thence on the floor, and scamper across it with a squeak. Agitated as I was, my companion almost made my soul die within me; for, turning over in his berth, he said, in a half-awake tone, "Why don't you lie still? they're only rats."

I shall not tell the reader how long I sat up in the dark, trying to scare the vermin away. Not all the shirs and hissings I could make, nor the lashings of the bed and floor with a jacket, seemed to incommode them. On the foot of the bed some sprang every few moments, and I felt them pulling my garments out of my grasp. To confess the truth, I was half frightened to death, assured, if I laid down, they would be on my head and face. The first dawn never was more welcomed than was it this morning to me. It was the signal for the troop to decamp. They made a rush, then all was silent; next followed the scampering over the roof, and they were gone.

What a scene the light brought forth! The entire floor was sprinkled, but the altar-table was fairly covered with their dung. It is no exaggeration to say that the cloth and writing-paper resembled, at the distance, thick spotted calico. The flat candlestick, and even H———'s snuff-box, in like manner covered. One half of a new pair of soft leather braces was carried off; its mate had gone also, but the burglars not having eaten quite through the loop that held it to H———'s pants, the latter prevented them from taking it; still, had the opening through which they had dragged it been somewhat larger, the more essential part of my companion's dress had vanished. Every atom of the candle was gone, wick and all. "Why, here's a miracle," I exclaimed; "our candle has vanished, but these three before the images are untouched." "Oh," replied my companion, "the devils know better than touch them: they can not digest wax; it kills them." This nightly defilement of the family sanctuary is horrible; so far from the images being any protection, glass alone prevents their being devoured. Not till now had I any adequate idea of this terrible plague, nor of the worth of Ulrich, the canonized rat-killer of Augsburg.

There was much hearty laughing at breakfast at my dread of the nocturnal marauders. They abound throughout the country, do not harbor in houses, but come down from the hills at nightfall, and retreat at daybreak. Once a year poison is laid for them. Garcilasso la Vega has a chapter on the "incredible number" of rats in his day. He mentions how they swarmed in Peru, Panama, and Nombre de Dios, refers to an annual proclamation commanding every householder, on a certain day, to poison them, and quotes the fact of the crew of a vessel going ashore at Truxillo, and leaving a sick man aboard, who was attacked by them. He managed to get a spit from the cook's berth, and with it, on his bed, protected himself the whole of that day and night. When his associates returned, they found three hundred and eighty rats killed by his spit, besides many wounded.

The estate of our hosts is considered a small one, being only half a league square. Inclosed by neighboring mountains, a considerable part is forest-land. The stock consists of thirty-six mules, forty oxen and cows, and seventy slaves, old and young—about thirty are able-bodied. Four first-rate hands and two children, valued at $800, recently died of fever. Mandioca, coffee, beans, pork, and mutton are raised in sufficient quantities for the family and negroes. The staple of the farm is sugar. Nothing else is cultivated for sale. The crop this season is a fair one, and is expected to yield four hundred moulds of eighty pounds each, which, at 5 cents, will yield only $1600—a miserable sum for the investment of so much capital, for the product of the wear and tear of so many men, and animals, and other costly instrumentalities—a sum, too, which has to be diminished by the cost of boxes, transportation to market, commissions, and taxes.

The mill, driven by mules, is the one of the last century—the first European form of the Asiatic original—consisting of three vertical wooden rollers cased with iron. The expressed juice passed through a log into the adjoining boiling-house, where the ordinary process of concentration was followed. Between the mill and the mansion are the slaves' huts. Against one were stuck up two small cigar-boxes — hives of *Abelhas jurutys*, little bees. Jurutys is an Indian diminutive. These honey-making insects are slightly thicker in the head and body than musquitoes, for which I at first took them. Their cells bear no resemblance to those of our bees. The comb is, in color, a dark brown, and in construction it reminds one of that of ants' nests. Extremely sensitive to atmospheric influences, they close every joint of their dwellings, and at night lock themselves so close that neither robbers nor damp air can invade them, the only door being as regularly opened and closed as the gates of a fortified city. They never open it till the sun has been some time up, and invariably close it before the evening dew begins to fall. I made it a point to observe, morning and evening, the door-keepers at work.

A quarter-inch gimlet-hole made through one side of each hive is the only place of exit and entrance. Over it the little artists form a short tube of wax, and curve it upward till the aperture is horizontal. In a morning the orifice is opened and the edges flared out; in the evening the material is gathered into a bulb or dome, like the sealed end of a barometer-tube. These bees are stingless, but singularly courageous, since they drive from their neighborhoods the common bee.

I have mentioned the general appearance of Brazilian sheep. The ram on this estate was of the Mozambique breed—black, except the nose and tip of the tail; small and sharp ears; agile, and with very little hair or wool on his body, but with a mane full and shaggy as a lion's. A noble animal, he stood nearly six inches higher than the tallest ewes.

Here is a herd of large dogs, something between the greyhound and the wolf, of a dun color, short hair, and without the least indication of tails. They have four large fangs in front, two above and two below. A smaller species have two or three inches of tail, appearing to a stranger as docked. At Sampaio was a mastiff-looking pup without the shadow of one. If I believed in man's quadrumanous descent, I would quote these to sustain the hypothesis, since all the dogs of the earth are derived by naturalists from long-tailed progenitors. Of Brazilian quadrupeds destitute of a caudal appendage, the paca is one. It has given rise to a popular form of rebuke: A vaunting emigrant, returning from a hunt without game, asserted that he had run to its burrow one of these animals, which escaped him, though not till he had deprived it of its tail. Hence of a vain boaster it is said, "He'll cut off a paca's tail."

Accompanied by Senhor J——, and mounted on mules, Messrs. M——, H——, and myself started to visit some neighboring fazendas. At a league's distance we came to the *Sumidouro* estate, the property of an ex-deputy and state councilor. The mill, of the latest construction, was, with the steam-engine that drives it, imported from England. The crushing cylinders are horizontal, and the cane passes through twice at one operation. Here were four evaporating pans. At every sugar plantation the molasses is distilled into cachaça; and here, as at others, were enormous hogsheads in which the spirit is stored, and whence it is drawn for sale.

Here 200 slaves are employed and 100 oxen. About fourteen moulds are filled daily (=1200 lbs. of sugar) during the season. The proprietor, a fine, fat old gentleman, was sitting in the engine-house. He has recently buried his wife, and is paralytic. Infant negroes were playing about him, and one stood between his knees. His negroes, he said, were his children, and truly he seemed to treat them as such. One of the oldest fabricas in the province, this is admitted to be the best conducted; yet he said it yielded no profit. He dislikes slavery, but thinks white laborers can not supersede it in Brazil.

Leaving, we came to the borders of a lake, where the dogs started an alligator. Here waved the conical lilac crests of the matured sugar-plant, towering from ten to fifteen feet above the ground—a beautiful sight. We came to a shanty, which turned out a venda for the sale of soap, shoes, cachaça, and straw and willow wares made by tamed Indians. Continuing on, we passed under a tree, from which a flock of parrakeets flew chattering away. Near by was an ant's nest, built on a fence of stakes— an irregular, hard, and brown mass of clay, three feet high, as many wide, and two feet thick. I stopped at another, of the form of a huge pine-apple, nearly four feet in diameter, and full five feet high, built in a tree. It is wonderful how creatures so minute manage to carry these masses of matter to such elevations.

At the "Engenho d'Agoa," a twelve-foot undershot wheel, with buckets only fifteen inches wide, drove three jacaranda stampers for husking rice in wooden mortars. In the carpenter's shop wagons were being made by slaves, the little adze in their hands bringing wheels and felloes into form to admiration. Old rose-wood axle-trees lay about, rendered useless by fire evolved from their friction. We returned before dark, after as picturesque a ramble as man ever enjoyed.

Determined to have what I so greatly needed, some rest, I began to block out our midnight tormentors. The flooring-planks were eaten away, more or less, along the four sides of the room. A tin trunk, old shoes, chair-feet, walking-sticks, and umbrellas, were put in requisition. M—— and H—— came in and assisted. There was a small library in a closet, and a score of octavos and quartos were employed. To my surprise, Senhor M—— did not hesitate to fold up an old missal to plug one hole. The butt-end of a musket was dropped into a corner cavity, that the invaders probably deemed the key of the fortress.

The light had certainly not been out a minute before the roof rattled as before; a pause ensued, during which the burglars were descending by unknown passages to the under side of the floor; anon they were working at our barricades. First one, and then another gave way. A few spies entered, scampered over the floor, jumped on the table and the beds, squeaked intelligence to those that sent them, and in a twinkling the horde rushed in. I was at my wits' end, while my acclimated dozing friend cared not one whit whether they were in or out. They drew off at 4 A.M., and not till then did I get a wink of sleep. It is a curious fact, that an individual or two led off in the retreat every night, while a couple of whippers-in staid a few moments behind, their tread being quite distinct.

16*th*. By 9 A.M. five of us were mounted for another day's ride, accompanied by the manager of the slaves, himself a Pardo, and, therefore, not allowed to wear shoes. To his naked heels spurs were strapped. The popular *bentivee*, a bird as large as a robin, ever and anon saluted us, while flocks of the tiniest of the parrot family flew about us. We entered at one spot the primeval forest by what seemed a foot-path, having constantly to stop to avoid being unhorsed by the branches. A few trees were from three to six feet in diameter, and rose to great elevations; such were the sapocaias, favorite haunts of monkeys. Our dogs started pacas and other game, but neither horsemen nor footmen could follow them, so dense and dark the interior became. The eye could not penetrate over twenty feet, and sometimes not ten.

Sipos, or vegetable cordage, of every size, from thread to cables, hung down from aloft, and ran hither and thither, thick almost as the rigging of ships, and quite as flexible. They constitute quite a feature of Brazilian forests, and are used throughout the country as ligatures in buildings, in fences, and a thousand other purposes. They are known as the "*nails* of Brazil." A story is current that the Jesuits sought to obtain from the crown of Portugal a monopoly in them, and that the monarch was no little surprised to hear that the Indians used pregos, which he supposed were like those of Europe, made of iron.

Emerging from the woods, we met a mounted party, a lady,

four gentlemen, and a monk, whose wide and white felt hat, cassock, scapulary, and bare legs gave a piquant feature to the group. They were members of the Araujo family, to one of whose fazendas we were traveling; one named after the stream on which it is located, Rio das Pedras. Its sugar product this season is estimated at two thousand moulds of eighty pounds each. Here we found a water-wheel forty feet in diameter and only three wide; also another species, common in the Middle Ages: from a vertical or inclined shaft spokes radiate, and have their extremities formed into *spoons*. Water brought down a deep descent in a close tube is directed against these, and by its impulse drives them round.

Belidor figures and describes similar wheels used for driving grist-mills in Provence and Dauphiny in his time, but they are met with in authors centuries before he wrote. Thus Dante:

> "Never ran water with such hurrying pace
> Adown the tube to turn a land-mill's wheel,
> When nearest it approaches to the spokes,
> As then along that edge my master ran."—*Hell*, canto 23.

Brick and tiles are made on this estate in large quantities. Under a shed were young and middle-aged negras, naked save a piece of skirt tied on, and some with infants slung at their backs, bending over benches and pressing the clay into moulds, their arms and legs covered and their faces marked with it.

Chigres swarmed on the hot sand; they ran up our legs and walking-sticks. Black and small as dots of the letter i on this page, they quickly burrow under the skin. There is not a slave but has more or less in his feet. When not extracted within two days, each forms a bag and fills it with eggs. Even then little inconvenience is felt; but care is taken to extract the tough sack (about the size of a small pea) before its living contents are ready to burst forth. An old slave is charged on every plantation with this duty.

After leaving the "Collegio," another splendid estate belonging to the same wealthy owners, we came up with three troops of muleteers, who had unloaded their beasts and encamped for the night. Each had formed with their hampers and bags three sides of a quadrangle, within which some were lounging, while others were kindling a fire in front. Their animals, not less than a hundred, were grazing close by. The whole was vividly illustrative of scenes in Spanish life, and of incidents in Don Quixote.

We had to ride through several large sheets of water. In the middle of one, a negro stood quenching his thirst by using both hands as a cup. We knelt on our saddles when crossing the river "Embohy," and forded another deep stream like so many praying equestrians. At length we arrived at the Macacu estate of the Carmelite monks of the Lapa Church in Rio. A league square of fine land, it was willed to them by an old planter in exchange for an apanage they promised him in heaven. Mandioca, rice, and beans alone are cultivated, but none for sale. The greater part is consumed on the place, the balance by the fathers in the city. Of the slaves, excluding children, only six are men; the rest, some fifty odd, are women. The owners find it more profitable to raise negroes than coffee, or aught else. The lads, at a certain age, are sent to the city and bound out to trades, by which "twice as much is made out of them as if they were employed on the soil." The manager is a slave; he led us into a barn, with mud floor and walls, in which thirty women and children were huddled around a pile of mandioca tubers, which they were scraping, while others washed them. Such distorted, mutilated, hard, and horny fingers as many of these women had, I never saw. Like the hands of some slaves, they seemed losing their human characteristics.

All were comfortably and uniformly clothed—black skirts and a species of short and dark-blue cloak. I believe the latter, as well as the prohibition of shoes, iron collars, flogging men with leather thongs, and women with ferules, is derived from the ancient policy respecting slaves. Those of the Gauls and Romans wore blue. Beggars wore the same, and were thence named "Blue-gowns."

17*th*. A Paulista called on his way home. He passed by a week ago with two hundred mules, young and mostly unbroken, which he has sold at prices varying from fifteen to twenty dollars. He returns in December with another drove. These animals cost planters nothing to keep. Turned into the woods, they are caught when wanted, and that is chiefly in the sugar season. Here are no stables in which to house them; neither hay nor oats are grown for them, and no blacksmith's bill to pay for shoeing them.

CHAPTER XXXIV.

Macacu.—A large Tree.—Its Form, Dimensions, and extraordinary Roots.—Why so few old Trees.—Vegetable Origin of Forms and Ornaments.—Singular Forms of Boles.—Natural Moulding.—The Sloth-tree and Sloth.—Fabrication of Farinha.—Cultivation of the Plant.—Grating and pressing the Pulp.—The Tipiti. —Musical Wagons.—Rats keeping Carnival.—Return to the City.

June 18. Manoel, a Portuguese employed on the estate, while descanting on gunning and game, mentioned a tree that he had often passed in his hunts, whose bole would require sixteen men with outstretched arms to encircle it. Senhor J—— had heard of it in his father's lifetime, but had never visited it, although located within two or three miles of the house. The spot where its highest branches mingle with others half way up the mountain is seen from the door. Alleged difficulties of the ascent, and passage through jungles and gulleys, rather whetted than blunted the desire to see it, and a party was arranged to start at seven this morning. As we were moving, two sportsmen came up and joined us, with three more uncouth-looking tailless hounds, whose barking, quoth Manoel, will scare off every monkey—his favorite game. He was right, for not one was seen.

Reaching the base of the forest acclivity, we began to climb by grasping hold of creepers, shoots, and saplings, pulling ourselves up, and stopping every few yards to breathe, while leaning against the upper sides of the trees. The slaves were with us, and barefooted of course, liable, as I supposed, to be stung every moment by poisonous reptiles; but two gentlemen threw off their shoes and boots, and scaled their way over the slippery leaves in their stocking-feet. Another left hat, jacket, shoes, and stockings below, and spent the day with gun in hand without them. All my fear of snakes and scorpions was gone.

Three of us pushed ahead and reached a level spot, on which we were glad to rest, although it scarcely afforded room. The hunters were below; their shouts, baying of dogs, and reports of guns kept reverberating through the otherwise silent woods, frightening pacas and armadillos to their holes, of which we passed several, and scaring away birds, among which toucans were the largest we saw. The first thing observable in getting into the forest is the absence of the sun. While glowing in brightness without, twilight reigns within. Not a beam reached the ground through the intercepting foliage, which, spreading at great elevations, forms a perfect and perpetual screen. As the brilliance of the solar rays is supposed to diminish in intensity as they travel onward, so we have experienced a diminution of light in coming thus far, and have attained a degree that possibly resembles morning on Herschel and noon on Neptune.

The trees are straight, rising from sixty to one hundred feet, and void of branches two thirds up. Their average thickness is under two feet; some occur of three, four, and even five feet, but thousands do not exceed fifteen inches. Large and small grow some six or seven feet apart, and the open spaces are, on the whole, free from scrub or brushwood. Occasionally the slaves had to cut the way for us. The most novel feature to me was the vegetable cordage hanging down from the topmost branches, often numerous and various as the ropes and rigging of a frigate. These sipos are not parasitic; their roots are in the soil, whence they run up the highest poles, descend like plumb-lines where nothing intervenes, run along the ground for hundreds of feet, and rise and drop again. At one place a four-inch sipo—a cable—formed a natural swing, which most of us used. It reached within four feet of the ground, while the upper ends were lost to sight, after rising eighty feet perpendicularly. Monkeys are said to be as fond as children of the exercise.

But for creepers, and trees to hold on and rest by, there would be no scaling these mountains. The angle of our ascent was not less than 45°, while the leaves, thick on the ground, exceedingly embarrassed us. When the foot did not slip over them, they slid down under it. After a short rest, we started again, passing huge rocks, that might have come down from above before the epoch of vegetation began. Our pioneers cleared the way into a gorge, where fresh trails and beaten tracks of pacas crossed and recrossed. Passing over a gulley, whose depth was concealed, we mounted again, and the mammoth tree rose up before us. Is that it? all shouted. "Si, senhors," quoth Manoel. We were disappointed. It was a noble one, but not near the smallest size he had named. Streaming with perspiration, and panting like overdriven cattle, the first thing was to find seats. While one was flashing some powder to light cigars, the cry or whistle of a sloth was heard, and away went guns and gunners.

The bole was straight, tapered very slowly, rose nearly a hundred feet, and there divided into three diverging branches, the parents of numerous others. We passed a sipo cord round three feet above the ground, and found its circumference twenty-seven feet; close to it, thirty-two. This was at the upper side, where the cord, though then close to the ground, was ten feet above it at the lowest side. On approaching from below, the spreading base at the right merges into a line of rocks extending twenty feet or more, and then sinks out of sight; their faces were upright, smooth, and of unequal elevation, from three to ten feet; their upper surfaces, shelving off, disappeared in the sides of the mount. On drawing near, with hatchets in hand, lo! this apparent wall of granite turned out *wood!*—the continuation of the base of the shaft. At the left, the slope of the mountain, or the changes it had undergone, had not required the development of such an extraordinary buttress to insure stability to the ponderous and stately trunk. For a hundred feet on either hand, and also above it, long stretches of roots appeared here and there above the surface—one three feet in diameter, and several two feet!

This sylvan Goliah was a jequetiba, the Indian medicine-tree. The bark is kept on sale by the druggists; the wood is easy to work, reminding one of whitewood, which it resembles. Interposing objects were cut away till we had a clear view of it, and two sketches were taken from different points. The branches are remarkably angular, and abruptly change their direction almost every foot; the leaves are small, and the foliage limited. Where the branches start from the trunk, scarlet parasites were flourishing, and there came down a sipo thick as my arm, that hung loosely within six inches of the tree, as if let down to plumb it. No better means of rising into the upper regions could be required by young sailors than these "monkey-ladders."

The age of this majestic column could not be ascertained. I thought at first it was in its prime, but that period had long passed—probably before Cabral came in sight of the coast. Three feet above the ground there appeared a circular hole, four inches in diameter, with edges handsomely rounded. I pushed in the end of a rod seven feet before it was stopped at the opposite side. The bole was a mere shell or tube, standing on a capacious chamber, whose front wall faced us below.

The thought may occur to others as it occurred to me: How is it that, in primitive forests, so few very large trees are found? Ought not a majority, at least, to be as venerable for age and dimensions as this? A brief reflection answers no, and with it reason as well as fact coincides. This one has outlived the usual age; its compeers, that rose with it, are gone, and left it to linger in the midst of a strange generation. A virgin forest has never been found stocked with old trees, any more than a nation with ancient men. Both spring up, mature, decline, and give place to their offspring, because in that way only could either be perpetuated. Forest giants are, therefore, like human Anaks, exceptions to a beneficent law that limits their stature and bulk, like the one which restricts those of men.

Before reaching and after leaving this tree, we were environed by striking proofs that the cardinal forms and ornaments of architects, joiners, and carvers were derived from Nature's carpentry. I do not say she elaborates her materials into finished mouldings, columns, and capitals. It would have been no advantage to her apprentice-man if she had, since her mission is not to anticipate his efforts, but to awaken and direct them. Hence, like a wise teacher, she suggests ideas, and incites him to work them out. Architectural contours and embellishments revealed to David for the temple, and patterns shown to Moses in the mount, are still found on Oriental hills, and abound in every forest here—"pillars and chapiters," "lily-work," "network," "wreaths of flowers," "pomegranates," "palm-trees," and "almonds," &c. Plain round columns occur in trees in all countries, but here are twisted, wreathed, fluted, and clustered or Gothic types.

At one spot I rested against a bole nearly two feet in diameter, about which a four-inch sipo was wound, from bottom to top, as regular as if carved on the straight shaft by art. Grown together, both appeared of one substance. A still finer example occurred on our way down, but I could not stop to examine and sketch it. On another bole, a couple of sipos gave more than a hint of the double spiral, and in one case they were coiled so closely as to conceal the trunk entirely, exhibiting the peculiarity of another artistic shaft.

Here are an outline and section of a fluted or Gothic shaft.
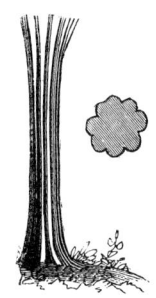
Its expression partakes of, and would, had they not been known, suggest both. Over three feet thick, its upper part expands into a capital regular as the base, thus showing us how the early builders were taught to combine elegance of forms with fitness for enlarged support. Like a word to the wise, the merest glance at such an object sufficed. In the twinkling of an eye the idea and its application were realized. The flutes were not of one thickness, but the difference was not great; few were less than four inches, and all were straight, round, and smooth. This tree belongs to a numerous family, but so far excelled in regularity other members we fell in with, that I begged the party to hold on a few minutes near it.

I had previously caused some delay at a stately one, four feet
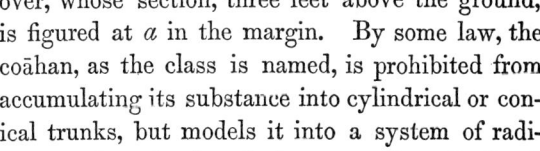
over, whose section, three feet above the ground, is figured at *a* in the margin. By some law, the coāhan, as the class is named, is prohibited from accumulating its substance into cylindrical or conical trunks, but models it into a system of radiating planks more or less developed, thus extending the fluted and Gothic features into other varieties. In another tree, the distance between two adjoining plates was six, and their depth five feet, leaving a space in which five men could stand. Here, thought I, are planks actually growing. The tree had hardly any centre.

In rose-wood the feature exists in a modified form. A very fine tree stood near where we dined, its upper branches waving from seventy to eighty feet above our heads; *a* shows a section

six feet from the ground, the extreme diameter five. The same form continued some forty feet, when the trunk gave birth to two perpendicular stems, from which spring all above them. On account of breaks and twists in the radiating slabs, a good-sized plank could hardly be got out of them.

I add the section of another tree near which we happened to

halt. It was neither a jacaranda nor a coāhan. It took forty feet of withe to go round it. This trunk is a very high one, and preserved the same strange form most of the way up. It was apparently in its prime; nothing like decay to be seen about it.

Here were dwarf and other cocoas, that present almost perfect columns, and one species with successive swellings at the upper parts reminded one of Hindoo and other Oriental architectural characteristics.

But none of these surprised me more agreeably than a nearly full-developed moulding. It was on a fallen stem upon which some of us sat a while to rest. A $\frac{5}{8}$ inch sipo had coiled itself

three times round, and then, turning away, disappeared in the distance. The part in contact with the stem was flattened, and in yielding to that shape the displaced substance was pushed out at either hand into fillets, as in the figure. Where the sipo took its departure, at *a*, the flat part continued a little way, and then the half circular boundary swelled again into the circular. The fillets vanished earlier. It was clear that the evolution of the fillets was due to the compressure (perhaps by shrinking) of the soft sipo upon the hard and unyielding surface of the larger body; for it approached as a cord, and left as one. As the coils tightened, a lateral direction was imparted to the fibres. No fact is more obvious than that vegetation here obeys the slightest impulses, and is ready to run into all sorts of forms. Its plasticity is such that it only wants moulds to produce planks, busts, and statues. In one convolution a single fillet only was produced, and in the others the angles were not wrought out sharp. But what then? A blind man could not fail to recognize in them the astragal and popular mouldings. Other, and probably much better, examples are to be met with in the forests.

In numerous instances the vegetable ropes united with each other, where circumstances had thrown them in contact; thus branches became soldered at every angle. Frequently the rope is divided into five or six strands for a foot or two, and then the whole unite in a single one. But besides these round sipos, here is another species, which at first I took for long stretches of collapsed leather hose. Some were singularly impressed with indentations at regular intervals, and corresponding elevations on the opposite side. There was another variety, unembossed, and bent as at *c*. The sipos proper present themselves also in long spiral stretches, exhibiting and diversifying a similar feature in our vine-tendrils.

The descent of the mountain was even more laborious than climbing it. More care and activity were required. In the latter a stick was useful, but on going down essential, to prevent one falling headlong. But for the trees and shrubbery there could be no descending, for no one could keep his feet. Once started, the momentum of the body could not be controlled till thrown down, and with the force of a cannon ball. Although trees of one kind or other occurred every six or seven feet, if we missed bringing up at every one in our way—if we passed over ten feet or twelve without stopping, we brought up with a terrible squelch against the next. I perspired quite as much in coming down as in going up. With specimens of sipos, rods for walking-sticks, and medicinal bark from the jiquetiba, we arrived with the hunters at home by 5 P.M., well pleased, though tired with the trip.

The general aspect of a Brazilian forest is brownish rather

than bright green. The trees cast their leaves all the year round.

The imbaiba, or "sloth-tree," is among the picturesque. The bole is straight, smooth, and bare of branches except at the top. The leaves are large and pentagonous, which, with young shoots, are the animal's favorite food. It resembles the mamão-tree, for which I often mistook it. It varies in diameter from nine inches to two feet, and rises from twenty to forty. The flesh of the sloth is sweetish, and, to persons unused to it, sickly. When one is within reach of a pole, it will slowly take hold, and is often thus captured, and borne off on the shoulders of the hunter. A more harmless creature can not be imagined—a hiss and a grin are its only weapons. Its face is the index of helpless old age.

A person with a low frontal region is said to have the forehead of a preguiça. Sloths have little or no forehead.

It is remarkable that the two species most allied to man, and with attributes so diverse—the most active and inert, the most harmless and mischievous — should thus be found together. But, in fact, all things are relieved by comparison and contrast, whether properties of matter, qualities of mind, or the influences of morals. Of minerals, plants, and animals, one class parodies another, while the living genus which approaches nearest to the human form exhibits it in the lowest stages of brutalization. What apes are to men, demons are to angels—distorted, degenerate, mischievous caricatures, and then the devil himself is the ape or imitator of God—" O demonio em tudo pretende ser simia de Deos."

I shall here insert the substance of my notes and observations on the fabrication of farinha. This word is Portuguese for flour or meal, but when used without any qualifying noun, is universally understood as designating that of mandioca. The procedure is *one* throughout the country, and substantially the same as was and is practiced by the aborigines. This root is, next to the potato, the greatest of the red man's gifts to his white brother, and one reflecting no small credit on the donor, inasmuch as it would have been valueless had it not been accompanied with information on its culture and conversion into bread. Naturally fatal to life, it has, by primitive researches, been rendered innoxious and nutritious. But for this early and invaluable discovery, the farinha of South America and cassava of the West Indies might not, and probably would not, have been known to this day. When, by whom, and under what circumstances it was made, can now never be known, albeit there was picked up by the early settlers a tradition of a venerable stranger, draped in white, and with a flowing beard—another Manco Capac—teaching the people the use of fire, to clothe themselves, and dwell in houses (neither of which they yet do), and the *cultivation and preparation of mandioca.*

A field of ripe mandioca looks like a nursery of hazels. The stem of each plant is isolated, and has only a few palmated leaves at top. A bud, or projecting nucleus of a sprout, occurs at nearly every inch on the otherwise naked stem, the length of which is from six to seven feet, and an inch thick at the base. When a field is reaped, the stems are chopped into pieces three, or at most four inches long. These are planted, and quickly take root, sending forth shoots from the buds, and in two years mature a new crop. The tubers yielded by each stem average five in number, the largest six to seven inches long, and four thick; the shape irregular, and in substance resembling the parsnip. After being scraped and rinsed, they are prepared for the "mill." Of the same plan and dimensions every where, this machine is nothing more than a revolving grater. Imagine a small carriage-wheel, three feet in diameter, mounted on an axle, one end of which is bent into a crank handle. Instead of iron tire, a strip of sheet brass, four inches wide, and punched full of holes, is nailed on the felloes, the rough side outward. One slave turns it, while another pushes a single root at a time against it. When the part left in the hand becomes too small to be held steadily, a fresh root is used to press it forward till it is wholly ground up.*

The pulp is put into bags of hair or cloth, and subjected to a press. The pressed matter, resembling cheese-cake in consistence, is rubbed through a coarse sieve, and thrown into shallow copper pans moderately heated, and stirred up for a few minutes,

* This rasping-mill is identical with the one used over two hundred years ago, as appears from Piso's History of Brazil, in Latin. Amster., 1648. At page 53 is a figure of the machine that might serve for every one now used in the country.

when its manufacture is completed. It is now not unlike Indian-meal or oat-meal. Thus in half an hour the root is converted into what is every where known as "the bread of Brazil."

The poisonous expressed juice is not immediately thrown away. Received into vessels, a beautiful white precipitate collects at the bottom. Senhor J——, plunging his hand in a tub, brought up a specimen. "That," said he, "when dried, is tapioca."

Such is the white man's mode of preparing farinha. The rasp of the aborigines consists of a board, say a foot or fifteen inches wide, and two feet long. One face is smeared over with a thick coating of gum—a natural glue that hardens like stone, and in it is inserted, often in regular and fancy figures, a multitude of sharp particles of granite, selected from pieces broken up for the purpose. On this board each root, after being washed and the skin scraped off, is reduced to pulp by rubbing it to and fro over the teeth. When the desired quantity is rasped down, the next thing is to compress it in order to get rid of the water, and after it is expelled, the mass is laid on a heated stone griddle and stirred till dry.

The press possesses more interest. Imagine a coarse, basket-like tube, made of split cane (the slips thin, three fourths of an inch wide, and rather loosely plaited or interwoven). A common size is five feet in length, five or six inches diameter at the mouth or open end, and three or four at the bottom or closed one. A large loop or a couple of strong withes is left at each end. When used, the first thing is to wet it, if dry. The operator then grasps the edges of the mouth with both hands, and, resting the bottom on the ground, throws the weight of his body on the basket till he has crushed it down to about half its previous height; the lower parts, meanwhile, swell out in diameter larger than the mouth. A smooth stick, like one of our broom-handles, is now introduced, held upright in the middle, and the pulp put in and packed round it till the tube is nearly filled. It is next suspended by the upper loop from a hook, or the limb of a tree, and a heavy stone or basket of stones fastened to the bottom loop, so that the weight may gradually stretch the tube till it becomes six or seven feet in length; *the internal capacity diminishing with the extension,* and the contracting sides powerfully forcing the pulp against the unyielding central stick, and consequently driving out the liquid. Instead of stones, one end of a heavy log is sometimes inserted through the lower loop, and loaded with a papoose or two, or any thing else at hand. Indians, again, will put one foot or both in the loop, as in a stirrup, and serve themselves as the weights.

Such is the original mandioca or cassava press. It was as common among the Caribs of the islands as it was and is with Indians on the Oronoco and Amazon, and throughout the immense regions between those rivers and the Plata. In Brazil there are those who prefer it to the massive and clumsy screw-press imported from Lisbon and Malaga at a cost of $200 to $300 each. I purchased one at a venda for 16 cents, of the dimensions given above, and for it the Indian manufacturer probably received only three or four, certainly not over five or six.

The carboclos, or tamed Indians, supply the venders or country stores with it in all the provinces.

This basket-press is the *tepiti*, and if there is a current primitive invention evincing closer and happier reasoning out of common tracks, and which exhibits neater and cheaper results, we do not know where to look for it.

The wagons and oxen are not without interest. The former are Portuguese, Spanish, medieval, and classical. Their construction is the same as those made by Grecian and Roman wheelwrights. The axle-tree is invariably fastened to the wheels, and consequently turns with them. The latter are made of two, sometimes three thick slabs, commonly five feet in diameter, four inches thick at the periphery, and between seven and nine at the centre, where they receive the squared and tapered ends of the axle. Two journals are formed on the axle just within the wheels, by making six or eight inches of the timber round and smooth, to receive two forked pieces, or inverted plummet-blocks of hard wood, secured to the bottom or under side of the wagon body. The axles are generally of rosewood. But the most singular feature of these carriages is, they are all musical, giving out an incessant moaning, more or less soft or sharp, and broken by every jolt or depression in the road. This arises from the friction of the forked piece on the journals;

it is modified but not destroyed by grease, nor is the noise unpleasant. There is no saw-filing, teeth-drilling, or flesh-creeping power in it.

For a full half hour, as we trotted along yesterday, the sounds of music far ahead came on us, swelling and subsiding as hills and valleys intervened, now like the humming of bees, and anon sharpened like the singing of musquitoes at one's ears. As we passed on, the tones might be compared to a score of Æolian harps—soft, clear, and continuous. At length we overtook the instruments and musicians—twelve wagons, laden with cane, on their way to the Engenho. Every one had a tone of its own, and the mingling of the whole was not ungrateful. To the animals in the shafts it is said to be as delightful as to the drivers. Cervantes, the most graphic portrayer of Spanish life, throws Sancho into a swoon of fear by the creaking of the same kind of wagon in the dark. The oxen frequently seen in these wagons, both in the city and country, are such as would make glad the hearts of our farmers. Allied to the buffalo of India, nobler-looking creatures are not to be found.

19*th*. Last night the rats kept carnival as usual. Leaping on and off the beds and altar-table, their fall on the floor sounded like that of so many cats. They smelled and pulled at our shoes and garments, and squealed and scampered as if they were the very imps of mischief. Repeatedly I sprang up with horror as they were tugging at my clothes. H—— was snoring before I had finished some writing, and, as this was the last night of our stay, I determined to reward him for his indifference to the intensity of my sufferings. Instead of putting the extinguished light outside of the door on retiring, I placed it on his bed, and quickly covered myself up in my own. A minute, and our familiars, who had been waiting till the light was out, were rushing through defiles behind the plaster; a twinkling more, and a score were on his coverlet, quarreling over the tallow. A violent splutter, a round oath in Portuguese, and a convulsive shake sent rats, candle, his own clothes, and those belonging to the bed into the air.

At 5 A.M., H——, M——, and I took leave of our kind hosts, by ten reached Sampaio, and were soon after steaming down the muddy Macacu. Millions of handsome tufts, on stems of three to five feet, like palm-trees in miniature, border the river and occupy the swamps. This graceful weed is known among the aborigines as the piripiri. H—— says he has met with it in most of the provinces. When we were about forty miles from the Organ Mountains they did not appear to be one fourth of the distance. By four we landed at the city. The captain, much to his satisfaction, succeeded in mortally wounding some harmless gulls; two splendid white cranes will not, however, rise in judgment against him, for he missed them.

CHAPTER XXXV.

Apollonia and Carasco.—Divinations.—Beatified Galens.—The Mizericordia.—Meeting of Isabel and Mary.—The Chapel.—Emperor.—Foundlings.—Isabel the Representative of a Pagan Goddess.—Manual and tibial Worship.—Fourth of July.—Lame leading the Blind.—British Chapel, Preacher, and Prayer-Book.—Nictherohy.—Fine Estate and its small Cost.—A Paca.—The Nuncio denounced.—Lost Image.—Shrine in a Brothel.—Legislation invoked.—Theatrical and sacerdotal Exhibitions.

June 22. Yesterday was the feast of Apollonia, the great dentista of the faithful. I might as well have attended, had it been only to learn the invocation, which the most waggish of clerical bachelors ordered an acquaintance of the reader to repeat in behalf of her master, and the fitness of which she presumed to question.

"The prayer of Saint Apollonia, say you? That might do something if my master's distemper lay in his gums, but, alas! it is in his brains."

"I know what I say, Mistress Housekeeper," quoth Carasco. "You go home and prepare me something warm for breakfast, and don't stand disputing with me, a bachelor of Salamanca, for there is no bachelorizing beyond that."

The conjuring season has opened. Booksellers advertise *The Diviner of the Future*, containing 1600 Sortes; *The Lady's Oracle*, with infallible modes of ascertaining the future; *The New Sibyl*, proper to be consulted on the nights of St. John, Peter, Anthony, and many others. The unmarried, I am told, apply to John, because he was a bachelor. Peter was married, and to him those who have lost their mates look for fresh ones.

24*th.* This is the day when the sun comes leaping and laughing up the horizon, instead of his wonted snail-like pace. Public business is suspended. I observed parties practicing divination after an old custom: they threw dice, and then turned to figures on a card corresponding with the numbers thrown. A lady neighbor went at twelve o'clock last night to the Cattete Brook to ascertain if she would live another year. Her shadow was doubled in the stream, and she will live two.

25th. The anniversary of "San Tude, advogado contra a tosse." Tude and Braz hold much the same rank in sacred therapeutics as Blase once held in England. He was a great friend to asthmatic people, and famous for removing obstructions from the windpipe. His fee was a couple of tapers, and even they "were good for the tooth-ache and diseased cattle." Of other beatified Galens, St. Servulo cures paralysis, and Liborio removes stones from the bladder—dor de pedra. St. Miguel dos Santos eradicates, without caustics, cancers and tumors, and St. Rita cures incurable complaints. The surpassing bull, that this lady makes impossible things possible, is seriously accepted by many; hence a pilgrimage to her shrine is the very thing for projectors, squarers of circles (I was introduced to one), inventors of perpetual motions, and compounders of universal panaceas.

29th. The coldest day. Thermometer at 6 A.M. 68°, from which it did not vary one degree to 8 P.M.

The Santa Casa da Mizericordia dates from 1582, and is as noble an institution of the kind as any people can boast of—a specimen of genuine catholicity, unstained and untrammeled with qualifying adjectives. Its blessings, like those descending from above, are showered alike on every age, sex, creed, and condition; on bond and free, foreigners and natives. It is also an asylum for foundlings. The boys are provided for at Boto-Fogo, and at a certain age are put out to trades; the girls reside in the city establishment, and are taught to read, write, sew, etc. At each anniversary, bachelors in want of wives often find partners for life. When two agree to be united, the managers inquire into the character and prospects of the man, and, if all is satisfactory, the marriage takes place, when a dowry of 400 milreis is given from the funds of the institution.

Having heard much about the daily exposure of infants, and facilities afforded those who drop them to escape unnoticed, I concluded to walk over to the place of reception. This, till recently, was at the Hospital, but is now in a thinly-occupied street, to the scandal of the Holy Mother of Nuns, after whom it is named. The device for receiving the infants is an upright hollow cylinder, revolving on pivots. One third of the side is removed to give access to the inside, and the bottom is covered

with a mattress. As the width of the opening is less than the

thickness of the wall, it is impossible for those on one side to see through into the other. I walked the entire length of Rua Santa Tereza without perceiving any thing of the kind; but on returning, a board, only a few inches square, over the closed door of an ordinary-looking building, caught my attention. The inscription was decisive, "*Expostos da Miz^a, No. 30.*" While reading it, corroborative sounds came forth. The only window in front was near the door, and was, in fact, the receptacle. What I had taken, on first passing, for a green inside shutter, I now saw was slightly curved. I touched it, found it turned readily, and the opening came in view, when a bell connected to it within sounded violently! For a moment I hesitated, but, when the inmates of a house opposite raised their lattices to see who was dropping a foundling in the daytime, I beat a quick retreat.

The 2d of July is the anniversary, when an interesting interview takes place between two church ladies. "Who is Isabel?" repeated E——, in replying to my inquiry; "why, she is the mother of St. John and the protectress of hospitals. To-day is THE VISITATION. Our Lady will leave her home in the Carmo Church to visit her cousin, but Isabel will meet her half way in Dereita Street, and after embracing, they will proceed together to the Mizericordia. The apartments of the female foundlings will be opened to the public, young men will attend to select wives, the emperor and court will be present. You had better go."

The procession is advertised for half past nine A.M. Allowing half an hour for the walk, we can reach the place by ten— and here, at the House of Mercy, we are. The Largo in front is covered with leaves, a regiment of the line is drawn up and its fine band playing, but the preparations are not finished, for workmen are busy hanging tapestries from the upper windows. The troops are an assemblage of the three marked varieties of our race, black, red, and white skins, with every shade from Indian-ink to chocolate, and from cinnamon to chalk. One of the officers is very pale and wan. Spectators begin to assemble; among them flocks of ladies, plump as partridges, with their heads dressed as for fancy balls, and no covering on their bosoms but amulets and jewelry.

The Carmo is one fourth of a mile off. Suppose, instead of standing here, we turn in that direction, and see what the friends of Our Lady are doing. We go, and meet her as she issues from her sanctuary. The procession is headed by three men abreast, the middle one bearing on a stave a cross, and each of his companions an artificial bouquet surmounted with a burning candle. The Carmelites, in cream-colored copes, follow with lighted tapers. Priests, monks, and chanting functionaries, a goodly number, come next, some in white and some in black sutains; several wear scarlet stockings, and not a few have cambric tippets. The next official is a Thurifer, swinging his censer. Behind him, and last of all, comes the lady, leaning on the arm of a bishop, whose conical mitre is decked with rubies, or stones resembling them.

There! they're past, but how's this? Not fifty spectators following, and hardly a dozen decent-looking persons among them! Business people are obviously getting tired of such things, and often, as in this case, pay little attention to them. I hesitated about joining the shabby escort, but a wish to view the affair minutely induced me to raise my hat and fall in immediately behind the lady. After passing the distance of a couple of blocks, I would have given a dollar to have got decently out of the business, for we were all brought to a dead stand by the bishop. Stopping as deliberately as if he had been in his private chamber, he handed the lady to one of his associates, slowly drew forth a handkerchief, and blew his nose *secundum artem*. Full a minute elapsed ere he resumed his sacred charge, and we moved on again. It has been suggested that this delay was possibly intended to give time for Isabel and her friends to come up, that the meeting might take place in a convenient part of the street.

Continuing along, music at length was heard, and presently a banner, a cross, and a crowd were seen approaching—Isabel and her servants. She had heard of her cousin being on the way, and came thus far to meet her. (I quote popular language on the subject.) There she is; and see! both ladies fly into each other's arms, and remain locked together for nearly a minute. Now they draw back, gaze a moment on each other's faces, and Isabel once more throws herself on her kinswoman's neck, Our Lady meekly receiving the caresses. The patroness of the hospital recovers herself, goes to the left of her guest, a little in advance, and with open hands invites her onward. Thus they procceeded, Isabel turning every few yards to repeat the graceful welcome. As soon as we arrived at the Largo, the troops presented arms to the cousins, the band struck up a lively

THE MEETING OF OUR LADY AND ISABEL.

tune, and the clapper of the chapel bell rattled most lustily. People thronged to salute the saints until they got inside.

After resting a little, Isabel is to conduct her visitor through the wards of the sick and convalescent, and introduce her to the foundlings. While thus engaged we can minute down their appearance. The contrast of their dresses with those of their attendants must have struck every stranger like myself. Their gowns were neither new nor newly washed: originally straw-colored, age had dyed them brown, scattered specks of gold flitted about the skirts, relics of rich flounces, made matters worse. It seemed unaccountable, where public reverence was to be excited, how the managers could allow them to appear in drapery so unbecoming. The feeling elicited was exceedingly disagreeable, and even rendered still more so by their soiled—decidedly soiled arms, necks, and faces. Had they been ragged street-girls, picked up for an emergency, less attention could not have been expended on their persons and attire. To be sure, they were low in stature, and little folks are apt to be neglected, especially when dumb. Neither exceeded twenty-five inches. The bishop bore his charge reclining on his arm, as an image-boy carries a plaster statue in our streets, and when she was about to meet her cousin, he raised her upright, like a soldier presenting arms, and held her by the ankles till Isabel came up. Both were then inclined till their faces met, and they had taken a long embrace. While they were in contact their bearers brought their own faces nearly to touch, and, speaking for their wooden ladies in an under-tone, exchanged salutations for them. The bishop spoke first: he stammered and smiled, and when he got through, the other, a hard-featured man, with no ornament on his head but his tonsure, replied in behalf of Isabel, and finished by causing her to make a low obeisance to her visitor.

I now entered the chapel between guards with fixed bayonets. Large as some churches, it has four subsidiary shrines. After trying in vain to recognize the presiding deities, I turned to go out, but lo! all exit was prevented by transverse rows, deep and wide, of kneeling ladies—a phalanx there was no breaking through. I therefore retreated, with others, into the vestry, where halberdiers were waiting for the emperor. He shortly made his appearance, passed through, and took a seat in a pew near the high altar. He was in plain dress, except a blue coat with epaulets large enough for Goliah's shoulders. The empress, in black, sat by him, and her ladies behind them. One of the managers read the annual report, and then mass began, at which the young ruler was perfectly at home, anticipating every kneeling and rising movement, and crossing himself with marvelous rapidity: he was through the operation before members of the cabinet near him were half through.

Twice a priest came from the altar with the Missal for him and his spouse to kiss; they buried for a moment their faces in its leaves. A small gilt case was passed to them for the same purpose, and then carried up and down a double row of senators and ministers of state, whose lips the priest touched with it; not, however, till they had received a preparatory purification from the censer. The services became exceedingly tedious, and the air so noxious, that every one was weary, and Pedro and his wife rose to depart. A few boys and women snatched their hands to kiss, at which they were not a little annoyed, and with reason, for the empress appeared haggard and ready to faint.

Before mass began the two cousins were brought in, when a small accident happened to Isabel. Her bearer was prevented by the crowd from placing her steadily on her shrine, and she fell, knocked over a couple of sacred candlesticks, and would have tumbled with them to the ground had not a gentleman in front of me caught her. Upward of one hundred girls, mostly under twelve years of age, were ranged along the four sides of a room. They were neatly dressed, and their apartments were every thing that could be wished. In the school-room were superior specimens of writing. Applicants for wives must leave their name and address, that their characters and circumstances may be ascertained.

The reader need not be told that Isabel is the modern representative of the goddess *Mizericordia*, to whom Greeks and Romans dedicated hospitals. In the early adoption of heathen deities under Christian appellations, the attributes and functions of that popular deity were assigned to Elizabeth, the mother of the Baptist.

One word on the performances in the chapel and church

services generally. I may be prejudiced—most of us are when out of the circle of influences in which our habits and opinions have been formed; but this manual, labial, tibial; this sprinkling, smoking, painted, pantomimic worship of the Creator; this system of externalage and gilded similitudes which sensible mortals would sicken to be complimented with, does seem out of character with the present times. In some respects it surpasses in grossness the grossest idolatry. The communion of North American Indians with the Great Spirit appears more consistent and refined. True, it was practiced by our forefathers, but that was when they were little better informed than are modern barbarians. The images are better carved and more neatly dressed than those of Fetichism, but the principle involved in their introduction is the same in both.

However well intentioned the unknown authors of the physical worship of gods and dead men by means of images and their accessories may have been, and however expedient or justifiable, if either term be admissible, its application to Christianity in darker times, it surely is not necessary now; but national and minor hierarchies never purged themselves: enlightened only from without, they are ever the last to yield to conviction. Still, the world in religious matters is advancing; it can not do otherwise where science is cultivated and Galileos left free to pursue it; and what is true science but a manifestation of the Creator in his works, and what are they but "revealed truths," which no one can study aright without becoming wiser and better—without feeling his nature rising into higher phases of existence, and his affections throbbing with gratitude to the Parent of the universe for the ceaseless wonders of his beneficence here displayed?

In the absence of uniformity in human organizations, and in the influences of climate and climatic productions, religious differences are unavoidable. Races will have congenial rituals, and homogeneity in them is impossible. Moreover, on every subject the sea of thought must be ruffled to prevent a stagnant and putrescent calm. Even with the soul, action is life, and with it there can be no action without reaction. Controversial gales, like material storms, may occasion temporary evils, but they are prescribed means of attaining enduring good.

4th. The American men-of-war, in gala dress, made the waters of the Bay flash and the air reverberate among the mountains in honor of the day when the world's exodus from thraldom began.

A living picture of the lame leading the blind passed this morning, in two slaves with baskets of clothes on their heads. One in advance moved slowly and sorely from elephantiasis; she had hold of a long horizontal stick, whose other extremity was grasped by a feeble old man, whom she thus drew along.

5th. Went with T—— to the British Chapel. The lesson for the day, 1 Sam., xii., was an unlucky one for the reader—a furious stickler for monarchy, and an upholder of the withering curses it has heaped on his native land. An Irishman by birth, he maintains England's right to rule the conquered country as she pleases; justifies the wholesale confiscation of the soil to the invaders, from whom he boasts of being descended; denies, with a slap on the table, that the English Church is a burden to the Irish people, and with another challenges you to cite an example of a lord, bishop, or vicar distressing a family for tithes, or removing one to make room for sheep; and by a third thump, that sets the glasses ringing, proves "it was right if they did." Half his salary is paid by the British government. His theme to-day was "The Love of God."

The prayer-book handed me was one of those issued "by authority," polluted with royal mandates, enjoining upon its owner what he is to believe and whom he is to pray for. Besides thirty-nine items of faith prepared for him, reminding him of forty stripes lacking one administered to old unbelievers, it contains a creed, accompanied with a profusion of damnatory clauses, enough to make a savage shudder. It tells every one who doubts its dicta "without doubt he shall perish everlastingly." I would not stay a week in heaven with the red bigots that conceived it, or the intriguing ones that perpetuate it.

6th. J—— proposed a visit to Nictherohy, and in half an hour we were skimming the Bay in a four-oared barge. Like some state capitals with us, this imperial city is yet a small one. After calling on General C—— and chatting a while, we passed on to the beautiful chateau and grounds of Senhor P——o, with whom and his amiable family we spent the day.

A smart Indian youth waited at table. I understood he was not considered a slave.

The place belonged to Pedro I., and on his withdrawal to Europe was purchased by the present proprietor for seven thousand five hundred dollars. Only to think! a handsome mansion, on an eminence commanding one of the finest of earth's landscapes, a plantation extending half a mile one way and nearly a mile in another, rich in every tropical treasure, adjacent to, and, in fact, included in the capital of the province, with all necessary out-houses, for so small a sum! While wandering through its teeming fields and forest groves, reclining under its shady trees (among which were bread-fruit and weeping-willows), quenching one's thirst by overhanging oranges, and a plum-like, cooling fruit, so plentiful as in some spots to have dropped from the stems and covered the ground, inhaling the soft and grateful air, I thought, if any earthly homestead may be likened to an inheritance in heaven, this one surely might.

On reaching the Bay our boats were in waiting. The men pulled like heroes, and landed us by moonlight at the Gloria Beach in an hour and fifteen minutes.

A present of game had arrived from Alagoas—a paca, which, instead of being consigned to the murderous knife of the cook, is to accompany me to the States.

9*th.* Bedini has been to Pedropolis, where he has caused no small trouble. The colonists are mostly German Protestants, and in a sermon he declared that all married Catholics among them are living in concubinage; that their marriages are void, and their children illegitimate. A storm of indignation rages there and has reached here. The *Diario* denounces him in strong but respectful language, insisting that it is the highest imprudence thus to kindle the fires of religious intolerance. It says, "Propositions like those emitted from the Chair of Truth by a priest of the character of M. Bedini are eminently censurable." The bishop is invoked to act promptly in the matter, as one that threatens to compromise the interests of Brazil.

10*th.* An advertisement in to-day's paper reminds one of Laban's stolen gods. "A black porter disappeared with a bundle intrusted to him in Ajuda Street on the 7th inst., containing three frocks, one shirt, a shawl, and an image of St. John, having one of the hands broken. If offered for sale, a gratification will be given for the information."

" O devoção de Nossa Senhora da Conceição erecta na Rua de S. Pedro, No. 226, tem de fazer seu beneficio no Theatrinho da Rua Flores, No. 55, Sabbado, 11 do corrente; os administradores do beneficio pedem ao respeitavel publico que queirao honrar com a sua presença: e os cartazes marcarão os divertismentos. Rio de Janeiro, 4 de Julho, de 1846. O Secretario: M. J. Borges."

In addition to this notice in a morning paper, hand-bills soliciting alms and inviting the respectable public and devout persons to attend at the Theatre, are stuck up on the corners of streets. One has a significant mark of some person's opinion of the establishment it celebrates—a coat of mud. The house is a brothel, which, from ignorance of its character, the bishop has licensed to have a shrine in one of its rooms.

A writer in the *Jornal* calls on the reverend deputies in the Legislature to bring forward measures for putting an end to the official connection between religion, churches, and theatres, and refers to this place. From play-bills he quotes, "A tragedy for the benefit of N. S. Conceição in Soap Street, namely, the much-applauded drama of *The Jealous Wife, Dance of the Polka*, and the comic farce of *The Brother of Souls*. Again, in the Theatre of Nictherohy, the farce of *The Brother of Souls* will be performed *for the benefit of souls in Purgatory*. And recently, in the Theatre San Pedro, in this city, the same was played *in honor of the divine Holy Ghost of Sta. Anna;* besides others, equally objectionable, advertised daily. What a satire on religion is this! What impudence!"

The union between theatrical and sacerdotal performances is too intimate to be easily severed. There is a real affinity between them. Take the Capuchins, who, as reformers, are held to be in advance in spiritual matters, frequently closing their advertisements with some mystic or moral apophthegm, and how near do they approach their histrionic brethren. Announcements of their festival to-morrow rival any play-bill in praising their grand displays of fire-works and martial music, to attract purchasers to their auction, and to exchange money for small portraits of Veronica. While ecclesiastics thus compete with lay showmen for public patronage, it is natural for the latter to retaliate where they can; hence the plays and farces in which the former are satirized. The evening's entertainments to-morrow at the Tereza Theatre are " the much-applauded drama, in five acts, of THE GRACE OF GOD; after which, a *Polka Dance;* to conclude with the *Three Women and Three Secrets.*"

CHAPTER XXXVI.

Capuchin Attractions: Fireworks, Music, Auction, etc.—The Mint.—Lantern-bellows.—Lady of Lampadoza.—Balthazar.—Peter Coelho.—A winged Monk.—A dead Christ by a Negro Artist.—Ceara.—How the Emperor was anointed.—More Galas.—Conveying Presents.—Interior of a Drawing-room.—Proverbs.—The Neckcloth.—Bedini.—British Embassador.—Chamber of Deputies.—Jaunt to the Gavia.—Inscriptions.—Tailor.—Dead Slave.—Pride and Piggishness.—God's Grandmother.—Bedini again.—Lady of Snows.—Birth of a Princess.—A Wizard's Stock in Trade.

July 12. The Capuchins' great festa comes off to-night. As it is the last spectacle of the kind I shall have an opportunity to witness, T—— kindly accompanied me up Castle Hill. Crowds were climbing up the steep, others hastening down faster than they wished. As we rose, gusts of music reached us, and now and then the pinnacle of the little church was seen flickering behind the glare and curling smoke of bonfires, while bombs shook the air, and rockets kept rushing into the fast-darkening vault. Arriving at the scene, and borne hither and thither by the crowds, there was no resisting the excitement.

Two sets of entertainments were going on—within and without. The latter consisted of music, auctioneering, and pyrotechnics. A military band of thirty-two instruments occupied a stage on one side of the church door, and kept playing, at short intervals, national and popular airs. On the other side was the auctioneer's platform, which accommodated a committee and a small black band—twelve negro musicians, in white jackets and blue caps, who played when the other company—a white one—was called inside to perform. Having spoken of auctions in other churches, I shall add nothing here, except that one of the committee cut long candles into short pieces by way of adding variety to the salesman's stock, and affording opportunities for persons of small means to obtain bits of holy tapers.

An accident nearly put an end to the business. A slave was relighting steeple lamps which the wind had blown out, and some sparks fell from his torch on the canopy over the stage. It took fire and was partially destroyed. The auctioneer, preternaturally alarmed, sprang from the boards, to the great diversion of the crowd. I was told that hundreds of young fellows present would not have hesitated to burn down the whole concern. A strong police force was on the ground, and the chief of police is head of the new brotherhood.

The fiery attractions included, 1. The usual twenty-foot pole, with its zigzag train of bombs, for giving the sacred salutes. Large and small balls alternate at the angles of the train, from top to bottom of the pole. One gives out reports equal to muskets; the others drop and explode on the ground with a noise that almost bursts the tympanum of one's ears; and when the fire reaches the last, it starts into life, an inverted cone of rockets. 2. A long line of taller poles on the ridge of the mount, and on the top of each some elaborated device—reels, wheels, stars, and full-grown men and women. Such might be called the chandeliers of the stage, while the foot-lights consisted of, 3. An extended row of flaming negroes' heads, alternating with tar-barrels.

We squeezed into the church. The committee on portraits were run down with customers. Veronica stood on their table: a handsome four-foot figure, draped like a nun in russet gown, and with thick folds of linen round her throat. She held a bouquet in one hand, and in the palm of the other a minute baby. Ladies young and old, gentlemen and lads, pressed to buy her picture. Colored women came up with two-foot candles, which they reverently laid down, and received likenesses of the Capuchin abbess.

All this time the business at the altars was going on, and eunuchs borrowed from the Imperial Chapel were chanting. When they got through, a monk entered the pulpit. His theme was Veronica—her virtues, sufferings, and her glory; the kiss Our Lady gave her, the value of her as a patroness, and the advantages of joining the brotherhood just instituted in honor of her. T—— said the whole was a perfect rhapsody, and not caring to hear more, we left.

14th. H—— and I went to the Mint, and yet an old resident of Rio did not know there was one. He had never seen a Brazilian dollar. The currency is now wholly confined to copper and paper. Neither silver nor gold is seen. The smallest denomination of bills are milreis, and all change below them is made in copper.

The building is in the form of a hollow square; its front has little to distinguish it from adjoining houses. The second is devoted to engraving and die-sinking. An American transferring and a medal-ruling machine were in one room. One of the artists showed us a small figure on a copper plate half engraved. I observed it was designed for Washington; on hearing which, he brought out a two-dollar Newark bill, from the margin of which he was copying it. I did not understand that any bills had as yet been engraved here. The plates of those in circulation were executed in England.

The melting-rooms are on the ground floor, where are three modern air furnaces and two old ones, with the ancient mode of supplying the blast by lantern bellows—a form of the popular instrument of the highest antiquity, and still in vogue throughout the Oriental world in one rude shape or another. The specimens here are similar to the one noticed at the arsenal, and present perhaps the best modification of the old pneumatic device. To literary readers a sketch can impart no interest, but there are others who will thank the writer for inserting one.

A, an upright hollow plank or chest, to whose opposite sides the ends of the leathern tubes or sacks, *b, b,* are nailed. It answers the purpose of two bellows-boards, and is secured to a fixed base. The nozzle proceeds from the

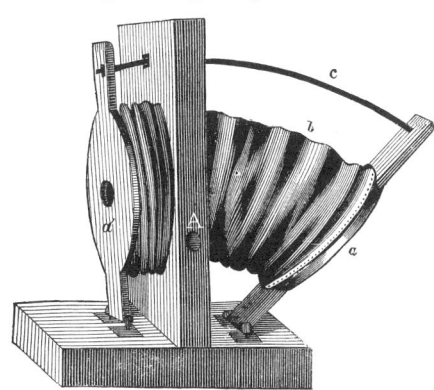

LANTERN BELLOWS IN THE MINT AT RIO DE JANEIRO.

opening at A, which communicates with the cavity within. a, a' are the movable boards, whose lower extremities turn on pins or pivots as represented, and the upper ends or handles are secured to each other by the curved iron rod c, which passes through a slit in a solid part of A. The clacks or valves of a, a' of course open inward, and so do two others within the cavity of A. Hence, by pushing a or a', one bellows or bag is inflated, the other collapsed, and vice versa on reversing the motion; thus a continuous though not uniform blast is kept up.

But for the rod c there would be two *separate* instruments, which, if placed side by side, and the front boards alternately pushed to and fro by each hand of the blower, would constitute the dual bellows of the early Greeks, Romans, Celts, Germans, and Anglo-Saxons, and would resemble those of modern India, Egypt, Greece, Asia, and Africa generally.

Every thing is neat and neatly arranged about the Mint, but no business connected with coining was going on. The furnaces were cold, the presses silent, and the small steam-engine for driving the machinery was motionless.

The famous Lady of Lampadoza having her residence close by, we stepped in. Like the temple of St. George, it is a small and mean affair, the floor rotten and level with the street. The altars and their wooden candlesticks, denuded of gilt and paint, are clouded brown with age and handling; the walls frown on the ebony sacristan as he lounges at the doorway, and the low roof scowls on him for withholding a coat of whitewash; but the varlet heeds them not, and possibly thinks colors increase in beauty as they approach his own.

Over the chief altar stands the patrona nursing a child, her occupation and regalia queerly contrasting with her fanciful, but faded, worn-out costume, her soiled hands and smutty face. At her right stands "Balthazar, king of Congo," whose white varnished eye-balls peer on her from sockets of jet. Confessing ignorance of this person's biography, I was told he was one of the three wise men, or kings as they are said to have been, guided by the star to the infant Christ in Bethlehem. Why he was brought here will appear presently. On her left is popular Anthony, his military sash, black cassock, and the light blue frock of his baby assisting to relieve each other.

The baby's stature does not exceed six inches, nor the monk's nor monarch's twenty-four. The "patrona" is properly made taller than her guests—she is four feet. Of all the faces, Balthazar's is the only one that does not cry for soap and water.

Passing through a side door, we entered the vestry, a large, airy, well-conditioned room, worth half a dozen such as we just had left. A young man gave us the history of the establishment, and showed us the original "Rules and By-laws," dated 1743—a fine specimen of old penmanship. The illustrated title, in purple, red, and gold, represented the patrona, and each chapter begins with an illumined letter. The ground was not obtained till 1748. The donor's portrait hangs against the wall, and close to it is a wooden tablet, on which is written, "It is the duty of the brotherhood, whenever a priest performs mass here, to ask him to pray for the souls of Pedro Coelho da Silva and his wife, who gave the ground on which this church is built."

This was the second fane given to the blacks, that of the Rosary being the first. The policy of having a negro patron in each was obvious, and hence Balthazar in one and Benedict in the other. In 1828 this one was taken from them. In the bureaus were festival suits for the images, including artificial bouquets and trimmings, dating from Peter Coelho's days. Here stood Our Lady of Pains, large as life, and in less antiquated costume than her sister over the altar. Here, too, was St. Vincente Ferrea, of full stature. I could not learn who he was. He looks like a nondescript—half monk, half angel. His head is shaved, and his plump body robed in a cassock, while from his shoulders sprout a pair of splendid wings. Judging from his name, he may have been a blacksmith before he joined a monastery and learned to read the Missal in his hands.

Our informant offered to show us as fine a piece of sculpture as is in Rio. We went into the church, the front of an altar was removed, and lo! a dead Christ lay on a checked mattress. "There," said he, "that was carved out of cedar more than eighty years ago by a slave named Fulah, the same who made the colossal crucifix in the Jesuits' College on Castle Hill." The general effect was not bad; the falling in of the chest, and other indications of life's departure, were tolerably in character. The image had been fresh painted. Its general ghastly hue was set off with deep carmine gashes in the breast, arms, thighs, and legs, besides smaller ones. The knees and shoulders are sorely bruised. Each wound is surrounded with a bluish tint, while vivid gore trickles or streams from all. I examined the figure minutely. It is six feet long, and the head has a slight movement. The joint is in the neck, and so neatly covered with a band of skin or parchment (painted like the rest of the body) as to require more than a casual inspection to detect. The arms are attached in like manner. This image is exposed for public veneration every Friday. Pious negroes and others then crowd to kiss its hand and feet, and leave their alms in a dish placed near it. A wig of flowing locks is then put on the now bare head, and a coverlet thrown over the body.

The young man finished by giving us an account of himself. He has been brought up to the law, but is about leaving it to devote himself wholly, as he said, "to God's blessed Mother."

17*th*. The papers announce assassinations and famine still prevalent in Ceara. Yesterday public business was suspended, and the pageantry at the Imperial Chapel increased by extra masses and other doings, in view of the approaching birth of another royal baby.

18*th*. A gala day—the anniversary of the consecration and coronation of Pedro II. A spectator tells me the consecrating unguent was rubbed on the emperor's bare breast and shoulders, and on the nape of his neck, according to the ritual, very much as the two lads were consecrated to the Capuchins by Bedini.

19*th*. Another gala in honor of the protecting angel of the empire. To compliment this nameless spirit, a procession was got up in the Imperial Chapel, which I did not think worth going to see.

The usual mode of conveying presents, and the taste with which their value is enhanced, was exemplified this evening. A messenger was announced, and presently a young man stood at the parlor door with a covered tray on his left palm, and holding forth his right one, asked a blessing.* The salver was

---

* When a slave enters the parlor to light the candles, he salutes the members of the family present by holding out his right hand and saying, "Louvado seja Nossa Senhor Jesus Christ—a benção." To neglect it would be deemed impertinent and deserving the lash.

heaped up with flowers, and in the centre an orbicular something, enveloped in fancy punctured paper, gathered up with green ribbon, and set off at the corners with white and red roses. The object inclosed was a large apple. This fruit is rare, and consequently much prized. Yesterday a barefooted young slave in livery passed by with a bilhête, the mode of carrying which struck me as a pretty one. The slender stems of a purple flower and of two yellow roses were passed through the folds of the envelope, so that the letter was borne between the bearer's hand and the flowers.

Ladies preparing for a ball send for a perruquier to plait their tresses and set them off with flowers. With the other sex things are different. The opinion of St. Paul, that it is a shame for men to wear long hair, is universally accepted. All are so closely cropped that with some the pile looks as if recovering from the razor rather than the shears.

Called with H—— on a corpulent and commanding widow of sixty, in a fine old mansion in Mata Cavallos. Stately and singularly punctilious, she is said to be a Semiramis in her family. We found her in the drawing-room on the second floor, which resembled in its fittings those of other old first-rate houses. The ceiling was raised and painted; the walls stenciled for three feet above the floor, and then papered. No glass in the windows, which were mere frames, with outside lattices, and heavy inside door-like shutters and massive bolts. Each of the interior doors was formed of three planks tied together with the usual dovetailed battens; they were painted (white), but not planed; their only finish had been given by the popular adze. Broad wrought-iron hinges, iron locks without knobs, and bolts extending from top to bottom, are capital fastenings for bank vaults and warehouses, but rather antique as fittings for a fashionable apartment. The facts, however, are worth recording for their relationship to the history of the arts.

In the day's table-talk some proverbial sayings occurred worth noting. "Carrying a lance into Africa" is applied to successful moves in business, at cards, etc. One fearful of imaginary dangers has "seen Moors on the coast." A person not easily excited "has the blood of a barata"—a roach. Of the thoughtless and unscrupulous it is said, "Presumption and holy water cost nothing." A person in low spirits is "jururu"—an Indian word. When people are frightened, "they have seen Medusa's head." Of a dull person, "He will go to the sea and not find water." Of a fortunate one, "His bread fell into the honey-pot." When a solicited favor is not granted, "Well, it requires one hand to wash the other, and both to clean the face," intimating that the refuser will want the aid of friends sooner or later.

The neckcloth is a mark of gentility, the want of it of servitude. This doctrine of the old Portuguese is still enforced on white young men. In Quitanda Street, the chief mart for dry goods, one is sure to encounter clerks passing rapidly along without hat or neckcloth, and their bare feet pushed into wooden slippers.

20*th*. St. Elias the Prophet's day was kept up by the White Friars, and indulgences issued.

A hot dispute is raging respecting the troubles Bedini has created among the mixed population of Pedropolis. He, or a friend who echoes his sentiments, complains of the emperor not taking sides in the controversy, and using his influence to prevent the spread of Protestant heresies. It is insinuated that Pedro does not attend mass as often as his father and grandfather did. Brazilians are pretty well chained to Rome, and Bedini is determined to give them no chance of breaking loose, if they were even so inclined. According to a promise it is rumored he gave the Pope, he is determined to bind the largest portion of the Western World faster than ever to St. Peter's chair. It was suggested that a public meeting should be called at the Campo to express the sense of the citizens on the interference of Bedini, but it was replied that no public assembly of the kind would be allowed: it would be deemed revolutionary.

The British embassador begged the loan of a medical electromagnetic machine I had brought from the United States, and, at the request of Mr. Hamilton, I assisted the doctor in applying it. Had Miranda, Bedini, or the Capuchins known that this gentleman was seized with an affliction that has disfigured his features and deprived him of the use of one arm *while witnessing the procession of Priscilliana*, and probably laughing at the farce, they would have made no small capital out of it—a heretic sneering at the newly-imported saint, and instantly struck dumb by her! It would have formed a twin transaction to that of the wicked painter.

22*d.* Remarkable for having only a single saint assigned it. To-morrow is more fortunate; it has several, and among them one to whom all afflicted with concretions in the kidneys might do well to apply. H—— and I spent some time in the House of Representatives. Several deputies are colored; some are priests, and among them the Bishop of Rio. A few are physicians, but the greater part are lawyers and military men. There is not a merchant in the House, nor a manufacturer; as for mechanics, they are out of the question.

23*d.* Another gala day, which H—— and I spent in a jaunt to the Gavia Mountains. Starting early, we tripped through Boto-Fogo, and left the Botanic Garden behind. So elastic and bright was the morning, that, before leaving home, the Corcovado seemed close to us, and now the distant "Two Brothers" appeared at our elbows. Cochineal cactuses occurred; breadtrees, laden with fruit, stood by the road side; and among floral treasures were "Flowers of Venus," of which a singular use, considering their name, is made. The leaves, rubbed on leather, impart to it the color of jet, and hence are employed as blacking for boots and shoes—a hint to chemists and dyers.

Black streaks crossed the road, as if a wide tar-brush had been drawn over the yellow soil: these were armies of ants passing with forage to their camps. Occasionally a green leaf, two or three inches over, is seen gliding along without any apparent mover: turn it over, and you find a Herculean emmet bearing it away—a load vastly more disproportioned to the bearer than the gates of Ascalon on Samson's shoulders.

The Gavia peak is nine miles from the city by land, and twice that distance by sea. The elevation has been calculated at three hundred feet above the Corcovado. Close to the ocean, the Gavia presents a prominent mark for navigators, and is supposed to furnish evidence that the coast was visited by Phœnician or earlier adventurers. One part of the pinnacle is a colossal cubical mass, with a comparatively regular face overlooking the ocean, and on that face is the alleged record—an inscription of between twenty and thirty gigantic characters, deeply cut in the granite, and generally perpendicular and parallel.

After passing over an excessively rugged road, we arrived at and rested on a summit, appropriately named *Boa Vista.* The largest of the Irmaões, a bare, black, overwhelming mountain, faced us. At our left were the valley we had come through, and the glorious country between us and the Bay. At our right the mighty Gavia towered, appearing close by, the sculptured tablet exposed above, and the white surf rolling and roaring at the base. Here we took a sketch of the scene and of the writing, which appears in two lines extending across the middle of the stupendous page. With a telescope we examined it minutely as we passed on. As we progressed, the table form contemplated from the city wholly vanished, and the largest and highest mass resembled a pointed helmet, up which no mortals could climb without the ascending powers of lizards.

In 1839, a committee of the Geographical Institute visited the Gavia, and copied the fancied writing. Their report oscillates between a natural and artificial origin. A second and more satisfactory investigation was promised, but has not been made. It is admitted that the characters bear little resemblance to those of any known people of old; that the face of the rock is inaccessible; that marks more or less like them are met with elsewhere, and that imaginary figures of animals and hunting scenes are found on the faces of mountains in other provinces.

Like profiles of men in mountain outlines, or figures in coal fires, these grooves in the Gavia may be interpreted into aught imaginative beholders please. They have, I should say, as much connection with primitive sea rovers as the Roman characters noticed on the Tejuca, and no more. If they were chiseled by human fingers, so was Anthony's Nose, shown to travelers on the Hudson River; the famous Virginia bridge was built by antediluvian masons; the Niagara was a dam constructed by Titan millers, and the Devil's Letters, impressed on a rock near Cape Frio, are the veritable handy-work of the Wicked One. But how were they produced? With a telescope we detected kindred indentations in process of development on the Greater Irmão, and on others of those cloud-crested quarries. Veins, striæ, cracks, and crevices pervade most, and into them *vegetable fibrils* creep, grow, and burst off portions whose figures and dimensions are governed by the directions and extent of previous fissures, the texture or grain at the place of rupture, etc. On the face, as on the summit of the highest and barest rocks, these thread-like borers hunt for lodgments in the minutest chasms, creep into every interior ramification, and swell till they displace the walls in front of them. Such, I believe, were the sculptors of the Gavian hieroglyphics. Instances occur where dislodged portions are protruded, but not sufficiently so to fall: they are waiting till the powers behind expand again to give them another push. In rocks partly decomposed these slow drillers and silent blasters abound. They raise the material in shelves, air and water then enter, and assist to break and crumble the layers up.

We rested a while and refreshed us near a venda at the base of the awful pile. Half-naked children were playing about; one had bone figas hanging at her ears. A man sat by the door patching a jacket—an itinerant tailor. His whole dress consisted of a shirt, and pants that barely covered his knees; his feet and legs were greatly swelled, and occupied his attention as much as his needle.

On our return, two negroes came suddenly on us out of a side path, bearing a pole on their shoulders. To it was slung the body of a brother slave they were going to bury. A white man, dressed like the tailor, met us—a picture of idleness, dirt, and distress: a specimen, it is said, of thousands in Brazil, whom slavery, with the feelings it has generated, makes wretched. Labor is degrading, and as they have not the means to live respectably without it, what can they do? Custom, instead of honoring useful toil, withholds all stimulus to exertion, and in a manner compels them to degenerate into worse than Indian habits. If they had land they could not cultivate it without slaves, and these they can not buy. The climate favors them: dwellings are hardly necessary, fuel and fire can be dispensed with, and, excepting fig-leaves, so might clothing. The poor of Brazil are poor indeed.

Pretty well used up, we got home soon after dark, with hands swelled with the bites of borrachudos.

25*th*. Public business suspended in honor of San Tiago.
26*th*. Anniversary of "Sta. Anna, mãe da Mãe de Deos."

Festas are announced at her sanctuary in the Campo, and at several others. As she is a favorite advocate, she has a shrine in most of the churches.

The president of the province of Rio has required the attendance of the master of the school at Pedropolis (a German and Roman Catholic) to explain the language used by Bedini in an address to the scholars. It appears that, not content with throwing a firebrand among their parents in the Church, he charged the boys of papists to hold no communication with their Protestant school-fellows. The master has arrived. He called at J——'s to-day.

28*th*. Thermometer early this morning, 63°. Of the whimsical incarnations of the Virgin, the novenas of a rare one began yesterday—Our Lady of Snows!

30*th*. Yesterday a princess was born, and to-day hundreds are off to Christoval; not only army and navy officers, priests, monks, and diplomatists, but almost all that can raise a suitable dress, and hire or borrow a carriage for the occasion. The road is thronged with parties hastening to leave their salutations for "her serene highness, the imperial princess Doña Isabel Christina Leopoldina Augusta Michaela Gabriela Raphaela Gonsago"—a lady one day old! There are, however, enlightened spirits in Brazil who scorn the practice. A deputy, in offering a complimentary resolution, dwelt on "the inappreciable honor of congratulating his imperial majesty on Divine Providence having conceded to him another pledge of felicity, and to the empire another glorious safeguard to monarchy." The Solomon was listened to, and the Chamber endorsed his wisdom.

31*st*. We called at the Police-office to look over the budget of an African conjurer just arrested. There was enough to load a cart. A large jar, concealed by skirts, constituted the body of the chief idol; two smaller ones were of wood, with jointed arms, their faces and heads smeared with blood and feathers—a fowl being required of every inquirer; iron prongs and stone knives, used as sacrificial implements; goats' horns, ivory tusks, skeleton heads of animals, a string of jaw-bones, small boxes of colored dust, rattles, a ferula, bundles of herbs (one of rue), the scarlet cap and gown of the enchanter, and the curtain behind which he acted the part of a ventriloquist in raising spirits and conversing with them. Being a slave—a shrewd Minas—he is to be flogged. The justice says the apparatus of a wizard's den is known as a *Candombe,* and that these fellows are successful in plundering slaves of their little savings, and stimulating them to rob their owners. Besides furnishing harmless powders as love-potions to insure milder treatment, they sometimes give out ground glass and other noxious matters to be dropped into the master's food.

CHAPTER XXXVII.

The Corcovado Mountain and Carioco Aqueduct: View from chamber Window.—Aqueduct Arches.—Ascent of the Tereza Hill.—Conduit and receiving Basins.—Romantic Character of the Work —Section of Conduit.—Mother of Waters.—Paineiras and Pic-nic.—Forest Features.—Ascent of the Corcovado.—Vegetable Instincts.—Summit of the Mountain.—Prospects from it.—Descent.—The Paineiras tributary to the Mother of Waters.—Reach Home by Lamp-light.—Subsequent Visits to the Aqueduct.—Its Length and Fall.—Section of Channel over the Arches.—Entire Length of the Aqueduct and Feeders.—Water furnished by it.—Might be conveyed through Tubes into every dwelling.—No Reservoirs.

J—— and I having agreed to visit the hunchback, the great natural lion of Rio, I awoke early amid such streams of golden light as poets invest celestials with. Before leaving the room, let us raise the ponderous sash and take a peep outside. Apparently not more than a mile off, yonder rises, at the left, beautiful Mount Martha, a perfect cone, and the most conspicuous of an insulated crowd. In its rear a somewhat similar formed pile towers over all the country and the ocean near. Its apex is a pinnacle, abrupt, on one side precipitous. To mount it seems impossible, and yet it is said to have been scaled on horseback, though where the animal found standing-room, save for his hind feet in a rearing attitude, does not appear. That is the Corcovado, and to its very summit we are bound. Scarcely a cloud dots the blue vault of heaven, but, as usual, milk-white fleeces are floating half way down the gigantic range, while one, pure as driven snow and dense as chalk, has within the last few moments cut off the black peak from the body.*

---

* This trip to the Corcovado was made in the latter end of March, but the MS. account of it having been mislaid, it is inserted here. It had been unnecessary to mention this but for references to some winter flowers.

THE CORCOVADO.

We were soon off, in white roundabouts and wide straw hats. "But how is this?" I inquired; "we are going from, not toward the mountain." "The longest way is the shortest," was the sententious reply. We soon came to Arcos Street, so named from the double tier of arches on which the Carioco stream is conveyed from the lower part of Tereza to Antonio Hill. Collected in the Corcovado glens, I now learned that only on the artificial elevations, made to bring the water to the city, can that mountain be approached. Our way, therefore, lies along the most picturesque of aqueducts, and thus a double pleasure attends us. While waiting in Arcos Street for our saddle-horses, the outlines of the scene were taken. At our right towered a part of the aqueduct arches; facing us arose the dead wall of the Tereza Convent garden, and over it banana-trees hanging; at its left extremity began the steep road we had to travel. Above the garden appeared a grassy hill, and beyond it the convent church. Projecting from the wall are spouts to supply the vicinity with water. Not less than two dozen slaves, of both sexes, came to fill their barils during the few minutes we waited, several of whom carried the liquid high up the hill down which it comes.

Though one of the most interesting structures through which life's liquid ever ran, the aqueduct has never been described; it will therefore be considered the principal object of the trip, and of other trips, for a week might be profitably devoted to it alone. The Tereza is the highest of the city hills, and from its summit the fluid descends. This hill, which in most lands would be called a mountain, is not insulated, but joins more aspiring peaks in its rear. We are now about to scale it. The

ARCOS STREET.

lower part of the road, beginning at Arcos Street, is paved, the rest is broken and rugged as a gully. Up the long and tortuous steep we ride, grasping the pommels of our saddles to prevent sliding off behind.

As we proceeded, a stone fence or stuccoed wall, varying from five to eight feet in height, was at our right. It turned with the road, and rose and fell with it. I supposed it was designed to keep the high ground behind it from caving in and blocking up the pathway, but at certain distances it was capped with peaked ridges extending across it, and their ends flush with its face. An opening appeared in each ridge. Asking for an explanation, I was quite taken by surprise on being told that this wall, as I called it, was hollow, and neither more nor less than a part of the famous conduit. I dismounted, put my ear to one of the openings, and, sure enough, heard the sound of rushing water. The difference in the height of the structure arose from the irregularity of the ground. With us, such works—the Croton, for example—have a slight and nearly uniform descent, but here they glide along gentle inclinations in one place, and dash down declivities steep as old Dutch roofs in another.

We had now risen between seventy and eighty feet above the pavement in Arcos Street, a few feet above the upper tier of arches, and were but a short distance from them, when, at a turn in the road, we came to the first "caixa"—the name of a structure built over a receiving-basin, where great changes in the direction or descent of the channel occur. Before reaching it, the wall-like structure had left the road, but here it appeared again, ascending from the caixa in two stretches, and disappearing in the side of a hill, upon which the Tereza Church and Convent stand, as seen in the sketch on the next page. The upper stretch has a fall (as I subsequently ascertained) of fifty inches in fifteen feet; the lower one enters the caixa with a descent of thirty-nine inches in fifteen feet. From this caixa the channel passes directly to the arches.

After passing the convent, the conduit appeared again, and accompanied us up to the summit of the Tereza Mountain, where we stood something like three hundred feet above the pavement below, and here is only the beginning, as it were, of this romantic specimen of engineering. It takes a turn at right

AQUEDUCT AND CAIXA.

angles on the right, and wriggling zigzag fashion, like a worm-fence, is soon lost to view in the forest. To accommodate the inhabitants of a few houses on the summit, an iron grating is let into the face of the work, through which slaves lade out the fluid with a calabash or cocoa-shell into their barils. The interior dimensions being thus open to the light, I dismounted and made a minute of them. I subsequently found they were the same throughout the entire length of the work. Now let the reader imagine the vast consumption of water in so populous a city within the tropics as Rio Janeiro, and try to infer the capacity of this, the chief source of its supply. Perhaps with me, when I first viewed yon extensive range of forty massive arches below, elevated as they are upon an equal number, for conveying the fluid across a valley of near a thousand feet, and at an elevation of some sixty feet above the heads of citizens in the streets, he will be inclined to assign to it the capacity of a canal.

But, speculate as he may, he could hardly realize or even approach the reality. So interesting in its course, its deviations, and descents as this aqueduct is, its volume of liquid took me with the most surprise. I may as well give a section here, for without one the peculiarities of this chief of Brazilian waterworks can not be understood.

The figure represents a cross section at a spot where the whole was beneath the surface, showing the interior, where a person can conveniently walk upright, while the width is almost sufficient for two to go abreast. The space is six feet by three. The walls, of ordinary masonry, are twenty-one inches thick, the dome is arched with brick and covered with a peaked roof of gravel and mortar, and the whole plastered with a coat of lime and clay—the same as all rough walls in the city, and which, from the humidity of the climate, never hardens sufficiently to resist a pointed stick or the end of an umbrella. The work appears at different elevations above the surface, and sometimes, though rarely, disappears beneath it.

SECTION OF THE CARIOCO AQUEDUCT.

Is it asked how high the water rises up the walls? It does does not touch them. Its surface is below them. It flows through a semicircular channel, cut in granite slabs laid at the bottom. The extreme depth of the channel is nine and a half inches, and the width at the widest part is nine inches—a mere gutter! and, small as it is, seldom over two thirds full—that is, except where the inclination is very moderate. These gutters were brought from Portugal: the blocks vary from three to eight feet in length, and are seldom less than two in width. A course of bricks on each side fills the space between them and the walls. We passed several blocks lying about; in some the channel is elbowed, in others a small one crosses the main one. Some of these weighed not less than half a ton. Their conveyance up here in early times must have been an immense labor.

We now continued along a narrow and grassy road cut in

the breast of mountains—a forest precipice at one hand, and the aqueduct, presenting a wall seldom less than five feet high, at the other. A velvet foot-path occasionally runs along its roof, while rocks and trees tower far above it. A solitary chacara appears now and then, and gratings in the conduit. They are doors composed of bars five or six inches apart, their lower edges being level with the water-channel. To facilitate the dipping of the fluid, a lateral basin adjoining the bars communicates with the current. When the water is below the surface of the ground, a few steps lead down to the grating, wherever chacaras in the vicinity require one.

We came to one of these that was unlocked. It was four feet square, so I stepped inside of the aqueduct, and walked some distance along it. There is sufficient light to go from one extremity to the other, for openings ten inches by seven occur every fifteen or twenty feet. The fall was here not less than two feet in twenty; the little stream gurgled as it rushed between my feet, and boiled and foamed in the basin at the grating. The wall seldom continues over a hundred feet without turning. It consists of a succession of short stretches, invariably in right lines, and broken laterally into every diversity of angles.

The Humpback occasionally rises above the forest, reminding us that our visit is also to him. Away down below us is a real Buena Vista—Engenho Velha and the Christoval Palace, which latter looks small enough to put in one's pocket. A little farther, and we ride over the aqueduct between two triangular columns, like the posts of a gateway. Both alike, they are named brothers. We passed between a similar pair before. The prospect soon becomes circumscribed, and the scenery wilder. Little but trees and sky is visible. Close at our right, the mountain forests reach to heaven, and immediately at our left descend to depths that make one shudder. A false step, and horse and rider are plunged to destruction. The place is rendered still more dangerous, it is alleged, by runaway slaves, who harbor here, and prowl about for means to live. At one spot we caught a sight of the Larangeiras valley, its road reduced to a thread of vermilion in a web of green baize.

Proceeding, the air becomes damper, and the overhanging

trees seem about to rain. Their dense foliage prevents the sun from penetrating, and the conduit becomes coated with moss. Its roof has in some places disappeared, leaving the arch exposed, and here and there fallen in. The old imported bricks that compose it are of the same dimensions as those now made in the country. At a turn in the work a tiny stream—the Lagoinha feeder—comes down the overhanging mountains, broken into spray in the fall, and, gathered at the bottom, joins the aqueduct in an open tile. Brought from a distance of between six and seven hundred Brazilian fathoms in tile channels, it would at present scarcely fill an inch tube.

Wishing a thousand times that I was on foot, we came at length to *Mai de Agua,* "The Mother of Waters," a rude ba-

THE MOTHER OF WATERS.

sin, some thirty feet by twelve, formed in the rock, and having a rural roof over it. The water, fifteen inches deep, does not spring up within it, but comes down, a miniature cataract, from projecting precipices, the place from where it leaps being concealed by trees and dense foliage.

Here, at a tortuous distance of between four and five miles from the city, and some seven hundred feet above it, the aqueduct, as I supposed, terminated; but no, not even here. This is simply the spot where tributary streams unite, and whence they descend in one volume to the town. The idea of a river or rivulet running through a little stone gutter may excite a smile, and yet that gutter is the outlet of several. The Carioco River, as it is called, brings in the principal supply to the Mother of Waters. Its source is in the mountain fastnesses, and all but inaccessible: it has five branches—the Corcovado, des Velhas, Serra, Lagurnal, and Regilio. These, with the parent stream, are brought in open tiles. Two other rivulets are also diverted hither—the Silvestre and Paineiras. The length of the latter is said to be some thousand fathoms, and an expensive work. Properly speaking, all these waters are springs, whose trickling treasures are thus gathered together. Each is named after the mountain from whose sides, or the cavern out of which, it gushes. In wet weather they become torrents, and hence provision is made at the mother reservoir to discharge the surplus down the dark yawning gulf at the edge of which it is located.

There is here a grating in the side of the conduit which enabled me again to mark and measure the interior. The dimensions and character of the whole were found precisely as represented in the section taken on the Tereza Hill. The descent of the channel is here moderate, and the water rises to the brim. At the junction of the conduit with the reservoir there is a corroded marble tablet let into the end wall of the latter. The inscription is in old and abbreviated Portuguese. With some difficulty we made out the letters: they are to this effect: "Under our Lord King John V., Gomes Freire de Andrade, Governor and Captain General, and Councilor to the King, 1744." Here is no intimation when the work was begun, or by whom it was projected and executed. This is to be regretted, since there is not a line in the public archives relating to its history. Agreeably to monarchical modesty, every thing eminently useful and honorable must be ascribed to royalty and its satraps.

It is not easy to impart an adequate idea of the Mother of Waters, buried as it is in a tropical forest, amid scenes indescribably picturesque and sublime. As for that portion of the aqueduct along which we have come, another time must be taken to examine it particularly. There is a moral influence about it in such a day as this. An emblem of youth and innocence, its crystal current gushes and sparkles as from excess of joy, running, leaping, and changing its course and its speed as in wantonness of play. A kindred feeling arises, we wot not how, within us. Buoyant and elastic, pleased with ourselves and all about us, heaven and earth seem one. Exulting in our being, emotions such as swell in angels' breasts heave in ours, and burst out into ejaculations of praise. To hypochondriacs the Mai de Agua would prove a fountain of health, and efficacious as the pool of Siloam. Melancholy would leave them ere they reached it. Like the lepers of old, they would be healed by the way.

Having so much work before us, we could linger no longer. As we pressed on, the road became less and less inviting. It was well enough for men who have tame tigers to ride on, but not for timid travelers on nags of the equus genus. I preferred leading mine to mounting him. After a while, a neat little line of embankment appeared, running along the right of the path. It formed a low grassy wall, on the top of which an uncovered line of bright red tiles was imbedded—the channel through which the Silvestre's tribute was borne along to the Mai de Agua. The liquid volume was scarcely equal to the bore of a three-inch tube. A little farther, and a feeder of like construction came out of the dark woods, and joined it. The path widened, but close to our right rocks and trees shot up to heaven, while at our left the scene was awfully precipitous. A few minutes more, and we were completely hid in the forest. Trees were above, below, behind, before, and all but in contact with us. Nothing else was visible except, now and then, a few inches of sky between translucent leaves, quivering hundreds of feet above us—Nature's green lattices.

We had got out of the track, and, fortunately, a loud *hilloa!* caused us to stand. The warning came from Pompey, who left home before us with a basket of provisions, and was resting near by. Now both in the stirrups, we sprung our horses up a gulley—a feat that a circus-rider might boast of—and rode past a mud-built house, in front of which lay a heap of coffee-berries drying in the sun. Slaves were picking clusters from trees in the rear and bringing them in baskets to the pile. Continuing on, the Corcovado peak, which we have scarcely seen or thought of for some time, now frowns in front, and looks as if inclined to tumble on us. The little tile conduit appears once more, and the scenery is quite enchanting. Every few yards' advance produces a new view. Still the forest occasionally ascends to the clouds on one side, and sinks at the other into depths and darkness. Far ahead, and at least a hundred feet above me, his white dress finely contrasting with the forest's livery, J—— is passing a turn in the road, which is so crooked and so up and down that his horse's head is in the opposite direction to mine: he is leaning back over the animal's rump, while my face is touching the mane of my steed.

The saints be praised! a level spot, on which to rest a moment, is at length attained. My poor nag blows as if his lungs, like a damaged pair of bellows, were ruptured. The road we have just climbed must at least be on an angle of $40°$—a heavy drag for horses, and not less for our peon. Yet slaves, it is said, consider the job a treat, and enjoy it as much as their masters. Hark! J—— is calling; the only sound, save that from my horse's nostrils, which I've heard for some time. The animal is, I believe, familiar with the route, and I've begun to yield up the reins to him. He tacks from side to side as he creeps up, and now and then passes into a twelve-inch track on the very verge of the gulf. Till he gets off it I instinctively incline my body the other way. J—— is shouting again, but I have no idea of saving a minute at the risk of being sent, by a false step, on a flying visit to forests which, for aught I know, are a thousand fathoms beneath me, taking a leap terrible as that of Curtius.

A feeble sound of water comes up from glens into which the solar light for unnumbered ages has probably never shone, so deep and dense the screen that intervenes. Here two trunks of trees extend diagonally across the road, and are partly sunk in it—terrible traps for the feet of men and cattle in the dark. Six inches apart, they form a gutter to convey part of the water streaming down in wet weather to cultivated spots of ground. Other agricultural indications occur. The ugly gutters become more frequent, and demand constant attention on our part. The road descends, and presently we cross the stream whose murmurs we had heard—one of the tributaries to the Mother of Waters, three feet wide and three to five inches deep. The limpid fluid, which our horses were glad to taste, gurgles for a few yards among pebbles, whirls in tiny eddies by moss-covered boulders, and darts out of sight.

Crossing the brooklet once more, and this time on a wooden bridge, the road improves. Here another tile conduit occurred, nearly level with our horses' feet, but quite dry; a handsome row of coffee-trees and another of oranges now inclose us, the ridge of a roof is visible above, and soon we dismount on a level spot, and join a party of gentlemen from the city in a delicious pic-nic.

This place is called "The Paineiras," from trees of that name, for which the adjoining mountains once were famous. Numbers still are flourishing, resembling grown oaks in size, and producing, in place of acorns, snow-balls of cotton. Each is a genuine noli me tangere, its bole being closely studded with cones half an inch at the base, projecting about the same distance, and compared with whose sharp points cambric needles are blunt as one's fingers.

The Paineiras branch of the aqueduct comes in here on its way to join the Mai de Agua. A small building accommodates the overseer of the work. Here are stables in which to leave our steeds, the rest of the journey having to be done on foot. This platform is, to some extent, artificial. At the extremity opposite to the one by which we reached it, the view opens down a huge gorge to the sea. It connects the Corcovado and Paineiras Mountains, and may be taken as part of either, as it rests on both. On our left the former rises, and at the right the latter stretch away past the Botanic Garden, which they overhang in awful grandeur.

In coming thus far, one feature of the forest was observable: the general green foliage was dotted with patches of light and dark purple, and here and there with masses of yellow flowers. These are Brazilian "signs of winter." The purple gems are "the flowers of Lent;" of the mourning color, and opening at the commencement of the long fast, Nature is supposed to sympathize with that season of mortification. The yellows ripen at Easter, and, being of "the color of joy," are aptly named "Allelulias." The "martyr flower" grows on a small plant, is shaped like a lily, and of a deep purple approaching to indigo. Two varieties of the passion flower are also cherished, purple and crimson: they open in Lent, and in each the devout see the spear that pierced the Savior, the nails that fastened him to the tree, the whip that scourged him and ten of the apostles. We passed many "silver trees," the entire foliage white and glistening.

Invigorated, and provided with stout walking-sticks, we now began the zigzag ascent of the Corcovado. Roots, large and small, run quite across the road, and some, resembling taut ropes, a foot above it; primitive gutters, like those below, and boulders also, interrupt us; still, it is considered in good condition, late heavy rains having cleared away the worst obstruction, viz., leaves. They are so slippery as to make the ascent troublesome in the extreme, and the descent more so.

Here I first observed, and stopped to admire, large trees, the horizontal sections of whose boles present cusped or star-shaped figures, and here I beheld a fine example of vegetable instinct. Every where trees, when prevented from growing upright, seek to recover their natural position, and to equalize the strain on their roots by sending them and branches out in the opposite direction. Where the face of the mountain rises at an angle of 50°, a noble tree partially inclines down for eight or ten feet, and then, as if the original obstacle had there been overcome, ascends perpendicularly sixty feet before throwing out its branches. How enormous the strain on the upper roots that prevent its prostration! After passing it, I was surprised to see a large vertical triangular slab protruding from it behind, and entering the ground. Not knowing what to make of it, and almost thinking it an artificial bracket, I clambered up and found it a natural one—a sheet of plank of a uniform thickness throughout, viz., 2½ inches.

The higher we mount, the steeper becomes the path, the quicker and shorter our breath. The trees diminish in number and dimensions, scrub bushes appear, and at length we emerge on the base of the peak. The sun is broiling hot, and not an inch of shade to be had. My companion declares he can not stand the grilling, and after cautioning me not to venture near the surrounding precipices, he dove at once into the forest, leaving me solus on the mighty pinnacle.

A sense of loneliness and a slight tinge of fear crept over me, but I was mistaken in anticipating naught but still-life here. A heavy bird, white underneath, came sailing up from the Larangeiras glens, wheeled and floated high overhead, then suddenly swept down again—I suppose an eagle on the hunt. Numerous swallows darted hither and thither close to me, and twice a gorgeous green beetle lit on my arm. Ants—the great domestic pest—have colonies here. They kept running over the paper in my hand, though how they got on it puzzled me. Other natives of the place not less vindictive attacked me. An ear began to pain me—I found it inflamed and bleeding.

The prospect from where I stood was so striking, that I determined, before advancing, to preserve it in memory for a sketch. Four upright sticks, over which some party had stretched a sheet or other screen, were standing near. I tried to spread a handkerchief at one corner, and subsequently my jacket, but, having nothing properly to secure them, they were so repeatedly displaced by currents of air that I returned them to their former places, and mentally told Apollo to do his worst.

In front the rock rises sixty or seventy feet above me—a dark, irregular, ruptured cone, relieved by the sky. At its edges a few shrubs and creeping plants hang over the abyss. Rails to guard people from falling over precipitous portions of the rock are seen at the summit. To the left the pile rounds quickly off into awful declivities at the side up which we have come, exposing to view the city suburbs in distant depths, the Bay, and the mountains of Nictherohy, which last look like a broken wall as seen through mist. At the right the ocean forms the horizon, and touches the Gavia at the extreme right. Four

SUMMIT OF THE CORCOVADO.

islands rise out of the placid water. On one the light-house—a diminutive thing—glistens like a pin stuck in a dark velvet cushion. Between these and a nearly level line of precipice running within twenty feet of me, nothing is visible but an assemblage of isolated peaks, rivaling in vain the eminence on which I stand. I drew near and glanced down among them, but drew back with a shudder.

Climbing higher up the contracting rock, its outline and appearance were so changed that I stopped and took another sketch. The two widely-extended wings of the low wooden railing opened before me, the rest being concealed behind the peak, which now appears a rounded and uneven swelling. All is bleak and bare of vegetation save where a few minute blades are struggling through crevices in the granite, and a withered stump leaning over the precipice at the right. Upon its extremity sat a bird of the color and size of a thrush, whose pewit voice drew my attention to it. It remained, turning its head and eyeing me for some time. Once or twice it darted off, and as suddenly changing its mind, returned. At length, at the call of its mate, it dropped out of sight. From it I turned and contemplated some pebbles at my feet, varying from half an inch to four inches over. Surprised, at first I wondered how they came here. A slight examination explained all. Fragments of feldspar, one of the chief constituents of the Corcovado, they have been cut from its surface, and their angles rounded by the elements, and have progressed thus far on their journey down, and in the process of disintegration and transmutation into soil.

The ascent is overcome with little difficulty and with less danger, provided one keep midway between the precipices at either hand. On stepping up within the railing, the origin of the pebbles was evident. The entire surface of the rock was paved with white roundish stones imbedded in black cement, and looking at a short distance not unlike the floor of an artificial grotto. The dark matrix, being a more dissoluble ingredient of the granite than the feldspar, is soon worn and washed away, and leaves the latter in relief. Then the dissolving agents, after penetrating beneath the surface, extend their influence horizontally. After breaking the blade of a strong knife in endeavoring to obtain specimens, I succeeded in raising a piece three feet by two, and three inches thick where it parted from the general mass. Part crumbled in my hands, and portions had already assumed the tint of the loam beneath.

Such is the process by which nature has been lowering the Corcovado Peak, and converting it into vegetable mould from epochs anterior to the birth of animals, and possibly of plants. Its nude, mottled, dissolving crest doubtless presents, in these respects, the same appearances it has ever shown since heat and moisture began to act on it, and since winds and rains, thunders and lightnings have played round it. What its elevation was originally, who can tell? Still, the idea has repeatedly forced itself on me, that something like data from which to calculate the age of these insulated granitic piles might possibly be derived from the depth of soil collected on the sides and bases, compared with the detritus borne down during a few centuries, if proper means were taken to ascertain the amount.

While engaged with the specimens I intended to take, the movements of a small creature drew me close to the rails. It was a lizard at the very edge of the cliff, down which the tail and part of its body hung. Gazing a moment at me, it darted out of sight—perished, as I supposed; but no; in a twinkling it appeared at the brink some ten feet off, and, raising its head, turned its beautiful orbs again on me. While looking at it I forgot the awful chasms; but now the sight, on drawing near, made me recoil with giddiness.

A few yards more, and I stood on the swelled protuberance, the apex of the mountain, as I imagined; but lo! two distinct peaks now appeared, separated by a cleft whose sides present frightful perpendicular terminations. The railing now gathered in, and descended to a wooden bridge, seven or eight paces long, stretched over a chasm of fearful depth at one side, but only twenty feet at the other. I stepped down on the bridge by rude steps or notches cut in the rock, and, crossing over, ascended the farther peak by many more. This, then, is the highest point of the Corcovado. The area is smaller than the first one affords, but here is uneven standing-ground 25 feet by 15. In the centre a hole is sunk, 12 inches deep by 7 inches, and full of water, probably for a flag-staff. For the statue of a South American Washington or Franklin, this is the spot. The black and white mosaic pavement is here repeated, a specimen of which I took. At the extreme end, and beyond the rails, eight rocky steps descend to a little grassy plot at the very verge of the most precipitous part of the mount. Fatigued, I was glad to descend and lie down while viewing a scene more sublime than any I had beheld on shore—one such as eagles see when soaring.

I had not a very distinct idea of the jutting coast inside and out of the harbor's mouth, but now every line is defined and every object depicted on a superbly-tinted map. The widespreading ocean appears slate-colored till it reaches the tortuous and shallow shores, and there it every where presents a vivid border of light green, fringed with a frill of surf white as driven snow. This raised edging, too, is pleasantly relieved by a rim of yellow sand. The Sugar-loaf, no longer leaning, is now bolt upright, more like its namesake than ever. That brown patch down yonder is the city. It might be taken for an abandoned brick-yard. Near it a few dots denote the shipping. How minute the Bay and villa of Boto-Fogo—the Cattete, Gloria, and Luzia Strands—the pretty Larangeiras dales and white chacaras! All things visible conspire to please one. Earth, sea, and sky enrich the landscape with their varied hues. That bright streak of red winding through the verdant grounds is a turnpike. Yon distant mountains are draped in blue; those nearer are all but black; while close by, Mount Martha and her sisters shine in emerald robes, decked with spangles from silver trees and flowers of Lent and allelulias.

The elevation[*] is quite moderate compared with many peaks, but the surface of the earth and sea immediately below are so visible through the transparent air that nothing is lost by intervening objects, and the full impression due to the height is felt.

As I sat and silent gazed, swallows came fluttering up, then twittering and twirling, floated down the enchanted valleys. Almost lost in ecstasy, I soared and dove in fancy with them, till a butterfly aroused me, when I rose and made one step to swing my hat over it, forgetting the contracted spot on which I was. Heaven only knows my feeling as I awoke to the danger. Instinctively leaning backward, I crept to the steps, and some moments transpired before I felt sufficiently composed to mount them and get within the railing.

My stick was missing, and as it was folly to attempt a descent without one—not to facilitate, but to retard progress, for when one's momentum gets beyond control, and that a few unwary steps bring about, there is no stopping until brought up by a rock or tree, or by a fall that would most likely end one's earthly journeyings—I got an apology for a staff from a large shrub, and descended, slowly as a hermit, to a decayed trunk lying across the road. Here we had rested on coming up, and here my companion had left my stick. In half an hour I joined him at the Paineiras, and there took leave of the Corcovado. Bathing my hands and face in the conduit basin, I sucked an

---

[*] There are discrepancies in the measurements. Beechey, in his "Voyage to the Pacific and Behring's Straits," made the peak of the Corcovado, in 1825, by barometer, 2308 feet above half tide; by trigonometrical measurement, 2306 feet; in 1828, by barometer, 2291½ feet; by trigonometrical measurement, 2305 feet. I am indebted to the politeness of Commodore Wilkes, who makes it 2332 feet.

orange and ate a slice of bread and butter with a relish that epicures never knew, seasoned as it was with the mustard of St. Bernard.

I was desirous, before leaving, of following the Paineiras tributary to its source. From this place it flows to the Mother of Waters through a string of tiles laid mostly on the ground, but comes in here in a more imposing manner. As we had no time to spare, we lost none by delay, and soon were walking along a thick low wall, in which a bright red groove of tile was imbedded, contrasting agreeably with the green velvet path, encircling forests, and white stucco of the wall. This was the conduit:

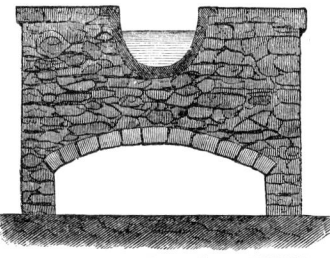

SECTION OF THE PAINEIRAS FEEDER.

built of rough stone, three feet four inches high, and three feet nine inches wide. To save material, the lower half consists of a succession of flattened arches, three and a half feet span, with an equal extent of solid work between every two adjacent ones. The top is flat, and finished at the side with a projecting cornice of plaster. The tiles are sunk flush with it, and form a clean and lively feature of the work. They are nine and a half inches deep, and twelve inches across their upper edges.

This pretty channel, on its snow-white bed, stretches away in the direction of the ocean, suspended on the precipitous faces of the Paineiras Mountains. Immense labor has been expended on it. We were careful to keep near it at the right, where the rocky forest shoots upward, to avoid slipping into the gulfs at the left. At first the path led us past coffee-trees laden with their scarlet clusters, and after leaving a few bananas and picturesque mamãos behind, we came to a terrible-looking precipice, where a wall sufficient to support the conduit and a safe path has been artificially raised. Here the silence was suddenly broken by parrots chattering down below. We next came to where the face of the mountain had been removed by blasting—a great undertaking to carry so small a trough along the all but perpendicular sides of these everlasting hills.

Next the trees shut out the sun, and the conduit is overgrown with moss. Much of the plaster has disappeared, and plants are springing from every part of the wall. Leaves are in the channel; insects, snakes, and other things, one would suppose, must occasionally be found in it too. The path is now delightful, and the prospect grand indeed. We next came to a small feeder. The fluid falls down from above, and, collecting behind a short wall, joins the main channel, as usual, through a tile. Rocks and trees here rise to heaven, and, within a few feet, sink to dark and impenetrable gulfs.

The Botanic Garden is somewhere beneath us, and the white surf rolling on the ocean shore is visible. We pass on, and the scene becomes, if possible, more romantic; the damp has caused every particle of plaster to drop off; the surplus water is pouring down the precipice at several points. Continuing, we come to the end of the tile channel and masonry—to wooden gutters, propped at irregular distances on rude piles of loose stones—box gutters nine inches deep and wide. The depth of water in them is three inches, and passing rapidly. Trees are growing two hundred feet above our heads. Things look wilder than ever, and verily they are so. We are no longer on the ground, but creeping on long rows of planks, that rest on iron rods let into and projecting from the face of the rock. Each rod is turned up an inch or two at its outer end, to keep the gutter from being pushed off. Between the gutter and the rock there is just room to pass. This is the most ticklish situation I was ever in.

I took one glimpse below, and that nearly upset me. After passing it, I asked how deep the fall was. "God only knows," was the reply. Stepping once more on rugged and uneven paths cut in the face of the mountain, the wooden channel kept us company, now at our feet, and now propped up four feet high. At length we came to a stretch of tiles again, where a side tributary came in; and not far off we were finally brought up at a place where, the channel ascending a steep, we could not mount, even if the dense forest had left an opening. A large tree marks the spot where the tile channel again ends, and the wooden gutter, shooting upward, left us to conjecture what jungle-scenes it passes through. We were now two miles, or perhaps more, from the Paineiras. Plunging our mouths into the tile channel, we drank and hastened back, fearful we should not get down the mountains before dark. Reaching the Paineiras, we found a slight refreshment prepared by our peon from the relics of his larder. While partaking of it he brought out our steeds, which we mounted, and, winding our way past the Mother of Waters, reached home by lamplight.

I subsequently devoted several days to the aqueduct. Provided with instruments, assistants, and an order from Colonel Frias, the distinguished superintendent of the Public Works, opening every part to inspection, we measured the length of every stretch between the Mai de Agua to Tereza Hill. They were two hundred and fourteen in number, all in right lines, and joined by angles more or less obtuse, seldom acute. Most of them were under a hundred feet long, and some did not exceed thirty. The fall of each was taken with a fifteen-foot pole or straight-edge, and a spirit level. In none was the descent less than four inches in fifteen feet, often two feet; in one, four feet and a half, and in another five feet, or one in three! We made the length from the Mother of Waters to Tereza Hill 18,128 feet, with a fall of 520 feet. From Tereza Hill down to the caixa near the arches—figured on page 411—the lengths of channel amount to 1290 feet, with a fall approaching to one in five, or 230 feet.

A section of the top of the long range of arches will be acceptable to professional readers.

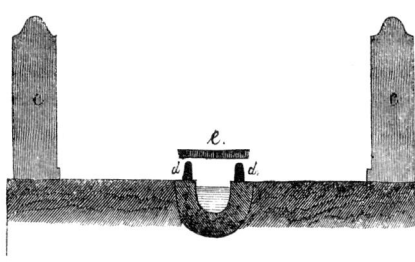

c, c, parapet walls, from outside to outside of which is nine feet. The water-channel is partly cut in granite, but mostly of tiles nine inches across, the same in depth, and two feet long. A small stuccoed wall, *d, d*, six inches high, runs along each side of the channel to prevent its overflowing, and upon them loose boards (*e*) rest. As there is no frost here, the stucco work, which never hardens much, lasts many years. A pathway, twenty-seven inches wide, and coated with stucco, is left on each side of the channel. The whole length of this stretch of archway is 833 feet; the fall of the channel five feet. At sixty feet from the Tereza side the work turns at a slight angle; at 300 feet it passes over Mata Cavallos and Arcos Street, where the elevation is sixty feet above the pavement. After passing Arcos Street, it goes over private yards and gardens to Antonio Hill, where it enters another vaulted passage about sixteen feet above the ground. I counted forty arches, and I think there are two more under the last-named covered passage. The fall, when the channel begins to wind round Antonio Hill, is one and a half inches in fifteen feet.

It will have been observed that the Mai de Agua is simply a caixa, or receiving basin, into which the tributaries bring their portions. The Office of Public Works has no account of the inclination of any part of the work, but the length of artificial conduit is recorded thus:

From the Hill Tereza to Mai de Agua	2589	Brazilian braças.
" Silvestre Stream to do.	321	" "
" Paineiras do., not known (at least)	1000	" "
" Lagoinha Feeder	633	" "

Thus the length of channel from Mai de Agua to Antonio Hill=20,305 feet; fall. 749 feet; length of feeders, as far as known.............. 14,166 "

Making the entire length of the Carioco Aqueduct .... 34,471 feet, with a fall of about 1000 feet.

The last day spent over the aqueduct I was alone, and of sketches then taken was one which, more than any other, is calculated to impart to the reader a correct idea of it. A copy is subjoined. It shows how erratic is the course of this famous conduit in limited spaces; how it is seen coming down a steep eminence into a caixa, and running zigzag from it at ever-varying descents and directions. Over the grated door of the caixa is a marble tablet, with the inscription "Por Ordem do Principe Reg^e No Sr Foi Reparada Esta Obra em 1814." The entire landscape, except this building, is a wild mountain forest.

Twilight began while I was some miles in the woods, and a sensation of fear crept over me from recollections of stories of runaway slaves robbing stray wanderers after nightfall. Having no stick, I stepped aside at an angle of the path, and cut one from a paineira-tree. While removing the spines with a knife, a tall negro with an ominous-looking staff burst suddenly

CARIOCO AQUEDUCT.

on me. He stood, gazed, passed on, and anon returned with club upraised. I tried to look bold, and asked what he wanted. He understood not the words, but comprehended my wants. Seeing I had got a poor branch—one not worth dressing, and whose prickles had drawn blood from my fingers—with a smile he drew near and offered me his. I hesitated, when he gently put it in my hand and went on his way. Ashamed of my suspicions, I called after him, and with difficulty got the kind-hearted man to accept a slight acknowledgment of his goodwill. It was dark when I arrived in the artificial world below.

The interest excited by the Carioco Aqueduct is augmented by its simple construction; its erratic and fitful courses; the wild, dark, and often awful scenery through which it passes; the elevations at which it receives the fluid, and the extent to which it meets the wishes of the people for "beaten" or agitated water, by causing it to leap and dance, to run, and boil, and sparkle in its passage down. Besides some others, it supplies four fountains in the oldest part of the city, viz., the Carioco, Marecas, Moura, and the one in Palace Square. To the first it gives (according to the account in the Office of Public Works) 37,420 barils in twenty-four hours; to the second, 1800 do.; to the third, 600 do.; and to the last, 6840. The baril is estimated at seven gallons.

Nature supplies this necessary of life in abundance, and would, if permitted, deliver it freely at the door of every dwelling, and raise it into every garret. In place of accepting her offer, it is drawn down in open gutters to the lowest streets, and thence borne upward, day and night, to the highest, by thousands of slaves, at an annual cost little exceeding that at which an ever-present stream in every house might be permanently attained. No city on earth is more favored in this respect than Rio.

There are no reservoirs in case of drought or damage to the works, so that when the supply is interrupted in the mountains it ceases in the city.

CHAPTER XXXVIII.

Population of Brazil.—Diseases—National Income.—Police.—Literature.—Library.—Newspapers.—Character of Brazilians.—Slaves.—Voyage Home.

BRAZIL is poor in population, and must be till she adopt a comprehensive and liberal system of immigration; but this is dreaded on account of the leveling spirit of the age, and a fear that both the Church and the throne would be endangered. No subject is more involved in uncertainty than the census. Official accounts, it is alleged, are often based on imperfect data, and not seldom on mere assumptions. As respects certain portions of the inhabitants, it is considered discreet in the authorities to say little; thus no reliable comparison of the numbers of whites and free colored are given, on account of the alleged overwhelming proportion of the latter. In the maritime cities and provinces the mixture of blood is obvious, but in the interior the preponderance of color is awful (I use the words of a native). In the city of Tejuco, the most thriving one in Minas and of the interior of Brazil, are only five pure white families among twelve thousand inhabitants.

I am indebted to a senator for a copy of a report made to the Chamber, July 21, 1847. It appears to be simply a reprint of a report by the Councilor Velloso in 1819, entitled "THE CHURCH OF BRAZIL, or Information to serve as a Basis for Dividing the Empire into Bishoprics," etc. He *estimates*, from isolated computations of previous years, the total da povoação Brazilense in 1819 at 4,396,231,* including 800,000 wild Indians, their conjectural number.

The *Diario* of December 11, 1847, contains an interesting article on the Political Geography of Brazil, by Senhor de Sousa, a native statician. I subjoin a few particulars.

"In 1766 the population was................... 1,500,000
1798 3,000,000
1815 (1819?) according to Velloso 4,396,000
1845 (assumed to be) .... 7,360,000."

In the ten northern provinces he estimates 3,480,000, being 29 persons to a square league. To the principal city, Bahia, he awards 150,000.

It is agreed, he observes, that the five southern provinces contain 2,530,000, being 84 to each square league. Rio de Janeiro, the chief city, he says, contains 250,000. (In 1807 its population was 50,000.)

População aproximada das provincias.	Em 1815.	Em 1845.
Paris	173,000	260,000
Maranhao	200,000	280,000
Piauhy	61,000	150,000
Ceara	210,000	350,000
Rio Grande do Norte..	71,000	160,000
Parahiba	96,000	240,000
Pernambuco	369,000	800,000
Alagoas	112,000	200,000
Sergipe	115,000	140,000
Bahia	478,000	900,000
Espirito Santo.......	73,000	60,000
Rio de Janeiro†......	510,000	1,400,000
S. Paulo.............	321,000	800,000
Santa Catharina	44,000	80,000
Rio Grande	79,000	190,000
Minas Geraes	622,000	1,130,000
Goyaz................	33,000	120,000
Matto Grosso	38,000	100,000
Indios nao domestic ...	800,000	
Total da povoação..	4,396,000	7,360,000

* This number is said, on what authority I know not, to be less than that of the aborigines at the period of the conquest.

† "It is very difficult to arrive at a correct knowledge of the population of

To the three central provinces Sousa assigns 1,350,000, being 14 to each league. The most considerable town, Ouro-Preto (Black Gold), the capital of Minas Geraes, has 20,000 inhabitants.

As nothing like positive data was within this writer's reach, the above, it will be perceived, is given merely as an approximation. Had the untamed Indians been carried over to the latter column of the preceding table, the number would have been swelled to over eight millions. Of subdivisions he makes

2,160,000 Whites.	3,120,000 Negro Slaves.
1,100,000 Free Colored.	180,000 Free Blacks.
800,000 Domesticated Indians.	

He here introduces the same number of tamed Indians as wild ones were counted by Velloso. From reliable sources of information, I should say the figures opposite the whites and free colored should be transposed. The number of inhabitants he assigns to Rio appears to me too high, and it would still appear so had he included the army in it.

Diseases.—The worst forms of rheumatism occur in Rio—of persons utterly deprived of the use of their limbs. One lady of my acquaintance has lain for years in that condition. Persons living on ground floors, in low situations, one would think could hardly escape. The air is so excessively moist, almost all the streets low and flooded during the rainy season, while the soil is saturated with water, which, on digging two or three feet, every where oozes up.

But that which most startles a stranger is the hydrocele and some kindred affections. At first he will be inclined to think every third or fourth man he meets is ruptured. Many are so, especially among the blacks, but the cause of the enlargement is generally dropsy of the parts—a complaint that is universal, and worse in Bahia than in Rio. It is not confined to adults: boys are afflicted by it. Young men from Europe seldom escape over a year or two. It is so common as to be

---

Brazil. According to the Political Annual of 1846 and correct information, the province of Rio de Janeiro contains a million of slaves. Before consulting that work, I had supposed the whole population of the province was nine hundred thousand.   F. NUNES DE SOUSA."

Nothing can be more expressive of uncertainty than this note.

little thought of by those troubled with it. Comparatively few undergo what is termed the radical cure, but have the water drawn off every few months.

Examples of what is named elephantiasis of the parts—excrescent accumulations within the scrotum—are somewhat common. Successful removals of these by the knife frequently occur in the Mizericordia. In a recent case a mass weighing thirty pounds was removed. There is a poor fellow, a Western Islander, seen about the streets, in whom the tumor reaches nearly to his ankles. Another man, about forty years of age, is unable to go on his feet, but is drawn on a four-wheeled truck by a negro.

Some ascribe these maladies to the water drunk: the Paulistas attribute the bronchocele among them to the same cause; but there is no doubt among the most enlightened physicians that the hydrocele is wholly due to the combined influence of the heat and moisture of the climate. These so relax the system that it becomes essential for young and old to wear bandages.

Girls, from diseases peculiar to them, eat earth, chalk, wax, and even the red crockery-ware or water-pots, breaking off portions and nibbling it. This appears more common than in temperate zones. The passion for these things is often so strong, and so secretly gratified, that the victims often die before their friends are aware of the cause. Some are saved by the timely application of masks. Negro girls are equally subject to this disease.

The first examples of goître I ever saw met me here—white women with monstrous swellings in front of their necks. The complaint does not appear extensively prevalent, but in the adjoining province of St. Paul's the greater part of the population is said to be subject to it.

The *Diario* of May 6th, 1846, gives the number of deaths in Rio for one year preceding, viz., 4498. Of these there were,

White males	1839	Black males		1020
" females	997	" females		642

The largest number of deaths occurred in December, and the least in March. Six hundred and sixty-seven died of tuberculosis pulmonalis. Seven hundred and ninety-five perished under the age of one year; twenty-eight had seen eighty-one years, and twelve nearly ninety; one had reached his hundred and eighth year, and three departed in their hundred and fourteenth. Very nearly two fifths of the whole expired in public institutions: one thousand and sixty-two in the Mizericordia; seventeen in the Lazaretto; one hundred and sixty-one in the Marine Hospital, and one hundred and one in the Military Hospital; thirty eight in the House of Correction; three hundred and forty-five in the House of Exposed Infants; five in the City Prison; and fifty-one bodies "found drowned." Nineteen died in religious convents.

From this account of Death's doings, the population of Rio may, to a certain extent, be inferred. That the climate is favorable to prolonged life is evident from the foregoing facts.

The national income is stated at nearly thirteen millions of dollars, and the expenses at fourteen and a quarter millions. Last year (1845) the deficit was about four millions. The emperor's salary is four hundred thousand dollars; the empress receives forty-eight thousand; the emperor's sister, Joinville's wife, has a pension of fifty one thousand dollars per annum, and the emperor's mother-in-law twenty-five thousand; the infant prince, six thousand; Amelia, a half-sister, three thousand, etc. Such is the provision for the bodies of the imperial family, while for their souls forty-five thousand four hundred and thirty-eight dollars are expended annually on the little Imperial Chapel alone. There are forty-eight public schools in the Municipio da Corte, thirty-one for girls and seventeen for boys, which are sustained at a cost of eighteen thousand four hundred and sixty dollars. In last year's budget the amount was nineteen thousand two hundred dollars.

The police of Rio is military. The men, enlisted for some years, are drilled and commanded by army officers. They are mostly colored. They are considered expert, and so, indeed, are the thieves. A rich old lady at Boto-Fogo was often visited by the old king and his family. One evening a number of carriages drove up, with attendants in regal livery. The party entered, seized and secured the lady and servants, rifled the house, and departed. Two of them, in livery, stood at the door the whole time, as if in attendance on their masters. Last year, on the eve of St. Anthony, a gang entered a house, and while some plundered it, others stood on the balcony firing off rockets, like the neighbors, in honor of the saint.

There are few capital punishments in Rio. Several years have elapsed since a white person was executed.

It is said there is little demand for native literature, and less encouragement to meet that little. The *Minerva Brasiliense*, a very interesting miscellany, has, after a feeble existence of two years, recently expired.

I was shown seven beautiful colored lithographs of native birds, the first of a contemplated series by a Brazilian Audubon. I regret that his name has escaped me. Rich in enthusiasm, but poor in pecuniary means, he no sooner realizes a few milreis than he starts for the woods, studies the habits and attitudes of each living subject, draws it, shoots it, and returns to transfer his figures to stone. He has not subscribers enough to meet his very moderate wants.

The public library contains about eighty thousand volumes, and occupies a building formerly belonging to the Carmelites. As these friars, in the contest for independence, adhered to Portugal, the premises were seized for public purposes, Pedro at that time being strongly disposed to rid the country of every monk in it. The library is an honor to the city. Every person in decent attire, white or colored, has free access; and if he wishes to make extracts, pens, ink, and paper are furnished. I seldom found more than half a dozen visitors, and the majority were young men of color—a fact corroborative of what I had repeatedly heard of the ambitious character of this part of the population.

Rio has four daily (morning) papers. The *Diario* is the oldest one in Brazil, being in its twenty-fifth year. It is a sheet twenty-six inches by eighteen, and has an extensive patronage. Devoted chiefly to domestic affairs, its notices of Church and other matters are interesting to inquiring strangers. To city subscribers twelve, and to country do. sixteen milreis per annum.

The *Sentinel of Monarchy*, of limited circulation.

The *Jornal do Commercio*, the largest sheet, has the widest circulation. It is twenty-nine by twenty-two inches, in its twenty-first year, ably edited by its French proprietor, and justly considered the best conducted and chief commercial paper in the country. It is the organ of the government, and published every morning except on holy days, a term which does not include Sundays. To its city patrons the charge is twenty milreis, and when sent into the provinces twenty-four do.

O Mercantil, of the same dimensions, is put at a lower price, sixteen milreis. It is eleven years old, and is pushing its claims to official patronage on the ground of being entirely a native sheet.

The character of the Brazilians, I should say, is that of a hospitable, affectionate, intelligent, and aspiring people. They are in advance of their Portuguese progenitors in liberality of sentiment and in enterprise. Many of their young men visit Europe, others are educated in the United States; add to this an increasing intercourse with foreigners — the means ordained by Divine Providence for human improvement — and who does not rejoice in their honorable ambition, and in the career opened before them? It must be remembered, however, that no one people can be a standard for any other, for no two are in the same circumstances and conditions. The influence of climate, we know, is omnipotent, and from their occupying one of the largest and finest portions of the equatorial regions, it is for them to determine how far science and the arts within the tropics can compete with their progress in the temperate zones. As respects progress, they are, of Latin nations, next to the French. In the Chambers are able and enlightened statesmen, and the representatives of the empire abroad are conceded to rank in talent with the embassadors of any other country. As for material elements of greatness, no people under the sun are more highly favored, and none have a higher destiny opened before them. May they have the wisdom to achieve it.

Among lithographic scenes of life in Rio, designed and published by native artists, those relating to the slaves are not the least conspicuous. There is no more fastidiousness, that I observed, about portraying them in shackles than in their labors and their pastimes. The one at the head of the opposite page represents common punishments: a negra in a mask, and a negro wearing the usual pronged collar, with a shackle round one ankle, and secured to a chain suspended from his waist.

LIFE IN BRAZIL.

It is said slaves in masks are not so often encountered in the streets as formerly, because of a growing public feeling against them. I met but three or four, and in each case the sufferer was a female. The mask is the reputed ordinary punishment and preventative of drunkenness. As the baril is often chained to the slave that bears it, to prevent him from selling it for rum, so the mask is to hinder him or her from conveying the liquor to the mouth, below which the metal is continued, and opposite to which there is no opening.

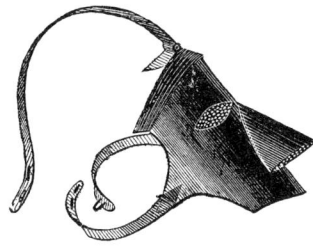

Observing one day masks hanging out for sale at a tin and sheet iron store, I stopped to examine them, and subsequently borrowed one, from which the annexed sketch is taken. Except a projecting piece for the nose, the metal is simply bent cylinder-wise. Minute holes are punched to admit air to the nostrils, and similar ones in front of the eyes. A jointed strap (of metal) on each side goes round below the ears (sometimes two), and meets one that passes over the crown of the head. A staple unites and a padlock secures them.

At most of the smiths' shops collars are exposed, as horse-shoes are with our blacksmiths; at one shop in Rua das Violas there was quite a variety, with gyves, chains, etc. Most of the collars were of five-eighths-inch round iron, some with one prong, others with two, and some with none except a short upright tubular lock.

Here, too, were the heaviest and cruelest instruments of torture—shackles for binding the ankles and wrists close together, and consequently doubling the bodies of the victims into the most painful and unnatural positions. Had I not seen them, I could hardly have thought such things were. While making a memorandum of their form and dimensions, the proprietor or his adjutant, a black man, in his shirt sleeves, came from the rear, and handling them, spoke by way of recommending them, supposing I was a customer. They were made of bar iron, *three inches wide and three eighths of an inch thick!*

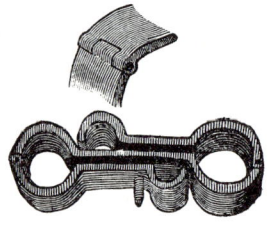

Each consisted of three pieces, bent, jointed, and fastened, as shown in the margin. The large openings were for the legs, the smaller for the wrists. A screw-bolt drew the straight parts close together. One of the joints is shown above. The distance from joint to joint was two feet.

Such are the tortures which slaves privately endure in the cellars, garrets, and out-houses of their masters. T——, a native merchant, says another common punishment is to inclose the legs in wooden shackles or stocks. Some owners fasten their hands in similar devices, and some, again, retain relics of the old thumb-screws to lock those members together. In the northern provinces, he says, the slaves are much worse used than in Rio; that it is no uncommon thing to tie their hands and feet together, hoist them off the ground, and then " beat them as near to death as possible." A heavy log fastened by a chain to the neck or leg of a slave who has absconded, or who is supposed to be inclined to run away, is a usual punishment and precaution. He is compelled to labor with it, laying it on the ground when at work, and bearing it under his arm or on his shoulder when he moves.

I observed one day a slave wearing a collar, the largest and roughest of hundreds I have seen. It is represented in the margin. Of inch round iron, with a hinge in the middle, made by bending the metal of its full size into loops, the open ends flattened and connected by a half-inch rivet. The upright bar terminated in a *death's head*, which reached above that of the wearer, and to it another piece,

in the form of the letter S, was welded. The joint galled him, for he kept gathering portions of his canvas shirt under it. Rest or sleep would seem impossible.

A Bahian planter, the brother of an ex-councilor, dined with us one day, and spoke with much freedom on slavery. With most men, he thinks the land can never be cultivated in the northern provinces by whites. The city slaves of Bahia, he said, are principally Minas. Shrewd and intelligent, they preserve their own language, and by that means organize clubs and mature schemes of revolution which their brethren of Pernambuco have repeatedly attempted to carry out. Some write Arabic fluently, and are vastly superior to most of their masters. In the interior, he remarked, the slaves are badly fed, worse clothed, and worked so hard that the average duration of their lives does not exceed six years. In some districts it reaches to eight, while the number that see ten years after leaving Africa is small indeed. Deceptions are played off on foreign agents of the Slavery Commissions. These visit the Engenhos once or twice a year. The planters, informed when they set out, have their slaves decently garbed and *well oiled*, to make them look supple and in good condition. On a late visit, the examiners were so highly gratified that one left, and wrote home a flattering account of the treatment of the helots. The other continued his inquiries, came to a fazenda where he was not looked for, and there beheld what he did not expect—a negro about to be *boiled to death* for some act of insubordination. His owner had invited, according to custom in such cases, neighboring proprietors to witness the tragedy.

From the little I have seen, I should suppose the country slaves are the worst off. Every morning, while nature was enshrouded in blackness of darkness, did I hear them driving wagons through the thick mist, and as late as ten at night were they shouting at the oxen as the jolting and groaning wheels rolled by. (This was, however, in the busiest season.) I often wondered how they found their way over the horrid roads, how their naked feet and limbs escaped unharmed, and how they then worked in the fields, unless their pupils had the expansile and contractile powers of night animals.

On large estates, a few days' rest are given them every three or four weeks during the sugar season, but on smaller ones, where owners commonly have difficulty to keep out of debt, they fare badly, and are worked to death. Staggering into their huts, or dropping where their labors close, hardly do their aching bones allow the Angel of Sleep to drive away the memory of their sorrows, than two demons, lurking in the bell and lash, awaken them to fresh tortures. To say these poor creatures are better off than when ranging their native lands is an assertion that language lacks the power justly to describe. It may be true, if the life of an omnibus hack is better than that of a wild horse of Texas. I would rather, a thousand times, be a sheep, pig, or ox, have freedom, food, and rest for a season, and then be knocked on the head, than be a serf on some plantations. I say *some,* because there are in Brazil, as in other lands, humane planters.

Suicides continually occur, and owners wonder. The high-souled Minas, both men and women, are given to self-destruction. Rather than endure life on the terms it is offered, many of them end it. Then they that bought them grind their teeth and curse them, hurl imprecations after their flying spirits, and execrate the saints that let them go. If individuals are ever justified in using the power Heaven has placed in their hands to terminate at once their earthly existence, it must be these. Those who blame them for putting the only barrier between them and oppression could not endure half their woes. And how characteristic of human frailties! Here are slave-dealers who weep over the legendary sufferings of a saint, and laugh at worse tortures they themselves inflict; who shudder at the names of old persecutors, and dream not of the armies of martyrs they make yearly; who cry over Protestants as sinners doomed to perdition, and smile in anticipation of their own reception in the realms above by Anthony and Loyala, Benedict and Becket.

Rich people who lose a slave by suicide or flight scarcely feel the loss, but to many families the loss is ruinous. There are not a few that live on the earnings of one or two helots. The papers are constantly noticing the flight of slaves who have manumitted themselves by escaping across a river their oppressors dare not attempt, since they there become denizens of a country in which Brazilian process can not be served. They unsheath their spirits, and leave the scabbards for their masters.

It is only suicides reported by the police that become publicly known. Were all recorded, every issue of the daily press would, I am told, contain more or less. Instances that have occurred within the last few weeks are here taken from the *Diario*.

June 22–24. " In the parish of Sta. Anna, an inquest was held on the body of the black, Justo, who killed himself by hanging. He was the slave of Major José de Paiva e Silva. Also on the body of the slave Rita, who destroyed herself by drowning. The body of a black, in a state of putrefaction, was found, thrown ashore by the tide, on the beach near the Public Garden."

July 1. The body of one was found near the Carioco Fountain; another, a female, in another parish, had released her spirit with a rope—" suicidou-se com um baraço." *July* 5. Another, in a fit of despair, precipitated himself from an upper window upon a mass of granite. 23*d*. The slave Luiz Pharoux killed himself with a rope. 24*th*. The slaves Pedro and Camillo by strangulation. *August* 1. Another drowned himself on the Praya Manoel. On the 4th, my last day in Brazil, one was lying on the rocks at the city end of the Gloria Beach, washed up by the tide. He was apparently under thirty years of age. As I stood looking down on him, a Mozambique girl came along, put her basket on the low wall near me, dropped a tear on the corpse, and passed on.

When the means of suspension are not at hand, it is no unusual thing for high-minded Africans, of both sexes, to expire under circumstances surpassing aught that history records. Some draw ligatures tight round their throats, lie down, and deliberately die. Others, I am told, have the art of folding back their tongues so as to prevent respiration, and thus resolutely perish.

I dined one Sunday with a party at the beautiful and hospitable retreat of Messrs. M—— and M'G——, at Boto-Fogo. Strolling alone up an adjacent mount, I was very much startled by two of the most frightful-looking and importunate of human beings rushing suddenly out of the bushes in front of me. Negroes of middle age, and wholly naked, except filthy rags round their loins, each had an iron ring about his neck connected by an ox-chain to shackles at his ankles. By another chain one hand of each were locked together. They bent forward, kneeled, held out their arms, sobbed, cried, screamed, and made such frightfully agonizing supplications, that I have often thought neither criminals condemned to die, nor even souls in Purgatory, could make more moving appeals. Poor fellows! I did not make out what they asked for—money, victuals, or intercession with their master, the owner of the hill and of a neighboring quarry, in which he employed over two hundred slaves. These two had attempted to escape, and, when not at work, were ordered to this sequestered spot and forbidden to leave it.

August 5. After taking leave of friends, communion with whom will ever be among the most precious of reminiscences, I went on board the Mazeppa, and bade farewell to one of the richest sections of the planet.

Rumors of war with Mexico rendered a convoy desirable, and the old Constitution escorted us home. Besides our vessel, there were five others, brigs and barks, bound for Baltimore, Philadelphia, and New York. To each vessel the commodore sent instructions and drawings of flags by which he would communicate with her. It may interest landsmen to know how an intelligent correspondence is kept up between vessels at great distances apart. A red flag hoisted on board the frigate was an intimation that she was about to communicate with our vessel; a blue one told us to "*wear ship;*" a red one, with a square patch in the centre, to "*tack ship;*" a flag half blue and half white, diagonally separated, "*close in with the Constitution;*" a white flag, with a blue cross extending over it, "*come within hail;*" red and blue, diagonally divided, "*heave to;*" red and white, diagonal, "*make sail;*" all white, "*shorten sail;*" a flag of four equal squares, two diagonal ones red and two white, "*haul by the wind,*" etc.

Our night-signals were guns and blue-lights. If we fell in with a strange vessel in the night, we were to signal the frigate with two of the latter.

At 4 P.M. the Constitution showed the jack at the fore and

fired a gun—the signal for sailing—and presently every vessel was under weigh, following the frigate out.

Rough weather set in, and dispersed us as chaff; it continued, and swept away our fowls, turkeys, and boats, and five days after starting, so far from having progressed a mile homeward, we were leagues south of Rio. On the ninth the frigate was in sight, or, as the sailors expressed themselves, the old hen and four of her chickens, from her gathering the fleet about her. I had a sloth, a large lizard, and a paca on board. The former began to strengthen the prophecies of some friends that it would not live through half the voyage; the others seemed unaffected by the sea.

One day I was much interested for two hours in watching a couple of Cape pigeons playing round the ship. They wheeled across the bows, turned close under the stern, sometimes within seven feet of me, tame, apparently, as street pigeons. Their movements, and those of the small gulls in Rio Bay, almost convinced me that some element of buoyancy and of progress, other than the mechanical operation of their wings, is called into action. Without vibrating their expanded wings (I was close enough to detect the slightest flicker), they rose, descended, skimmed along the water surface, shot up, and wheeled again and again. They move those organs less than any birds I have seen, though I am told the albatross resembles them in that respect.

We crossed the line on the 19th of August, with all the fleet in sight. On the 27th the sloth died. I fed it with thin slices of yam after bananas gave out, but it pined gradually away, hanging by the stick on which it was brought out of the woods. After a voyage of fifty days we landed at New York, our comrades having dropped off at Chesapeake Bay and Cape Henlopen, while the frigate passed on to Boston.

APPENDIX.

A.

ILLUSTRATIONS OF ANCIENT SOUTH AMERICAN ARTS: POTTERY.—STONE-WARE AND WORKS IN METAL UNDER THE INCAS.—MODERN CARVINGS.

Relics of American arts are of peculiar interest, inasmuch as they are connected with the solution of one of the greatest problems in human history. Here is one half of the planet without a page of written record, without legends or traditions. From its first occupancy, at a period whose date no one can tell or even conjecture, down to comparatively recent days, it presents to the historian, instead of a chronicle of dynasties, of stirring actions and mighty events, a huge and silent blank—not the name of an individual, nor the sound of a footfall, preserved. Comparatively speaking, it was but yesterday that the continents were discovered, and the fact of their being in possession of a peculiar race proclaimed to the rest of the world; and now, as then, there is little more information to be obtained from the Indians respecting their predecessors than from the native quadrupeds. Whatever is to be known has to be drawn out of the ground; out of what the plow turns up; what mounds, graves, and existing earth-works may disclose, and what architectural ruins may afford. These are the only archives remaining of the deeds and destinies of the old inhabitants of the hemisphere; and hence every thing registered in them, however trifling under other circumstances it might be considered, has a value proportioned to the insight it may give into national or social habits and conditions.

The American aborigines are melting away. A change in terrestrial occupancy on such a scale is an episode unparalleled in the history of our globe; and though we who live during its accomplishment are in a manner indifferent to its magnitude, and to its bearings on the destinies of the species in coming times, it will be discussed and referred to in the distant future as one of ever-memorable significance.

Poor themselves, the red tribes have made others wealthy. Besides bequeathing to us the richest of earthly inheritances, their contributions to the great staples of commerce are unprecedented. To say nothing of the fur-trade, nor of the metals in unparalleled profusion, of bread-plants they gave us the potato, maize, and mandioca; of poultry, the turkey is an example; and of raw materials for manufactures, india-rubber is another. Of timber for ship-building and furniture, we are indebted to them for mahogany, rose, satin, and at least two hundred varieties of ornamental and dye woods. In medicine, quinine, jalap, and ipecacuanha readily occur, besides a list of plants, including tobacco, which have become necessities to such a degree that nations would stand aghast if threatened to be deprived of them. To a people to whom we owe so much, the least we can do is to gather up for posterity whatever memorials of them may fall in our way.

General Alvares, the last Spanish political chief and commandant of the province of Cuzco, made up during his administration a varied and valuable collection of antiques. Arriving at Rio de Janeiro (on his way to Spain), he disposed of them there. To the politeness of the purchaser—Señhor Barboza, a Brazilian gentleman of great learning and of antiquarian tastes—I was indebted for opportunities to examine them. No account of them has been published till now, and it is doubtful if any modern volume contains a finer assemblage of antiquities of the kind.

For the purposes of classification and description, the articles are arranged in groups, according to the principal material in each, while the accompanying illustrations may be viewed as so many pattern-cards of pottery, stoneware, hardware, works in silver, gold, and *champi* (said to be an alloy of copper and gold, or of copper and silver).

Earthenware.

The first figure, *a*, is of special interest, from its historical associations, and the light it reflects upon one of the modes by which Peruvians perpetuated the features and characters of prominent men. A drinking-vessel of a reddish clay, it stands nine inches high, has an internal depth of six inches, and is two inches across the mouth. It belongs to a class of vessels of which, it is supposed, there are not over two or three extant, viz., vase-busts. It represents the head of the famous Cacique *Ruminhauy*. The features are strongly developed, and with indisputable traits of an individual's portrait. A deep wound is shown on the right cheek; the eyes and upper teeth are prominent; a front tooth is left out, and the place for it distinctly marked. The hair is dressed in plaited cords. The ears are small, unpierced, and well modeled, the upper lobes being level with the under eyelids. The border of the tire or head-dress is handsomely notched in front and twisted behind. The round base, as well as the rest, was modeled by hand, and by the hand of an expert too. It will be remembered that in the Old World baked clay busts and relievos preceded marble statuary.

Instead of carousing, like the savage Scandinavians, and others professing more refinement, from the skulls of the conquered, the Peruvians employed these harmless imitations, and anticipated a branch of art which modern potters might usefully extend much farther than they have yet attempted.

Ruminhauy, or Rumminaui, stands out in horrid relief in the Commentaries of Garcilasso de la Vega. After the death of Atahualpa, he schemed to succeed him. With this view he invited the brother of the murdered Inca, his sons and daughters, and some chiefs whom he could not rely on, to a feast, at which he introduced, besides the ordinary drinks, a spirituous liquor named *sora*. His object was accomplished. His guests indulged in it, became intoxicated and helpless, and he slew them. He covered a drum with the skin of Atahualpa's brother, leaving the scalp hanging to it. He subsequently buried alive a number of females, old and young, under circumstances of unusual barbarity. "Thus did this barbarous tyrant discover more unhumane cruelty and relentless bowels by this murther committed on poor silly women, who knew nothing but how to spin and weave, than by his bloody treachery practiced on stout soldiers and martial men. And what farther aggravates his crime was, that he was there present to see the execution of his detestable sentence, being more pleased with the objects of his cruelty, and his eyes more delighted with the sad and dismal sight of so many perishing virgins, than with any other prospect. * * * * * Thus ended these poor virgins, dying only for a little feigned laughter, which transported the tyrant beyond his senses. But this villainy passed not unpunished, for after many other outrages he had committed during the time of his rebellion against the Spaniards, and after some skir-

APPENDIX. 447

EARTHENWARE.

mishes with Sebastian Belalcaçar (who was sent to suppress him, as we shall hereafter relate), and after he had found by experience that he was neither able to resist the Spaniards, nor yet, by reason of his detestable cruelties, to live among the Indians, he was forced to retire with his family to the mountains of *Antis*, where he suffered the fate of other tyrannical usurpers, and then most miserably perished."

The second figure, *b*, has been modeled after the head of the jaguar. Of a darker red than the preceding, it is ornamented with black lines and spots. There are two openings into this vessel, one at the left ear, through which it was charged, and a small one at the back, near the bottom, to draw off the contents. Capacity, three pints. *c*, another red vase, whose form and ornaments indicate good taste in the artist, whoever he was. On the opposite side the remains of a painted panel are visible, and within it the figures marked *c'*. *d*, *d'*, are front and edge views of a flat bottle, eight inches in diameter. Of a bright red, the upper half is ornamented with black, white, greenish, and purple lines (not shown in the figure). Two cobras, or double-headed snakes, are on each side. The vase *e* is ornamented all round, but less on the side represented. It has three features characteristic of vessels carried about the person: loops to sling it by, a conical bottom, and a stud projecting from the swell equidistant from each loop. Whatever was the object of these studs, they seem to have been carried next the person, since they are always found on the plain or least decorated sides. Besides the loops, a couple of small holes are made in ears close to the rim, as if to pass twine through. The vase *f* has been employed in heating liquids; marks of fire are perceptible. Most of the colored ornaments are gone. *g* is a beautifully-formed vase. The stud is colored white, and the panel is drawn in black on the usual pale-red surface. The capacity about three pints. *h* is somewhat smaller, of the same general outlines, but differing in colored ornaments. *i*, a square bottle of the same material as all the preceding. It is seven inches high, and four across each side. The top is flat, projects a little all round, and more so at the corners. The contents were poured in at the top, and drawn out at the small opening near the bottom. Both openings are protected by raised borders. This vase, so like those in modern liquor-cases (the second figure *b*, and probably others), was certainly not designed to hold water, but for keeping more precious liquids, and spirituous liquors in all probability. That the Peruvians had such is well known. Acosta says of one that it induced intoxication much quicker than wine; and the strength of *sora* was such as almost instantly to prostrate those that indulged in it. Its use was prohibited by several of the Incas, under the penalty of death. *j*, *j'* are front and end views of a vase in the form of a shield, of very small dimensions. *k*, a minute bottle, rather roughly formed, decorated with lines sunk in the surface. *l*, a traveling-vase. The face is well brought out, and the whole elaborately painted. *m*, a larger one, holding near two quarts, and elaborately ornamented. *n* is of a yellowish clay, and has been profusely embellished; but, except traces of the pencil here and there, all is obliterated. The lip has a recess to receive a plug. This bottle is supposed to be the oldest in the collection. *o*, a minute pitcher, but prettily embellished in black and yellow. Having a rounded and convex bottom, it was necessarily suspended by the handle. *p*, another bottle with a flat bottom, nearly five inches in diameter, and of the same height, neck included. The front part has been tastefully painted, and the large handle also. The weight scarcely exceeds a quarter of a pound. *q*, a long-necked bottle without a handle, and designed for a traveler, as the loops and stud declare. The opposite side is decorated; the one shown is left plain. This vase is nearly eight inches high, of which the neck makes four inches. At the swell it is four and a half inches in diameter. *r*, a drinking-cup not quite four inches high. The diameter at top is rather less, and at bottom two inches. A golden cup from the tomb of an Inca is of precisely the same figure, but less than half the size, and raised without solder from a flat piece of exceedingly thin metal. *s*, *t*, *u*, *v*, *w*, *x*, *y*, are specimens of thirteen plates or shallow pipkins, varying from three to thirteen inches across, and rarely exceeding half an inch in depth. Most of them have handles, terminating with the head of a bird.

All are ornamented within, none without. The colors are black, red, white, and yellow, the last looking like unburnished gold. Except such as have recurved or ring-shaped handles, all have studs at the rims ; and some of these projections have small perforations, probably to insert loops of twine to suspend them against the walls, instead of resting them on shelves. Those marked s, t, were found in 1820 in a huaca near Saint Sebastian, one league from Cuzco. z and a 1 are of stone-like texture. a 3, a pot or crucible cover ; a fox's head imitated on the handle. To this ancient pottery I have added a modern Peruvian specimen, a 2, a small vase in my possession. Its material, a red clay, is similar to that of the preceding. It is rudely formed, ill burnt, and the ornamental work immeasurably worse done than what the old potters turned out.

There were a few other small matters intended for the preceding group of figures, but which have been accidentally omitted. One was a whistle formed in the body of a small bird of baked clay. The relic was very old, and the head missing. The tone was shrill and clear, and was pleasantly modified by partially or wholly closing with the finger an opening in the breast. There were also two whistles of cocoa-wood ; one gave a triple sound, and was little larger than a thimble.

On casting a parting glance over this invoice of pottery, and bearing in mind that only samples of plates and saucers are inserted, it may appear surprising that such numbers of fragile articles should have reached us without being damaged, after passing through dark, turbulent, and indefinite periods of time. But there is something which explains that. By a superstition indigenous to all lands, people without records have left their annals in their graves. In the belief that their wants and occupations would be the same in the spirit land as they were here, they had their household and personal effects interred with them. Every Inca had his cooking utensils in his cemetery ; not only his gold and silver ware, but, observes the native historian, "the plates and dishes of his kitchen." We can scarcely regret the prevalence of a delusion which has been the means of making us acquainted with the arts and habits of peoples of whom we could otherwise have known little, and posterity nothing—that is, by our making a proper use in this life of things which they foolishly laid up for another. Indeed, those things seem intended by Providence as agents for preserving a knowledge of the successive stages of human progress till barbarism is no more.

Utensils in Stone and Wood.

I have here thrown together in outline a number of utensils whose use is not ascertained. All, save one, are carved in stone, and, with a single exception, modeled after the llama and its relatives—the alpaca, huanaco, and vicuna. It is difficult to imagine them any thing else than mortars or salt-cellars. The cavities are represented by dotted lines. The bottoms of all are flat, and hence they were evidently designed to stand alone, and to be used in the positions in which they are figured. There were *twenty-one* in the collection. Those omitted presented no peculiar features. (See next page for illustrations.)

The first one, marked C, is the largest, being six and a half inches long and four inches deep. It is of gray basalt. The cavity is two inches deep, and three fourths of an inch in diameter at the top, but rather wider below. The whole is well polished, and the surface mottled. B is three inches long, one and a half deep, and as wide across the body. The stone is veined, and of a yellow tint, inclining to green. It is jasper. A. Polished schistus ; the upper half black, and the under a palish yellow. The body two inches long, and not quite so deep. (It is drawn too large). D and K. Both of schist ; the former black, the latter darkish brown.

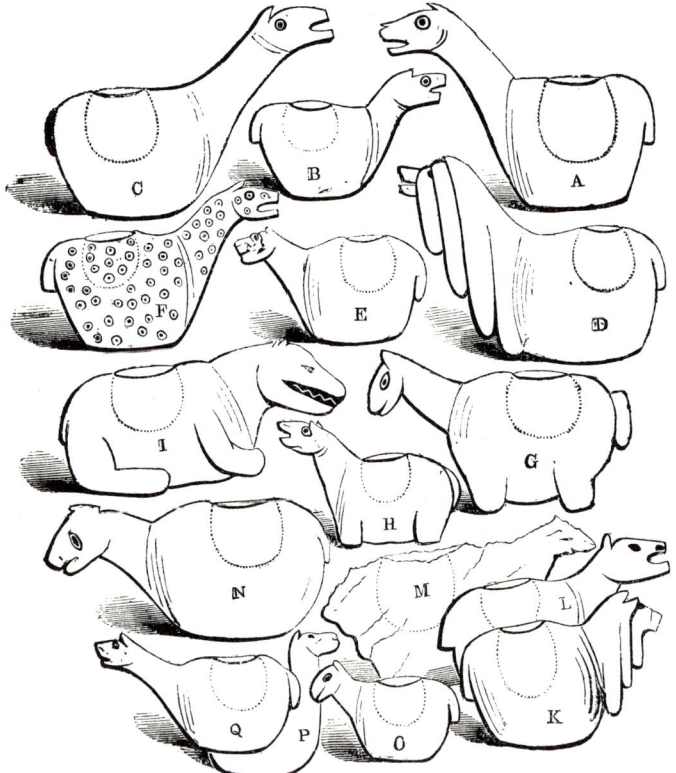

UTENSILS IN STONE AND WOOD.

E, of alabaster; the cavity is less than an inch in depth, and not quite half an inch in diameter. F is schist, or soapstone; surface black, and covered with rings scratched on it, with dots in their centres. G, H, L, O, P, Q, of various stones— two of steatite; and the rest as easily cut, except one of granite. Their dimensions vary but slightly from those already given. I, a calcareous stone, wrought in imitation of a bear or hippopotamus. N is of hard *wood*, four and a half inches long, and two inches deep. The eyes are plugs of *gold*, of the form and position represented. M is one of a couple whose lineaments have become almost entirely destroyed by time.

An extract from Von Tschudi will add to the interest of these relics:

"Under the dynasty of the Incas, when any useful plant and animal was an object of veneration, the Peruvians rendered almost divine worship to the llama and his relatives, which exclusively furnished them with wool for clothing, and with flesh for food. The temples were adorned with large figures of these animals, made of gold and silver, and their forms were represented in domestic utensils of stone and clay. In the valuable collection of B. C. Von Hägel, of Vienna, there are *four* of these vessels, composed of porphyry, basalt, and granite, representing the four species, viz., the llama, alpaca, huanaco, and vicuna. These antiquities are exceedingly scarce, and when I was in Peru I was unable to obtain any of them.

APPENDIX. 451

How the ancient Peruvians, without the aid of iron tools, were able to carve stone so beautifully, is inconceivable."

Implements and Utensils in Stone.

In the following group, the first figure, A, represents a small and neatly-cut stone vessel. I think it was used over the fire. It is only four inches in diameter, and one and a half inches in depth. B is a pestle, of hard and finely-grained granite, and black with age. A wild cat, or panther, is sculptured on the upper part, and forms a not inconvenient handle. C, a round, black, and exceedingly hard stone, regularly formed as in a lathe, is nearly seven inches in diameter, and three and a half inches deep. It is a mortar; the cavity indicated by the dotted lines. D, D', a view and section of a silversmith's crucible. E is another. One was of clay, the other of a species of soapstone. Neither exceeded two inches in depth or diameter.

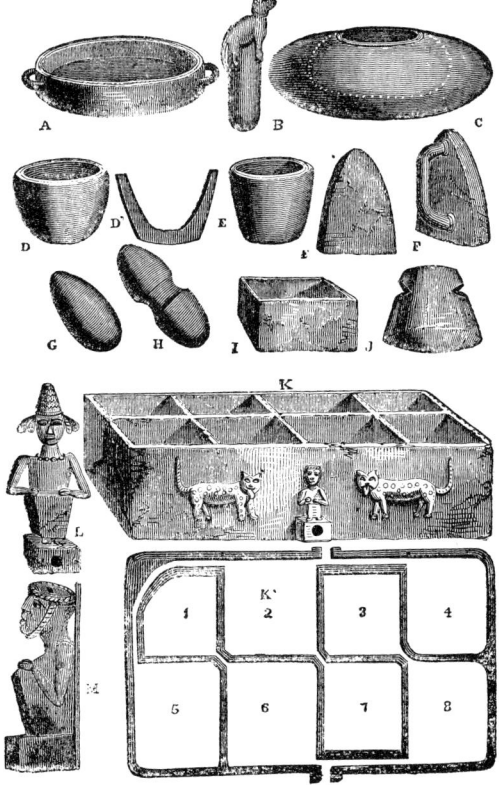

IMPLEMENTS AND UTENSILS IN STONE.

I am not aware of any large-sized ancient crucibles having been recovered; yet the old founders had them, since they turned out castings of several hundred pounds' weight. Examples abound in the early historians. Gomarra mentions basins in a bath belonging to Atabalipa, "one of which weighed eight arrobas of gold, which makes two hundred weight English." In a vault at Cuzco " an entire sepulchre [coffin] of silver was dug up, so thick and massive that it was worth fifty thousand pieces of eight." A vessel of gold was accidentally found, and it weighed between two and three hundred pounds; "for the Indians make greater or less of these, as occasion requires, using them *to boil drink or liquors in.*" Now, as they had no bellows, it may be asked how such masses of metal were fused. Garcilasso states that in reducing silver from the ore, "they melted it down in *earthen or clay pots*, which they carried from place to place;" and that, instead of bellows, they used blow-pipes "made of copper, and about a yard long, the ends of which were narrowed, that the breath might pass more forcibly by means of the contraction; and as the fire was to be more or less, so accordingly they used ten or twelve of these pipes at once, *as the quantity of metal did require*. And still they continue this way, though the invention of bellows much more easier and forcibly raises the fire."

The instrument represented at F F' I naturally enough took for a smoothing-iron, or an old American substitute for that indispensable implement of our laundresses, but I was greatly mistaken. It is an ancient plasterer's trowel, cut out of one stone, handle and all. Its dimensions are those of the common sad-iron; the face being four inches by three and a half, and a little over half an inch thick. This is another of those coincidences of thought in inventors, far separated from each other by distance or by time. Indeed, every discovery of new lands and strange people has shown the uniformity of human efforts at mental and material civilization, a result that has frequently excited surprise, but which ought not, since it it unavoidable, being due not less to the earth herself and the laws impressed on her materials, than to man's organic structure. There are no mechanical, chemical, or other principles provided for one part of the globe, or for one race of men, to the exclusion of others; and hence, wherever invoked, feebly or with power, their manifestations must be more or less alike. To smooth the interior surfaces of the walls of dwellings with a coating of plaster or clay was an instinctive suggestion, and coeval with it was the idea of the plasterer's trowel, in one or more of its forms. From the remains of smooth and polished walls in Peru, Central America, and Mexico, it is probable that a finer finishing instrument than this stone one was employed—most likely one of copper or silver: modern plasterers use trowels of wood, and polish with blades of steel.

Figure G is a black, hard, and smoothly-polished stone, resembling an egg in shape, used for working sheet-metal. H is another "hollowing hammer" of ironstone, and one that might be employed with advantage by our tin, copper, and silver smiths. The groove worked round the middle was the universal device by which handles were secured to primeval stone axes and hammers, viz., by bending a hazel or other pliable rod twice round the indentation, and then twisting or lashing the two ends together. Blacksmiths to this day every where thus handle their punches and chisels. I, a box two inches long, one deep, and seven eighths wide, cut out of a soft, greenish-tinted stone. A Peruvian Indian from Cuzco says it was a salt-box. J, an axe or hatchet, two inches deep, and two wide at the blade, which is brought to a fine edge. The stone, though well polished, is not hard. K, a box or chest, divided into eight equal compartments. The material is a stone known as "Aza de Mosca," Fly's Wing. At the ends serpents are figured, and at the sides a man and woman in high relief in a sitting posture. At their feet the liquid contents were drawn out at two orifices, to which plugs or faucets were adapted. On each side a couple of tigers are sculptured, whose heads and protruded tongues stand out full an inch, their bodies being in low relief. For the

APPENDIX. 453

sake of the head-dresses, the human figures—supposed to represent an Inca and his wife—are enlarged and figured separately at L, M.

The object of this vessel is not obvious, except that it was for mixing liquids, but whether for innocent or deceptive purposes does not appear. A plan of it is below at K', showing channels of communication between the partitions at the bottom and along the sides. It will be perceived that the contents of cells 1, 6, 8, 3 were discharged at one orifice, while those of 2, 5, 4, 7 ran out at the other.

Works in Bronze.

Next in interest to a personal interview with half a dozen ancient Peruvian founders—could they be called up from the dead to hold communion with us—would be a daguerreotype picture of them in the midst of their implements and processes, and next to that are opportunities of examining articles produced by them. The information thus obtained is reliable as far as it goes; and as metallic antiques accumulate, so will our knowledge of their authors, until we shall be in possession of details of their fabrication. All the articles in the following group have been cast, and some are remarkable specimens of casting.

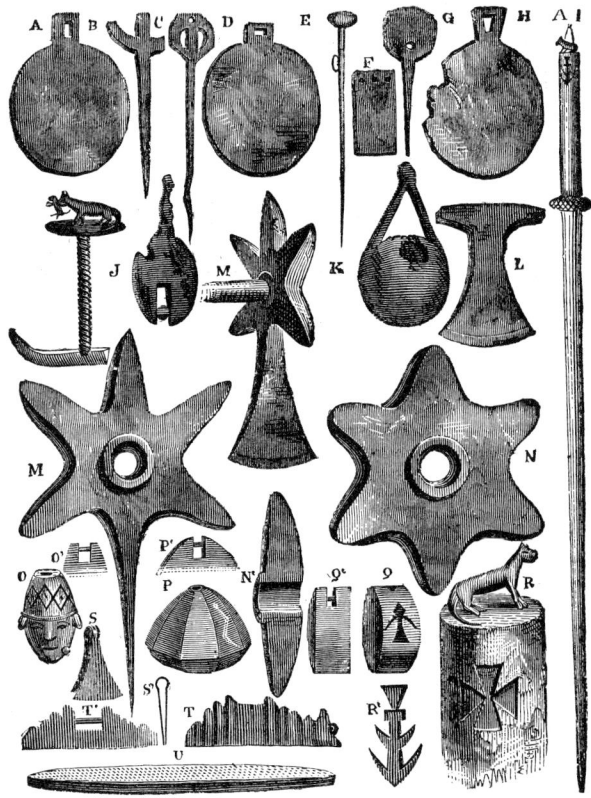

IMPLEMENTS IN COPPER AND BRONZE.

A 1, a staff of solid bronze, two feet and a half long, exclusive of the wild-cat on the end of the handle. See this end enlarged at R. The part grasped by the hand was six inches long, and nearly an inch and a half thick. Two crosses were sunk deep in it, one opposite the other, and between them two other indentations of the figure of R'. The handle terminates below in a handsome bulge or swell, inlaid with net-work of silver. The rest, being plain and tapered, requires no notice. The cord by which the staff was slung over the arm or secured to the wrist remained attached: it passed between the feet of the animal. The entire instrument was one casting.

Three kinds of official batons have been found, viz., in gold, silver, and bronze — supposed to have been borne respectively by Incas, Curacas, and Caciques — a classification that awards the one described to a chieftain of the latter class. The crosses cast in the handle recall those met with by the early discoverers, to account for which the legend of St. Thomas preaching in America was introduced. As a mythic symbol, the figure is known to be more ancient than Christianity, both in the East and the West. Whether employed as one by the aboriginies Garcilasso was uncertain. He describes a cross of jasper or marble, suspended by a *golden chain*, in the Inca's apartments at Cuzco, and much esteemed. The Spaniards seized it; and when he left his native city for Europe (in 1560), it was hanging by a *ribbon* in the vestry of the cathedral church. It was only a few fingers' breadth in size, and in form resembled that figured at R, the transverse bar being equal to and running across the middle of the upright one.

The plates A, D, H are respectively three, three and a half, and four inches in diameter, and vary from one sixteenth to three sixteenths of an inch in thickness. They are slightly concave on one side, and convex on the other. Two are of copper, and one of bronze. The difference is perceptible in their weight—the alloyed one being, of course, the lightest. One is so covered with rust as to resemble iron. I took them for mirrors; but they do not seem to have been polished. In the catalogue they are named breastplates. They are cast; and marks where the two halves of the moulds met are visible in the holes by which they were suspended. F is one of two plates of silver. B, C, E, G are bronze hair or dress pins. E, the most perfect, is four inches long, with a solid head and a rude wire ring *soldered* to the shank with *silver solder*, the first marked example of hard soldering I have met with among old American metal wares. I, a knife. A cylindrical haft three inches long, and not quite half an inch thick, connects the curved blade with a disc or button, on which a fox or *gamba* is mounted, with a prey or young one in its mouth. The surface of the haft is dented, to imitate a cord, or something like the plaited covering of a whip handle. In this particular the engraving does not do it justice. The blade is half an inch deep, and not quite one eighth of an inch thick at the back. There is positively no soldering, the whole having been cast complete. The alloy approaches, though it does not reach, the composition known as gun-metal, whose ingredients for small articles are, an ounce and a half of tin to a pound of copper, or about 10 per cent. The edge was rather easily cut by a penknife, and yet I think it was harder than gun-metal; but the difference, if any, in this respect, is satisfactorily accounted for by the well-known impurity of South American copper and tin. Both have to be refined before being used by European and American manufacturers. This was the common form of the old Peruvian knife, for numbers have been found, all bearing the same general outline. I have seen two, recently brought from Peru, which approach still nearer to the cutting instrument of saddlers, the hafts being equidistant from the ends of the blades, and the edges curved uniformly. The blade of one is two inches long, three fourths of an inch wide in the middle, and at the back is a little over one sixteenth of an inch thick; the haft is imperfectly cylindrical, an inch long, and three sixteenths thick, with the head of a llama at the end, and has a small ring for a thread, to suspend it over the wearer's neck. J, K, two views of the same thing—a minute bell, three fourths of an inch in its longest diameter, rude in fabrication, much corroded, and consequently its sonorous powers weak. A shapeless hole is in the upper part, from the metal not having been sufficiently fluid at the time of casting. A loose pebble of copper is within, and forms the clapper. This interesting article was disinterred near Cuzco in 1821. Hawks' bells, we know, were among the chief presents by which Columbus gratified the Indians of the Antilles; but it is not the less true that brass-founders on the Pacific possessed the art of making similar things, and this certainly might have been inferred from their familiarity in mixing the ingredients. They had but to double the proportion of tin used in the compounds of which their edge-tools were made. L, an axe or chopper, four inches deep, and three wide at the cutting edge, which is well formed and sharp. It has been used as a chisel, for the upper surface is partly spread out by blows, probably from a wooden mallet. The extension of the head on either side was most likely designed to serve as handles when thus employed. Though harder than copper, the edge yielded readily to a penknife. N, the bronze head of a war-club, or six-pointed mace; one of three discovered in a grave in the province of Cuzco. Two are in fine preservation, but this is somewhat corroded. The extreme diameter between two opposite rays is nearly four inches. The hole for the handle is of one inch bore, and slightly tapers. A collar is cast on the side toward the handle. (See section N'.) M has one of the rays lengthened and formed into a hatchet or war-axe, the blade of which equals in hardness I and L. The side-view, on a smaller scale, in the middle of the group, represents the same instrument. The third specimen resembled N; the rays were a little longer, and not so thick. Though less than either N or M, it was heavier and softer, being nearly pure copper.

Weapons identical with these are mentioned by old historians among arms stored for public emergencies during the sway of the Incas. "Pikes," says Garcilasso, "clubs, halberts, and pole-axes, made of silver, copper, and some of gold, having sharp points, and some hardened by the fire." Carpenters, he observes, had axes and hatchets of copper, and the sculptors cut stone with flints and hard pebbles ground to an edge.

Blas Valera, one of the earliest Spanish writers, remarks that the copper which the natives called *anta* served them in the place of iron. Of it they made knives, carpenters' tools, pins used by women on their heads and dresses, their polished mirrors, "and all their rakes and hammers," so that they worked more in mines of copper than in others, preferring it to gold and silver. It is very evident that this *anta* was bronze. Persons not practically acquainted with it would pronounce it copper, from its resemblance to that metal. The native word was probably expressive of its true character, but misunderstood by the invaders.

O, P, Q, T differ in form, yet were evidently designed for the same purpose, whatever that was. A perpendicular hole is formed on the top of each, and across it a transverse wire has been cast in a little below the surface. (See the sections O', P', Q', T'.) The one representing the head of an Indian (O) is the smallest. Solid like the rest, its weight is less than an ounce; and, though corroded, the features are well defined. The truncated conical cap is ornamented as figured; and the acullico in the mouth, or quid of coca, is shown by the little bulb or swelling. P is one inch and a quarter high, and as wide across the widest part. It is of copper. At two of its six sides a couple of minute serpents are inlaid. Q is a short cylinder, nearly an inch in diameter. An anchor-looking figure is sunk in at two opposite parts of the periphery. T is not unlike the mummy of a cat. It represents the animal "quinquincho;" is nearly two inches long. The metal is shrunk at the under side as if it had been poured into an open mould with that part uppermost. S, S', a pair of spring pincers or tweezers, one inch and a quarter long. The metal is thickest at the bend. They are little better than a bent piece of sheet copper. U, a rough ingot of bronze, sixteen inches long. It was found with the war-clubs.

Gold, Silver, Champi, &c.

1, a full-length figure of a female, in silver. It is two and a half inches high, but does not weigh as much as a quarter of a dollar, being one of those thin specimens mentioned by the early historians. I could not detect traces of soldering except at the feet. At the inside of the legs the metal laps, and is unsoldered. The head is large beyond all proportion. This mode of dressing the hair is the same in all the figures of females. Figure 2 shows how it was secured behind. 3, a bust of a hunchback, in bronze, not quite two inches high, and much corroded. The bulb in the cheek denotes the quid of coca. The weight is light in proportion to the bulk, showing that tin preponderates in the alloy. It is the best proportioned figure of the whole, and apparently the oldest. 4 and 5 are solid images, in "*champi*," one and a half inches high, and smooth and bright, as if just finished. 4 is a male, with the coca quid, and a cap with horizontal folds. The hands (imperfectly developed) are placed on the breast, the prevailing attitude. 6 shows the disposition of the hair of figure 5. The ears, large and stretched in the man, are invisible in the female. The two figures are supposed to represent a man and his wife. 7, an Indian seated on his hams, the hands resting on the ground. The cap is similar to that on figure 4; the features are rude and imperfect, and the whole much corroded. 8 and 9, two views of one image, in silver; an Inca or Cacique, with the dress and badges of his office, and the best finished, if not the best modeled figure of the whole. The head, as usual, is too large, and the arms are withered. The height is two inches, and the whole solid. Eight golden spokes radiate from the rim of the conical hat or cap, the front of which is ornamented with dotted rays. Two convex plates of gold are worn at the ears. A species of cassock passes over the shoulders, and reaches to the knees in the front and rear. An outer robe passes over it, but descends only half way. Plaits of hair, or hat-strings, hang down upon the breast. A silver baton with a swell on it is in the right hand, and something appears to have once occupied the other. 10, solid silver; a llama, size of the sketch. The joints of the moulds in which it was cast are indicated. 11, a llama or one of its congeners, two inches high, and as long. It has been worn as an ornament or jewel. A loop of silver wire is soldered at the junction of the neck and trunk, while the tail is bent to form another. Two ingots, one of silver, the other of gold, are soldered on the back of the animal, clearly showing the ancient use of the llama in transporting blocks of these metals. (The ingots are figured beneath.) At the present time llamas are of the greatest utility, as they frequently carry the metals from the mines in places where declivities are so steep that neither asses nor mules could find footing. 12 and 12*a*, another image of solid silver, less than two inches high. It is rudely formed, with the eyes, nose, and hands preternaturally large. The head is remarkably flattened, and the lobes of the ears are stretched down to the shoulders. 14, a statuette of a man, solid, nine and a half inches high, very heavy, and black with age. The nose is large and aquiline; the ears slit and stretched; the cap ribbed horizontally as in figures

APPENDIX

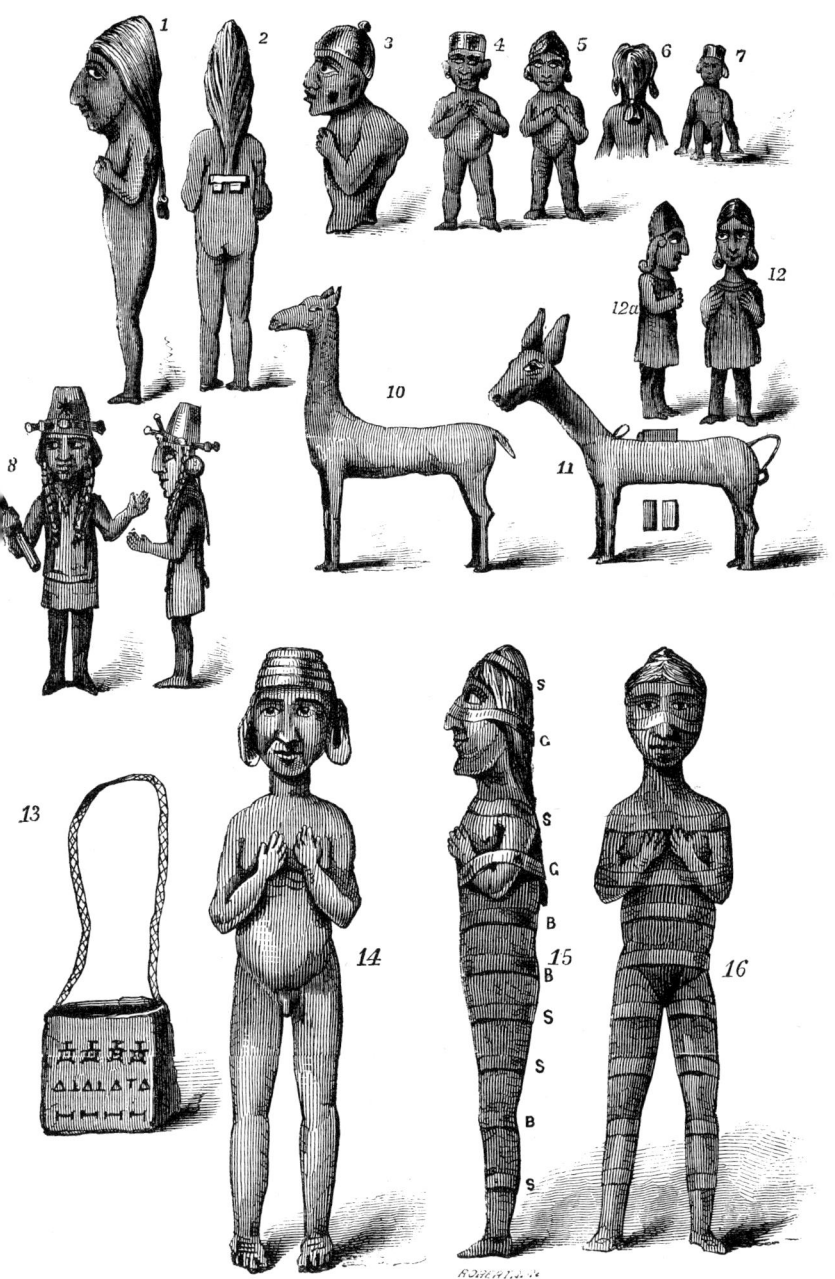

4 and 7. The material of this casting, according to the catalogue, is "*champi*," but from examination it appeared to me to be pure copper, coated or plated by some means with silver, for when the latter was cut through the copper appeared. Ridges on the inside of the thighs and legs show the meeting of the moulds. 15 and 16 are two sketches of one subject. The image is that of a female, and of the same material and dimensions as the preceding one. Both were discovered together, and are supposed to represent an Inca or cacique and his wife. A number of gold, silver, and bronze bands are let in flush with the surface. Perhaps they were places in the moulds before the metal was run in. By looking at the initial letters placed opposite these bands in figure 15, it will be seen that two are of gold, five of silver, and three of baser metal. The eyes and paps are of gold. The bands vary from three eighths to three sixteenths of an inch in width, and their ends lap over each other and are imperfectly united. Their thickness appeared in one place over an eighth of an inch. The whole figure is black; but, if scratched any where, silver appears, and when cut through, copper comes to view. The ankle-bones were quite prominent, the fingers poorly portrayed, the feet flat above, with sand-holes in several parts, and the joints of the flasks were observable, leaving no room to doubt that those essential devices in our foundries were used by old Peruvian craftsmen. 13, a *chuspa* for carrying tobacco or coca. The weft is cotton; the warp Alpaca wool. The front is eight inches square, and ornamented with figures wrought in the fabric as represented. The strap is a species of knitted work, very similar to what modern Indians produce. These bags were suspended at the left side, the straps going over the right shoulder. This relic is in tolerable preservation, although the owner, from whose body it was taken, had long been reduced to dust.

The magic effects ascribed by old writers to the use of coca—enabling men to pass days without food, and under severe labors—are testified to by modern travelers. Von Tschudi says it is in the highest degree nutritious; that with its aid miners and others undergo incredible fatigue on very spare diet; that those who are in the habit of masticating it require little food, &c. Though a powerful stimulant, and its effects on the looks of inveterate chewers any thing but attractive, its moderate use, he thinks, is not merely innoxious, but conducive to health. An Indian employed by him in laboriously digging for five days and nights, tasted no food during that time. Every three hours he chewed half an ounce of coca-leaves, and kept a quid continually in his mouth. Individuals of great age have chewed it from infancy. He refers to Indians who have attained 130 years. One, living in 1839, was 142 years old, and for 90 years had never tasted water—not a drop! During that time he had drunk only *chicha*—a filthy and intoxicating liquor. When eleven years of age, he began to chew coca three times a day, and continued the practice through the rest of his life.

The testimony of early writers is confirmed in other particulars by the preceding figures. Three things were instituted by Manco Capac to distinguish his successors—shaving the head except a single lock, wearing large ear-ornaments, and the llautu — a species of turban composed of a long strip of cloth of divers colors. The hair was removed by sharp flints; and the operation, being a painful one, led a young Inca who had undergone it to observe that, had the Spaniards introduced no other inventions than scissors, looking-glasses, and combs, they deserved all the gold and silver in the country. The llautu is seen in Figures 4, 7, 14, page 457.

When the native historian speaks of ear-rings, he means, generally, round or elliptical discs, not pendent from, but embraced within the outstretched lobe, the opening in which "was so wide that it is wonderful to conceive how it is possible

APPENDIX. 459

for the velvet of the ear to be extended so far as to receive an ear-ring as large as the block of a pulley, for it was made in the form of those with which we draw up water from a well." Figures 4, 5, 7, 8, 12, 14, page 457, show enlarged lobes, but not so perfectly as the originals. The mode of wearing jewels in them is still followed by South American tribes. The subjoined cut represents a Brazilian Indian with discs of pito wood, three inches in diameter and an inch thick, in his ears and under lip. I obtained specimens of these ligneous gems. To the tribes on

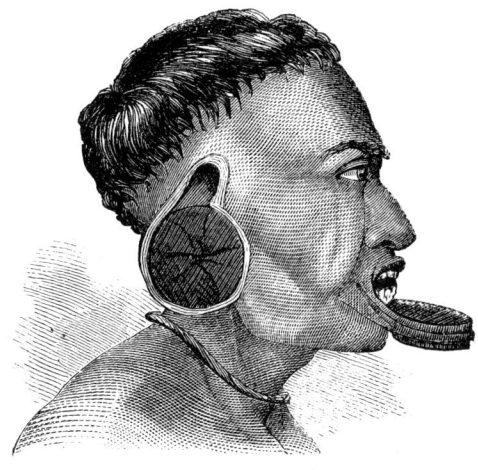

the Pacific, which had their ears thus preternaturally enlarged, the Spaniards applied the term *Oregons* or *Orejones*.* The figures on page 457, just quoted, are all thus designated in the catalogue of General Alvares. Figure 12, which, as already stated, has the lobes stretched to the shoulders, illustrates another historical passage, which informs us that barbarous tribes subdued by the Incas were accustomed to flatten the heads of their children between two boards.

Besides ordinary relics in stone, as chisels, maize-pounders, etc., there was in Mr. Barboza's collection a beautifully-wrought lip-ornament, of a bright green jade. It is a button or disc of the size of a cent, but thicker, and with a shank enlarged into a crescent, as represented in the margin. A slit is cut through the lower lip parallel with the mouth, and the shank inserted endwise, and then turned, so that the curved part rests against the gums within the lip, while the round and polished face remains without. These discs are therefore not worn horizon-

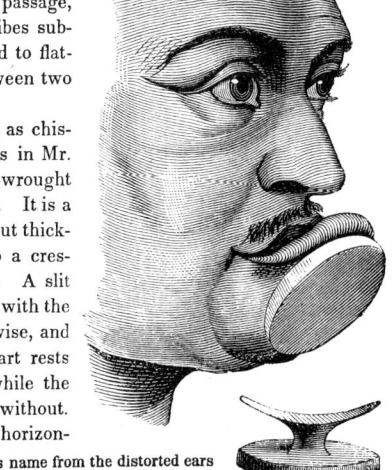

* Has the territory of Oregon derived its name from the distorted ears of its early inhabitants?

460   APPENDIX.

tally, like those of the Boto-Cudos in the preceding figure. The Chiriviones of Paraguay, as well as Brazilian tribes, still wear them; in fact, they form quite an item in the early accounts of the Amazons. Jasper lip-jewels are noted by early travelers, some of whom, when they first beheld the openings in the under lips, imagined they had found men with two mouths.

A modern founder would be puzzled to cast complete—that is, without the application of a file, chisel, or other tool after the articles had left the sand—such things as figure I and A 1, page 453, and figure 8, page 457—to say nothing of others still more intricate. It is very evident that the most elaborate works in metal were solely produced by the crucible, hammer, and abrasion, to which the blowpipe in soldering, and the process of chasing must be added. The secret lies in one word—*patterns of wax*. These, plain or intricate in detail, were modeled by hand, and buried in moulds of plaster or clay, which, when dried, were heated, the wax run out, and its place filled with molten metal. Inlaid material was imbedded in the waxen type, and thereby became imbedded in the metal. This explanation accords with every ancient piece of work. It removes every difficulty, and is the only one that does.

Specimens of carving by modern Peruvians are subjoined. Figures 1 and 2 are spoons, each cut out of one piece of wood. Figure 3 is one of their knives. The blade, hammered out of hoop-iron, was secured in a slit in the haft by strong cotton twine. It is not unusual for Peruvian Indians to pass over into the southwestern provinces of Brazil with little ventures of carved wood. The specimens figured were purchased from one of the traveling artists.

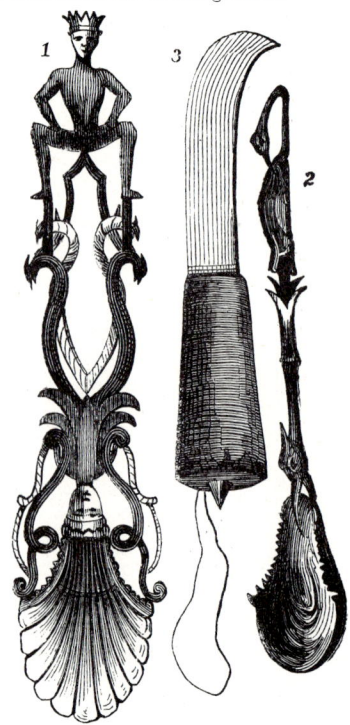

APPENDIX. 461

An appendix, by the author of this volume, to the report of the United States Naval Astronomical Expedition, now in the press, contains a description of antiquities brought from Chile and Peru by Lieutenant J. M. Gillies, commander of the expedition. The contents of an ancient huaca, near Arica, discovered and forwarded by W. W. Evans, Esq., engineer of the Arica and Tacna Rail-road, were received too late to be illustrated in the report. Some of the relics are of unusual interest in an ethnological point of view, and are introduced here.

The skulls of old Peruvians, it is said, are indicative of a peaceful people—the moral preponderating over the animal organs—and certainly their graves afford ample evidence of the fact. We find household furniture, plain and ornamental pottery, knives, spoons, pipkins, basket and wooden ware, pestles and mortars, hammers, chisels, hatchets, whetstones, agricultural products, implements of spinning and weaving, pins, needles, bodkins, caps and clothing, whistles and toys for children—these, and other instruments of male and female industry, taken in connection with the general absence of weapons of war, are pleasing tokens of domestic habits and pacific inclinations.

Seldom are data met with from which to infer the age to which ancient huacas belong. They are found in soils and locations as well calculated to preserve their contents as the catacombs of Egypt. From the character and condition of the following relics, they may have been interred, not only centuries, but decades of centuries. They consist of the household and personal effects of a family—of movables never left behind on a change of residence. Valuable on earth, they were believed to be equally desirable in the country beyond the setting sun, and were therefore packed up to accompany them thither—ears of corn, and also grains carefully sewed up in bags, to plant there, vessels to hold liquids, and others in which to boil water there, spindles to spin thread there, *bronze hooks* to catch fish, and arrows to kill game there.

Of pottery, there are several vases, some whole, others in fragments. Nos. 1 and 3 in the above group are nearly of equal capacity—about seven inches high, and six across the swelled parts. Designed for heating water, they have conical bottoms to drop into the perforated stone slabs which formed the top of old Peruvian stoves; hence the lower halves are not painted, nor are such vases ever found glazed. In texture, hardness, and material, they resemble our sand crucibles, and are possibly as well adapted to endure heat. The colors are black and red on a pale yellow ground. No. 4 is a cover or stopper to the first vase, of the same material, hollow, and pretty uniform in thickness—from one eighth to three sixteenths of an inch. Such covers are in some respects superior to our close-fitting pot-lids, since boilers could never be exploded by an accumulation of steam. While a sudden evolution of vapor might partially raise them, they could never be blown out of their seats during the absence or in the presence of the cook. No. 2 is a more perfect pitcher than I have ever met with among American antiques. It is flat-bottomed, has a loop handle, but not a contracted lip. The ground color is a dark chocolate, upon which are displayed, with considerable effect, white lines, stars, and circles. The rim is painted inside and out. Taken altogether, this vase is worthy of a place on modern tables. The material is a light reddish clay. No. 5, a small wide-mouthed and flat-bottomed bowl. No. 6, possibly a toy, since its capacity hardly exceeds that of a wine-glass.

Of the above, No. 1 resembles a tankard or quart measure in dimensions and form, with the mitred head of an Inca for a handle. The colors are black and brown on a red ground. A similar vessel, with the head and body of a monkey for a handle, was found in a grave, eleven feet below the surface, near Ariquipe, during the past year, and presented to the Smithsonian Institution by Mr. Eckel, United States Consul at Talcahuana, Chile. It is better painted and in better preservation than the one represented here. No. 2, a boiler, twice the capacity of those on the preceding page: it shows marks of the fire, and is destitute of ornament. A painted stopper closes the mouth. No. 3, a small vase for heating liquids, and No. 4, a still smaller one. No. 5, a very rough little pot, which may have served for a lamp, if lamps were used by ancient Peruvians.

The six objects in the following group are of bronze. No. 1 is a singular-looking article, and one whose use it is next to impossible to divine. At the first glance, upon its arrival, when its general and rough contour only was observable, for it was imbedded in a thick envelope of green oxide, it bore some resemblance to a sword-handle; but when the incrusted covering was removed, the relic assumed another appearance—one as much of an enigma as before. It is an elliptical band, with an opening three and a half inches one way, and an inch the other. The or-

APPENDIX. 463

namental projection at one end is slit down the middle. The figures of Incas on the broad face of the band are in a sitting posture, holding cups to their mouths, and, minute as they are, their legs, arms, and thighs are singularly relieved, considering that the article has been *cast complete*. None of our founders could produce any thing like it from their moulds. No. 2, the triangular blade of a knife, rather more than two inches across the cutting edge. A small wooden haft had been secured to it by twine, but it dropped to dust on being handled. No. 3, a fishhook, covered with blossoms of green oxide. It retains the lashing that secured it to the line, and was found on the centre of a handsome coil formed of the latter. Its shank is one inch and a quarter long. No. 4, another, about the size of a mackerel-hook. The shorter end is one inch and a half. On removing the oxide, the metallic part was found to be one eighth of an inch thick at the middle, and to taper thence to both ends. If there had been a barb at one end, and a notch or eye at the other, they were rusted away. This hook is stiff, and as difficult to bend as if made of iron. No. 5, a straight hook, the shank a little over two inches long, with a barb neatly tied on. The finely-twisted line has disappeared, except small portions imbedded in the copper rust. No. 6, a small hook, half imbedded in a portion of the line. Its size resembles those temporary hooks made by boys of pins. An attempt to remove its green envelope would destroy it.

Of the four figures on the engraving on the following page, No. 1 is a prettily-carved snuff or other mill for rubbing dry leaves to powder. It resembles current Brazilian apparatus. The shallow recess is two and a half inches by one inch. The blade is cracked in three places, and each crack has been prevented from spreading by drilling holes on each side, and binding the parts together by twine or wire. No. 2, a thin piece of hard wood, three and three quarter inches long, one and three eighths wide, three sixteenths thick at the centre, and reduced thence to the edges. In a hole in the centre a short rod remained. There were dust marks round the hole, as if the rod had been charged with thread. No. 3, a genuine ancient spindle, in good preservation. It consists of a round tapered stick, eleven inches long, pointed at both ends, with no slit or notch at the upper end. The little stone weight, a truncated cone, is identical in form with some figured on Aztec paintings. Broken and decayed pieces of thread, of llama wool, remain on the stem. No. 4, a portion of a small stone, which, from the notch cut round its pointed end, may have been used as a plumb-line or as a spindle.

464 APPENDIX.

Among other matters, there were quartz arrow-heads in a reed quiver, and remains of a sling woven in black and white squares. A variety of slings were anciently in vogue, and considerable labor and skill laid out on them. This specimen is a proof of the correctness of old historians on the subject. There were also the remains of a bronze adze in a forked stick, the fork presenting an acute angle; the film of green oxide remains attached to the part to which the blade had been attached by thongs. The implement, when perfect, resembled some recovered from Egyptian tombs. Then there were interesting remains of clothing, plain and ornamental; a child's cap, with a loop to pass under the chin; fragments of netting, of round and plaited cords; a handsomely-wrought bag, with pendent tassels, very like a modern lady's reticule; and, lastly, a *skull*, which, from its long plaited locks, may have belonged to the mother of the family. Probably within it sat the mind that contrived the useful and ornamental fabrics just mentioned, and in it revolved the eyes that watched their progressive development, from the twisting of the thread with the spindle to the finishing touches given to them by her fingers.

There is something affecting in the members of a family being thus accompanied with their little stock of valuables on their exodus from this world and their journeyings to another. Happily, they had no idea that their treasures would be stolen, and even their own bodies borne off as curiosities by people of another race.

B.

NOTICIA HISTORICA DE SANTA PRISCILLIANA VIRGEM MARTYR.

São os subterraneos de Roma uma das cousas que inspirão curiosidade a todo o estrangeiro e religioso respeito ao christão que visita a Cidade Eterna. Vinte e tantos destes lugares abertos no seio da terra, dos quaes o maior é o que tem hoje o nome de Catacumbas de S. Sebastião, que tem doze milhas de extensão nas suas diversas ruas subterraneas, onde estão enterrados cento e setenta mil christãos, martyres e não martyres, fórmão uma segunda Roma subterranea. E' inconcebivel como e para que se perfurou em todos os sentidos o baixo da terra de Roma emquanto se ignora a origem disto: desde o principio da fundação da cidade que os Romanos edificão com um barro, que chamão hoje Pozzolana, que só se encontra em uma camada geral algumas braças ao fundo da terra; e para esta extracção ião cavando o terreno em fórma de corredores de abobada; e é de tal sorte glutinoso e consistente, que não se vê um só desmoronamento no cabo de tantos seculos.

Como estas barreiras pertencião a particulares, aquelles dos proprietarios que erão christãos nos tres primeiros seculos de perseguição contra o christianismo, as convertião em asylos religiosos, onde a furto se reunião ao clarão das alampadas, exercião todos os officios da religião e enterravão os seus mortos em catacumbas abertas de um e outro lado ao longo dos corredores, como ainda hoje se conservão e se vêm; notando porém que nos jazigos dos christãos que morrêrão de morte natural não se encontra nem emblema nem epitaphio ou signal algum que o distinga; naquelles porém ondo jazem os corpos dos que morrêrão pelo martyrio lê-se o seu nome aberto em uma lapida, ou na parede que fecha a catacumba, o dia e o anno em que soffreu o martyrio, e uma palma esculpida, que o symbolisa; e em grande numero delles se encontra dentro, junto á cabeça do cadaver, um vaso com sangue e arêa, quando o podião apanhar no lugar ende o martyr cahira morto; as chronicas e as legendas dos escriptores sagrados desse tempo narrão então a historia da vida e genero de tormentos que soffrêrão esses martyres, cujos corpos se achão nesses subterraneos.

Foi só depois de trezentos annos que a religião sahio debaixo da terra e ergueu os seus altares no meio da Roma pagãa: desde então até hoje estes lugares subterraneos forão tidos na maior veneração e cuidado, porque pertencem ao dominio da historia e da religião.

Santa Priscilliana, Virgem Romano, no tempo em que Julianno Apostata, imperador, perseguia com mais raiva os discipulos da Cruz, não tinha senão 16 annos de idade, e sempre em companhia de sua piedoza mãi Santa Priscilla, que consagrára o rendimento de todos os seus bens ao serviço da caridade, se occupava fervorosamente com ella nestes exercicios pios e em prestar soccorros aos martyres durante o tempo de suas prisões e tormentos, e depois de mortos, em fazer recolher os seus cadaveres e as reliquias de seu sangue para lhes dar jazigo nas catacumbas: sorprendida na pratica desta devoção e exercicios de caridade, presa e interrogada pela sua religião, confessou a Cruz, e todos os tormentos e torturas empregadas nos debeis membros da delicada virgem de 16 annos não podérão conseguir abater a sua fé, que sustentou no meio de dôres horriveis, até que o ministro do tyranno, desesperado de nada conseguir da heroica virtude da virgem, mandou-lhe atravessar uma espada pelo pescoço, o que a fez cahir morta no meio da praça, no dia 16 de janeiro, para ir viver eternamente no céo, e na terra ser venerada como uma heroina da religião.

Os virginaes restos mortaes de Santa Virgem Martyr Priscilliana jazião em uma das catacumbas do cemiterio subterraneo de Ciriaca na via Tiburtina, e dahi forão tirados por sua eminencia o cardeal patricio, vigario geral de Roma, e concedidos, por muito especial graça de sua santidade o papa Gregorio XVI. ao Dr. Manoel Joaquim de Miranda Rego, parocho da freguezia de Santa Anna desta côrte, para os collocar na sua igreja parochial. Dentro da catacumba junto ao esqueleto de Santa Virgem, do lado da cabeça, estava um vaso de barro contendo o seu sangue com arêa, assim como foi apanhado no dia do seu martyrio, e o nome da Virgem gravado no bojo do mesmo vaso, o qual tambem foi concedido por sua santidade e se acha dentro da arca que contém as santas reliquias. O ossos de Santa Virgem

Martyr estão vestidos de um envoltorio de cêra, que a representa na sua idade de 16 annos, e só o alto da cabeça está descoberto e deixa ver o craneo da Santa Virgem.

A solemnidade da trasladação e exposição deste precioso monumento da religião, que a cidade de S. Sebastião tem a fortuna de possuir pela primeira vez, vai ter lugar logo que SS. MM. Imperiaes tenhão regressado a esta capital, na forma que dispozer a pastoral de S. Ex. Revma.

Nesse mesmo dia terá lugar a installação da irmandade de Santa Priscilliana Virgem Martyr : a sua vocação é o culto e a caridade fraterna ; cuidando da decencia da arca, onde estão depositadas as reliquias santas, fazendo celebrar uma missa solemne no dia de sua festividade ; e dotando, cada anno, segundo os fundos do cofre, a donzellas pobres, para casamento, com o dote de 600$ rs. a cada uma, em honra e gloria da Santa Virgem Martyr.

C.

CARTA PASTORAL DO EXM. SR. BISPO DO RIO DE JANEIRO, ANNUNCIANDO A PRESENÇA DO SAGRADO CORPO DA VIRGEM E MARTYR SANTA PRISCILLIANA, E ESTABELECENDO O CEREMONIAL DA TRASLADAÇÃO E DA FESTA DAS SANTAS RELIQUIAS.

D. Manoel do Monte Rodrigues de Araujo, por mercê de Deos e da Santa Sé Apostolica, bispo do Rio de Janeiro, conde de Irajá, do conselho de S. M. o Imperador, seu capellão-mór, deputado á assembléa geral legislativa pela provincia do Rio de Janeiro, grão-cruz das ordens de S. Januario e de Francisco I. do reino das Duas Sicilias, grande dignitario da imperial ordem da Roso, commendador da de Christo, etc., etc., etc.

Aos fieis que habitão esta cidade do Rio de Janeiro, graça e paz da parte de Deos Padre, e da de Nosso Senhor Jesus Christo.

Bemdizendo ao Senhor pelos beneficios que não cessa de fazer-nos, nós vamos annunciar-vos, M. C. F., um dos seus grandes favores, qui muito póde contribuir para a nosso salvação. Ao dar-vos a noticia que pretendemos, nós nos possuimos dos mesmos sentimentos, e empregaremos as mesmas palavras de S. João Chrysostomo em uma occasião semelhante : " Eu exulto de felicidade, disse elle, e o meu prazer chega até a loucura ; porém uma loucura que vale mais que a sabedoria do mundo. Eu triumpho, eu estou transportado de alegria, e o meu espirito em uma especie de arrebatamento. Que direi eu ? Como exprimir os sentimentos da minha alma ! Direi o poder dos martyres, a derrota dos demonios, a dignidade da Igreja, a virtude da Cruz, os milagres de Jesus crucificado, a gloria do Pai, a graça do Espirito Santo, a fé de todo o povo, os transportes de toda a cidade, o coro das virgens, a bella ordem dos sacerdotes, o ardor dos homens de todos os estados, dos magistrados, dos pobres e dos ricos, dos cidadãos e dos estrangeiros ?"

Assim se exprimia o grande pontifice de Constantinopla, por occasião da trasladação das reliquias de um santo martyr ; e da mesma maneira, nós vos annunciamos hoje, M. C. F., que se acha no meio de nós o corpo da virgem e martyr Santa Priscilliana ! Estes sagrados despojos, *tirados desses lugares subterraneos onde a nova Roma*, mãi dos martyres, *encerra nas suas entranhas áquelles a quem Roma idolatra*, e embriagada do sangue dos martyres perseguio ; estes sagrados despojos, nós os devemos á devoção do nosso irmão o digno parocho da freguezia de Santa Anna, e á liberalidade do pontifice reinante Gregorio XVI. !

Feliz cidade do Rio de Janeiro, que possues uma tão consideravel reliquia ! Con-

templando esses *ossos inanimados*, mas que forão objecto de uma providencia particular que os guardou, que exemplos de virtude não tens tu que aprender? Que valimento não te alcançarão elles, e quantos beneficios tu não recolherás por sua intercessão, junto áquelle que assim tem honrado aos seus santos! Abre, abre as tuas portas, e recebe com alegria, com pompa, e sobretudo com devoção, um tão precioso dom. Que os teus sentimentos nesta occasião sejão os mesmos que outr' ora animárão a população, experimentou e descreveu o santo bispo de Constantinopla.

..... S. Ex. continúa longamente tratando da vemeração e do culto que desde o principio do christianismo se tributou ás reliquias dos martyres; das heresias que no seculo XVI. se suscitárão a este respeito: da constante doutrina da igreja ensinada pelos concilios e santos padres sobre este ponto, e depois conclue assim:

..... Ainda uma reflexão sobre o culto das santas reliquias, e nós concluiremos este nosso trabalho. O culto das reliquias, será certamente mui agradavel aos Santos, cujos restos preciosos nós veneramos; mui agradavel a Deos, a quem nós louvamos, louvando aos seus santos, se por ventura esse culto tiver por objecto imitar as virtudes desses santos. Em verdade que a virtude do martyrio é heroica, e não é dado a todos aspira-la; mas quando os martyres chegavão a este gráo da fortaleza christãa, outras virtudes os havião disposto e preparado para isto. A oração, o jejum, a penitencia, a vigilancia, a piedade, a caridade, eis-aqui o que, desapegando-os desta vida, levava-os a sacrifica-la por amor de Jesus Christo. Ora, estas virtudes nós podemos imitar. Assim honravão os nosses maiores aos santos martyres, e assim cumpre que nós igualmente os honremos. Quando a celebre Agláe mandava de Roma o seu domestico Bonifacio procurar as reliquias dos martyres no Oriente, dizia lhe: "Sabei, o Bonifacio, que os corpos dos fieis que vão buscar os dos martyres devem ser puros e sem mancha; não seria honra-los não imitar as suas virtudes!

"Santa Priscilliana, cuja reliquia nós hoje veneramos, brilhou na Igreja de Deos, especialmente pelo exercicio da caridade christãa. O seu nome acha-se associado ao dessas illustres virgens e matronas romanas que nesses dias infaustos para a religiao, quando a perseguição desfechava desapiedados golpes sobre os confessores da fé, ellas os assistião com as suas orações com auxilios temporaes, pensavão-lhes as suas chagas, davão sepultura aos seus corpos. Santa Priscilliana e sua mãi Santa Priscilla tinhão applicado todos os seus bens á pratica de uma tão louvavel caridade; e foi em odio desta virtude que o imperador Juliano Apostata mandou traspassar com uma espada o pescoço da joven Priscilliana, que por este modo ajuntou á aureola da virgindade a palma do martyrio! A caridade portanto, a beneficencia christãa deve ser a virtude pela qual especialmente honremos a memoria da santa, veneremos as suas reliquias. Nós ouvimos com prazer que uma associação religiosa vai estabelecer-se sob a protecção da Virgem e Martyr Santa Priscilliana, cujo fim é, além do culto á sagrada reliquia, a dotação para casamento a donzellas pobres. Digne-se o Senhor, que é a mesma caridade, de aceitar esta homenagem em honra da gloriosa Virgem e Martyr Priscilliana; digne-se de animar e sustentar os esforços dos fundadores de tão pia e util instituição, e que ella encontre a mais viva sympathia e efficaz cooperação nos fieis desta diocese, como nós o esperamos."

Depois destas considerações, nós vamos estabelecer o seguinte ceremonial que se deve observar na trasladação e festa da reliquia de Santa Priscilliana, em conformidade do que prescreve a instrucção de S. Carlos Borromea no concilio provincial 4° mediolanense, a rubrica do ritual romano, e os preceitos liturgicos em casos taes, e de accordo com o nosso Illm. e Revm. Cabido, e em virtude de algumas concessões pontificias.

APPENDIX.

Jesu Christi Nomine invocato.

Art. 1°. A trasladação do corpo da Virgem e Martyr Santa Priscilliana, da capella, onde se acha, de S. Francisco na Prainha para a igreja matriz de Santa Anna, onde ha de ser collocado, terá lugar no dia 10 do proximo futuro mez de maio, ás 4 horas da tarde. Na vespera desse dia esta solemnidade será annunciada com repiques na matriz e capella sobreditas.

Art. 2°. As 3 horas da tarde do referido dia 10, na mencionada capella de S. Francisco, na nossa presença ou do nosso Illm. e Revm. monsenhor vigario-geral, do nosso Revm. conego notario, Revm. vigario e Rev. clero da igreja de Santa Anna, far-se-ha o reconhecimento, e se verificará a authenticidade de santa reliquia, abrindose a caixa que a contém, e lendo se o Breve da sua concessão, do que se fará auto. Depois desta ceremonia, a reliquia será thurificada e patente á veneração do clero e dos circumstantes.

Art. 3°. Feito o reconhecimento, seguir-se-ha a procissão. Pela presente carta pastoral nós convidamos as irmandades, ordens terceiras, e o reverendo clero secular e regular deste côrte a tomar parte em um acto religioso de tanta gravidade. Para o mesmo fim convidaremos tambem o nosso Illm. e Revm. Cabido.

Art. 4°. As irmandades, ordens terceiras, e reverendo clero secular e regular guardaráõ nesta procissão a mesma ordem relativamente aos seus lugares que guardão nas procissões de *Corpus Christi* e de S. Sebastião. Fechara o prestito o corpo da Santa, que irá debaixo do pallio, precedendo dous acolytos thurificando.

Art. 5°. Ao sahir da capella de S. Francisco, e por algum espaço de tempo nós carregaremos a arca da santa reliquia, juntamente com alguns membros do nosso Illm. e Revm. Cabido. Seguir-se-hão ao depois a fazer este officio sacerdotes que irão paramentados.

Art. 6°. Sahindo da capella de S. Francisco, o prestito tomará pela rua da Imperatriz e rua Larga de S. Joaquim para entrar na matriz de Santa Anna. Pelo caminho cantar-se-hão as litanias dos SS., accrescentando-se no lugar proprio a invocação de Santa Priscilliana; e depois os canticos *Benedictus e Magnificat* ou algum psalmo festivo.

Art. 7°. Recommendamos e pedimos a todos os moradores das ruas sobremencionadas, pelas quaes a procissão ha de passar, tenhão as mesmas ruas limpas e asseiadas, e ornadas, como é de estylo, as frentes das suas casas, em testemunho de devoção aos sagrados objectos do nosso culto.

Art. 8°. Ao recolher-se a procissão, posta a reliquia sobre o altar mór e thurificada, cantar-se-ha *Te-Deum*, e ao depois a antiphona, versiculos e oração do *Commum das Virgens*. Seguir-se-ha a predica. A reliquia se conservará patente á veneração publica.

Art. 9°. No sobredito dia 10 e no seu oitavario, haverá indulgencia plenaria, que começará da tarde desse dia até o pôr do sol do dia oitavo, em favor de todos os fieis de um e outro sexo, verdadeiramente penitentes, que se tenhão confessado e commungado, os quaes visitarem a matriz de Santa Anna, em qualquer dos oito dias, e orarem por algum tempo, segundo a intenção de Sua Santidade. Esta indulgencia póde ser applicada em suffragio pelos mortos.

Art. 10. O auto do reconhecimento e o que se fizer, memorando a trasladação, será registado no livro a que pertencer a parochia, e se conservará copia em um retabulo que se collocará em lugar proximo ao em que ficar a santa reliquia.

Art. 11. O dia 30 de agosto deste anno é o designado para a festa da reliquia de Santa Priscilliana. Nesse dia cantar-se-ha na igreja de Santa Anna a missa

Loquebar, pro Virgine et Martyre; e desde a tarde do dito dia até o pôr do sol do oitavo haverá indulgencia plenaria, que poderá ser applicada pelos mortos, em favor dos fieis de um e outro sexo, verdadeiramente penitentes, que se tenhão confessado e commungado, os quaes visitarem a matriz de Santa Anna em qualquer dos oito dias, e orarem por algum tempo, segundo a intenção do santissimo padre.

E para que chegue á noticia de todos, mandamos expedir a presente carta pastoral, que terá a necessaria publicidade.

Dada nesta residencia episcopal da Conceição, sob o nosso signal e sello das nossas armas, no sabbado antes do domingo da Paixão, 28 de Março de 1846. E eu o conego José Antonio da Silva Chaves, secretario do bispado e da camara ecclesiastica, a subscrevi. +Manoel, bispo capellão-mór, conde de Irajá.

D.

The storm of red dust, sweeping over the ocean, noticed in Chapter III., is said to have been, in extent and duration, one of the most remarkable on record. As the peculiar tint and predominating character of the sky-scenes at the time were believed to be due to it, I submitted to the Smithsonian Institution the expediency of preparing in chromo-lithography sketches of the singularly beautiful illustrations, by Nature herself, of the meteorological phenomenon; and the rather, as I supposed they would be pioneer paintings in a department of physics that is destined to call to its aid the pencil and palette. Celestial landscapes have yet to be studied. They are full of instruction, and those referred to were charged with a special lesson.

THE END.

204475

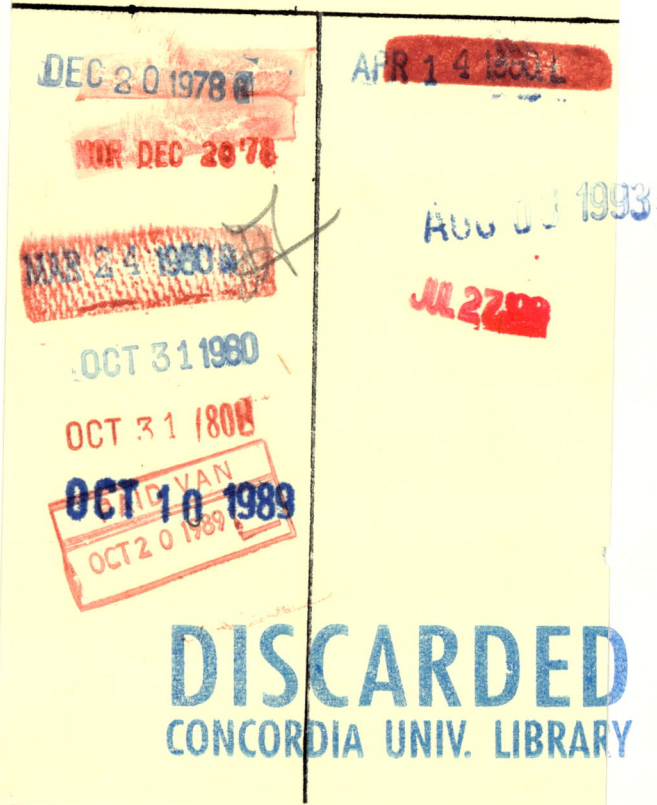